Feminist Theory

Also by Josephine Donovan

Uncle Tom's Cabin: Evil, Affliction, and Redemptive Love

After the Fall: The Demeter-Persephone Myth in Cather, Wharton, and Glasgow

New England Local Color Literature: A Women's Tradition

Sarah Orne Jewett

Feminist Literary Criticism: Explorations in Theory (edited)

Gnosticism in Modern Literature

Animals and Women: Feminist Theoretical Explorations (edited with Carol J. Adams)

Beyond Animal Rights: A Feminist Caring Ethic for the Treatment of Animals (edited with Carol J. Adams)

P.O.W. in the Pacific: Memoirs of an American Doctor in World War II by William N. Donovan (edited)

Women and the Rise of the Novel, 1405–1726

Feminist Theory

The Intellectual Traditions

THIRD EDITION

Josephine Donovan

2004

The Continuum International Publishing Group Inc.
15 East 26 Street, New York, NY 10010

The Continuum International Publishing Group Ltd
The Tower Building, 11 York Road, London SE1 7NX

Printed in the United States of America

Library of Congress Cataloging-in-Publication Data

Donovan, Josephine, 1941–
Feminist theory : the intellectual traditions / Josephine Donovan.—3rd ed.
p. cm.
Includes bibliographical references and index.
ISBN 0-8264-1248-3 (alk. paper)
1. Feminist theory. 2. Feminism—United States. I. Title.

HQ1190 .D66 2000
305.42'01—dc21 00-027957

To
Anne Rhodenbaugh Barrett
(1946–1997)

Resistance to tyranny is obedience to God
—Susan B. Anthony

Contents

Preface to the Third Edition (2000)

I write this preface late in 1999 as the twentieth century—the most violent and destructive ever, with over 100 million people killed in wars and genocide—comes to an end.

At this historical moment, the renaissance of feminist theory that I noted in the second preface continues to flourish, while feminism as a political and social movement continues its slow but steady progress.

Some are now saying that a "third wave" of feminism has begun. Although it is true that the high tide of the "second wave"—the explosion of feminist theory and activism of the late 1960s, 1970s, and early 1980s—seems to have crested, it has not receded. Many of the ideas of these theorists have become mainstream: they are now commonplace features of the political landscape.

The concept of "waves" of feminism, although a useful device (that I continue to use), is in fact somewhat inaccurate. The "first wave," that is, feminism of the nineteenth century, was really not the *first* wave of feminism. My studies in the early modern period, which resulted in my book *Women and the Rise of the Novel, 1405–1726,* have made it clear to me that there was an earlier feminist wave in the fifteenth, sixteenth, and seventeenth centuries in Western Europe. Many of the issues that feminists are concerned about today—rape, sexual harassment, violence against women—were issues for women then. Likewise, women then articulated demands for equitable education and for respectful treatment as rational, dignified subjects. This wave of feminism, which peaked in the late seventeenth and early eighteenth century, was followed by a counterrevolution that lasted though much of the eighteenth century during which feminist claims were ridiculed and, finally, suppressed.

The next wave, which we now call the "first wave," began in the late eighteenth century and continued until the early twentieth. It too precipitated a kind of backlash and suppression, even though it succeeded in institutionalizing many of its central claims.

Now, at the advent of the twenty-first century, some say we are at the conclusion of the so-called second wave. Certainly, the past several years have seen the rise of another backlash or counterrevolution. My sense, however, as noted, is that the second wave is really a rising tide that will not recede. Feminists of the second wave did not just theorize; they institutionalized as well. Numerous feminist institutions, such as rape crisis centers, wife abuse shelters, Women's Studies programs, feminist publishing networks, and the growing global feminist organizations, are in place and continue to grow. They will ensure, I believe, that feminism will continue as a major cultural force in the coming millennium.

My hope remains the one that motivated me to write this book in the first place (during the height of the second wave)—that it may help keep alive feminism's historical identity and its historic promise.

JOSEPHINE DONOVAN
Portsmouth, New Hampshire

Preface to the Second Edition (1992)

I write the preface to this updated, revised edition of *Feminist Theory* in the summer of 1991, eight years after the manuscript of the first edition was completed. The volume and quality of feminist theory produced during this period—roughly the decade of the 1980s—is staggering. We are in the midst of, and part of, a historic intellectual renaissance.

The main change between the first and second editions is the addition of a final chapter (8), in which I attempt to indicate the major directions in the most recent feminist theory. I have made no changes in the main text of the first edition, except for a few necessary updates, especially in the notes, and a few minor stylistic revisions and corrections.

In addition to the persons I acknowledged in the preface to the first edition, I would like to thank the following for their contributions—whether intellectual, moral, or material—to the production of this second edition: Evelyn Newlyn, Jana Sawicki, Carol Adams, Barbara White, Marilyn Emerick, Evander Lomke, and my students at the University of Maine.

JOSEPHINE DONOVAN

Preface to the First Edition (1985)

Illiterate people will not
keep their freedom.
Nikki Giovanni, 1977

Literacy can imply more than the ability to read. It can mean having a knowledge of one's history, of one's origins; having a world view that is indigenous to one's people and not imposed by others.

George Santayana reminded an earlier generation that those who are ignorant of their history are condemned to repeat it. Nikki Giovanni's more recent observation underscores that freedom is sustained by critical knowledge of one's self, one's community, and the world.

Women will remain trapped in age-old patterns of enslavement and they will lose hard-won freedoms unless they learn and transmit their history. An important part of that history is the extensive body of feminist theory that has been developed over the centuries. Women remain illiterate without a knowledge of this theory.

This book is the result of a seminar on feminist theory I have taught at various universities for over a decade. As such, it is a teaching book meant to present and interpret the main traditions of feminist theory in the context of their historical and philosophical roots.

The book is designed for the student and general reader who wish to gain an understanding of the intellectual traditions of American feminist theory. It should also be of use to scholars, for it provides a convenient and comprehensive summary of the diverse philosophical strains that make up the intellectual heritage of modern feminism.

I hope too that it may serve as a kind of handbook for the feminist activist who wishes to learn more about feminist theory, and for women (and men) in all walks of life who want to know what feminism really is. For it has little or nothing to do with the frivolous notion of "women's liberation" perpetrated in the media. Nor, ultimately, is it about "dressing for success" or becoming the first woman to have a finger on the nuclear trigger.

Finally, I hope that this book may help in the formulation of future feminist theory. One of the sad conclusions I have reached in writing this book is that feminists have re-invented the wheel a number of times. While the theories developed in the late 1960s and early 1970s came as a kind of revelation to many of us at the time, it has since become clear, as we have learned about earlier feminist movements, that there was little really new in what these "radicals" had to say. Much of it had been said, repeatedly, over a century before. This eclipse of feminist theory must not happen again.

To an extent this is a personal book. I have stressed those works and ideas that seemed to me, intellectually and emotionally, the most significant. While it includes the major theoretical traditions and is therefore a comprehensive study, the book does not purport to be exhaustively complete, nor to detail each particular group's oppression. I have attempted to be objective, in the sense of being faithful to the demands of rigorous intellectual standards of judgment, but the opinions and views expressed, as well as the selections, emphases, and arrangement, are obviously my own. In this sense no scholarship can claim to be wholly objective.

A few notes of explanation are in order. The book is about the American feminist tradition; it includes only those British or European theories that have had a significant influence on American feminism. Second, I have elected to include liberal citations from the theorists themselves because I wanted to convey the flavor of their rhetoric as well as the substance of their ideas, and so as to be as faithful as possible to the detail of their thought. Third, I have used the terms "first wave" and "second wave" to designate the nineteenth-century women's rights movement and contemporary movement, respectively. I have called the nineteenth-century campaign the "women's rights," rather than the "woman's rights" movement, as it was then called, because the latter term seems awkward now. Similarly, I use the term "feminist" even though it was not then current. Also, for convenience I often use the term "American" as an adjective instead of "United States."

I would like to thank the students who participated in my seminars on feminist theory at the Universities of Kentucky and New Hampshire, Bowdoin College, and George Washington University; Pam Elam and Barbara White who carefully read the manuscript and provided helpful suggestions and criticism; the following people for their various contributions to the making of this book: Karen Beckwith, Greta Reed, Charlotte Stewart, and Philip Winsor; and to thank for their encouragement over the years: Fannie J. LeMoine, Nelly Furman, Robert O. Evans, Gail Pass, Carolyn G. Heilbrun, my parents, and especially my sister, Ann Devigne Donovan.

JOSEPHINE DONOVAN

1 Enlightenment Liberal Feminism

All I ask of our brethren is, that they will take their feet from off our necks . . .
Sarah Grimké, 1837

On January 3, 1792, Mary Wollstonecraft completed the first major work of feminist theory in history: *A Vindication of the Rights of Woman.* It was to dominate subsequent feminist thought. Four months previously, in September 1791, during the early phases of the French Revolution, Olympe de Gouges had issued a street pamphlet in Paris entitled *Les Droits de la femme* (The Rights of Woman). She was later guillotined. The year before, in 1790, Judith Sargent Murray, an American, had published "On the Equality of the Sexes" in Massachusetts. And even earlier, in the midst of the American Revolution, Abigail Adams suggested to her husband, John, that women should have some "voice, or Representation," in the "new Code of Laws" being drawn for the nation.[1]

These eighteenth-century feminists were responding to the tide of revolutionary fervor that was sweeping the Western world. Theories developed during the so-called Enlightenment or Age of Reason were being put into practice: the idea, for example, that people have certain inalienable or "natural" rights upon which governments may not intrude was at the philosophical heart of both the American Declaration of Independence (1776) and the French Declaration of the Rights of Man (1789). Feminists hoped to assure that women be considered entitled to the same natural rights as men. Indeed, Mary Wollstonecraft dedicated the *Vindication* to French minister Talleyrand, urging him that if women were excluded from the new French constitution, France would remain a tyranny.[2] But the male theorists who developed and enforced the natural rights doctrine unfortunately did not accept the feminist position. In order to understand why this was and to specify the nature of Enlightenment feminist theory, it is necessary to study the theoretical origins of the natural rights doctrine and the intellectual world of Enlightenment liberalism in which it arose.

Thinkers in the Age of Enlightenment—a period which may be loosely defined as the late seventeenth through the late eighteenth centuries—were concerned to re-impose an order on a world which had philosophically "fallen apart" due to various scientific discoveries. The hierarchical "great chain of being" which ordered the medieval cosmos had been fatally challenged by such discoveries as Galileo's of the movement of the earth, published in 1632, which disproved the geocentric basis of Ptolemaic astronomy, itself the backbone of the medieval cosmological system.

A new synthesis was developed by Sir Isaac Newton whose *Principia Mathematica* (1687) laid down the fundamental paradigm of the Enlightenment world view: that the entire cosmos is governed by a few simple, immutable mathematical laws. Indeed, these laws were themselves reducible to one fundamental theorem, the law of universal gravitation. The Newtonian paradigm—that the physical universe operates according to simple, rational laws—became the governing metaphor of the age. If the physical world were ordered by a few basic laws, knowable through human reason, so too must be the moral world, the political world, and the aesthetic world. Descartes, for example, in his *Discourse on Method* (1637) had determined that a few "clear and distinct ideas," known through the "light of reason," provide irrefutable principles of knowledge. In each area theorists ascertained the basic principles that describe or prescribe behavior.

Political philosophers developed the idea that certain natural rights or natural laws, known through the exercise of reason, exist a priori. They thus established one of the most important moral ideas of the modern world: that each individual has certain inherent or "natural" rights. This premise is stated most eloquently in the American Declaration of Independence:

> We hold these truths to be self-evident, that all men are created equal, that they are endowed by their Creator with certain inalienable rights; that among these are life, liberty & the pursuit of happiness. . . .[3]

Ernst Cassirer characterized the Enlightenment rationalist world view as neo-Stoic.[4] As in the ancient Stoic view, the world was seen to work rationally, according to mathematical, "natural" laws. Each individual had access, autarchically, to these laws, because each individual had a God-given rational faculty. Each, independently, could extract from the particulars of the situation the fundamental general laws or principles held to exist a priori. All minds, therefore, while fundamentally isolated and independent, were presumed nevertheless to work in the same mechanical way. All could follow reason to the same conclusions.

The mechanical metaphor, which saw the world essentially as a great clock and God as the great clock-winder, was in many ways a deficient paradigm; for, it left out—because it could not explain—basic areas of reality. It neglected, most importantly, what we might call the subjective world: the realm of the emotions and the nonrational to which were relegated questions of aesthetic and moral value. The Newtonian paradigm presumed that all which did not operate according to reason, according to mathematical principles of mechanism, was Other, that is, secondary, not significant, less than real, not nameable. Into this category fell women, according to the view of male liberal thinkers.

The Newtonian world view therefore postulated a fundamental dissociation or split between the public world and physical world of the cosmos, on the one hand, which were governed by reason, and on the other hand, the fringe marginal world to which were relegated such nonrational matters as emotional engagements, personal idiosyncrasies, questions of faith, questions of aesthetic and moral judgment, and women.

This neo-Stoical view also included the presumption that the rational world is superior to, and must control, the nonrational; that order must be imposed upon the non-ordered, the marginal, the Other world. Descartes, for example, wrote a treatise on the passions in which he argued that one must learn to master one's emotions, to keep them subdued.[5]

The assertion of the primacy of human reason and of its right to rule all other aspects of reality led to a certain conceit or arrogance, indeed to a kind of "species," or male, chauvinism. For, inherent in the vaunting of human (male) reason is the idea that rational beings are the lords of creation and have the right to impose their "reason" on all who lack it—women, nonhuman creatures, and the earth itself. The pernicious implications of this arrogation will be discussed below.

Through the seventeenth and eighteenth centuries—as before and since—the assumption that women belonged in the home as wives and mothers was nearly universal. By the middle and late eighteenth century, and particularly into the nineteenth century, historical circumstances, notably the industrial revolution, separated the work place from the home, isolating women in the domestic sphere. With mechanized factories and the decline of cottage industries the public world of work became split off from the private world of the home as never before. Such tendencies, too, reinforced the Enlightenment identification of rationalism with the public sphere, and the non-rational and the moral with the private sphere and with women.[6]

Blackstone's *Commentaries on the Laws of England,* which appeared first in 1765–69, codified the view that women had no legal, public existence. As Susan Moller Okin points out, "The exclusion of women, particularly after marriage, from legal personhood, had a firm foundation in the common law fiction of coverture."[7] This fiction was articulated by Blackstone as follows:

> By marriage, the husband and wife are one person in law: that is, the very being or legal existence of the woman is suspended during

> marriage, or at least is incorporated and consolidated into that of the husband: under whose wing, protection, and *cover* she performs everything. . . .[8]

This meant in effect that married women had no property rights, no control over inheritance, no control over custody, and no right to bring civil suit. All these points became central issues in the nineteenth-century women's rights movement.

The presumption that women belong in the family under the aegis of their husband was central to male liberal theorists, even those like John Locke who espoused, at least theoretically, natural rights for all people. Locke's second *Treatise of Government* (1690) is considered the gospel of natural rights doctrine and is the main ideological source of the Declaration of Independence. In it he states unequivocally:

> The state of nature has a law of nature to govern it, which obliges everyone; and reason, which is that law, teaches all mankind which will but consult it, that, being all equal and independent, no one ought to harm another in his life, health, liberty, or possessions (II.6).[9]
>
> The natural liberty of man is to be free from any superior power on earth, and not to be under the will or legislative authority of man, but to have only the law of nature for his rule (IV. 22, p. 411).

Unfortunately, Locke did not mean man in the generic sense, but in the specific sense of the male of the species. For, later in the *Treatise* he states quite specifically that husbands are to be allowed authority over their wives and children, and although this is not an absolute authority, he does not spell out its limits. "But the husband and wife . . . will unavoidably sometimes have different wills too. It being necessary that . . . the rule . . . be placed somewhere, it naturally falls to the man's share as the abler and the stronger" (VII. 82, p. 435).

Several scholars have pointed out that Locke's theory necessitates conjugal subordination of women because it is rooted in the concept of private property. Locke stressed the importance of private property as a central factor in self-determination, in part as a means of wresting power from the crown and of securing a place protected from monarchical intrusion. But central to the protection of private property was the right of (male) inheritance. For this reason monogamy and the control of one's wife became of paramount importance, so that the property would remain within the family.[10]

Thus, the "individuals" who form a social contract for the protection of their lives, their fortunes and their property are in Locke's and subsequent liberal theorists' view male heads of households.[11] The "persons" mentioned in the United States Bill of Rights meant to the framers: "only the male heads of families, each of whom was understood to represent the interests of those who constituted his patriarchal entourage" (Okin, 249).

Moreover, Locke presumed a primary qualification for citizenship, the right to participate in public affairs, to be rationality. Only when (male) children had reached a level of adult rationality could they become citizens (VI. 55–63, pp. 425–27). Women were presupposed lacking in rationality, and were excluded from the role of citizens.

> Every male is assumed to be sufficiently rational, or "naturally" to have the capacity, to govern a family. . . . In Locke's theory it is women who are seen as "naturally" lacking in rationality and as "naturally" excluded from the status of "free and equal individual," and so unfit to participate in public life (Brennan, 195).

The supposition by male liberal theorists was that the persons who had natural rights were male property owning heads of families. This proposition held in American jurisprudence until well into the twentieth century. Okin asserts, "the male-headed family has been regarded by both legislators and courts as the fundamental basis of U.S. society" (248). One of the reasons an Equal Rights Amendment was deemed necessary is that the U.S. Supreme Court refused to apply the strictest standards of scrutiny in considering women's right to due process and equal protection under the Fourteenth Amendment, seeing by implication that there are aspects to being a female (usually her role within the family) which may properly intrude upon her natural rights as a person.[12]

Feminist theorists in the natural rights tradition sought to argue, however, that women were citizens, were "persons" entitled to the same basic rights as men. Because women were so rooted in the home, however, and subject to male authority therein, it was difficult for even liberal theorists to avoid a critique of the home that had more radical implications than a limited liberal position—that of simply granting women rights—might entail.

The most dramatic early attempt to apply the basic natural rights doctrine to women is the Declaration of Sentiments, drafted primarily by Elizabeth Cady Stanton and issued July 19–20, 1848, in Seneca Falls, New York. It was signed by 100 women and men. This document, rooted in natural rights theory, is modeled nearly word for word on the Declaration of Independence. And yet, as one historian noted, "it was . . . a decidedly radical document . . . [because] it made demands that could not be satisfied without profound changes in the social order."[13]

The opening sentence includes an appeal to natural law:

> When, in the course of human events, it becomes necessary for one portion of the family of man to assume among the peoples of the earth *a position different from that which they have hitherto occupied,* but one to which *the laws of nature and of nature's God entitle them,* a decent respect for the opinions of mankind requires that they should declare the causes that impel them to such a course.[14]

Note the potentially radical implications of the idea that women deserve to assume "a position different from that which they have hitherto occupied." Such assertions necessarily challenged the status quo of women belonging in the domestic sphere, and they help to explain why even a demand that today we consider innocuous, such as the right to vote, was seen by opponents as revolutionary.

The Declaration continues:

> We hold these truths to be self-evident: that all men and women are created equal; that they are endowed by their Creator with certain inalienable rights; that among these are life, liberty and the pursuit of happiness; that to secure these rights governments are instituted, deriving their just powers from the consent of the governed.

This nearly verbatim transcription of the Declaration of Independence takes on new meaning when applied to women, for women did not consent in their government. That they did not was held to constitute a violation of natural rights, which to be remedied would require that women have a voice in public affairs hitherto denied them: it implied the right to suffrage, the right to serve in government and the right to proper training to enable such service.

The Declaration of Sentiments proceeds to assert the right to overthrow "absolute despotism," as urged in the original document. The despot in the women's document is not, however, "the present King of Great Britain," but rather "man." "The history of mankind is a history of repeated injuries and usurpations on the part of man toward woman, having in direct object the establishment of an absolute tyranny over her." Again, the implications of this statement go beyond simply granting rights to women, the traditional liberal feminist position. It suggests that the oppression of women as a class or group has been an historically pervasive, systematic subjugation by men. This idea, first clearly developed by Sarah Grimké (see below), approaches contemporary radical feminist theory that roots women's oppression in patriarchal systems, an analogue to the "absolute tyranny" specified in the 1848 document.[15]

Following the preamble, the authors of the Declaration of Sentiments catalogue fifteen grievances. The first two concern the denial of suffrage and the right of the governed to consent in their laws. The next several concern the injustice of coverture:

> He has made her, if married, in the eye of the law, civilly dead. He has taken from her all right in property, even to the wages she earns. . . . In the covenant of marriage, she is compelled to promise obedience to her husband, he becoming . . . her master—the law giving him power to deprive her of liberty, and to administer chastisement.

The final several grievances are not about political rights but societal prejudices: the framers deemed that these too contribute to woman's subjugation. She is barred from "profitable employment" and does not receive equitable pay. She is excluded from the professions of theology, medicine, and law. All universities are closed to her. She is allowed no leadership positions in the church. A double standard of morality condemns women to public obloquy while exonerating men for the same (sexual) misdeeds. A woman is conditioned "to lead a dependent and abject life," her self-confidence systematically undermined along with her self-respect.

The Seneca Falls convention passed several resolutions, all of them unanimously, except the suffrage demand. But Stanton and Frederick Douglass, a leading black abolitionist and supporter of women's rights, pushed through the suffrage resolution by a small majority. The resolutions, too, are imbued with natural rights philosophy. Citing the "natural right" to pursue one's "own true and substantial happiness," the document asserts "that such laws as conflict . . . with the true and substantial happiness of woman, are contrary to the great precept of nature." Stanton later used this concept to justify divorce. "All laws which prevent woman from occupying such a station in society as her conscience shall dictate, or which place her in a position inferior to man, are contrary to the great precept of nature." The essence of the resolutions was simply "that woman is man's equal. . . ."

The Seneca Falls statements serve as a useful summary of the central liberal doctrines of the nineteenth-century women's rights movement in the United States. The theoretical way to Seneca Falls was, however, paved by the theories of several powerful feminist thinkers who are most properly placed in the Enlightenment tradition. They are Mary Wollstonecraft (1759–1797), Frances Wright (1795–1852), and Sarah Grimké (1792–1873). The ideas of Sojourner Truth (1795–1883), Elizabeth Cady Stanton (1815–1902), Susan B. Anthony (1820–1906), Harriet Taylor (1807–1858), and John Stuart Mill (1806–1873) were articulated for the most part after Seneca Falls. Their theories will be discussed later in this chapter.

The Enlightenment liberal feminists shared the following basic tenets:

(1) A faith in rationality. With some thinkers, such as Wollstonecraft, Reason and God are nearly synonymous. The individual's reason is the divine spark within; it is one's conscience. With feminists such as Frances Wright and Sarah Grimké the individual conscience is regarded as a more reliable source of truth than any established institution or tradition. (A similar antinomianism had been branded a heresy when expressed by Anne Hutchinson (1591–1643) in colonial Massachusetts.)

(2) A belief that women's and men's souls and rational faculties are the same; in other words, that women and men are ontologically identical.

(3) A belief in education—especially training in critical thinking—as the most effective means to effect social change and transform society.

(4) A view of the individual as an isolated being, who seeks the truth apart from others, who operates as a rational, independent agent, and whose dignity depends on such independence.

(5) Finally, Enlightenment theorists subscribed to the natural rights doctrine, and while the most important theorists did not limit themselves to demanding political rights, the mainstream of the nineteenth-century women's movement settled upon these demands, in particular the demand for the vote.

Mary Wollstonecraft's *Vindication* remains a classic of feminist theory. Imbued with revolutionary passion, its rhetoric still rings today in stirring and convincing tones. Its central argument is that women remain enslaved because of a corrupt process of socialization which stunts their intellect and teaches them that their proper purpose in life is to serve men.

Wollstonecraft is particularly exercised over the empty, frivolous lives that upper-class leisured women were encouraged to lead. "Confined . . . in cages like the feathered race, they have nothing to do but to plume themselves" (146). "Strength of body and mind are sacrificed to libertine notions of beauty, to the desire of establishing themselves—the only way women can rise in the world—by marriage" (83).

Wollstonecraft is aware that women must cultivate their beauty and "their senses" at the expense of their minds, because their only means of establishing themselves economically and of obtaining a measure of power is by attracting a husband. But that, Wollstonecraft maintains, is prostitution: "to their senses, are women made slaves, because it is by their sensibility that they obtain present power" (153). And: "To rise in the world . . . they must marry advantageously, and to this object their time is sacrificed, and their persons often legally prostituted" (151).

> Pleasure is the business of woman's life . . . they have, to maintain their power, resigned the natural rights which the exercise of reason might have procured them, and have chosen rather to be short-lived queens than labour to obtain the sober pleasures that arise from equality (145).

"She was created to be the toy of man, his rattle, and it must jingle in his ears whenever, dismissing reason, he chooses to be amused" (118).

Wollstonecraft embraces the Enlightenment view of the person as divided between reason and "the senses." Life is similarly divided: the world's important business is conducted in the public arena where reason obtains, while frivolous, unimportant pleasures are confined to the private sphere where women live. Women's sole purpose is therefore to cultivate the nonrational, sensuous side of life in order to please men. Such a role, according to Wollstonecraft, lacks dignity.

> Surely she has not an immortal soul who can loiter life away merely employed to adorn her person, that she may amuse the languid hours, and soften the cares of a fellow-creature who is willing to be enlivened by her smiles and tricks, when the serious business of life is over (113).

Not only does such an existence lack dignity, it also prevents women from developing their critical faculty, their reason, which itself is the means by which they must prepare their "immortal soul."

Wollstonecraft believes that proper education, proper training in critical thinking, is the most important single item on the feminist agenda. She projects a two-fold benefit. First, it will enable women to think clearly and sensibly about their own situation, which will make them less gullible and less likely to forget their own self-interest and to become slavish prostitutes.

> Strengthen the female mind by enlarging it, and there will be an end to blind obedience; but as blind obedience is ever sought for by power, tyrants and sensualists are in the right when they endeavour to keep women in the dark, because the former only want slaves, and the latter a plaything (107).

Second, the cultivation of women's powers of critical thinking will enable them to grow spiritually, to develop their souls. It is the latter issue that most concerns Wollstonecraft. For, in the tradition of Christian rationalism, of Thomas Aquinas and Augustine, she believes that the sine qua non of moral growth is the ability to make moral judgments. "Reason [is] . . . the power of discerning good from evil" (153). "Every being may become virtuous by the exercise of its own reason" (103). One achieves virtue by using one's reason and subduing one's passions (91). For, "the stamen of immortality . . . is the perfectibility of human reason" (142).

> Reason is, consequently, the simple power of improvement . . . of discerning truth. Every individual is in this respect a world in itself. . . . The nature of reason must be the same in all, if it be an emanation of divinity, the tie that connects the creature with the Creator (142).

Thus, any system of education that prevents a woman from developing her reason is denying her access to immortality, is condemning her to a materialistic vegetative limbo. It seems likely that in speaking of immortality Wollstonecraft is not thinking of a literal heaven; rather she is asserting that human dignity is bound up with the ability to transcend physical existence spiritually and intellectually. The spark of reason is therefore the "god within" by which each person independently achieves spiritual growth.

Women are denied access to reason, according to Wollstonecraft, because they must always deal with an intermediary—man—who obscures its truth. Instead, women "must be permitted to turn to the fountain of light [directly], and not forced to shape their course by the twinkling of a mere satellite" (101). "Man [is] ever placed between her and reason, she is [permitted only] to see through a gross medium, and to take things on trust" (142). These statements are undoubtedly meant as a refutation of Milton's celebrated line in *Paradise Lost* (1667): "He for God only, she for God in him." But, they also reflect the rationalist faith that each individual can achieve truth by dealing immediately and critically with reality, not by relying on trust or on authorities. And they express the fundamentally Protestant view that each individual conscience connects directly to God, that establishment hierarchies only impede such communication.

Wollstonecraft also reflects the Stoic bias of the age. It is by subduing one's "animal nature," through the imposition of disciplined reason that one achieves dignity and virtue. "When we are gathering the flowers of the day, and revelling in pleasure, the solid fruit of toil and wisdom should not be caught at the same time" (114). "He who will pass life away in bounding from one pleasure to another [will] . . . acquire neither wisdom nor respectability of character" (115).

Since men and women have the same moral and intellectual core (there is no "sex in souls," 151), they should receive the same mental and spiritual training. Wollstonecraft rejects Rousseau's idea that men and women think differently (124–25). In this she establishes a central liberal feminist position: reason is the same in all persons. When women do reason differently or incorrectly, it is due to a lack of training. Wollstonecraft acknowledges that women sometimes sees the trees and not the forest (151). They fail to think in an orderly fashion (104). They have not developed "the power of generalizing ideas"; "merely to observe" is not enough (144). Lack of education prevents women from perceiving the general principles behind the facts; this keeps them from analyzing their own situation critically. Such myopia condemns women to meaningless repetition: "So they do today what they did yesterday, merely because they did it yesterday" (104). Critical reason is, therefore, the means by which women may rise out of the vegetative slough in which they perpetually languish.

Wollstonecraft also shares the Enlightenment faith in individualism. One of the benefits of critical thinking for women is that it will facilitate their self-determination. It will enable them to think for themselves who they want to be, to control their lives. "I do not wish," Wollstonecraft asserts, women "to have power over men; but over themselves" (154). Such self-empowerment can happen only when women have separated themselves and become "independent of men" (253). Women need to have the chance to think in solitude in order "to acquire that strength of character on which great resolves are built" (149).

Finally, women should have access into the "great enterprises" of public life, and not be confined to the domestic sphere (294). As a means of establishing their moral and economic independence, they should be allowed into various professions, such fields as medicine, scholarship, and business (261).

> How many women thus waste life away the prey of discontent, who might have practised as physicians, regulated a farm, managed a shop,

> and stood erect, supported by their own industry, instead of hanging their heads surcharged with the dew of sensibility (262).

Wollstonecraft fully believes in the dignity of work. "How much more respectable is the woman who earns her own bread by fulfilling any duty, than the most accomplished beauty!" (262).

There are many other minor changes that Wollstonecraft urges, such as proper physical training for women and ending the double standard in morality (like most nineteenth-century feminists she proposed male chastity), but the core of her position is that outlined here. She was a rationalist and a Stoic who firmly believed that critical thinking can liberate the individual from the mindless repetition of mere physical existence, and that proper education could liberate women from subjugation to their conditioned role of serving men.

Frances Wright, a Scotswoman, presented her views in a series of lectures in Cincinnati in 1829. The *Course of Popular Lectures* shows her to be an empiricist in the tradition of Locke and Jeremy Bentham (Wright knew and studied with the latter). Unlike rationalists, empiricists believed that all knowledge came through the senses—Locke, for example, rejected the Cartesian notion of innate "clear and distinct ideas"—but the rationalist assumption of the age was so powerful that even empiricists assumed the objective world was rational and that the human mind, though a "tabula rasa" at birth, could come to a knowledge of the general principles that underlie appearance.

In spite of their different philosophical orientations, Wright and Wollstonecraft share a passionate belief that critical thinking can break through the mystifications by which women are duped into accepting a subjugated status. Like Wollstonecraft's, Wright's rhetoric is charged with revolutionary zeal. In Lecture 1, "On the Nature of Knowledge," Wright argues that truth can be reached only through skeptical and thoughtful evaluation of evidence by each individual. She debunks "truths" presented by established institutions and those perpetuated by custom or tradition—an indication of her fundamentally antinomian position. She asserts that only by thinking clearly about their situations will women be able to recognize age-old prejudices for what they are.

"All real knowledge," she argues empirically *"is derived from positive sensations."* Only "a vigorous intellect" "in the free exercise of its powers, is . . . likely to collect accurate knowledge, [not] those who are methodically fed with learned error and learnedly disguised truth."[16] True knowledge can only be achieved by the individual in direct contact with reality. "Things which we have not ourselves examined, and occurrences which we have not ourselves witnessed, but which we receive on the attested sensations of others, we may *believe,* but we do not *know*" (10).

Wright is suspicious of anyone connected with an established institution, including all teachers, scholars, and lawyers who are in its pay. Because they are financially dependent, they are "*compelled* to the support of existing opinions, whether right or wrong" (18). One should decide for one's self the truth of any proposition. Only through "a fearless spirit of inquiry" and "a just system of education" will progress and reform occur.

"Let us inquire!" she cries,

> What mighty consequences, are involved in these little words! . . . Before them thrones have given way. Hierarchies have fallen. . . . Iron bars, and iron laws, and more iron prejudices, have given way; the prison house of the mind hath burst its fetters (34).

Unlike Wollstonecraft, Sarah Grimké, and many other feminists, Wright was an atheist. Indeed, she saw religion as one of the main forces that keep women subjugated—a point with which, however, Sarah Grimké, Elizabeth Cady Stanton, and others concurred (see chapter 2). Wright rages against the "insatiate priestcraft," which succeeds in keeping women in "mental bondage" (20).

> Above, her agitated fancy hears the voice of a god in thunders; below, she sees the yawning pit; and before, behind, around, a thousand plantoms, conjured from the prolific brain of insatiate priestcraft, confound, alarm and overwhelm her reason! (20)

Like Grimké and Maria Stewart (see below), Wright had to deal with the prejudice against women speaking in public. Her liberal rejoinder was to deny that "truth had any sex" (15). However, she did suggest that as outsiders to various establishments, women may be closer to the truth than corrupt insiders (16).

Reflecting Bentham's influence, Wright developed utilitarian arguments for women's equality. Utilitarianism proposed an eudaimonistic ethic, based on happiness as the highest good, and evaluated human progress quantitatively by whether a society provided the greatest good for the greatest number. For example, Wright rejected the idea that it was "useful" for society to keep women subordinate. Such an argument, she claimed, could only come from the oppressor class for whom such suppression was indeed "useful."

> There is a vulgar persuasion that the ignorance of women, by favoring their subordination, ensures their utility. 'Tis the same argument employed by the ruling few against the subject many in aristocracies; by the rich against the poor in democracies; by the learned professions against the people in all countries (32).

"Let us have done with abstractions!" Wright argued, "Truth is fact." A central means of determining the validity of fact is, she maintained, the pleasure-pain principle (a utilitarian prescript): "virtuous feelings are those which impart pleasure to the bosom; bad feelings those which disturb and torment it" (50). Using such guidelines one can determine that keeping half the human race in a state of ignorance retards the progress of the entire race. The oppression of women does not provide the greatest good for the greatest number. "Until women assume the place in society which good sense and good feeling alike assign to them, human improvement must advance but feebly" (24). John Stuart Mill, also a utilitarian, was to use a similar argument. Wright, therefore, like Wollstonecraft, expressed the Enlightenment faith in the power of critical thinking to dispel ignorance and liberate women and other oppressed groups from subjugation.

Sarah Grimké's *Letters on Equality* (1838) presents the most cogent and elegant arguments against women's subordination developed in the liberal tradition. At times they move in a decidedly radical direction. The letters were written during a lecture tour through northern Massachusetts which Grimké had undertaken in 1837 on behalf of the abolitionist cause. During the tour she had been excoriated for daring to violate the biblical injunction against women speaking in public (I Cor. 14:34 and I Tim. 2:12). Earlier a black woman abolitionist, Maria Stewart, had been subjected to the same prejudice and had been forced off the podium—not, however, without protest: "What if I am a woman? St. Paul declared that it was a shame for a woman to speak in public . . . Did St. Paul but know of our wrongs and deprivations, I presume he would make no objection to our pleading in public for our rights."[17]

Like Wollstonecraft and Wright, Grimké believed strongly in the efficacy of critical thinking; she asserted that women's natural rights had been denied them by men, and argued that women and men were moral and intellectual equals.

Grimké's own critical powers are brought to bear in her close textual analysis of central biblical passages used to justify women's oppression. Indeed, Grimké was one of the first to bring critical thinking to Biblical exegesis—a practice that came to dominate nineteenth-century biblical scholarship. Grimké's central point is that an erroneous view of scripture has evolved through "perverted interpretation of Holy Writ."[18] And in an antinomian spirit she rejects (male) clerical intermediaries as necessary to the reception of spiritual truth. On the contrary, they impede it.

> I . . . claim to judge for myself what is the meaning of the inspired writers, because I believe it to be the solemn duty of every individual to search the Scriptures for themselves, with the aid of the Holy Spirit, and not be governed by the views of any man, or set of men (4).
>
> . . . False construction [of scripture] has no weight with me: they are the opinions of interested judges, and I have no particular reverence for them, *merely* because they have been regarded with veneration from gen-

> eration to generation. So far from this being the case, I examine any opinion of centuries standing . . . as if they were of yesterday. I was educated to think for myself, and it is a privilege I shall always claim to exercise (91).

Grimké sees that in order to combat the weight of centuries of received opinion and custom, women are going to have to articulate and legitimate their own truths. Such legitimation comes for Grimké, as for Wollstonecraft, out of the radical Protestant tradition. Women should receive their instruction from direct communication with divine wisdom and not from the clergy (Letter 3).

Grimké's *Letters* had an obvious influence on Stanton in the drafting of the Declaration of Sentiments (indeed Stanton was a personal friend). For Grimké was among the first to apply American natural rights principles to women. Curiously, however, she claims that it is the Bible that declared that "men and women were CREATED EQUAL" (16). But it is in language derived form the natural rights tradition that she urges that men's laws have systematically stripped women of their rights: "laws . . . have been enacted to destroy her independence, and crush her individuality; laws, which she had no voice in establishing and which rob her of some of her *essential* rights" (74).

Grimké also provided the first systematic feminist critique of Blackstone, in particular the concept of coverture under which, Grimké urges, "the very being of a woman, like that of a slave is absorbed in her master" (75). She is also the first to argue that women suffer "taxation without representation" (80), another thesis that became central to the nineteenth-century women's rights campaign. And she deplores the fact that working women do not receive equal pay for equal work (50). Oddly enough, though, while Grimké firmly believed in women's right and duty to speak out on public issues, she shrank from the idea of women participating in government (81), reflecting perhaps the Victorian notion that public affairs were too sordid for women.

Grimké's overall analysis is similar to Wollstonecraft's, but she develops the radical feminist position more fully: the view that men as a class keep women as a class in a subordinate position because it is in their interest to do so. To this end, Grimké notes, men condition women to please them, men deny women the possibility of a decent education and prevent their developing powers of critical analysis.

> As [men] have determined that Jehovah has placed woman on a lower platform than man, they of course wish to keep her there; and hence the noble faculties of our minds are crushed, and our reasoning powers are almost wholly uncultivated (61).

> He has adorned the creature whom God gave him as a companion, with baubles and geegaws, turned her attention to personal attractions, of-

> fered incense to her vanity, and made her the instrument of his selfish gratification, a plaything to please his eye and amuse his hours of leisure (17).

Grimké castigates feminine concern with external appearance and considers that the frivolity of most women's dress means that they will not be taken seriously as dignified moral beings. Then "know that so long as we submit to be dressed like dolls, we never can rise to the stations of duty and usefulness from which they desire to exclude us" (71).

Rather than allowing women to "stand upright on that ground which God designed us to occupy" and to speak out on moral issues like slavery, the clergy would return women to the harem. "We find our clerical brethren . . . endeavoring to drive woman from the field of moral labor and intellectual culture, to occupy her talents in the pursuit of those employments which will enable her to regale the palate of her lord with the delicacies of the table, and in every possible way minister to his animal comfort and gratification" (39).

Her own southern belle adolescence is recalled when Grimké decries the way women are socialized only to catch husbands.

> During the early part of my life, my lot was cast among the butterflies of the *fashionable* world; and of this class of women, I am constrained to say, both from experience and observation, that their education is miserably deficient, that they are taught to regard marriage as the one thing needful, the only avenue to distinction; hence to attract the notice and win the attentions of men, by their external charms, is the chief business of fashionable girls (46–47).

She denounces the notion that women belong in the domestic sphere, and that any evidence of rational thinking about public matters is inappropriate. "Where any mental superiority exists, a woman is generally shunned and regarded as stepping out of her 'appropriate sphere,' which . . . is to dress, to dance, to set out to the best possible advantage her person" (47).

In fact, Grimké argues, in the first major feminist critique of the home, for married women the domestic sphere is usually a tyranny. "Man has exercised the most unlimited and brutal power over woman, in the peculiar character of husband,—a word in most countries synonymous with tyrant" (85). And she deplores "the vast amount of secret suffering endured, from the forced submission of women to the opinions and whims of their husbands" (86).

The consignment of men and women to public and private spheres respectively is an arbitrary matter of custom, according to Grimké. For, since men and women are moral and intellectual equals, they have the same moral and intellectual rights and responsibilities.

> Intellect is not sexed; . . . strength of mind is not sexed, and . . . our views about the duties of men and the duties of women, the sphere of man and the sphere of woman, are mere arbitrary opinions (60).

Moreover, because of their basic equality, women have a responsibility to express their views, have a duty to preach. Grimké uses the language of the Declaration of Independence to make her point.

> According to the principle which I have laid down, that man and woman were created equal, and endowed by their beneficent Creator with the same intellectual powers and the same moral responsibilities, and that consequently whatever is *morally* right for a man to do, is *morally* right for a woman, it follows as a necessary corollary, that if it is the duty of a man to preach . . . it is the duty also of a woman (98).

In Letter 7 Grimké urges the "social gospel" on women. They have a moral obligation to get out of their homes to help those less fortunate than they, in particular black slaves. The social gospel had been reemphasized during the Second Great Awakening (1797–1831), which had so greatly affected American theology in the early nineteenth century. It encouraged Christians to engage in moral and social reform. Many of the reform movements of the period, including to some extent the women's movement, sprang out of this "awakening."[19]

Finally, Grimké's analysis depended on the Enlightenment assumption that men and women are naturally equal and ontologically the same. Indeed, Grimké insists that it is pernicious to look upon a woman as a female first and a person second. "Nothing . . . has tended more to destroy the true dignity of woman, than the fact that she is approached by man in the character of a female" (22). To claim her dignity as a person a woman must assure that "all she does and says must be done and said irrespective of sex" (25). For,

> she is now called upon to rise from the station where *man*, not God, has placed her, and claim those sacred and inalienable rights, as a moral and responsible being, with which her Creator has invested her (24).

Elizabeth Cady Stanton and Susan B. Anthony, two of the great leaders of the American nineteenth-century women's rights movement, developed and refined the Enlightenment theory articulated by their predecessors, Wollstonecraft, Wright, and Grimké. They also—Stanton particularly—formulated original theory that went beyond liberal doctrine. This will be discussed in chapter 2.

Stanton's liberal position is exemplified in three important statements made over the course of her career: the "Address to the New York State Legislature" (1854), "Address to the New York State Legislature" (1860), and

"Solitude of Self" (1892). Both the 1854 and the 1860 addresses rely on natural rights theory.

> There are certain natural rights as inalienable to civilization as are the rights of air. . . . The natural rights of the civilized man and woman are government, property, the harmonious development of all their powers, and the gratification of their desires (1: 679).

> [Women] are persons; native, free-born citizens; property-holders, taxpayers; yet we are denied the exercise of our right to the elective franchise. . . . We have every qualification required by the Constitution, necessary to the legal voter, but the one of sex. We are moral, virtuous, and intelligent, and in all respects quite equal to the proud white man himself (1: 595).

"The sexes are alike," she argues, and therefore deserve equal rights (1: 604).

In the 1854 address Stanton enumerates various grievances, in particular the taxation without representation of the unmarried woman (1:597), and the "instant civil death" (1:599) of the woman in marriage. She demands not just the right of franchise, however, but also the right to a jury of one's peers (1:597–98). Wollstonecraft had briefly touched upon this idea in the *Vindication.* The implication of this thesis is, however, that women are different from men, and are to be seen as a separate group better able to understand one another's motives. It contradicts, therefore, the liberal belief that all people are fundamentally similar and capable of similarly "objective" reasoning.

Stanton also debunked the then prevalent "cult of true womanhood," which held, among other things, that women were weak, incompetent, and pure, and therefore needed male protection from the evils of the world.[20] Women hardly need such protection, Stanton argues, when their home life is often anything but a blissful haven. There women experience many of the horrors they are supposedly being protected against (1: 682). Sojourner Truth had pointed out the hypocrisy of the idea that women belong on a pedestal in her 1851 remarks to the Akron Woman's Rights Convention (see below); Margaret Fuller, as will be discussed in chapter 2, made similar points in *Woman in the Nineteenth Century* (1845).

Stanton's central liberal thesis is that women, as individuals, need rights in order to stand on their own. Grant us minimal basic rights and then "let us take care of ourselves, our property, our children, and our homes" (1: 683). In the Lockean tradition Stanton sees government as a protection against tyranny: it should allow the individual woman to function freely, to enjoy her natural rights. Two moving expressions of Stanton's individualism are a letter to the 1851 convention, in which she urges educating daughters in "courage" and "self-dependence" (1: 815), and her final address, the

"Solitude of Self." In the latter she states her conviction that because every person is isolated, a woman must learn to take responsibility for herself. Stanton rightly notes that the concept of "the individuality of each human soul" is rooted in part in the Protestant idea, "the right of individual conscience and judgment."[21] Positing a natural law environment, Stanton projects each woman as "an imaginary Robinson Crusoe with her woman Friday on a solitary island." She is "in a world of her own, the arbiter of her own destiny. . . . Her rights . . . are to use all her faculties for her own safety and happiness" (4: 189).

Women as isolated agents are persons first and only incidentally wives, mothers, sisters, and daughters (4: 190). Since women, indeed all people, are fundamentally alone, they need equal opportunities and government protection to enable them to chart their own course.

> The strongest reason for giving woman all the opportunities for higher education, for the full development of her faculties . . . ; for . . . a complete emancipation from all forms of bondage, of custom, dependence, superstition; from all the crippling influences of fear—is the solitude and personal responsibility of her own life (4: 190).

> The strongest reason why we ask for woman a voice in the government under which she lives; in the religion she is asked to believe; equality in social life . . . ; a place in the trades and professions, . . . is because of her birthright to self-sovereignty; because as an individual she must rely on herself . . . (4: 190).

Like Wollstonecraft, Stanton believes that "nothing adds such dignity to character as the recognition of one's self-sovereignty; the right to an equal place, everywhere conceded—a place earned by personal merit" (4: 191). Stanton concludes this powerful speech in a vein that is strikingly modern.

> We may have friends, love, kindness, sympathy and charity to smooth our pathway in everyday life, but in the tragedies and triumphs of human experience each mortal stands alone.[22]

Susan B. Anthony, less a theorist than a brilliant political organizer, elaborated on fundamental natural rights doctrine in some of her statements. Of particular interest are the arguments she developed in connection with her celebrated trial for civil disobedience on June 18, 1873. Anthony was under indictment for having voted in the 1872 Congressional election, a violation of the law.

In her pretrial statements Anthony used the Declaration of Independence and Constitution to argue that she "not only committed no crime but simply exercised [a] 'citizen's right,' guaranteed . . . by the National Constitution" (2: 631). Expressing the liberal theory of government she asserts,

> Our democratic republican government is based on the idea of the natural right of every individual member thereof to a voice and a vote in making and executing the laws. We assert the province of government to be to secure the people in the enjoyment of their inalienable rights.

The preamble to the Declaration implies the right of all citizens to vote, for it aims at establishing a government which will be responsive to the people's ideas of how best to ensure their "safety and happiness." But, Anthony argues, women have no means of expressing their views through government. Since her statement summarizes the basic grievances of nineteenth-century liberal feminists, I quote the passage *in toto* here.

> One half of the people of this Nation to-day are utterly powerless to blot from the statute books an unjust law, or to write there a new and a just one. The women, dissatisfied as they are with this form of government, that enforces taxation without representation,—that compels them to obey laws to which they have never given their consent—that imprisons and hangs them without a trial by a jury of their peers—that robs them, in marriage, of the custody of their own persons, wages, and children—are this half of the people left wholly at the mercy of the other half, in direct violation of the spirit and letter of the declarations of the framers of this government, every one of which was based on the immutable principle of equal rights to all (2: 631).

But Anthony goes beyond natural rights doctrine to adopt a radical feminist position. This government, in fact, is not a democracy, she alleges. It is a hateful "oligarchy of sex." In every household men are the "sovereigns, masters; the women subjects, slaves" (2: 635).

In her statement Anthony developed the rather novel thesis that under the recently passed Fourteenth and Fifteenth Amendments women have in effect been granted the vote. The first section of the Fourteenth Amendment, passed in 1868, reads:

> All persons born or naturalized in the United States and subject to the jurisdiction thereof, are citizens of the United States and of the State wherein they reside. No State shall make or enforce any law which shall abridge the privileges or immunities of citizens of the United States; nor shall any State deprive any person of life, liberty, or property, without due process of law; nor deny to any person within its jurisdiction the equal protection of the laws.

Anthony ascerbically notes, "the only question left to be settled now, is: Are women persons?" (2: 638). As noted above, the Supreme Court has not always chosen to answer this question affirmatively in interpreting the Fourteenth Amendment.[23] Certainly in 1873 the trial judge did not accept Anthony's contention. Indeed the editors of the *History of Woman Suffrage* argue that "with remarkable forethought" he had "penned his decision" before even hearing her arguments (2: 647).

Anthony maintained, further, that the first section of the Fifteenth Amendment, passed in 1870, also granted women the right to vote. It reads: "The right of citizens of the United States to vote shall not be denied or abridged by the United States or by any State on account of race, color, or previous condition of servitude." Anthony contended that women exist under a "condition of servitude" and therefore qualify under the terms of the amendment. Neither was this argument persuasive.

In her statement at her trial Anthony recapitulated these arguments and told the judge that she would never pay a penny of the $100 fine, and that she would continue to urge her sisters to "rebel against your manmade, unjust, unconstitutional forms of law," reminding women of "the old revolutionary maxim": " 'Resistance to tyranny is obedience to God' " (2: 689).

In her attempt to use the Fourteenth Amendment for her own purposes Anthony was challenging the second section of the amendment, which specified, "when the right to vote . . . is denied to any of the male inhabitants of such State . . . the basis of representation shall be reduced in . . . proportion." The ratification of this amendment in 1870 had inserted the word "male" into the Constitution for the first time, a serious setback for the suffragists. In the post-Civil War years a rift developed in the women's rights movement over this very issue. The Stanton-Anthony faction also split with the abolitionists, feeling that while they, the women, had worked fervently for the cause of liberating the slave, the abolitionists had backed down from their support of women's rights when the time came to frame the amendments which enfranchised ex-slaves. Abolitionists claimed it was "the Negro's hour." (To be more accurate they should have said it was the male Negro's hour.) Stanton and Anthony, however, refused to support the Fourteenth and Fifteenth Amendments and stated that from then on they would support no cause but the cause of women. To this end they formed the National Woman Suffrage Association in 1869, breaking off from the National Equal Rights Association, which itself reorganized later that year as the American Woman Suffrage Association.

The women's rights movement had its origins in the antislavery movement. This was partly because of the harassment that women activists like Maria Stewart and Sarah Grimké received when they attempted to advance the abolitionist cause. The idea of taking action on behalf of women's rights, which finally resulted in the 1848 Seneca Falls convention, was in fact born at the London World Anti-Slavery Convention in 1840 at which the women delegates, which included Lucretia Mott, were seated not on the floor with the other delegates but in the balcony. (Elizabeth Cady Stanton, whose husband was a delegate, joined them there and spent the week in discussion with Mott.) Frances Wright took personal anti-slavery action and established a utopian community in Tennessee (Nashoba) where the races and the sexes had equal footing.

The women's rights activists showed their abolitionist roots, too, in their ready use of the slave-woman analogy. The idea had been briefly suggested by Wollstonecraft, was used by Margaret Fuller, and by Sarah Grimké. The analogy was freely employed in women's rights literature. Stanton, for example, elaborated the idea in her 1854 and 1860 addresses: like the male slave, she said, a (white) woman has no name of her own, but takes the name of her master (slave wives were called by their husband's first name: Tom's Sue or Caesar's Jane, for example); like the slave the woman can own no property, has no right to custody of her children, has no legal existence, and can be chastised by her master. Indeed, Stanton argues, the free black male exceeds the white woman in civil rights (1: 680–81).[24]

The situation of the black woman slave was a central issue in the abolition movement and became central to women's rights theorists. In particular, Sojourner Truth, an ex-slave herself, and Sarah Grimké, who had grown up on a Southern plantation, publicized the plight of the black woman.

In the wake of the Civil War (1867) Sojourner Truth noted, "there is a great stir about colored men getting their rights, but not a word about colored women." She warns, however, "if colored men get their rights, and not colored women theirs, you see the colored men will be masters over the women, and it will be just as bad as it was before" (2: 193). Her words were prophetic, for during Reconstruction, as Bell Hooks notes, "as black men advanced . . . they encouraged black women to assume a more subservient role."[25] Sojourner Truth suggested that such subordination was already beginning in 1867. "[Colored women] go out washing . . . and their men go idle . . . and when the women come home, they ask for their money and take it all, and then scold because there is no food" (2: 193).

Earlier she had pointed to the difference between the situation of the black woman slave and the white woman. In doing so she rocked the shaky pedestal upon which white women were placed in antebellum America. Answering a heckler at the 1851 national convention she said:

> That man over there says that woman needs to be helped into carriages, and lifted over ditches, and to have the best place everywhere. Nobody ever helps me into carriages or over mud-puddles, or gives me any best place! . . . And a'n't I a woman?

Pointing to her muscular right arm she cried: "I have ploughed, and planted, and gathered into barns and no man could head me! And a'n't I a woman?" (1: 116).[26] As Angela Davis notes, "the alleged benefits of the ideology of femininity did not accrue to [the black woman slave]."

> She was not sheltered or protected; she would not remain oblivious to the desperate struggle for existence outside the "home." She was also there in the fields, alongside the man, toiling under the lash from sun-up to sun-down.[27]

In her eighth Letter on Equality, Sarah Grimké particularized the plight of the black woman on the plantation in most vivid terms. Not only do they work like men, they are used as property, as "brood mares." They are "often employed by the planter, or his friends, to administer to their sensual desires" (52). "If amid all her degradation and ignorance, a woman desires to preserve her virtue unsullied, she is either bribed or whipped into compliance, or if she dares resist her seducer," she is often killed (51–52). White women, too, were injured by this system, Grimké argues, because it was their husbands and sons who were engaging in rape.

It is clear, then, that the analysis developed by Enlightenment feminists did not apply without qualification to black women. Women slaves were not socialized into the behavior of leisure class white women; on the other hand, they were not immune to the ideology of the "cult of true womanhood" which held that women should properly be dependent, submissive, domestic, pious and feeble. For, as Hooks notes, most black women, unlike Sojourner Truth, were not able to ignore the cult and take pride in their physical strength as they did heavy labor outside the home. The "true womanhood" ideology "had an intense demoralizing impact on enslaved black females" for "they assimilated white American values . . . that it was debasing and degrading for women to work in the fields." "So great was the slave woman's desire to appear feminine and ladylike that many chose to wear dresses to work in the fields rather than don trousers" which were seen as masculine (48). And after emancipation and through the Reconstruction period, black women's groups sought to change their negative images—particularly that of sexual promiscuity—by stressing behavior that emulated the white "lady" (55).

Under slavery black women were not as confined to the domestic sphere as the white woman; nor, obviously, were they barred from heavy "masculine" physical labor. But like white women and black men they were civilly dead and had no political rights. Nor could they—with a few rare exceptions like Phillis Wheatley—hope to obtain a decent education or enter any profession. And after emancipation, as Sojourner Truth pointed out, they were relegated to menial labor, and did not receive equal pay even for that. The radical feminist analysis developed by Enlightenment theorists does, therefore, apply in these respects to black women; for like white women, they were subjugated to men who used them for their own interests.

Unfortunately, the women's movement in the nineteenth century did not sustain its early concern about the black woman. Perhaps in bitterness over what she regarded as the abolitionists' betrayal, perhaps as a political tactic, Stanton in particular engaged in racist rhetoric. And by the early years of the twentieth century women's suffrage organizations, hoping to woo white southern support, effectively abandoned the black woman.[28] Black women, however, continued to express their own feminist ideas. The most important African-American feminists were: Josephine St. Pierre Ruffin, Anna Julia

Cooper, Ida B. Wells, Frances E. W. Harper, and in the early twentieth century, Mary Church Terrell and Fannie Barrier Williams.

Not surprisingly, black feminists were not only concerned about women's rights issues such as the vote, but also with issues of racism, such as lynching and Jim Crow laws. They seemed concerned to establish the moral dignity and intellectual potential of the black woman and, in the tradition of Enlightenment liberalism, urged full educational opportunities for black women.

By the turn of the century some black feminists, notably Anna Julia Cooper, had developed an essentially cultural feminist perspective—that women had a special humanizing attribute to bring to the world of public discourse (see chapter 2). But, others, such as Frances E. W. Harper, were less sanguine. She questioned whether any group had a monopoly on purity and suggested that "moral and educational tests" be given to all persons to determine who should vote.[29]

One final piece of liberal theory introduced in the nineteenth century was that developed by Harriet Taylor and John Stuart Mill, the English philosophers. They engaged in a twenty-seven-year intellectual and personal liaison (they married in 1851) during which time they collaborated on three feminist tracts. While it is difficult to figure out who wrote what, I am following the judgment of Alice S. Rossi that Harriet wrote one of the early (1832) essays on marriage and divorce and "The Enfranchisement of Women" (1851), and that John Stuart wrote another of the 1832 essays and *The Subjection of Women* (1869).[30]

Harriet Taylor's 1832 article was one of the more radical proposed in the nineteenth century. Not only did it urge complete civil and political equality for women, including the opening of all public offices and occupations, but it also proposed the abolition of all laws relating to marriage. This meant the state would have no say in divorce proceedings—still a somewhat radical notion today.

Elizabeth Cady Stanton had early taken up the right of divorce as one of her central causes. In 1852 as president of the New York Woman's State Temperance Society she urged the passage of laws enabling divorce and custody of children for wives of "drunkards" (1: 481–82).[31] Later in her "Address on Marriage" before the 1860 National Woman's Rights Convention Stanton spelled out her demand for liberalized divorce laws, using natural rights doctrine once again (the natural right to the pursuit of happiness) to justify her claim (1: 716, n.)[32]

Harriet Taylor's "Enfranchisement of Women" (1851) borrowed heavily from American women's rights doctrine, particularly that issued at the 1850 Worcester convention. (Its resolutions are listed in *History of Woman Suffrage,* 1: 821.) Indeed, Taylor's treatise really served to publicize the Worcester declarations in England. Taking note of the natural rights basis of American feminism, Taylor states, "We do not imagine that any American democrat will evade the force of these expressions by the dishonest . . . subterfuge . . . that 'life, liberty, and the pursuit of happiness' are 'inalienable rights' of only one moiety of the human species" (96).

But Taylor echoes the more radical analysis developed by earlier theorists when she considers the reason for female subjugation.

> When . . . we ask why the existence of one-half the species should be merely ancillary to that of the other—why each woman should be a mere appendage to a man, allowed to have no interests of her own, that there may be nothing to compete in her mind with his interests and his pleasure; the only reason which can be given is that men like it (107).

Mill's *Subjection of Women* reflects its author's utilitarian principles and remains firmly in the English liberal tradition. Not only is "the legal subordination of one sex to the other . . . wrong in itself," it is "now one of the chief hindrances to human improvement" (125). The oppression of half the human race "dries up *pro tanto* the principal fountain of human happiness, and leaves the species less rich, to an inappreciable degree, in all that makes life valuable to the individual human being" (242). Thus Mill uses the utilitarian "greatest good for the greatest number" argument to protest women's situation.

Women's liberation is justified because it will enable each individual to experience the highest happiness. Such happiness derives from the full development of an individual's talents.

> But it is not only through the sentiment of personal dignity, that the free direction and disposal of their own faculties is a source of individual happiness, and to be fettered and restricted in it, a source of unhappiness, to human beings and not least to women. There is nothing, after disease, indigence, and guilt, so fatal to the pleasurable enjoyment of life as the want of a worthy outlet for the active faculties (239).

The individual indeed ought be allowed to grow to maximum potential and not be fixed to a prescribed place. "We ought . . . not to ordain that to be born a girl instead of a boy, any more than to be born black instead of white, or a commoner instead of a nobleman, shall decide the person's position through all life" (145). This remains the heart of liberal political theory today. In its 1966 Statement of Purpose the National Organization for Women (NOW), urged:

> NOW is dedicated to the proposition that women, first and foremost, are human beings, who like all other people in our society, must have the chance to develop their fullest human potential. We believe that women can achieve such equality only by accepting to the full the challenges and responsibilities they share with all other people in our society, as part

> of the decision-making mainstream of American political, economic and social life.[33]

Like other early theorists Mill criticizes irrational customs and prejudices and calls for rational analysis of such traditions as a means of opening up opportunities for women to move beyond their prescribed, limited sphere. "So long as an opinion is strongly rooted in the feelings, it gains rather than loses in stability by having a preponderating weight of argument against it" (126). The status quo, the subjection of women, was not "the result of deliberation or forethought, . . . or any notion whatever of what conduced to the benefit of humanity or the good of society" (129). In fact, Mill argues, continued subjection is rooted in a prehistoric disproportion in physical strength; while civilization has in other respects transcended "the law of the strongest" (131), it has not done so with respect to women.

Moving somewhat beyond Stanton's tentative critique of the home, Mill attacks it and the male-female relationship therein as the principal site of women's oppression. He perceives women's status in marriage as a tyranny. And, echoing Wollstonecraft, Mill notes that because of her moral and financial dependence, "being attractive to men [has] . . . become the polar star of feminine education and formation of character" (141).

Mill, too, concludes with a radical feminist analysis: the reason women continue in a state of subjection—apart from the continuance of traditional roles—is that it is in men's interest to keep them there. The root of public exclusion of women lies in the male desire "to maintain [women's] subordination in domestic life; because the generality of the male sex cannot yet tolerate the idea of living with an equal" (181). Mill did not seriously question the role of women within the family as sustainers of the domestic sphere, however, and some critics have pointed to this as a flaw in his feminist theory.[34]

Women in the United States finally succeeded in obtaining the right to vote in 1920 when the Nineteenth or Anthony Amendment to the Constitution was finally ratified. Unfortunately, it soon became clear that, just as the Emancipation Proclamation had not eliminated discrimination against blacks, neither had the suffrage amendment established equal rights for women. With this realization apparent in 1922 the National Woman's Party—originally a militant suffrage organization established as the Congressional Union by Alice Paul in 1914—issued a declaration of principles. This declaration reiterated many of the ideas of the original Declaration of Sentiments issued at Seneca Falls in 1848, including this summary resolution: "That Woman shall no longer be in any form of subjection to man in law or in custom, but shall in every way be on an equal plane in rights, as she has always been and will continue to be in responsibilities and obligations."[35] Paul codified this demand into the "Lucretia Mott Amendment" which was introduced in Congress in 1923. It read: "Men and women shall have equal rights throughout the United States and every place subject to its jurisdiction." Later the wording was modified to read: "Equality of rights under the law shall not be denied or abridged by the United States or by any state on account of sex." This succinct expression of liberal doctrine, now known as the Equal Rights Amendment, languished in the Congress until 1972, at which time both houses approved it, and the ratification process began. An extended ratification deadline expired in 1982; the amendment was immediately reintroduced in Congress, but it has never passed. The natural rights doctrine of the Enlightenment remains a central premise of the mainstream women's movement today (for further discussion, see chapter 2).

There has been a tendency among feminists to write off the nineteenth-century women's rights movement as a relative failure, partly because the vote did not end women's subordinate status and because it is clear that oppression still continues today. However, beside the vote, which was not a negligible achievement, the women's rights movement had a number of other significant successes. The most important of these was the drastic change in married women's status by mid-century, when nearly all states had adopted legislation protecting married women's property. This gave the married woman considerable leverage to establish her own economic base and also improved her legal position in child custody cases. Divorce laws were also liberalized. Finally, the doors to higher education and many professions began to open to women by the 1880s.

On the other hand, there are some basic problems with Enlightenment feminist theory. The first is that a strictly liberal analysis left the private sphere untouched. As noted, most liberal feminists veered toward a radical feminist position, attributing the subjection of women as a class to men and to patriarchal or male-serving systems of education and social organization. This necessarily led them to criticize the domestic sphere, the home, and marriage; but basically they thought that such legal changes as the married woman's property acts would equalize women's status within marriage. None seemed seriously to consider that the division of the world into public and private and the assumption that women uphold the domestic world—including the duty of child rearing—might interfere with women's ability to enjoy equal rights and opportunities, even if they were granted. As Zillah Eisenstein puts it, they did not seem to consider that women, because of the duties ascribed to them as a class, would necessarily start the race at a disadvantage.[36] Nor did they develop ideas for any instituational alternatives to traditional marriage and motherhood. It remained for Charlotte Perkins Gilman to develop this more radical feminist theory at the turn of the century (see chapter 2).

Another question liberals leave unanswered is whether there really are significant "ontological" differences between women and men. Mill addresses the question but generally concludes, as do other liberals, that what differences exist are minor and the result of conditioning. Nevertheless, a strong counter current in nineteenth-century feminism asserted just the opposite:

that women are different. The conclusions drawn from this premise are treated in chapter 2, while aspects of the contemporary discussions of "differentness" appear in chapters 7 and 8.

Finally, the public-private split presumed by Enlightenment theory involves further serious questions that are with us today and which touch upon the fundamental organization of our moral, social, and political life. For, aside from "natural rights" which appear like *dei ex machina,* the Newtonian world view provided no means of establishing or legitimizing qualities and values. The mechanistic public world was governed by mathematical laws and statistical facts; the only possible judgments were quantitative. Qualitative judgments and assessments of value had necessarily to be relegated to the marginal Other world of the private sphere. The medieval cosmos, by contrast, had incorporated values and qualitative properties into its hierarchical world-scheme. Good was at the top and Evil at the bottom, figuratively ranged in Dante's *Divine Comedy.* (I do not mean to imply that a woman was any better off under this system, only that the terms of her oppression and its theoretical justification had changed.)

It was Machiavelli who first codified this split between fact and value and described the public sphere as an amoral realm. As one historian puts it, "Machiavelli's chief contribution to political thought lies in his freeing political action from moral considerations." "Thus he established a cleavage between political conduct and personal morality—a cleavage that haunts the conscience . . . even to this day."[37] As Ernst Cassirer notes, in the Machiavellian view "the political world has lost its connection not only with religion or metaphysics but also with all other forms of . . . ethical and cultural life. It stands alone—in an empty space" (140). This divorce between ethics and politics also occurred in the economic sphere. It was indeed most congenial to the then-emerging system of economic organization, capitalism; for it relieved entrepreneurs of any moral scruples in conducting their affairs and allowed their machinations to proceed morally unchecked.

Cassirer notes that the only restraint on the fundamental amorality, or immorality, of the modern Machiavellian secular state has been the natural rights doctrine (141). (And that does not necessarily apply in the economic sphere, which is held to be an area of "private" enterprise.) In the United States today the only means of asserting moral judgments in the public sphere is either by relying on the Bill of Rights or by asserting one's individual moral truth, in the religious tradition of Sarah Grimké, and persuading enough others of its validity to form a majority. The rule of the majority is a quantitative judgment, which ultimately says nothing about the ethical legitimacy of its position. There is, indeed, no "absolute" way to validate that legitimacy.

In *The Prince,* Machiavelli asserts that a leader rules "either by fortune or by ability (virtú)" (13), the latter implying manipulative rationality and a certain macho willingness to exert military control. It was derived from the behavior of the much-admired Renaissance bully boys, the *condottieri.* Fortuna, on the other hand, represented the nonrational, that which is unpredictable, all that was *other* to the exertion of rational control and masculine domination.

Fortuna, to Machiavelli, was a woman who must be mastered either by "cold calculation" or by force. The latter, he notes, works better. "For fortune is a woman and in order to be mastered she must be jogged and beaten. And it may be noted that she submits more readily to boldness than to cold calculation" (86–87).

Machiavelli then articulates the central assumption of the post-medieval world view, of a division between the rational and the nonrational. Rational calculation governs the public world amorally; it is a masculine sphere. On the other hand is the nonrational sphere, the world of women, which must be kept in its place, or if it strays into the public realm, must be brutally subdued. The congruence between Newtonian-Cartesian rationalism, as explained above, and Machiavellian politics is clear.

In her excellent work, *The Death of Nature: Women, Ecology, and the Scientific Revolution,* Carolyn Merchant points out that the witch craze developed in Europe and in New England at the same time as the Newtonian world view was gaining ascendency. The witch was the quintessentially irrational woman who had mysterious powers beyond the scope of scientific rationality. She therefore symbolized the *other* marginal world that the rationalists feared and wished to subdue. Merchant notes that in their eyes "the witch, symbol of the violence of nature, raised storms, caused illness, destroyed crops, obstructed generation, and killed infants. Disorderly woman, like chaotic nature, needed to be controlled."[38]

The development of the scientific method, particularly by Francis Bacon, involved an attempt to impose rationality and scientific order upon vegetative, organic nature. It required that nature therefore be transformed into a spirit-less "it" in order that rational methodological procedures "work" as they do in predicting the motions of the heavenly bodies.[39] Merchant suggests that it was during this period that women became identified with resisting nature, and that, as with Machiavelli, scientists like Bacon came to desire to subdue an irrational ("feminized") nature. Bacon, indeed, lived during a period of an intense witch scare and used the analogy of a witch interrogation to explain his scientific method of extracting "truth" from nature. He wrote: "For you have but to follow and as it were hound nature in her wanderings, and you will be able when you like to lead and drive her afterward to the same place again" (168). As Merchant notes,

> The interrogation of witches as symbol for the interrogation of nature, the courtroom as model for its inquisition, and torture through mechanical devices as a tool for the subjugation of disorder was fundamental to the scientific method (172).

Nature in the scientific world view is therefore seen as a woman, according to Merchant, who "takes orders from man and works under his authority" (171).

The association of women with nature cannot, however, be accepted uncritically.[40] For, nature does not take on the personal qualities of a living woman in the scientific view; rather both nature and women take on the qualities of an Other to the rational I, the male subject. They become an It, profane, something to be controlled and manipulated to run as the physical cosmos does in the Newtonian hypothesis—that is, rationally.[41] The impulse in the scientific view is to impose rational order on all that is alive, unpredictable, and therefore nonrational. There is a perpetual tension, therefore, between the marginal, animated, sacred, thou-world of organic nature and women, and on the other hand, the rational predictable public world of Newtonian scientists and Machiavellian politicians. Contemporary Freudian feminists suggest that modern patriarchal civilization is indeed built upon this masculine impulse to repress, reject, and subdue the feminine (see chapter 4 for a further elaboration of these theories, as well as chapter 7, including note 15).

To the extent that liberal political theory ignores this situation, it sanctions the derogation of women and organic nature—the moral domination of the private sphere by the public and the feminine by the masculine. Critics of liberalism have noted the consequences of this assumption,[42] but none has proposed a satisfactory resolution of the divisions between public and private, fact and value, the secular and the religious, between men's and women's worlds. Theorists are understandably reluctant to alter the concept of limited government, despite the division of experience it entails, because of the horrendous consequences that resulted from "organic" totalitarian systems in the twentieth century. Nevertheless, liberalism is limited in that while it may provide for justice of means, it does not afford a morality of ends.

Contemporary feminist theorists urge that some integration between the two sides is necessary if the ultimate catastrophe, a nuclear holocaust or a biotic meltdown, is to be avoided. Following in the vein of Virginia Woolf's *Three Guineas* (1938), these feminists assert that there is a connection between the derogation of women, the compartmentalization of life, and the unbridled militarism and corporate imperialism at loose in the world today. They contend that a more holistic vision is necessary if women and their morality of ends are not to be perpetually consigned to an ineffective marginal sphere, excluded from the public realm and the scientific-industrial community, which continues largely unchecked by humane considerations for the future of organic life on earth.

2 Nineteenth-Century Cultural Feminism

I have an intense and
endless love for women.
Charlotte Perkins Gilman, 1898

The legacy of Enlightenment feminist theory is with us still. It provides an image of woman as a rational, responsible agent; one who is able, if given a chance, to take care of herself, to further her own possibilities. Mary Wollstonecraft and Sarah Grimké's indictment of women's socialization as servants of men still remains an important item on the feminist agenda. And the important legal changes brought about by liberal theory have been a significant factor in the improvement of women's status.

There are other veins of equal importance in nineteenth-century feminist theory, however, ideas that may be grouped under the label "cultural feminism," because they go beyond the fundamentally rationalist and legalistic thrust of Enlightenment liberal theory. Instead of focusing on political change, feminists holding these ideas look for a broader cultural transformation. While continuing to recognize the importance of critical thinking and self-development, they also stress the role of the nonrational, the intuitive, and often the collective side of life. Instead of emphasizing the similarities between men and women, they often stress the differences, ultimately affirming that feminine qualities may be a source of personal strength and pride and a fount of public regeneration. These feminists imagined alternatives to institutions the liberal theorists left more or less intact—religion, marriage, and the home. By the turn of the century this vein of feminist theory moved beyond a view of women's rights as ends in themselves and saw them finally as a means to effect larger social reform.[1] Feminist social reform theory held that women should and must enter the public sphere and have the vote because their moral perspective was needed to clean up the corrupt (masculine) world of politics.[2]

Underlying this cultural feminist theory was a matriarchal vision: the idea of a society of strong women guided by essentially female concerns and values. These included, most importantly, pacifism, cooperation, nonviolent settlement of differences, and a harmonious regulation of public life. In the latter part of the nineteenth century this utopian vision was expressed in the theory of the matriarchate, a period of mother-rule which was postulated by anthropologists to have existed in prehistoric times. It found fictional expression in the women's literature of the period,[3] most graphically in Charlotte Perkins Gilman's matriarchal utopia, *Herland* (1911).

It seems likely that this matriarchal vision arose at least in part as a response to the masculinist ideology of Social Darwinism that swept Western thinking in the latter part of the century. This ideology, discussed below, not only provided ammunition for antifeminists, it also espoused a philosophy of competition and war that was anathema to these feminists. The matriarchal vision may also have arisen as a means of perpetuating the experience of intense female-bonding that characterized nineteenth-century female society (see further discussion below). By the last quarter of the century those female networks—themselves segregated matriarchal islands—were beginning to disintegrate for reasons not yet fully understood.[4]

Margaret Fuller's *Woman in the Nineteenth Century* (1845) initiated the cultural feminist tradition. As a product of the European romantic movement, or more specifically of American transcendentalism, it stresses the emotional, intuitive side of knowledge and expresses an organic world view that is quite different from the mechanistic view of Enlightenment rationalists.

Romanticism (or transcendentalism) and liberalism do, however, share a fundamental individualism. The transcendentalists believed strongly that individuals should develop to their fullest and should be taught to take responsibility for their lives. Emerson's essay on "Self-Reliance" is the classic expression of this position. But the romantic concept of individualism differed from the liberal in that it posited the individual in the process of organic growth. Anything that impeded that growth was held to be evil, including society or government when it checked the free unfolding of the individual. The liberal view of government, on the other hand, was not so much as a barrier against self-development but as a shield that protected the individual from other tyrannizing forces.

Fuller, who had studied such German romantics as Goethe and Novalis, as well as the English poets Wordsworth, Coleridge, Shelley, and Keats, took over the romantic idea of the individual and applied it to women. "For human beings are not so constituted that they can live without expansion."[5] "We would have every arbitrary barrier thrown down. We would have every path laid open to Woman as freely as to Man" (37).

> What Woman needs is not as a woman to act or rule, but as a nature to grow, as an intellect to discern, as a soul to live freely and unimpeded, to unfold [her] powers . . . (38).

It is in the context of this idea of organic growth that Fuller declares women must develop "self-reliance." Too long, she urges, women have been "taught to learn their rule from without, not to unfold it from within" (40), a statement that recalls earlier feminist concern about socialization (Wollstonecraft and Grimké) and anticipates Stanton's "Solitude of Self" (which nevertheless remains more of a liberal than a romantic document). Fuller's idea is that each individual is born as a seed with a unique design imprinted within (a favorite romantic image); it must be allowed to unfold through one's life course. This is what she means when she states that women must learn to follow the rule within, and not be dictated to from without. Such self-determination enables a woman to develop personal strength in her encounters with the world, an observation similar to that made by Wollstonecraft, Grimké, and Stanton; it enables her to stand on her own.

Fuller borrows from Native American tradition[6] to illustrate separatism as a means of developing self-reliance: There was once an Indian woman, who believing herself betrothed to the sun, moved out of her camp, "built her a wigwam apart, filled it with emblems of her alliance, and means of an independent life. There she passed her days, sustained by her own exertions, and true to her supposed engagement" (101). Fuller lauds the fact that her tribe tolerated this eccentricity, and urges that she be considered a symbol of the way women should live—apart from the dictates of the crowd, alone in communion with their sun, their truth.

> I would have Woman lay aside all thought, such as she habitually cherishes, of being taught and led by men. I would have her, like the Indian girl, dedicate herself to the Sun, the Sun of Truth. . . . I would have her free from compromise, from complaisance, from helplessness, because I would have her good enough and strong enough to love . . . from the fulness, not the poverty of being (119–20).

Such isolation and self-development through communion with one's own truth, according to Fuller, make one better able to relate to others, to love out of strength, not weakness. Fuller's concern about loving relationships and connectedness to community is not something one finds in liberal Enlightenment theory.

Not only do women need to have the freedom to unfold their faculties and discover their own truths as individuals, they need, collectively as women, to discover who they really are. Such a process must be done separately, with other women: "I believe that, at present, women are the best helpers of one another" (172). Fuller contends that we will discover that women have their own unique character; that they are fundamentally different from men.

"Were they free, were they wise fully to develop the strength and beauty of Woman; they would never wish to be men, or manlike" (63).

Fuller urges therefore that women collectively retire or withdraw from the world in order to discover their true and distinct nature.

> Women must leave off asking [men] and being influenced by them, but retire within themselves, and explore the groundwork of life till they find their peculiar secret. Then, when they come forth again, renovated and baptized, they will know how to turn all dross to gold. (121)

Women's one special capacity which is already evident, according to Fuller, is an "electric nature." There is an electrical intensity about women that men do not have. But the present organization of society that relegates women to the domestic sphere and to mental duties does not allow this electricity to be expressed; consequently it goes awry in many women and becomes destructive (a proto-Freudian notion). "Yet, allow room enough, and the electric fluid will be found to invigorate and embellish, not destroy life" (104). In fact, however, "the electrical, the magnetic element in Woman has not been fairly brought out at any period. Everything might be expected from it; she has far more of it than Man" (103).

Beyond a personal quality of intensity Fuller seems to mean by this electric element an intuitive intellectual faculty: "The especial genius of Woman I believe to be electrical in movement, intuitive in function, spiritual in tendency" (115).

> [Women's] intuitions are more rapid and more correct. You will often see men of high intellect absolutely stupid in regard to the atmospheric changes, the fine invisible links which connect the forms of life around them, while common women . . . will seize and delineate these with unerring discrimination (103).

Women, in other words, have an intuitive perception that goes beyond reason to understand the subtle connections among people and among all life forms; today we would say, women's vision is holistic. But, because men do not see these subtle connections, women's perceptions are ridiculed and denied. "Their quick impulses seem folly" to those who do not comprehend the whole picture. Such denial of women's realities is, needless to say, oppressive and destructive to the women themselves.

Moreover, it deprives the public world of an element, a perception without which it remains one-sided and limited. Instead, Fuller argues, an influx of the feminine will radically change society. She wavers, however, as to what that change will be. It may result in a somewhat vaguely conceived cultural androgyny. Or, it may result in the "feminization" of culture.

The cultural androgyny Fuller envisages seems to be drawn to some extent from the theories of Emmanuel Swedenborg (1688–1772), a theosophist whose neo-Platonic notion of a correspondence between the microcosm and the macrocosm was an integral part of romantic theory. Fuller seems to feel that a psychic synthesis of masculine and feminine attributes would be reflected in the outer world, creating a dialectic of complementary opposites, like yin and yang, an organic, harmonic whole. "Male and female represent the two sides of the great radical dualism . . . they are perpetually passing into one another" (115–16).

> The growth of Man [the generic]
> is two-fold, masculine and feminine.
> So far as these two methods can
> be distinguished, they are so as
> Energy and Harmony;
> Power and Beauty;
> Intellect and Love (169).

"If these two developments were in perfect harmony, they would correspond to and fulfill one another, like hemispheres" (170); "a ravishing harmony of the spheres, would ensue" (37).

On the other hand, the result of integrating the feminine into the public world may be a desired feminization of culture. This would mean the reinstatement of a "plant-like gentleness," a harmonic, peaceful rule, an end to violence in all areas, including such violence against self as the use of alcohol and drugs and the slaughter of animals for food.[7] It would mean "the establishment of the reign of love and peace" (113). "For, Woman, if by a sympathy as to outward condition, she is led to the enfranchisement of the slave, must be no less so, by inward tendency, to favor measures which promise to bring the world more thoroughly and deeply in harmony with her nature" (114). Fuller argues that women's magnetic or electric nature is "identical" with the idea that woman is the "harmonizer of the vehement elements." This is apparent if one considers that women's intuitive faculties lead her toward a holistic vision; such a perspective is necessarily synthetic: it encompasses the reconciliation and binding together of elements that are thought to be disparate. Such a process appreciates and does not destroy "the singleness of life" (115).

Fuller, therefore, lays out the first theory of women's differentness, and of how their life and the life of society would be changed were their special qualities allowed expression. She therefore links the liberation of women with the amelioration of life on earth, as later feminists were to do.

While Stanton and Anthony's fundamental theoretical position always remained that of natural rights, they had by the 1870s begun analyzing women's issues that carried them beyond the pale of traditional liberal thought. Their journal, *The Revolution,* which was published from 1868 to 1870, included discussions of prostitution, venereal disease, rape, and working women's conditions. They also advocated dress reform and proper physical training for women.[8] In general, their analysis was that the root of women's oppression was their economic and moral dependence on men. Many of these issues had in fact been touched upon by earlier theorists. Margaret Fuller made sympathetic remarks in *Woman in the Nineteenth Century* about the plight of prostitutes; she had visited them in prison and contemplated establishing halfway houses for released female convicts.[9]

Sarah Grimké had called for equal pay for equal work for women wage earners, a demand repeated by Anthony in 1868, in *The Revolution* and as chair of the National Labor Union's Committee on Female Labor. This Committee's report, labeled "historic" by the historian Philip S. Foner, also demanded an eight-hour day and trade unions for women. The NLU, however, rejected the Committee's demand for women's suffrage. And from this point on the brief alliance between Stanton, Anthony, and the labor movement went rapidly downhill.[10] Thereafter, Anthony's position on women workers crystalized around the vote.

Perhaps the most radical of the cultural feminist positions developed by Stanton was her critique of religion, in particular Christianity. She was joined in this by Matilda Joslyn Gage (1826–98) whose *Woman, Church And State* (1893) remains one of the most powerful pieces of feminist theory produced in the nineteenth century, one that had fallen into obscurity until it was republished in 1980. Stanton's main assault on patriarchal Christianity is to be found in *The Woman's Bible,* published in two parts in 1895 and 1898, and in an 1891 article entitled "The Matriarchate."

The Woman's Bible illustrates the radical purposes to which natural rights doctrine could be put. For in it Stanton establishes that natural rights principles are on a higher moral plane—are closer to God, so to speak—than the Bible; she therefore uses natural rights theory to repudiate the validity of biblical ethics and, indeed, that of the entire ensuing Judeo-Christian tradition. "We cannot accept," she urges, "any code or creed that uniformly defrauds woman of all her natural rights."[11] With these words she dismisses the Ten Commandments as being unworthy of and irrelevant to women. Her overall position is that the Old Testament is an expression of a tribal morality of centuries past and has little or no contemporary ethical relevance. "The Pentateuch," she insists in truly incendiary language, must be seen as "emanating from the most obscene minds of a barbarous age" (1: 126).

> The question naturally suggests itself to any rational mind, why should the customs and opinions of this ignorant people, who lived centuries ago, have any influence in the religious thought of this generation? (1: 71)

By the 1890s Stanton had come to the conclusion that it was a mindless reliance on the Bible and its supposed doctrine of women's inferiority that was the central force in perpetuating an ideology of women's subjugation. Such a thesis implied that political rights would not be enough to change women's status; a revolution in social and religious attitudes was necessary.

Stanton begins *The Woman's Bible* by asserting that it is the Bible that is the ultimate source to which antifeminists always refer: "the Bible [is] used to hold [woman] in the 'divinely ordained sphere,' prescribed in the Old and New Testaments" (1: 7). "Creeds, codes, Scriptures and statutes, are all based" on the patriarchal idea "that woman was made after man, of man, and for man, an inferior being, subject to man" (1: 7).

The Woman's Bible is built on a series of commentaries Stanton and a panel of feminist scholars made on those passages of the Bible that concern women. It is clear that Stanton's strategy was, first, to discredit the authority of the Bible where it presents negative ideas about women, to laud its positive images of women, and finally, to develop alternative religious traditions more congenial to women. In her commentary on Genesis, for example, she points out, as had Sarah Grimké, that it includes two contradictory stories of the creation. Stanton chooses to focus on the first story (Gen. 1: 26–27) and dismisses the second (Gen. 2: 21–23), in which God made Eve out of Adam's rib, as an expression of the male supremacist ideology of its author. Subsequent tradition has focused on this version, which posits female inferiority, but Stanton urges that we return to the first where God created man and woman as equals "in his image."

From this Stanton elaborates one of her most important ideas; echoing Margaret Fuller, she urges that the Godhead be considered androgynous. Genesis 1: 27 implies that the "masculine and feminine elements were equally represented" in the deity (1: 14). (Stanton found a similarly androgynous god in the Jewish Kabbalah [2: 108].) Like Fuller, she postulates androgyny as the central rule of the cosmos.

> The masculine and feminine elements, exactly equal and balancing each other, are as essential to the maintenance of the equilibrium of the universe as positive and negative electricity, the centripetal and centrifugal forces, the laws of attraction which bind together all we know of this planet whereon we dwell and of the system in which we revolve (1: 15).

She suggests that the heavenly being is an androgynous one. "Scientists tell us that both the masculine and feminine elements were united in one person in the beginning, and will probably be reunited again for eternity" (2: 122). Stanton believes, therefore, that it is imperative to restore the concept of femininity to the deity. She advocates prayer to a "Heavenly Mother."

> The first step in the elevation of woman to her true position, as an equal factor in human progress, is the . . . recognition . . . of an ideal Heavenly Mother, to whom . . . prayers should be addressed, as well as to a Father (1: 14).

Stanton goes further in her search for a cultural tradition that reveres rather than denigrates women: she introduces the theory of the matriarchate. According to this anthropoligical theory there once existed a period in which "for centuries woman ruled supreme." After this came the patriarchate in which men rule, and after it will come an androgynous period, Stanton says, called the "Amphiarchate," in which both will reign as equals." It is, she predicts, "close at hand" (1: 25).

Stanton's thesis, which she elaborated in "The Matriarchate," derived from contemporaneous theories found in such works as J. J. Bachofen's *Das Mutterrecht* (1861), Henry Maine's *Ancient Law* (1870), and Lewis H. Morgan's *Ancient Society* (1877), works which were also used by Gage in *Woman, Church and State,* and by Frederick Engels in his feminist treatise (see chapter 3). Modeled in part on the American Iroquois nation, the idea of a matriarchate took hold among nineteenth-century cultural feminists and became an expression of their own utopian ideals.[12]

Stanton conceived the rule of the mothers as a period in which women "reigned supreme" as "arbiters of their own destiny, the protectors of their children, the acknowledged builders of all there was of home life, religion, and . . . of government."[13] Such a society reflected the values and concerns of the women who created it. All the early accomplishments of civilization were effected by mothers concerned about protecting and nourishing their children: homes, early agriculture, early medicine, and domestication of animals. Women also encouraged social behavior that made the community cohere; these included "the arts of peace, and the sentiments of kinship." "The necessities of motherhood were the real source of all the earliest attempts at civilization" (144).

Stanton's main interest in the idea of the matriarchate is that it will help to restore a "sense of dignity and self-respect" in women to know "that our mothers, during some periods in the long past, have been the ruling power, and that they used that power for the best interests of humanity" (147). Were women once again permitted to rule, we would have "a civilization at last in which ignorance, poverty, and crime will exist no more . . ." (147). In short, Stanton saw the matriarchate as "a golden age of peace and plenty" and the patriarchate as the "source of tyranny, wars and [all] social ills."[14]

In rejecting the Bible, therefore, Stanton is rejecting the patriarchate and advocating the creation of a new society in which mothers will rule, or at least participate in ruling. Because of their connection with the life-giving force women should be considered "as sacred as the priesthood" (*Woman's Bible* 1: 102), and their perspectives and values welcomed. She establishes (somewhat unrealistically) Queen Victoria as the model of a woman who could rule and be a mother at the same time. "Why should . . . American women be incapable of discharging similar public and private duties at the same time in an equally commendable manner?" (1: 78).

Stanton does not seem to want to consider that such a double task might be well nigh impossible for any but the most heroically organized individuals; the arrangement of the domestic sphere is left fundamentally unquestioned. She does, however, suggest that the home would be enriched if fathers were there more and the public world enhanced by the presence of mothers. For "the home is in a condition of half orphanage for want of fathers, and the State suffers for need of wise mothers" (1: 37).

Stanton introduced, or deepened (if Fuller is credited with first proposing the idea), an important new vein in feminist theory: the idea that women, and in particular mothers, have special experiences and capabilities that lead them to express a life-affirming, pacifist, creative world view. That perspective has been put in eclipse by the patriarchs, whose reign has been one of destruction, tryanny, and war. In order to bring about a new, positive era, women and their feminine perspective must once again be integrated into the public powers of government and religion.[15]

The Woman's Bible was not popular among suffragists; indeed the 1896 national woman's rights convention passed a resolution dissociating the NAWSA from it—a resolution which Anthony attempted to block, as did a newcomer to the feminist scene named Charlotte Perkins Stetson (later Gilman).

By this time Matilda Joslyn Gage, an important figure in the nineteenth-century movement, had split off from the NAWSA and from Stanton and Anthony since she believed their views had become too conservative. In particular, she rejected their pragmatic cohabitation with the Woman's Christian Temperance Union, a conservative group that to Gage was anathema. Earlier, Gage had collaborated with Anthony and Stanton in putting together the multivolume *History of Woman Suffrage*. She in fact wrote the first chapter, which is still a cogent statement of first-wave feminist theory. Her magnum opus, however, was *Woman, Church and State*. The book antedated the first part of *The Woman's Bible* by two years, but Gage carried her critique of the Judeo-Christian tradition much further than Stanton. Indeed, the work is a nineteenth-century version of Elizabeth Gould Davis's *The First Sex*, which also provides reams of information about the history of women's oppression and matriarchal societies of the past. Some or much of this material has been questioned by contemporary scholars, but enough of it is historically accurate for one to appreciate that, like Davis, Gage constructed what Mary Daly has called an "a-Mazing" theory.

Despite the radical implications of her ideas—she advocates no less than the overthrow of the established church and its doctrines—Gage's theory is, like Stanton's, rooted in natural rights theory and in the Protestant emphasis on individual conscience. Gage therefore carries on the radical antinomianism of such predecessors as Grimké and Wright, and the liberal individualism of her contemporary Stanton.

A resolution drafted by Gage and adopted by the 1878 woman's rights convention held in Rochester, New York, stated her theoretical position clearly:

> *Resolved:* That as the first duty of every individual is self-development, the lessons of self-sacrifice and obedience taught to woman by the Chris-

tian church have been fatal, not only to her own vital interests, but through her, to those of the race.

Resolved: That the great principle of the Protestant Reformation, the right of the individual conscience and judgment heretofore exercised by men alone, should now be claimed by women; that, in the interpretation of Scripture, she should be guided by her own reason, and not by the authority of the church.[16]

Believing firmly in "the political doctrine of the sovereignty of the individual" (240), Gage recommends that women follow Lucretia Mott's aphorism and accept "truth for authority and not authority for truth" (241).

Gage's theory is that the oppression of women is rooted in Christian doctrine and in particular the idea, derived from Genesis, of women's inferiority and wickedness. Even English common law, as seen in Blackstone, which codifies women's lack of legal status, is rooted in canon law and therefore ultimately in Christian doctrine (48). The centuries during which Christianity dominated were truly dark ages of "barbarism" from which "the world is slowly awakening to the fact that every human being stands upon the plane of equal rights" (133). Elsewhere, Gage hailed Magellan's circumnavigation of the earth as "the first step toward woman's enfranchisement" because it helped destroy the medieval Christian world view.[17] She therefore shares the rationalist belief that humans are progressing toward an enlightened state by rejecting the superstitions and customs of the past.

Unlike Grimké and Stanton, who criticized specific biblical passages, Gage regards biblical and Christian doctrine as products of the patriarchate and therefore tainted and expendable. Grimké had argued that God's curse on Eve was not really a curse but merely a prophecy (Letter 1). Gage moves beyond such casuistical nit-picking (as did Grimké herself) and mounts a condemnation of the entire Christian tradition.

During the Christian ages, the church has not alone shown cruelty and contempt for women, but has exhibited an impious and insolent disregard of her most common rights of humanity. It has robbed her of her responsibility, putting man in place of God. It has forbidden her the offices of the church. . . . It has denied her independent thought, declaring her a secondary creation for man's use. . . . It has anathematized her sex, teaching her to feel shame for the very fact of her being (*Woman, Church and State,* 241).

More than any previous theorists, Gage catalogues a series of historical atrocities done to women and lays the responsibility for them at the door of the church. These included the feudal marchette (chapter 4), witch persecutions (chapter 5), treatment of wives (chapter 6), polygamy (chapter 7), and the condition of working women (chapter 8). In her discussion of the feudal marchette (the *jus primae noctis* in which the lord of the manor had first night privileges with tenants' brides), Gage presents a lengthy analysis of prostitution and concludes that "Christianity created the modern brothel . . ." (84). This is because Christianity presents "a religious theory which . . . has trained men into a belief that woman was but created as a plaything for their passions" (85).

The persecution of witches Gage also attributes to the Christian notion of "woman's extraordinary wickedness, based on a false theory as to original sin" (98). Gage also saw the witches as bearers of alternative feminine traditions, which established them as community powers feared by the church.[18] The other chapters detail considerable specific evidence of brutal treatment of women through the ages—all of which she attributes to Christian doctrines that allege women's inferiority and polluted character.

Like Stanton, Gage postulates the existence of a pre-Christian matriarchy, an era of "mother-rule." It was a period of peace and beneficence. "During the Matriarchate all life was regarded as holy; even the sacrifice of animals was unknown" (21). With the patriarchate, however, came a host of evils: prostitution, enslavement of women, family discord, and war (21).

Gage also calls for the reinstatement of the feminine, indeed the motherly, in the deity. "It is through a recognition of the divine element of motherhood" that evil will cease—especially toward women (23). "When the femininity of the divine is once again acknowledged . . . the holiness (wholeness) of the divinity [will] be manifested" (32). Instead of accepting the Old Testament notion of women's "uncleanness" we should revere the "life-giving principle exemplified in motherhood" (28).

The feminine must be reinstated in our picture of the cosmos, Gage continues, and proclaims that "science now declares the feminine principle to inhere in plants, rocks, gems, and even in the minutest atoms" (23). It is not clear to what she is referring here, nevertheless she plainly wished to alter the Newtonian paradigm by seeing the "feminine" at work even within the inert world of the physical universe.[19]

It was the early church fathers who "denied the femininity of the divine equally with the divinity of the feminine" (24). Gage's thesis refers to a time when many Gnostic sects, labeled heretical by the church fathers, included feminine aspects in the divinity and allowed women much fuller participation in ritual than did what became orthodox Christianity.[20]

In one of her most intriguing ideas, Gage borrows from occult theories to postulate that the notion of a "lost word" or a "lost name" is really the lost memory of the divine attribute of motherhood—of the feminine. When that is back in its rightful place in the cosmos and in the culture, the lost power will be restored (109, 234). Gage suggests further that the "lost word" may be connected with the witch's traditional wisdom. This may be the lost lore, the lost knowledge of which the occultists speak. It is a women's tradition of herbal medicine, of magical healing powers. Like Fuller, Gage believed women to have special intellectual capacities that are unique to them—in particular, an intuitive faculty, a "practical reason" that does not "need a long process of [obfuscating] ratiocination" for its work (238). It is through the operation of this faculty and through the "a-Mazing" connections it may make that women may rediscover their lost past, their lost culture (238).

Gage believed, with Stanton, that the restoration of the feminine should be symbolized by prayer to a mother goddess. She stunned the 1888 International Council of Women by beginning her session with a prayer addressed to a female deity by Isabella Beecher Hooker. Gage urged the startled assemblage to recognize the "Divine Motherhood of God" and called for the establishment of a "new female clergy for women" (xxxi).

Charlotte Perkins Gilman, often considered the leading theorist of "first-wave" feminist theory, continues the traditions of cultural feminism. Her work, however, is based on the tenets of Social Darwinism—indeed, one may consider her work as the major feminist attempt to wrestle with the implications of that ideology, to refute what was inimical to women and to coopt the positive. To understand Gilman's theory it is therefore necessary to summarize Social Darwinism.

Charles Darwin's theory of evolution was first expressed in *The Origin of Species by Means of Natural Selection, or the Preservation of Favored Races in the Struggle for Life.* It appeared in England in 1859 and in the United States the following year. Like Newton's theory, the Darwinian thesis swiftly became the governing paradigm of the age (or perhaps also like Newton's theory, Darwin's simply gave expression to what was already the governing metaphor).

Darwin's theory was that the species of plant and animal life had evolved over the centuries, from the simple to the more complex, and mainly through the mechanism of natural selection. Through this process the environment "selected" those variants in the species that were better adapted; because of population pressures the less fit died out and the more fit survived to procreate a new variety or a new species. Another mechanism through which evolution occurred was through sexual selection of the "struggle of males for females."

> With animals having separated sexes, there will be in most cases a struggle between the males for the possession of the females. The most vigorous males, or those which have most successfuly struggled with their conditions of life, will generally leave most progeny.[21]

This theory was more fully developed in Darwin's second major work, *The Descent of Man: and Selection in Relation to Sex* (1871), which promulgates a doctrine of male superiority.

Social Darwinism was not necessarily implied in Darwin's own theory, but applied Darwinian notions—in particular the "survival of the fittest" (a phrase he did not use)—to societies, races, or individuals. It was necessarily a conservative philosophy for it implied that whatever or whoever was on top deserved by inexorable design to be there. It also implied that the race was furthered by aggressive and competitive males. Some Social Darwinists carried this farther to argue that evolution or "progress" is sustained by murderous competition and war. Herbert Spencer, the main exponent of Social Darwinism, concluded that wars were a mechanism of social evolution and progress. While acknowledging the horrors of war, he concluded "we must nevertheless admit that without it the world would still have been inhabited only by men of feeble types sheltering in caves and living on wild food."[22]

The theory that life progresses by means of vicious competition and war became a convenient justification for American capitalists like John D. Rockefeller and Andrew Carnegie who saw in them license to pursue their business machinations ruthlessly.[23] As Jacques Barzun noted in his study of Darwinism, it gave Machiavellianism a new lease on life.

> Darwin did not invent the Machiavellian image that the world is the playground of the lion and the fox, but thousands discovered that he had transformed political science. Their own tendencies to act like lions and foxes thereby became irresistable "laws of nature" and "factors of progress," while moral arguments against them were dubbed "pre-scientific."[24]

Beyond licensing unbridled economic competition, Social Darwinism was held to justify war. Again, to quote Barzun:

> War became the symbol, the image, the inducement, and the language of all human doings on the planet. No one who has not waded through some sizeable part of the literature of the period 1879–1914 has any conception of the extent to which it is one long call for blood (92).

There was, however, another less-heeded vein in Social Darwinist thought, even in Spencer's work. It saw the race evolving toward a more collective organization which required more cooperative than competitive skills.[25] It required altruism, not egoism. Peter Kropotkin's *Mutual Aid* (1890) was the primary exponent of this thesis, and it was this aspect of Social Darwinism that Charlotte Perkins Gilman came to stress.

Gilman's *Women and Economics* (1898), her first major work, is predicated upon the Social Darwinist hypothesis which she used to prove that women's subjugation is an unnatural aberration that is impeding the progress of the race. People, she argues, are determined by their social and economic environment. The human female's social and economic environment is unnatural and artificial—that of economic dependence on the male. This has warped her development and threatens to drag down the whole race.

> We are the only animal species in which the female depends upon the male for food, the only animal species in which the sex-relation is also an

> economic relation. With us an entire sex lives in a relation of economic dependence upon the other sex.[26]

Yet this dependency is not necessitated by nature: human motherhood does not require segregation from all other work nor protection by the male (19); indeed the time a mother actually spends mothering is rather small (21). It is "an erratic and morbid action" (26) that has gotten the human race off the path of proper evolution: that of "excessive sex-indulgence," which is rooted in an excessive "sex-distinction," or excessive development of "secondary sex-characteristics" (30–32). Secondary sex-characteristics are features such as the horns of the stag or the plumage of the peacock. When such characteristics are too highly developed they interfere with the individual's and the race's development. They may be labeled morbid, and "all morbid conditions tend to extinction" (72). Gilman makes an allegorical comment on the situation of the human female: Imagine a peacock whose tail becomes so big he perishes, or conversely, peahens who become so "small and dull" that they die (35). Such is the state of the human race, Gilman implies.

The human situation of female dependence on the male prevents natural selection from checking excessive sex-development (37). Consequently, women have become stunted in most of their faculties and have developed only one—the capacity to attract a male—because this is their primary means of survival. As a parasite, the human female has learned how to attract and keep a host (62). Thus, working through the convolutions of Social Darwinism, Gilman comes to much the same conclusion as Wollstonecraft, Grimké and Mill: that women's primary energy is wrongly channeled into making themselves pleasing to men, this because of their economic dependency.

Gilman argues that all women are therefore reduced to the level of prostitution to survive: "Woman's economic profit comes through the power of sex-attraction" (63). Marriage is a form of prostitution: "in both cases the female gets her food from the male by virtue of her sex-relationship to him" (64).

Moreover, this economic dependency has kept women in a retarded state of development. "Woman has been checked, starved, aborted in human growth" (75). Gilman catalogs the ways in which women are kept in an unnatural state of helpless femininity: they are denied physical development of their bodies (44–46), they are forced to be preoccupied with a minute sphere of life (43), all avenues of development are blocked (53), their dress is silly and confining (55), they are restricted to the home (65), and generally prevented from engaging in creative, transcending work (67).

Gilman therefore urges a variety of changes that will alter women's condition of economic dependence, the most important of which is "to break up that relic of the patriarchal age,—the family as an economic unit" (151).

Since this important aspect of Gilman's theory is spelled out in more detail in *The Home* (1903), its consideration will be deferred.

The other major theory that Gilman introduces in *Women and Economics* derives from Spencer's and Kropotkin's notion that the race is evolving into a cooperative phase. Gilman seizes upon this to argue that the feminine virtues of altruism are most needed in this phase of development.

> Social evolution tends to an increasing specialization in structure and function, and to an increasing interdependence of the component parts, with a correlative disuse of the once valuable process of individual struggle for success (103).

Gilman maintains that "there is no female mind. The brain is not an organ of sex" (149); she nevertheless believes that at this stage in evolution men and women are very different. "The tendency to fight is a sex-distinction of males in general: the tendency to protect and provide for, is a sex-distinction of females in general" (41).

Like the other matriarchal theorists she believes the powers of maternal energy, of mother-love, to be a socially cohesive force. These powers are what are needed for the construction of a new, progressive, cooperative society. We need "most the quality of coordination—the facility in union, the power to make and to save rather than to spend and to destroy. These [are] female qualities" (129). Gilman sees the women's movement—in particular, the feelings of what second-wave feminists called sisterhood—as a harbinger of this new phase in social development because it augurs a new cooperative "social consciousness." "The woman's movement rests . . . on the wide, deep sympathy of women for one another" (139).

Gilman's *The Man-Made World, or Our Androcentric Culture* (1911) presents the most comprehensive statement of her overall theory. In it she follows Stanton in arguing that we live in a patriarchy, or what she calls an androcentric, male-centered society, and that our culture in all its aspects reflects this androcentric bias. Gilman sees this bias as destructive because the male sensitivity is destructive. A woman-centered, or better a mother-centered, world would be very different, because it would express the positive, benign character of women's sensitivities. In this work and in *His Religion and Hers* (see below) Gilman presents her most extreme statement of the radical differences between men and women. These differences she attributes to prehistoric roles assigned the two sexes. "The male naturally fights, and naturally crows, triumphs over his rival and takes the prize—therefore was he made male. Maleness means war" (92). "The basic feminine impulse is to gather, to put together, to construct; the basic masculine impulse to scatter, to disseminate, to destroy" (114).

Gilman's central thesis in this work is that a male-centered culture reflects these negative masculine concerns in nearly every area of expression. Some of her most original contributions to feminist theory are contained in her discussion of the ideological warp impressed upon language, art, literature, sports, education, government, and religion by the androcentric perspective. Her chapter, "Masculine Literature," is the first modern example of feminist literary criticism. It exemplifies her approach throughout. We have a "masculized literature," she argues, in which two main plots predominate—the Story of Adventure and the Love Story (94). "All these stories of adventure, of struggle and difficulty, of hunting and fishing and fighting, of robbing and murdering, catching and punishing, are distinctly and essentially masculine . . . [they dwell on] the special field of predatory excitement so long the sole province of men" (95). Women's experience is not depicted. "Half the world consists of women . . . who are types of human life as well as men, and their major processes are not those of conflict and adventure, their love means more than mating" (96). "Fiction, under our androcentric culture, has not given any true picture of woman's life" (102).

Not only in cultural affairs but also in the domestic organization of society is androcentricity expressed. Here Gilman extends her radical critique of the private sphere, which she carries much farther in *The Home* (see below). While public society is organized as a democracy, the man-made home remains a "Despotism." "The male is esteemed 'the head of the family'; it belongs to him; he maintains it; and the rest of the world is a wide hunting ground and battlefield wherein he competes with other males as of old" (41).

In the "proprietary family" of the patriarchate, women remain men's property in the household; they are little more than objects whose purpose is "first and foremost . . . a means of pleasure to him" (32). "Every law and custom" of the "family relation" "is arranged from the masculine viewpoint" (35). "From this same viewpoint . . . comes the requirement that the woman shall serve the man" (35). "The dominant male, holding his women as property, and fiercely jealous of them . . . has hedged them in with restrictions of a thousand sorts" (38). "Being so kept, she cannot develop humanly, as he has, through social contact, social service, true social life" (39). As put forward in *Women and Economics,* Gilman's solution is to radically change the home.

Gilman concludes *The Man-Made World* by urging that society move away from androcentricity wherein "man, as a sex, has . . . deified his own qualities" (133) toward a matriarchal value system. Here Gilman returns to the matriarchal utopian vision of her predecessors, urging that a world governed by the maternal ideology would be one which reveres "the principle of loving service" (251). It would express "the lasting love, the ceaseless service, the ingenuity and courage of efficient motherhood" (152). "Government by women . . . would be influenced by motherhood; and that would mean care, nurture, provision, education" (190). Gilman urges further, as she did in *Women and Economics,* that women are "fitter" "for administration of constructive social interests" because of their holistic and collective orientation. And since "we are entering upon a period of social consciousness" (191), the feminocentric must replace the androcentric as the controlling cultural ideology.

Gilman acknowledged the influence of Stanton's *Woman's Bible* on *His Religion and Hers* (1923), which is an extended critique of androcentric religion and a proposal for a women's religion. The gist of her theory is that because of their prehistoric roles men have created a death-oriented religion where a women's religion would be life-affirming.[27]

The "death-basis for religion" lies in the fact of primitive man's preoccupation with death. "Their occupation was in hunting and fighting. They lived mainly by killing other animals" (37). "Death was something to celebrate" (38). What, on the other hand, would a woman's religion be? "The business of primitive woman was to work and to bear children" (45). "Her glory was in giving life, not in taking it. To her the miracle, the stimulus to thought, was birth" (46). Because her role dealt with the protection of the child the primitive woman's ethic reflected "an immediate altruism" (46). This would be the core of her religion. A female conception of the deity would be of "the Life-giver, the Teacher, the Provider, the Protector—not the proud, angry, jealous, vengeful deity men have imagined" (51). God would be "a power promoting endless growth" (247). To summarize:

> the most widely entertained religious misconceptions rest on a morbid preoccupation with death and "another world" . . . this is due mainly to the fact that they have been developed by . . . the male, in whose life as a hunter and a fighter death was the impressive crisis; . . . the female, the impressive crisis of whose life is birth, has an essentially different outlook, much more in line with social progress (6).

Gilman concludes, "A normal feminine influence in recasting our religious assumptions will do more than any other thing to improve the world" (7).

Gilman's matriarchal vision is embodied in her utopia, Herland, described in a novel of that title (1915). Matriarchal traditions govern in this all-female land (where women reproduce by parthenogenesis). Mother-love is the basis for their religion and a mother goddess or a "Maternal Pantheism" is the prime diety.[28]

The women in Herland live collectively, are peaceful and harmonic, vegetarian, physically strong, and competent. There are no "homes" as we know them; child rearing is a profession, wastes are recycled, and the country is dotted with "help" temples where people may drop in for loving care and attention when in need. *Herland* reflects the matriarchal value system, seen as early as Margaret Fuller, embodying a reverence for peace and harmony and an ecological concern for all forms of life. This vision was at the heart of the theory developed by the pacifist-feminists in the early twentieth century (discussed below).

Gilman's other major work, *The Home* (1903), was in many ways her most radical, for it attacked the institution of the home in iconoclastic tones reminiscent of Sarah Grimké and Frances Wright. ("What: Scrutinise the home, that sacred institution, and even question it? Sacrilegious!"[29]) With *The Home* we are far indeed from traditional liberal theory, which respected the sanctity of the private sphere. Gilman's thesis is that the home as an institution is an antiquated system that restricts women and retards social evolution; indeed it retards social progress largely because it crimps women's development—a theory adumbrated in *Women and Economics*. In this work, however, Gilman systematically demystifies the home, describing it as a chaotic hothouse governed by ignorance where the woman is overwhelmed with work and where her emotional and intellectual energies are frustrated to the point of neurosis. From an economic point of view the system is enormously wasteful.

The home, she argues, is in a state of "arrested development," a throwback. A new system must be created to keep apace with social evolution into a more collective age; it must be one which allows women to move beyond their current level of "social idiot" (315). In stripping the home of its sentimental mystique Gilman demolishes a number of suppositions that underlie liberal theory. "There is no privacy for the individual" (39) in the home—especially for women, so the liberal argument that the home is a "private" sphere free from tyrannical intrusion is shown to be untenable. Nor is the home governed by the principles of natural rights. "In the home is neither freedom nor equality. There is ownership throughout; the dominant father, the . . . subservient mother, the utterly dependent child" (171).

Gilman also cheerfully attacks several other popular notions about the home. Mothers are instinctively neither good nutritionists nor skilled child-rearers. In fact, many mothers are poor cooks and know next to nothing about proper nutrition (124–30). Nor does the home properly nourish children intellectually or morally. Children are oppressed by the overzealous attention of obsessive mothers (40). As often as not the home fosters cowardice ("constant shelter, protection . . . must breed cowardice") and deceitful manipulation (168). While it is true that love grows in the home, it should not be restricted to the private sphere: "Mother-love, *as limited by the home,* does not have the range and efficacy proper to our time" (167).

Gilman suggests a number of radical changes: domestic work should be professionalized. People should be trained in cooking, nutrition and child rearing and should be paid to perform these services (138, 339–41). Many of these services, such as laundry, should be collectivized. Child rearing should be done in collective nurseries. Collective kitchens should feed several families at once, thus ending the enormous waste of the current individualized system (118, 133). Through such reorganization of domestic labor women will be freed from their current twenty-four-hour, wage-less oppression and will work eight hours for pay. And they will be free to pursue work as their talents permit. Integration of women into the public world, and integration of the public and private, will end male domination of the public and therefore end the androcentric reign Gilman described in earlier works.

Moreover, ending the confinement of women in the home will make the public world of the streets safe again for women and children (254).

Gilman's *The Home* remains the most clearly articulated piece of radical feminist theory on the domestic sphere produced during the first wave of feminist thought. It was, however, not the only work of its kind. Indeed, Delores Hayden has brought to light a submerged tradition of such radical feminist theorizing in *The Grand Domestic Revolution: A History of Feminist Designs for American Homes, Neighborhoods, and Cities* (1981). Hayden calls such theorists "material feminists" because they were concerned to transform the material conditions of women's lives. Their central thesis, like Gilman's, was that "women must create feminist homes with socialized housework and child care before they could become truly equal members of society."[30] Among these feminists were Melusina Fay Pierce, Marie Stevens Howland, Victoria Woodhull, Mary Livermore, Ellen Swallow Richards, Mary Hinman Abel, Mary Kenney O'Sullivan, Henrietta Rodman, and Ellen Puffer Howes. They advocated many of the reforms Gilman urged, including socializing the domestic sphere. One of the earliest proponents of significant changes in the home (although not collective arrangements) was Gilman's great aunt Catharine Beecher whose *Treatise on Domestic Economy* appeared in 1841.[31]

Theories advocating socialized domestic work had been developed by early nineteenth-century utopian socialists such as Robert Owen and Charles Fourier. Wright, Fuller, and Stanton had been fully familiar with these theories. Wright knew Owen personally; Fuller and Stanton praised Fourier's ideas.[32] The material feminists also drew on the utopian socialist tradition. Hayden argues convincingly that nineteenth-century feminist ideology was more of a piece than has hitherto been recognized. Social reform feminism, which developed by the turn of the century, was just the other side of the coin of material feminism: "most feminists wished to increase women's rights in the home and simultaneously bring homelike nurturing into public life" (5). This, as noted, was the case with Gilman.

Two other first-wave feminists who deserved attention really belong in the romantic tradition initiated by Margaret Fuller. They are Victoria Woodhull and Emma Goldman. Woodhull, whose outspoken views won her a notorious reputation, was not an important theorist. Nevertheless, she did articulate a romantic, ultimately anarchistic, view of women's liberation in a series of articles printed in the 1870s in her own *Woodhull & Claflin's Weekly.*

Woodhull's main concern was that women be free of all restrictions, particularly any restraints on her freedom to love whom and when she chose. This "free love" position meant the abolition of marriage. Marriage, she urged, was a passé institution that like slavery and the monarchy should be abolished. "As it exists today [marriage] is nothing but a system of licensed prostitution and rape."[33] In the tradition of material feminists she urged "socialistic arrangements" to replace marriage and traditional domestic organization.

Woodhull ran for president (the first woman to do so) as the candidate of a new Equal Rights Party in 1872, which was soon dubbed the free love ticket because of her views. The year before she had obtained control of Sections 9 and 12 of the First International, but these sections were expelled by Marx himself shortly thereafter. Woodhull urged that other sections secede to form a new Communist Party with Woodhull replacing Karl Marx as the leader. *Woodhull & Claflin's Weekly* was the first journal to print the *Communist Manifesto* in the United States.

Emma Goldman also had an interest in Marxist-Leninism as a force promoting social revolution, but her orientation was essentially anarchist; she refused obeisance to any and all authority (her *Disillusionment With Russia* explains her rejection of Communism).[34] Anarchism, as articulated by Goldman, meant a kind of romantic individualism, the elimination of all social restraints and the replacement of current social arrangements with decentralized, organic communities. Like all anarchists she believed strongly in attitudinal change; the ends must be in the means. "Social revolution," she wrote, "is a *fundamental transvaluation of values.*" "Our institutions and conditions rest upon deep-seated ideas. To change those conditions and at the same time leave the underlying ideas and values intact means only a superficial transformation" (354).

Goldman's feminist theory must therefore be seen in the context of her anarchism which, as Alix Shulman notes, was really "a theory of organic growth" (30). Goldman's vision remains very much in the romantic tradition. The feminist predecessor whose theory hers most resembles is Margaret Fuller—this despite the extraordinary difference in their background, Fuller coming from a middle-class native New England family and Goldman, a working-class Jewish immigrant. Nevertheless, they share a basic belief in the organic process of growth as a fundamental good and in the importance of the ability of the individual "soul" to grow untrammeled by authority of any kind, and they imagine a world free of restrictions with a resulting natural harmony.

Freedom is the sine qua non of romantic anarchist theory, not freedom as an "end product" but as a process. "In the anarchist view freedom is not a commodity . . . it is a condition of living without sanctions and without domination."[35] "True emancipation," Goldman believed, "begins in woman's soul" (142). In rejecting the notion that suffrage will "free" women, Goldman (who nevertheless supported the right to vote) argued that legal changes will not effect freedom, for that comes from within. In a 1911 article Goldman reveals her exasperation with women's passivity and slavish behavior (an irritation reminiscent of Wollstonecraft and other feminists) and argues that until each individual asserts her own freedom and powers, she will never be free.[36]

At the same time, Goldman rejected institutions like government and marriage that restrict individual freedom and the expression of love, which to Goldman is the ultimate anarchic force (anticipating in this some of the neo-

Freudians of the twentieth century; see chapter 4). Like Woodhull she asserts that institutions like marriage tend to crush real love (*Red Emma,* 43).

> Love, the strongest and deepest element in all life . . . love, the defier of all laws, of all conventions, love, the most powerful moulder of human destiny; how can such an all-compelling force be synonymous with that poor little State- and Church-begotten weed, marriage (165).

Like Gilman, therefore, Goldman sees love as the ultimate regenerative force. But unlike Gilman, Goldman's notion is not just of mother-love but of romantic love between men and women (44). Goldman along with Woodhull was among the first feminists to espouse sexual freedom for women. She, with Crystal Eastman, Margaret Sanger, and other Greenwich Village feminists, became a strong advocate for birth control. Indeed, Goldman was imprisoned in 1916 for circulating birth control information.

Birth control became one of the major feminist issues of the early twentieth century. The subject had been raised in the nineteenth-century movement by such feminists as Elizabeth Cady Stanton who in the 1870s advocated "voluntary motherhood," or abstinence, as a means by which women could exert further control over their lives. See Linda Gordon, *Woman's Body, Woman's Right: A Social History of Birth Control in America* (New York: Grossman, 1976) for a full discussion.

Margaret Sanger became the champion of the cause in the early 1900s, believing that limited population growth would ease slum crowding, prevent abortions, and further enhance women's control over their own bodies. "No woman can call herself free who does not own and control her body. No woman can call herself free until she can choose consciously whether she will or will not be a mother."[37] Like Woodhull and Goldman, Sanger believed in a woman's right to sexual gratification and was not afraid to state so explicitly. In this she was a pioneer, for most feminists of the past from Wollstonecraft to Gilman remained somewhat disinterested in the problems of heterosexual relationships. This was probably because their own primary orientation was toward other women (see below). The going thesis among first-wave feminists was simply that men should exercise as much self-restraint as women and should for the most part remain celibate. Through the 1920s Gilman continued to resist strongly any identification of sexual emancipation with women's liberation. Indeed, she condemned the supposedly liberated "new woman," the flapper, in tones that recall Wollstonecraft's condemnation of upper-class butterflies. "It is sickening," she wrote in 1923, "to see so many of the newly freed using their freedom in a mere imitation of masculine vices" (*His Religion and Hers,* 54).

> No prisoned harem beauty, no victim of white-slavery, no dull-eyed kitchen drudge is so pitiful as these "new women," free, educated, independent, and just as much the slaves of fashion and the victims of license as they were before (95).

Goldman, too, though she endorsed sexual emancipation, condemned the socialization that led women to view themselves as strictly sexual objects. In one of her most important articles, "The Traffic in Women" (1911),[38] Goldman asserts, "Woman is reared as a sex commodity" (149). We need not therefore "be surprised if she becomes an easy prey to prostitution, or to any other form of a relationship which degrades her to the position of an object for mere sex gratification" (149).

Goldman, like Gilman and Fuller, envisioned ideal society as an organic community of persons contributing and receiving in mutual harmony. Both Goldman and Gilman relied on anarchist Kropotkin's idea of a society motivated by "mutual aid" (95). This organic vision is far indeed from the mechanistic model of isolated (qualitatively neutral) integers upon which the liberal Enlightenment view of society is predicated. Goldman rejects a state whose "highest attainment is the reduction of mankind to clockwork" (55). Rather

> [I]t is the harmony of organic growth which produces variety of color and form—the complete whole we admire in the flower. Analogously will the organized activity of free human beings endowed with the spirit of solidarity result in the perfection of social harmony—which is Anarchism (46).

Goldman especially condemns industrial capitalism which reduces human beings to objects, a critique offered by the early Marx (see chapter 3).

> It is the private dominion over things that condemns millions of people to be mere nonentities, living corpses without originality or power of initiative, human machines of flesh and blood, who pile up mountains of wealth for others and pay for it with gray, dull and wretched existence for themselves (36).

Liberation for women, as well as all subjugated persons, consists in their being emancipated—or in emancipating themselves—from reified forms that reduce them to mechanisms and stereotypes. "True civilization is to be measured by . . . the extent to which [the individual] is free to have its being, to grow and expand unhindered by invasive and coercive authority" (97). Not surprisingly perhaps, Goldman was the first American feminist who openly supported homosexual rights.[39] Goldman's central insight into the reason for women's oppression, therefore, is couched in the anarchist idea that they are turned into objects by the system; this prevents their souls from growing freely.

Unlike the "material" or social reform feminists, Goldman did not believe that women would purify politics. Indeed, she remains something of an anomaly among cultural feminists because her theory does not particularly revere or romanticize relationships between and among women, and because most of her major personal relationships were with men. The majority of the other first-wave feminists either had their primary relationships with women, were part of all-female networks, or they had intense crushes on or "romantic friendships" with other women. Scholars have by now established that these relationships, which were of an intensity that today we would call "lesbian," were a dominant social arrangement among nineteenth-century women.[40]

One of the most important relationships of Mary Wollstonecraft's life was with a woman, Fanny Blood; Margaret Fuller was infatuated with Anna Barker. Fuller, indeed, was possibly the first feminist to articulate the nature of these relationships. She did so in a journal extract first published in expurgated form in the 1855 posthumous edition of *Woman in the Nineteenth Century*. The unexpurgated version was first published thanks to Bell Gale Chevigny's scholarship, in 1976. "It is so true," Fuller writes, "that a woman may be in love with a woman and a man with a man. . . . Undoubtedly it is the same love as we shall feel when we are angels." She goes on to note "how natural" was her own love for an unidentified woman; what a "strange mystic thrill" she felt in her presence.[41]

The Stanton-Anthony bond is well known, as are Anthony's romantic attachments with several other women. Charlotte Perkins Gilman had at least two major affairs with women, and once wrote "I have an intense and endless love for women." Most of the social reform feminists, including Jane Addams, Lillian Wald, and Crystal Eastman, had central relationships with women.[42]

The participation of cultural feminists in woman-identified networks helps to explain the matriarchal character of their vision. They believed that women were different and that they had a separate cultural and ethical heritage, described by Fuller, Gilman et al. as maternal, cooperative, altruistic, and life-affirmative. This vision provided a fundamental motivation for the social reform-pacifist feminists of the turn-of-the-century—women like Jane Addams, Emily Greene Balch, Crystal Eastman, Lillian Wald, Sophonisba Breckinridge, and Florence Kelley.

These feminists had great influence in the first decades of the twentieth century. Their contribution must neither be minimized nor, as some scholars have in the past, denigrated.[43] As America's first generation of college-educated women they believed that women (especially educated women) had an obligation to commit themselves to bettering the world. They were seeking ways to utilize their talents and what they saw as their heritage of women's values to reform the masculine and corrupt public sector.

To an extent these feminists were also attempting to deal with their own anomalous and rootless situation as educated women in a world that had no place for them. It was Jane Addams who candidly articulated this personal dilemma and who like many great social reformers was able to translate personal unhappiness into a major social and political movement. In an 1892 article, "The Subjective Necessity for Social Settlements," Addams applies earlier feminist theory about women's need to grow, develop, and particpate fully in the world to her own situation and that of her peers. Citing John Stuart Mill she notes, "There is nothing after disease, indigence, and a sense of guilt so fatal to health and to life itself as the want of a proper outlet for active faculties."[44] Educated women of her generation lacked such an outlet. They needed to engage in meaningful work, and they in turn were needed by the deprived classes in society. It was out of this dialectic between what Addams called subjective and objective needs that the settlement movement was born.

The settlements were houses established in urban slums by educated women who lived there collectively to provide services for the poverty stricken populations that surrounded them. Addams later used essentially the same argument as that developed in "The Subjective Necessity" to promote women's full participation in international affairs. "Those primitive human urgings to foster life and to protect the helpless, of which women were the earliest custodians . . . must be given opportunities to expand and to have a recognized place in the formal organization of international relations" (131).

Addams' central position, however, is not just based on women's needs to express themselves. Rather it is that the world needs women's special moral sensitivities. This thesis was the central contention of the women pacifists who organized the Woman's Peace Party in 1915, which later became the Women's International League for Peace and Freedom (still in existence). Addams formulated her feminist theory in a series of articles, the most important of which were: "Why Women Should Vote" (1909), "The Larger Aspects of the Woman's Movement" (1914), "Women, War and Suffrage" (1915), and "Women and Internationalism" (1915).[45]

Aileen Kraditor calls Addams' theory (that women need the vote in order to carry out needed social reform) an "expediency" argument, expedient because it does not see the vote as an end in itself as does natural rights theory, but as a means toward another goal. Indeed, Kraditor suggests that natural rights and expediency are *the* two main types of suffragist theory.[46] Unfortunately, Kraditor's choice of the term "expediency" tends to denigrate the social reform position as being somehow less pure or less feminist than the natural rights position. In fact, the social reform theorists had come to a more comprehensive vision than those who continued to espouse a narrowly liberal position. The social reformers saw that women's lives, cut off as they were in the domestic world, could no longer be seen in isolation from other great social evils—war, poverty, and economic exploitation.

In "Why Women Should Vote" Addams argues that women in fact cannot properly function in isolation in the domestic sphere because so much of the public world impinges upon the private. Women's housekeeping must therefore extend into the public realm. An urban woman who lives in a tenement will find her life affected daily by exploitative landlords and ineffectual social legislation. "Her basement will not be dry, her stairways will not be fireproof, her house will not be provided . . . with sanitary plumbing" (144). She needs to participate in municipal life, if only to ensure that her home life will be decent and healthy. Similarly, her role as mother requires that she have a place on school boards and in effecting child-labor legislation. In this article and in "The Larger Aspects of the Woman's Movement" Addams essentially argues in the vein of liberal interest group theory. Women must see that their interests are reflected in government decisions. As Christopher Lasch comments, Addams believed "women to have a set of distinctive interests of their own, which could no more be served by men than the interests of the proletariat could be served by the *bourgeoisie*" (152).

At the same time Addams believed that there was an objective necessity for women's participation in public affairs at this stage in historical development: the world needed their humane perspective. In this she followed most closely the theory of Gilman (who had, by the way, spent a few months at Hull House with Addams in 1895; the two were familiar with one another's ideas). Like Gilman, she believed that society was evolving toward a more cooperative social phase and that women's altruistic moral bent, and especially mothers' nurturing care about life, were needed for this progress to occur. "Women's value to the modern states . . . lies in the fact that statesmen at the present moment are attempting to translate the new social sympathy into political action" ("The Larger Aspects," 157). The present social reforms are

> titanic pieces of social engineering in which the judgment of women is most necessary. Governmental commissions everywhere take woman's testimony as to legislation for better housing, for public health and education, for the care of dependents, and many other remedial measures, because it is obviously a perilous business to turn over delicate social experiments to men who have remained quite untouched by social compunctions and who have been elected to their legislative position solely upon the old political issues (157).

In "Women and Internationalism" Addams cautiously suggests that women, particularly mothers, have an innate aversion to war and therefore that their views, if incorporated into international public affairs, might lessen its possibility.

> Quite as an artist in an artillery corps commanded to fire upon a beautiful building like the *duomo* at Florence would be deterred by a compunction unknown to the man who had never given himself to creating beauty and did not know the intimate cost of it, so women, who have brought men into the world and nurtured them . . . must experience a peculiar revulsion when they see them destroyed, irrespective of the country in which these men may have been born (128).

Crystal Eastman was the other major theorist of the pacifist-social reform group. Like others of her feminist generation she was very much under the influence of Charlotte Perkins Gilman. Her basic theory is laid out in an article written in August 1920 at the moment the suffrage amendment finally became part of the Constitution. The article is perceptively entitled "Now We Can Begin." It seems in part to have been written to counter Emma Goldman's romantic notions about women's soul.

Agreeing conditionally that woman needs a "free soul"—if such is defined as "a certain emotional freedom, a strong healthy egotism, and some unpersonal sources of joy"[47]—Eastman nevertheless argues that such freedom cannot come only from within. "Conditions of outward freedom" must be created "in which a free woman's soul can be born and grow. It is these outward conditions with which an organized feminist movement must concern itself" (54).

Eastman believed the main social changes that would effect such "outward freedom" were: opening all professions to women, change in early socialization of boys and girls, government subsidies for child rearing, and "voluntary motherhood" or birth control (56). In an earlier article, "Birth Control in the Feminist Program" (1918), Eastman asserted that this must be a primary component of the feminist struggle. "Feminists," she says, "are not nuns" (47). By this she meant feminists are not asexual. Today, of course, there are many feminist nuns.

Crystal Eastman also contributed to the development of feminist pacifist theory. She organized the Woman's Peace Party of New York in 1914 and was later one of the founders and executive director of the American Union Against Militarism, which became the American Civil Liberties Union. The purpose of a pacifist, she wrote in 1915, must be "to establish new values, to create an overpowering sense of the sacredness of life; so that war will be unthinkable" (236). In her "Program for Voting Women," Eastman declares that the primary task of politically enfranchised women must be to end war.

> What we hope . . . is to bring thousands upon thousands of women—women of international mind—to dedicate their new political power, not to local reforms or personal ambitions, not to discovering the difference between the Democratic and Republican parties, but to *ridding the world of war* (267).

The pacifist-feminist position took its final form in the manifestoes of the Woman's Peace Party and in the declarations issued at the International Congress of Women at The Hague in May 1915. The Woman's Peace Party, which organized in 1915 with Jane Addams as its national chair, issued a platform that stated the special role women must play as proponents of pacifism. Its "Preamble" reads:

> As women, we feel a peculiar moral passion of revolt against both the cruelty and the waste of war. As women, we are especially the custodians

> of the life of the ages. We will no longer consent to its reckless destruction.[48]

The platform of the Woman's Peace Party included a series of proposals for ending the hostilities in Europe (World War I was by then well under way) and the establishment of a permanent peace. These proposals were incorporated into the resolutions adopted at The Hague conference. That conference was attended by 1,136 voting delegates (almost all women) from nearly every country in Europe as well as the United States. The American delegation included Jane Addams, Emily Greene Balch (both later received the Nobel Peace Prize), Sophonisba Breckinridge, and Alice Hamilton.

The Hague resolutions are of particular interest because many of them were adopted by Woodrow Wilson in his celebrated "Fourteen Points" doctrine. These included the following principles: no transfer of territory without consent of the inhabitants, recognition of the right of all peoples to autonomy, self-determination and democratic government, the organization of a Society of Nations with various permanent committees to promote peaceful international cooperation in diverse areas, establishment of a permanent International Court of Justice, freedom of the seas and of international commerce, and an open foreign policy, democratically determined.

The major proposals of The Hague conference which Wilson failed to specify in the "Fourteen Points" are also of significance. They include the right of women to vote—a demand repeated four times in The Hague document for the following reason.

> Since the combined influence of the women of all countries is one of the strongest forces for the prevention of war, and since women can only have full responsibility and effective influence when they have equal political rights with men, this International Congress of Women demands their political enfranchisement.[49]

The women also demanded they be included in the World War I peace conference and announced that in any event they would meet simultaneously with that conference, which they did. (Indeed, at their 1919 Zurich conference the International Congress of Women issued the first condemnation of the Versailles treaty, within days after it was issued; the women charged, prophetically, that the treaty did nothing but sow the seeds of future discord.)[50]

The Hague congress had also called for a general disarmament and the use of "collective sanctions" against aggressor nations, and stated that economic investments abroad be considered "at the risk of the investor, without claim to the official protection of his government."[51] It also urged that children be educated in the ideals of peace. In its preamble The Hague document once again stated women's special concern about the "reckless sacrifice of human life" and added the further point, derived from Addams' theory that no woman is an island, that women must protest against war because they are so often its victims.

> This International Congress of Women opposes the assumption that women can be protected under the conditions of modern warfare. It protests vehemently against the odious wrongs of which women are the victims in times of war, and especially against the horrible violation of women which attends all war.[52]

The International Congress of Women, itself, remains an embodiment of the cultural feminist ideal: a model separatist women's network, unified by a belief in common female interests and values, and dedicated to extending that heritage into the public, androcentric world. Its history is replete with moving incidents of women, the men of whose countries were at war, embracing in their common cause.

The cultural feminists in the Progressive Movement also were among the first to evince concern over environmental degradation and thus anticipated in certain respects the contemporary ecofeminist movement. In particular, Alice Hamilton, a physician and colleague of Jane Addams, recognized the negative effect that industrial pollution had on human health, foreshadowing in this respect Rachel Carson and the modern environmental movement. Her classic *Industrial Poisons in the United States* (1925), along with other works and her active political campaigns to end industrial pollution, did much to raise awareness about the issue.[53]

Nineteen-twenty is a landmark date in the history of American feminism. On August 18, the Anthony or Suffrage Amendment was ratified by Tennessee and became part of the Constitution. Most feminists and historians have come to regard 1920 as the end of "first-wave" feminism. However, this is not entirely accurate. Feminism did not simply die out in 1920 and reemerge in the 1960s. In fact, the 1920s and 1930s were a period of continuing feminist activity. While little was developed in the way of feminist theory during these years, much of the earlier theory was being put into practice.

In fact, it is becoming increasingly clear, as several historians have proposed, that the welfare-state reforms of the New Deal, such as Social Security, were to a considerable degree the result of the changed conception of government developed by Progressive Era cultural feminists like Jane Addams, who, broadly speaking, saw government in maternalistic terms, as a caring entity whose purpose was not just to protect people's liberties (as held in traditional liberal theory) but also to help provide for their basic needs. Linda Gordon, for example, asserts that "the whole welfare state . . . derived to a significant degree from the feminist agenda of the late nineteenth and early twentieth centuries."[54] "Women's organizations," Robyn Muncy notes, "play[ed] a particularly prominent part in bridging America's two periods of reform, the Progressive Era and . . . the New Deal."[55]

J. Stanley Lemons has similarly argued convincingly that the cultural feminists of the prewar period channeled their ideas into progressive legislation during the 1920s. Not all this legislation was enacted; some of it languished until the New Deal. Nevertheless, Lemons sees the cultural feminists of the 1920s, whom he calls the "social feminists," as "an important link in the chain from the progressive era to the New Deal."[56] "Social feminists," he claims, "worked up an agenda for reform in the Progressive Era and in the 1920s, which required the emergency climate of the New Deal for passage" (118).

Following Jane Addams' notion that women should purify politics, the social feminists of the 1920s urged the elimination of boss politics and political machines (85). They promoted the direct primary (133), civil service reform (134), and various pieces of social legislation. The vehicle for this political expression of cultural feminism was the Women's Joint Congressional Committee, an umbrella group formed in 1920 and comprised of ten women's organizations, including the newly formed League of Women Voters.

Typical of the legislation for which the WJCC lobbied was the Sheppard-Towner Maternity and Infancy-Protection Act (1921), which was later incorporated into the Social Security Act of 1935. The feminists also effected the passage of a Child Labor Amendment, which was never ratified by the states. These cultural feminists also fought for "government ownership and operation of Muscle Shoals [later TVA], federal regulation of marketing and distribution of food, the cooperative movement, aid to education . . . pure food and drugs . . . collective bargaining, hours and wages laws, equal pay for equal work, [and] federal employment service" (119).

What they did not support, however, was the Equal Rights Amendment, which had been formulated by the National Woman's Party and introduced in Congress in 1923. The WJCC opposed the ERA because it saw the amendment as a threat to protective legislation for women. Alice Paul and the National Woman's Party, on the other hand, opposed protective legislation and supported the ERA.

The clash between these two groups was in many respects a clash between liberal and cultural feminist theory. The supporters of the ERA believed that women were similar to men in capabilities and merely needed to be afforded equal opportunities and accorded natural rights. The opponents believed women were different and required special legislation to protect that differentness. Jane Addams, Florence Kelley, and other members of the National Women's Trade Union League, a reform-minded labor organization, had rejoiced over the 1908 Supreme Court decision *(Muller v. Oregon),* which upheld protective legislation for women (a ten-hour day).[57] That decision had been based on the famous Louis D. Brandeis brief which stressed women's physical inferiority.

The Brandeis brief points up a problem of the cultural feminist position. In the eyes of the law "different" is too often interpreted as "unequal," "inferior," or "incapable." An example may be made of the Wisconsin Equal Rights statute which passed in 1921. As part of its provisions, it exempted protective legislation. In 1923 the Wisconsin Attorney General ruled that because of this, the equal rights statute did not void a 1905 law prohibiting women from serving as legislative employees (Lemons, 189). Thus, protective legislation could easily be used in a discriminatory way to bar women from various occupations. As Crystal Eastman noted in 1924, "a good deal of tyranny goes by the name of protection" ("Equality or Protection").[58] This was the position of the National Woman's Party and why it supported an unadulterated Equal Rights Amendment. The question of "equality versus difference," as it is termed today, remains a major issue in contemporary feminist jurisprudence (see chapter 8).

There are other problems with cultural feminist theory that must be specified. Perhaps the most apparent issue is the question of what constitutes the "differentness" between the male and female identity and epistemology. Is it biologically based, or culturally constructed? At times, the contemporary cultural feminist vein of radical feminism, especially as expressed by Shulamith Firestone, has veered toward biological determinism: Difference lies in the genes, or in the hormones, or, as Gina Covina suggested, in women's "right-brainedness" (see chapter 6). Such a theory like any determinism, if carried to an extreme, obviates the possibility of human freedom, which is an essential feature of humanness.

If male-female difference is not in the genes, then the assumption is that it must be a matter of social environment; if this is the case, then the traits that we attribute to women and men must be seen as mutable. A change in socialization, or education, or social circumstance would produce different gender identities or no such identities at all. We would all be "persons" or androgynes. This is the liberal feminist position.

However, if gender identities and the cultures that go with them are historically a matter of social construction, then any political ideology based upon them, such as cultural feminism, seems less secure than if based upon an immutable construct such as biology. In other words, if women have developed a humane value system in the context of the domestic sphere, will they retain this system when they enter a different context, the public sphere? The nineteenth-century cultural feminists more or less assumed that women's pacifist, reformist nature was relatively innate and that women would bring this perspective with them into the public sphere to "purify politics."

Some have suggested that this idea was proven a failure when women did not act as a bloc after the passage of the suffrage amendment. As we have noted, however, women had some success in introducing progressive reform in the 1920s and 1930s. Moreover, the extraordinary socialization of women to not assert themselves cannot be overestimated in considering women's relative political reticence. Most women did not even vote, for example, in the 1920 presidential election, nor in the 1921 and 1922 local elections (Lemons, 51). There is, however, some evidence that women voters have favored pacifist and reform-minded candidates. And today, of course, numerous polls have shown that a "gender gap"—largely over issues of peace and social welfare—exists between the female and male electorate.[59]

Twentieth-century cultural feminists are for the most part leery of biological determinism, having seen the destructive purposes to which it was put by the American revisionist Freudians in the 1940s and 1950s, who used it to construct an ideology of female inferiority (see chapter 4). There is also the concern that stress upon women's differentness can lead back to an assertion that men and women belong in separate spheres, with women in the home away from the world of public politics—a position no contemporary feminist would support.[60]

Cultural feminists today believe that the traditional realm of women provides the basis for the articulation of a humane world view, one which can operate to change the destructive masculine ideologies that govern the public world. However, contemporary feminists do not believe that this transformation will happen automatically for (with the exception of certain French feminists) they do not believe that the differences between women and men are principally biological.

Contemporary cultural feminists therefore hold that a women's political value system may be derived from traditional women's culture and applied to the public realm. They also believe it is possible for men to learn the tenets of this system. Contemporary feminists are more aware of the need to systematize cultural feminist ideology, and to teach it, than were their nineteenth-century predecessors who, as noted, tended to feel that pacifist and reformist attitudes were inherent in women's nature. Cultural feminists today, therefore, bypass the nature versus nurture question by assuming that revolution is a matter of transforming ideology, and that all humans are ultimately educable. (For a further discussion of revolutionary strategy in the contemporary movement and the place of educational praxis therein, see chapters 3 and 5.) Cultural feminism remains one of the most important traditions of feminist theory, if somewhat more sophisticated in form and political consciousness today than in the nineteenth century.

The other important contemporary approach remains the liberal one, derived from natural rights theory and discussed in chapter 1. Because its theoretical premises were fully laid down in the nineteenth century, contemporary liberal feminism has been largely a matter of practical political activity. For this reason, I have chosen not to dwell upon it further in this book. However, it is important to note that because of their divergent theoretical histories, liberal feminism and cultural feminism occasionally clash. Two issues in particular bring this out: One is the question of women serving in the military; the liberal supports such service on the integrative theory that women should participate in public occupations the same as men, while a cultural feminist opposes such service on the grounds that feminism is a transformative philosophy rooted in the fundamentally pacifist character of the female value system.[61]

Another area of disagreement remains the question of protective legislation. Should laws be adapted to fit the contingencies of women's circumstances, or not? A proponent of the strictly liberal position would say no; a cultural feminist would say yes. The most important legal cases in this regard concern maternity leaves and the self-defense plea for women.[62]

The next section of this book examines those feminist traditions that constitute the theoretical base of the modern women's movement: the Marxist, Freudian, existentialist and radical feminist positions. The first three, like the natural rights doctrine, were originally developed to explain and ameliorate another social issue. We first present the essentials of these prefeminist theories and then examine how they were adapted to fit women's contingencies. Perhaps because there is some common ground among these contingencies, second-wave theorists converged in the 1980s toward a cultural feminist position. This development is discussed in chapter 7.

3 Feminism and Marxism

He is the bourgeoisie and
the wife represents the proletariat.
Frederick Engels, 1884

This chapter, and the following on Freudianism, concern revolutionary theories developed to analyze aspects of the modern condition, but without primary reference to women, the "woman question," or feminist theory. Many feminists have legitimately questioned whether theories developed under such circumstances can be sufficiently modified to merit feminist interest.

There is an inherent methodological weakness in taking a theory developed for one set of circumstances and transposing it to another, or modifying it so that it "fits" the second set. Moreover, both Marx and Freud were concentrating primarily on men and masculine circumstances when they developed their theories; the legitimacy of such concepts applied to women may be seen as intrinsically suspect.

Despite such reservations, which I share, I believe this chapter will show that there is much in Marx's and Engels' ideas, and in subsequent Marxist theory, that is of central importance in the development of feminist theory. Indeed, important aspects of contemporary feminist theory, such as the notion of "consciousness-raising," are rooted in Marxist premises.

This chapter is divided into two parts. The first describes and analyzes those theories of Karl Marx and Friedrich Engels that are relevant to contemporary feminist theory, and the second part takes up contemporary Marxist feminist and socialist feminist adaptations of Marxism. In truth, contemporary "Marxist feminism" is more appropriately called "socialist feminism" to point up that it no longer presents an undiluted Marxism but a Marxism modified (primarily) by radical feminism (see chapter 6). In order to understand contemporary socialist feminist theory and Marx and Engels' own limited speculations on the "woman question," it is necessary to sketch in elements of their overall theory. Three aspects in particular will be discussed: 1) the theory of materialist determinism (and the formation of ideology and class consciousness), 2) theories about labor and capitalism, specifically, about alienated labor, praxis, and the determination of economic value, and 3) the one sustained piece of feminist theory produced by Marx or Engels, the latter's *Origin of the Family, Private Property and the State* (1884).

One of Marx's central insights is the idea of materialist determinism, usually called historical materialism, which holds that culture and society are rooted in material or economic conditions. The idea is clearly stated by Engels in his 1888 preface to the *Communist Manifesto* (1848).

> In every historical epoch, the prevailing mode of economic production and exchange, and the social organisation necessarily following from it, form the basis upon which is built up, and from which alone can be explained, the political and intellectual history of that epoch.[1]

Marx stated this more explicitly in a preface to his *Critique of Political Economy* (1859): "the mode of production of material life conditions the social, political, and intellectual life process in general. It is not the consciousness of men that determines their being, but, on the contrary, their social being that determines their consciousness."[2]

Earlier, in *The German Ideology* (1846), Marx had developed the idea that economic conditions shape ideology by contrasting his materialist view with the idealism of earlier German philosophers, particularly Hegel.

> In direct contrast to German philosophy which descends from heaven to earth, here we ascend from earth to heaven. . . . We set out from real, active men, and on the basis of their real-life process we demonstrate the development of the ideological reflexes and echoes of this life-process. The phantoms formed in the human brain are also, necessarily, sublimates of their material life-process, which is empirically verifiable and bound to material premises. (*Writings*, 164).

Marx further believed that the governing ideology in a society is determined by the economic interests of the ruling class, the capitalists in the case of his own and contemporary society. This he states forcefully in *The German Ideology:*

> The ideas of the ruling class are in every epoch the ruling ideas, i.e. the class which is the ruling material force of society is at the same time its

> ruling intellectual force. The class which has the means of material production at its disposal, has control at the same time over the means of mental production, so that thereby, generally speaking, the ideas of those who lack the means of mental production are subject to it (*Writings*, 176).

Marx then reiterates the idea of material determinism: "the ruling ideas are nothing more than the ideal expression of the dominant material relationships" (176).

The ruled class, the proletariat, comes to consciousness in opposition to the ruling class or the bourgeoisie. (Marx occasionally argued that there were more than two classes, but for our purposes it is only necessary to note these two great class antagonists.) As one critic notes, "the criterion for belonging to a class is one's position in the prevailing mode of production."[3] "The bourgeoisie are defined as the owners of the means of production and the employers of wage-labour, the proletariat as those who own no means of production and live by selling their wage-labour" (*Thought*, 152).

Beyond the economic criterion for class membership, however, lies the difficult question of class consciousness. For Marx also held that "a class only existed when it was conscious of itself as such, and this always implied common hostility to another social group" (*Thought*, 155). In 1852 Marx defined class as follows:

> In so far as millions of families live under economic conditions of existence that separate their mode of life, their interests and their culture from those of the other classes and put them in hostile opposition to the latter, they form a class.[4]

Class consciousness therefore seems to form dialectically in opposition to the ideology of the ruling class. True class consciousness requires that class members see the world from the perspective of their own true class interests and not from the point of view of the interests of the oppressor class. To absorb uncritically that class's ideas is to operate in terms of "false consciousness."[5] Engaging in revolutionary praxis is one means Marx specifies by which consciousness of true class interests may be awakened. "In revolutionary activity, the changing of oneself coincides with the changing of circumstances."[6]

Many contemporary Marxists have seized upon the idea of praxis, some seeing it as an educational tool whereby groups may learn to become aware of their oppressed conditions, thus shedding "false consciousness" and moving toward changing their circumstances (see especially Paulo Freire's *Pedagogy of the Oppressed*, 1970). The relevance of these ideas to feminist theory is readily apparent. Socialist feminists have generally assumed (without always stating) an analogy between women and the proletariat, and have urged that women need to develop an analogous true consciousness of their own oppressed condition, in the process shedding "false consciousness," or "male-identified" ideologies that serve male, ruling-group interests. The further refinements in the concept of ideology and group consciousness which contemporary Marxists have developed will be discussed further in the second part of this chapter.

The second major aspect of Marx's theory is his analysis of modern industrial capitalism. Of particular relevance here are his concept of alienation, elaborations of the idea of praxis, and theories of value determination. The concept of alienation is central to Marx's overall theory. Many contemporary critics argue, indeed, that it is the germ from which the rest of his analysis proceeds. Many also believe it is one of the Marxist ideas that retains special contemporary significance. It is stated most clearly in the *Economic and Philosophical Manuscripts of 1844*, sometimes referred to as the "Dead Sea Scrolls of Marxism" because they were "lost" for decades until their recovery by the existentialists in the 1930s and 1940s. (They were not published until 1932 and not translated into English until 1959.)

Alienation generally refers to the modern experience of being cut off from oneself, from others, and from a sense of meaning. As noted in chapter 1, there is an inherent alienation built into the Newtonian world view with its dissociation of subjective and objective, private and public, spiritual and material. Hegel was the first modern philosopher to elaborate the concept of alienation.[7]

In the 1844 manuscripts Marx determines that the root cause of alienation is the condition of alienated labor created by industrial capitalism. In a factory, for example, workers are cut off from the final product of their labor. Usually they only see a minute part of the product. They have no say in its creation, or its use. They themselves become no more than cogs in the factory machine.

The product therefore becomes a thing that is alien to the worker. "The object produced by labor, its product, now stands opposed to it as an *alien being,* as a power *independent* of the producer . . . this product is an *objectification* of labor" (*Manuscripts,* 95).

> The *alienation* of the worker in his product means not only that his labor becomes an object, assumes an *external* existence, but that it exists independently, *outside himself,* and alien to him, and that it stands opposed to him as an autonomous power (96).

Workers feel unfulfilled by their work and deprived of a sense of participating in an integrated process. They feel "homeless" on the job, and only "at home" during leisure hours (98). Their work does not belong to them; it belongs to another person, to the capitalist owner (99). As a consequence of this original alienation "the worker sinks to the level of a commodity" (93). She or he turns into a thing. This process Marx labels *Verdinglichkeit,* translated as "reification" (from the Latin *res,* which means "thing"). All of the workers' social relationships are similarly affected by the reifying process.

> *Man* [becomes] alienated from other *men*. . . . What is true of man's relationship to his work, to the product of his work and to himself, is also true of his relationship to other men, to their labor, and to the objects of their labor (103).

The transformation of humans into commodities which is effected by capitalist industrialism, is a central theme of the *Communist Manifesto*. Here, as elsewhere, it is clear that Marx has a vision of a humane world and humane relationships that have been destroyed by capitalism. The bourgeoisie "has resolved personal worth into exchange value" (*Manifesto*, 11). "The bourgeoisie . . . has reduced the family relation to a mere money relation" (11). "All that is holy is profaned" (12).

The *Communist Manifesto* reiterates the concept of alienated labor seen in earlier manuscripts. Laborers under capitalism "who must sell themselves piecemeal, are a commodity" (15). "Owing to the extensive use of machinery, and to division of labour, the work of the proletarians has lost all individual character, and, consequently, all charm for the workman. He becomes an appendage of the machine" (15–16).

Note in the above passage Marx and Engels point to another factor that contributes to alienated labor, the division of labor. In *The German Ideology* Marx also suggested that specialization of labor and allocation of certain groups to certain tasks is fundamentally alienating. "For as soon as the distribution of labor comes into being, each man has a particular, exclusive sphere of activity, which is forced upon him and from which he cannot escape" (*Writings*, 169). Marx condemns this "fixation of social activity." Ideally, and under a communist system, Marx urges, labor will not be specialized. It will be "possible for me to do one thing today and another tomorrow, to hunt in the morning, fish in the afternoon, rear cattle in the evening, criticize after dinner, just as I have a mind, without ever becoming hunter, fisherman, cowherd, or critic" (*Writings*, 169).

In *The German Ideology* and later in *Capital* (1867) Marx roots the division of labor in what he calls the "natural division of labour in the family" (*Writings*, 168). In *Capital* he specifies again that one of the primary divisions of labor occurs in the family: "within a family . . . there springs up naturally a division of labour, caused by differences of sex and age, a division that is consequently based on a purely physiological foundation" (*Writings*, 476). In *The German Ideology* Marx had argued that this family division created the first form of ownership of one person by another; he saw the enslavement of the wife and children by the husband as the first form of private property.

> With the division of labour . . . which in its turn is based on the natural division of labour in the family and the separation of society into individual families opposed to one another, is given simultaneously . . . the unequal distribution, both quantitative and qualitative, of labour and its

> products, hence property: the nucleus, the first form of which lies in the family, where wife and children are the slaves of the husband. This latent slavery in the family . . . is the first property [that is,] . . . the power of disposing of the labour-power of others (*Writings*, 168).

Marx's overall view, as Edmund Wilson points out, is of a world where humans have been overpowered by things, in which "commodities command the human beings."[8] His most powerful condemnation of the mystification of commodities is found in *Capital*. There he perceives capitalism as an heretical, idolatrous religion. Under its reign commodities develop a "mystical character." "So soon as it steps forth as a commodity, it is changed into something transcendent" (*Writings*, 435). "This I call the Fetishism which attaches itself to the products of labour, so soon as they are produced as commodities" (*Writings*, 436). As Erich Fromm suggests, Marx seems to be talking about the Old Testament concepts of idolatry.

> The essence of what the prophets call "idolatry" . . . is that the idols are the work of man's own hands—they are things, and man bows down and worships things. . . . In doing so he transforms himself into a thing. He transfers to the things of his creation the attributes of his own life, and instead of experiencing himself as the creating person, he is in touch with himself . . . only in the indirect way of submission to life frozen in the idols.[9]

In contrast to the deplorable alienation inherent in industrial capitalist societies, Marx envisions an unalienated world, a communistic world where people will experience a more holistic relationship to the products of their labor, and where people will no longer be divided against one another because of their class relationship to the modes of production (the "classless society").

A central concept in this positive vision is the idea of praxis. Praxis in this connection means free, creative engagement in the world by the individual, who is changed by the experience and who thereby changes the world.[10] At times Marx seems to have as his model for praxis the idea of the artist who shapes the materials of the world into an expression of his or her own vision. Unlike the factory worker, the artist has control over the creation, the design, and the use of a product. In this sense the artist's relationship with the product is more integral, more holistic, and less alienated. In the process the artist transforms the world and is, as well, transformed.

In the 1844 *Manuscripts* Marx argues that the central defining characteristic of human beings is that they engage in creative activity. "Free, conscious activity is the species-character of human beings" (101). "Conscious life activity distinguishes man from the life of animals" (101). Unlike animals who are "one" with their life activity, humans have the ability to freely choose, to create their activities (101). Marx is here referring to the human reflective consciousness identified by Hegel and elaborated by phenomenologists. Humans can step back from the world, can plan and shape the environment according to their own interests and desires. Animals cannot. While "animals construct only in accordance with the standards and needs of the species to which they belong," humans can construct "also in accordance with the laws of beauty" (102). In *Capital* Marx notes, "what distinguishes the worst architect from the best of bees is . . . that the architect raises his structure in imagination before he erects it in reality. At the end of every labour process, we get a result that already existed in the imagination of the labourer at its commencement. He not only effects a change of form in the material on which he works, but he also realized a purpose of his own" (*Writings,* 456).

At times Marx's notion of praxis veers in the direction elaborated by later phenomenologists—that the human being constitutes the world, endows it with significance, humanizes it. In this way the split between subjective and objective (and its inherent alienation) is healed or fused into an integrated process. Products no longer have significance as commodities, but rather have the qualitative personal meaning endowed by human consciousness.

> It is only when objective reality everywhere becomes for man in society the reality of human faculties, human reality, and thus the reality of his own faculties, that all *objects* become for him the *objectification of himself.* The objects then confirm and realize his individuality, they are *his own* objects (*Manuscripts,* 133).

In this sense praxis transforms the world by means of the human consciousness which renders objects "sacred," to use the words of Mircea Eliade, rather than "profane." Sacred reality is that charged with personal, magical, or mythical significance, where profane reality remains dead, quantifiable, inert matter.[11]

In contradistinction to Hegel, who relied on an idealistic solution to the dissociation between subjective and objective (subsuming the material within absolute Mind), Marx insisted that it was by "practical means" or praxis that such alienation could be overcome.

> The fully constituted society produces man in all the plentitude of his being. . . . It is only in a social context that subjectivism and objectivism, spiritualism and materialism, activity and passivity, cease to be antinomies and thus cease to exist as such antinomies. The resolution of the *theoretical* contradictions is possible *only* through *practical* means, only through the practical energy of man (*Manuscripts,* 135).

With this idea of praxis Marx provides a response to the epistemological dilemmas of the post-medieval world alluded to in chapter 1. Unlike liberal theorists who more or less assume that alienation in inherent in the human condition and who construct government in accordance with that assumption, Marx envisaged a world where alienation would cease.

One further aspect of praxis should be stressed; namely, that it may be interpreted as revolutionary activity. As Gajo Petrović, a twentieth-century Yugoslav Marxist explains, "Marxist philosophy is a philosophy of revolutionary action because its nucleus is . . . the conception of man as a being of praxis who by his free creative action molds and changes his world and himself" (57). "Praxis is man's truth . . . the true life is life in the revolutionary transformation of the world" (193). Implicit in the idea of praxis as revolution is an analogy between the artist and the revolutionary; each imagines a new reality and transforms the givens into a new world.

The final aspect of Marx's philosophy relevant to feminist theory is his theories of economic value. In *Capital* Marx distinguishes three kinds: "use value," "exchange value," and "surplus value." Use value and exchange value had been identified as early as Aristotle (in the *Politics*), but capitalist surplus value is a modern phenomenon.

Use value refers to the worth of an article produced for (usually immediate) consumption, and usually by members of one's own group. Home labor such as cooking, knitting, weaving (generally women's work, though Marx does not note this) produces articles that have use value. Exchange value refers to articles produced for exchange. The inherent meaning of an article changes when it is to be used for exchange. It is valued for its abstract character as an exchange token, as a commodity, and not necessarily for its inherent qualitative worth. "Exchange-value . . . presents itself as a quantitative relation" (*Capital, Writings*, 422). On the other hand, "as use-values, commodities are, above all, of different qualities, but as exchange-values they are merely different quantities, and consequently do not contain an atom of use-value" (423). It is clear that Marx is drawing a distinction between the products of comparatively unalienated labor (use-value) and those of alienated labor (exchange-value). The very fact that it is produced for exchange strips an article of its qualitative, personally charged, "sacred" character and turns it into something "profane." Indeed, it is apparent in the *Grundrisse* (1858) that Marx saw the termination of exchange value as a precondition for the establishment of unalienated society.[12]

Beyond this Marx developed a labor theory of value to explain the worth of goods on the market and to explain the excess worth that accrued to the capitalist owner as profit. The worker's "labor-power" is itself abstracted "as a commodity" for sale on the market. This commodity is then factored into the determination of the total value of commodity goods, or the total gain from their sale (i. e., capital). "The value of each commodity is determined by the quantity of labour expended on and materialized in it, by the working-time necessary . . . for its production" (*Writings*, 462). But the labor power not only produces enough worth to pay for itself (i. e., wages paid to workers to keep them functional, or to "reproduce" them); "it also produces an excess, a surplus value" (472). The latter largely becomes the profit for the capitalist. Surplus value was therefore "the difference between the value of the products of labour and the cost of producing that labour power, i. e. the labourer's subsistence" (*Thought,* 86). In the second part of the chapter we will see that a considerable amount of contemporary Marxist feminist thought has gone into the question of where domestic labor or housework fits into this theory. Marx and Engels did not treat the issue.

Engels' *Origin of the Family* (1884) remains the only sustained piece of feminist theory produced in the "first wave" of Marxism. As with the matriarchal feminists discussed in chapter 2, Engels relied heavily on contemporaneous anthropological speculations. In particular, he depended on Bachofen's *Mutterrecht* (1861) and Lewis H. Morgan's *Ancient Society* (1877). The interest in Engels' theory lies not, however, in its anthropological base, or in the question of how valid that base is, but rather in his analysis of the family and women's role in it. Engels projects his utopian vision back to a prehistoric matriarchate rather than into the future like Marx, but his analysis of the oppression of women derives fully from Marx's own economic theories, especially those developed in *Capital.* (*Origin* was published after Marx's death, but Engels indicates in the preface that its theory had had Marx's blessing.)

Engels' central thesis in *Origin of the Family* is that the prehistoric, communistic matriarchate was overturned or superseded at a particular moment by the patriarchate. Unlike the matriarchal feminists, however, Engels associates this transition with economic developments, in particular, with the establishment of private property and the emergence of commodities to be used for exchange and profit. Before the change, however, society was organized in matriarchal fashion into matrilineal *gens,* or extended families, that revolved around the mother. Engels here relied upon Morgan's research on the American Iroquois nation.[13]

In the "communistic household" of the gens "most or all of the women belong to one and the same gens, while the men come from various gentes."[14] While there is a division of labor "between the sexes" (the man hunts, the woman tends the house), within those spheres they hold equal power. "They are each master in their own sphere" (145). The woman, however, appears to be a little more equal, because the material base of that society is centered in the woman-controlled gens. "The housekeeping is communal among several . . . families. What is made and used in common is common property" (145). This "communistic household . . . is the material foundation of that supremacy of the women which was general in primitive times" (43). Note that Engels is associating the realm of unalienated life and labor with women and the collective household.

The first great change in the mode of production that led to the patriarchal takeover and to the development of alienation (or evil, if one wishes to associate Engels' theory with the Judeo-Christian myth of the fall, which seems invited) was the taming of animals. Because there was a greater supply of food and animal products when cattle were herded rather than hunted, materials were available for exchange. Cattle therefore became a commodity privately owned (by men) and exchanged for other goods. Other inventions increased production and this "gave human labor-power the capacity to produce a larger product than was necessary for its maintenance" (147). Hence arose surplus value. To continue the growth of the system, however, more and cheaper labor was needed; this led to the use of slaves. Wives also acquired "an exchange value" at this time (48).

It was the male who benefited from this transition, for "all the surplus . . . fell to [him]" (147). The woman's domestic labor began to count less in comparison to the wealth he was accumulating. "The latter was everything, the former an unimportant extra" (147–48). "In proportion as wealth increased, it made the man's position . . . more important than the woman's" (49). "Mother-right, therefore, had to be overthrown" (49). This overthrow constituted "the *world historical defeat of the female sex*" (50).

Because he now had property to bequeath, the man became more concerned with ensuring paternity (55). For this reason, and because of the economic shift in power, the man "took command in the home also; the woman was degraded and reduced to servitude, she became the slave of his lust and a mere instrument for the production of children" (50). The woman was, therefore, in this sense reified into a tool for male purposes. The family was thus transformed into a monogamous male-dominated nuclear unit. Therein arose the first class struggle in history. "The first class opposition that appears in history coincides with the development of the antagonism between man and woman in monogamous marriage, and the first class oppression coincides with that of the female sex by the male" (58). The analogy is clear: "he is the bourgeoisie and the wife represents the proletariat" (66). This is because the man retains a stronger material base. It continues in the modern industrial family: "the husband is obliged to earn a living and support his family, and that in itself gives him a position of supremacy" (65).

With the development of the nuclear family came the privatization and the denigration of household labor. "Household management lost its public character. . . . It became a *private service;* the wife became the head servant, excluded from all participation in social production" (65). "The modern individual family is founded on the open or concealed domestic slavery of the wife, and modern society is a mass composed of these individual families as its molecules" (65). It remains "the economic unit of society" (149).

Engels' solution to the problem of women's oppression is to urge that women fully enter the public work force, thus eliminating their confinement to "private, domestic labor," which would be changed "into a public industry" (148). Engels thus urged "the abolition of the monogamous family as the economic unit of society" (66)—a position he and Marx had, of course, espoused most passionately in the *Communist Manifesto.* All of this would be accomplished under communism.

> With the transfer of the means of production into common ownership, the single family ceases to be the economic unit of society. Private house-

> keeping is transformed into a social industry. The care and education of children becomes a public affair; society looks after all children alike, whether they are legitimate or not (67).

In his concern to collectivize household labor and child rearing Engels came close to the vision of the material feminists discussed in chapter 2.

One might wish to challenge the logic of some of the linkages Engels specifies in the historical chain of circumstances that led to women's enslavement. Indeed, contemporary anthropologists such as Karen Sacks and Kathleen Gough have refined his speculations in light of current anthropological research,[15] but each agrees that his association of surplus wealth with male dominance is probably valid. Sacks finds of particular importance his stress on the fact that men's production for exchange eclipsed women's production for use, and that this forms an important basis of male power (217). "Engels is right in seeing public or social labor as the basis for social adulthood" (221). "The spouse who owns the property rules the household" (222).

Engels' determination is that a central solution to this economic (and therefore political) imbalance is to give women access to the area of public production, a position understandable in the context of the Marxist theory of material determinism, and one which Sacks and Gough appear to accept. However, his solution does not make sense when considered in the context of Marx's theories of alienation and of use and exchange value. For, the realm of industrial production into which Engels is inviting women's participation is par excellence the world of alienated labor. So, other than providing women with an economic base they otherwise would not have (in wage labor), a move into the factories can hardly be seen as a liberating step. Rather, one could argue in Marx's own terms that it is a step toward further alienation, although women might well develop more sense of class solidarity if they worked with others instead of being isolated in their homes.

Engels' two-pronged program—let women enter into the public sphere of production and communalize the realm of private production—became the central tenet of the Marxist, and eventually communist, program for the emancipation of women. In general, subsequent "first-wave" Marxist theorists who addressed the "woman question" subsumed it under communist theory; they saw that, as August Bebel put it, the "solution of the woman question [was] identical with the solution of the social question."[16] Lenin, Alexandra Kollontai, Clara Zetkin, and Rosa Luxemburg all generally adhered to this position.[17]

The contemporary women's movement has prompted Marxists to rethink the "woman question" in an attempt to develop a satisfactory Marxist theory of women's oppression. In general, this effort has endeavored to locate a material basis for women's subjugation; to find a relationship between the modes of production, or capitalism, and women's status; to determine, in other words, connections between the realms of production and reproduction (which refers not only to biological reproduction in Marxist thought but to the entire maintenance process that keeps workers functional; it is done mainly in the home by women).

A central concern of contemporary socialist feminism has therefore been to determine the role of the household in capitalist society: The most extensive analysis has revolved around the question of domestic labor and its contribution of capitalism. A second area of discussion on the "woman question" concerns the direct relationship women may have with the modes of production as wage-earners. Third is the connection between women and class. Fourth, theory has developed around the question of the home or family's role in ideological socialization. A final direction in contemporary feminist theory that derives from Marxist categories is that which focuses on the idea of praxis and on questions about ideology and the nature of consciousness. These ideas will also be addressed in this chapter.

The domestic labor "debate" was initiated in 1969 by Margaret Benston's "The Political Economy of Women's Liberation." Benston was the first to draw attention to the fact that housework must be taken seriously in any analysis of the workings of the economy, and not relegated to a marginal or non-existent status (as it was by Marx and Engels). Benston saw the labor performed in the household as a "pre-capitalist" survival (15), and stressed that under capitalism it is women who continue to produce use values that are consumed by their immediate family.[18] Because this work is "not wage labor" it is "not counted" (16). Women's "work is not worth money, is therefore valueless, is therefore not even work" (16). This fact is "the material basis for the inferior status of women. . . . In a society in which money determines value . . . women, who do this valueless work, can hardly be expected to be worth as much as men, who work for money" (16). As noted above, Engels and more recently Karen Sacks also identified the household as a producer of use values.

Lise Vogel in "The Earthly Family" (1973) elaborates upon this point but takes a different tack. She suggests that because it produces use values housework is "relatively unalienated."[19] Vogel develops this idea briefly but it deserves more extensive consideration by Marxists and feminists than it has received.[20] Vogel even urges that, as unalienated labor, housework may provide a glimpse of what a future society organized around unalienated labor would be like: "Because it is primarily useful labor, it has the power . . . to suggest a future society in which all labor would be primarily useful" (26). Housewives, therefore, "can . . . have access to a vision of a life of unalienated productive activity" (38). Indeed, such awareness is a source of "consciousness and strength that drives women into the forefront of revolutionary activity" (26). While one may question whether housewives have ever been at the forefront of revolutionary activity, Vogel's point is a valuable one, for it suggests that the experience of unalienated labor provides a point from which the housewife may criticize alienated labor; it provides her with the beginning of critical consciousness.

Other critics have made similar points. Angela Davis in her "Reflections on the Black Woman's Role in the Community of Slaves" (1971) urges that it was the black woman's dual awareness that created her critical consciousness and made her the center of the slave resistance movement. The dual awareness came from the fact that she engaged in both the public world of productive labor, which was alienated, and the private world of relatively unalienated labor. The latter was "the *only* labor of the slave community which could not be directly and immediately claimed by the oppressor. . . . Domestic labor was the only meaningful labor for the slave community."[21] This was because such labor produced articles for use by the community.

Other analysts have acknowledged that the household or private sphere provides the only unalienated space in a capitalist industrial society. Susan Sontag in her article "The Third World of Woman" (1973) suggests that "in capitalist society today . . . the family is often the only place where something approximating unalienated personal relations (of warmth, trust, dialogue, uncompetitiveness, loyalty, spontaneity, sexual pleasure, fun) are still permitted."[22] (Sontag is not urging the preservation of the nuclear family but rather that the "opposition" between home and world be ended [203].)

A more extensive treatment of the relationship between private, unalienated space and capitalism is provided by Eli Zaretsky in *Capitalism, the Family and Personal Life* (1976).[23] Zaretsky argues that it was the rise of capitalism that created the extreme dissociation between the public and private worlds that characterizes modern society. "With the rise of industry, capitalism 'split' material production between its socialized forms (the sphere of commodity production) and the private labour performed predominately by women within the home" (29). "As a result 'work' and 'life' were separated" (30). The transformation of workers into commodities, which Zaretsky calls "proletarianization," "split off the outer world of alienated labor from an inner world of personal feeling" (30).

Zaretsky argues that this process "created a historically new sphere of personal life" (31). Because public labor was reified, the only area left for personal, subjective existence was the private sphere, the home. "The rise of industrial capitalism . . . gave rise to a new search for personal identity which takes place outside [the realm of alienated labor]. In a phrase: proletarianization gave rise to subjectivity" (10). The family became a "utopian retreat" (61) from the "harsh [public industrial] world that no individual could hope to affect" (57).

As a result of this transformation of the household, "housewives and mothers were given new responsibility for maintaining the emotional and psychological realm of personal relations" (31). Moreover, "for women within the family 'work' and 'life' were not separated but were collapsed into one another" (31). This "collapse" suggests, once again, that housewives' labor remained essentially "unalienated." But as a result of the rise of capitalism, they had been given the primary role for the preservation of human values, which were impossible to sustain in the public world of alienated labor. Thus, Zaretsky attributes to capitalism the division of values along sex lines, an idea discussed in chapter 1. "The split in society between 'personal feelings' and 'economic production' was integrated with the sexual division of labour. Women were identified with emotional life, men with the struggle for existence" (64).

Ann Foreman follows an argument similar to Zaretsky's but maintains that the relegation of women to being custodians of emotional life constituted a gender construction—"femininity"—that was inherently alienating because it quickly became reified into an expected form, an Other in Simone de Beauvoir's sense of the term.[24] While Foreman stresses as aspects of femininity its passivity, physical delicacy, visual attractiveness, and an inherent masochism, it would seem more promising from a Marxist point of view to explore further the historical identification (recognized by Zaretsky) of women with caring labor and men with the uncaring world of commodity exchange. The dialectic inherent in this dynamic seems most interesting and worthy of further discussion in this vein of Marxist analysis.

Other socialist feminists have, like Foreman and unlike Vogel, seen the domestic sphere as inherently alienating to women. In particular, they have argued that housework is in fact alienated labor. Zillah Eisenstein (1979) urges that any tasks pre-assigned to a particular group are alienating because they are not freely chosen. And, "the sexual division of labor in society organizes noncreative and isolating work particularly for women."[25]

A more extensive statement of a similar position is provided by Mariarosa Dalla Costa in her article "Women and the Subversion of Community" (1972). Dalla Costa argues that women's isolation in the home and her dependency on men are alienating factors. Dalla Costa sees factory labor as potentially less alienating than housework because it is collective. "Participating with others in the production of a train, a car, or an airplane is not the same thing as using in isolation the same broom in the same few square feet of kitchen for centuries."[26] Because the housewife does not participate in the realm of social production she is cut off from "all . . . possibilities of creativity and of the development of her working activity" (77). Yet later in the same article Dalla Costa acknowledges that simply entering the realm of public production, as it is, will not end women's alienation. "Slavery to an assembly line is not a liberation from slavery to a kitchen sink" (81). Women must reject "the myth of liberation through work" (96). But, the actual experience of housework is alienating, Dalla Costa insists, because it is trivial and repetitive (89), as well as isolating.

It is clear that the question of whether housework is alienating or not may be answered by saying that some aspects of it are and others are not. The housewife has more control over her time than the factory laborer; generally she can choose when to do her projects. This would seem to allow a measure of creative planning that Marx said was a central factor in unalienated labor. On the other hand, her chores are prescribed, repetitive, and for the most part, trivial (excepting, of course, the overall process of childrearing, though many of the specific tasks in this process are also trivial and repetitive). The housewife is also cut off from the realm of ultimate political control, and this constitutes another element in her alienation. Finally, her economic dependency must be seen as an alienating factor. Nevertheless, the fact that her life and work are much more closely integrated than the industrial worker's, the fact that unlike the factory worker, she has creative control her her time and space, that she occasionally does truly creative, artistic labor such as knitting and needlework, and that as a significant part of her labor, she does interact emotionally with others, provide the basis for a "relatively unalienated" experience. In this sense, as Vogel notes, it suggests what an unalienated work environment might be like.

The main issue the domestic labor debate entails, however, is the question of what function housework plays in the capitalist system. In an early article (1971) Peggy Morton suggested the household be considered "a unit whose function [was] the maintenance and reproduction of labor power."[27] Mariarosa Dalla Costa, in the 1972 article cited, goes further: "domestic work not only produces use values but is an essential function in the production of surplus value" (79). The "family is the very pillar of the capitalist organization of work" (81). Dalla Costa rejects the idea of earlier Marxists that housework, because it produces only use values, is marginal to the capitalist system. Housewives contribute to the reproduction of labor power—itself a commodity that contributes to the accumulation of capital—and therefore contribute to surplus value. As noted, the determination of surplus value is the difference between the total price of the products and the cost of reproducing labor power. As Gayle Rubin explains, it is housewives who do this "reproductive" work. "Marx tends to make [the determination of what it takes to reproduce labor power] on the basis of the quantity of commodities—food, clothing, housing, fuel—which would be necessary to maintain the health, life and strength of a worker."

> But these commodities must be consumed before they can be sustenance, and they are not immediately in consumable form when they are purchased by the wage. Additional labor must be performed upon these things before they can be turned into people. Food must be cooked, clothes cleaned, beds made, wood chopped, etc. Housework is therefore a key element in the process of the reproduction of the laborer from whom surplus value is taken. Since it is usually women who do housework, it has been observed that it is through the reproduction of labor power that women are articulated into the surplus value nexus which is the *sine qua non* of capitalism.[28]

There has been considerable debate on whether housework really does contribute to surplus value or not, though much of it is a semantic exercise concerning the definitions of such key Marxist terms as "productive" and "unproductive" labor.[29] Most Marxists do agree, however, that housework is functional to the perpetuation of the capitalist system. As Zaretsky summarizes, "the wage labour system . . . is sustained by the socially necessary but private labour of housewives and mothers" (30).

One of the problems with this analysis, however, is that while it argues convincingly that domestic labor is an integral part of the capitalist system, it does not provide an overall explanation for women's oppression. The fatal flaw in this regard in all Marxist theory to date is that women's subjugation is linked to the rise of capitalism. It therefore does not explain why women are oppressed in precapitalist societies and in societies that are "post-capitalist," which have experienced socialist revolutions, such as the Soviet Union, Cuba, and China. Another problem with the Marxist "functionalist" approach to domestic labor (that it is necessary to capitalism) is that it assumes that capitalism could not "reproduce the working class without the nuclear family." As Michèle Barrett notes in her very useful book, *Women's Oppression Today* (1980), "this assertion is highly questionable."[30] Barrett points out that the sexual division of labor was not created by capitalism but preceded it; capitalism may have "built a more rigidly segregated division," but the "ideology of gender division" was there for capitalism to use. It was not "spontaneously generated by it" (137–38). Barrett thus rejects this part of Zaretsky's argument (180, 190–91).

Barrett is joined by a number of other socialist feminists (see especially many of those whose articles are included in *Women and Revolution,* ed. Lydia Sargent, 1981) in rejecting the notion of Engels and many subsequent Marxists that women enjoyed a relatively paradisiacal situation in precapitalist societies. As Gayle Rubin notes,

> Capitalism has taken over, and rewired, notions of male and female which predate it by centuries. No analysis of the reproduction of labor power under capitalism can explain foot-binding, chastity-belts, or any of the incredible array of Byzantine, fetishized indignities, let alone the more ordinary ones which have been inflicted upon women in various times and places (163).

There are, however, some structural differences between capitalist and precapitalist modes of production, as Barrett points out. "The first is the separation of home and workplace, brought about by the development of large-scale production under the wage labour system." The second is the increasing specialization and hierarchization of labor brought about by "the capitalist drive for increased productivity" (164–65). How these developments have specifically contributed to women's oppression needs to be more thoroughly discussed in future socialist feminist analysis. It is clear that analysis of the first point will hinge upon the question of the nature of housework alluded to earlier. The second question, that of the increased specialization of labor, relates back to Marx's theory of alienated labor—a worker who specializes in screwing on bolts is obviously experiencing alienation from the product and the process. How this relates specifically to women needs further clarification. One point that is clear, however, is that sexism and racism provide convenient ideological rationales for who fills the slots at the bottom of the economic hierarchy.

Most recent socialist feminist analyses have taken into account the preexistence of patriarchy (broadly defined as male-dominated society) to capitalism—a concept borrowed from the radical feminists. They nevertheless still attempt to locate a material base for patriarchy within the capitalist system. Christine Delphy (1977), for example, defines patriarchy as "the exploitation of wives' labour by their husbands."[31] Heidi Hartmann in her important article, "The Unhappy Marriage of Marxism and Feminism: Towards a More Progressive Union" (1981), urges that "the material base upon which patriarchy rests lies most fundamentally in men's control over women's labor power."[32] Socialist feminists like Hartmann, however, veer toward a radical feminist analysis when they acknowledge that it is not just capitalists who benefit from women's role in the labor market; it is also "surely men, who as husbands and fathers receive personalized services at home" (9). "Men," she urges in a play on words in the *Communist Manifesto,* "have more to lose than their chains" from a truly feminist revolution (33).

Some socialist feminists have drawn attention to another aspect of women's relationhip to capitalism, which is their status as wage laborers. Especially in recent years, when women make up a good portion of wage earners, this has become a central issue. Indeed, one of the most trenchant criticisms of Juliet Mitchell's *Woman's Estate* (1974) has been that it neglects this aspect of women's economic condition.[33] As most analysts point out, far from being liberated by their entrance into the public work force, as Engels had predicted, women have found themselves consigned to double duty: work for wages in the public sphere but continued unpaid domestic labor in the private sphere. Some socialist feminists, notably Zillah Eisenstein, have seen this as a potentially radicalizing experience, which may mean a "radical future" for "liberal feminism." This is because housewives, while they may accept the ideology of gender division of labor, also accept the American ideology of equal rights. The two ideologies clash in the capitalist market. "Feminist demands uncover the truth that capitalist patriarchal society cannot deliver on its 'liberal' promises of equality or even equal rights for women without destabilizing itself."[34]

In other words, the housewives' expectation of equal pay, as well as such logical concomitants to working mothers' labor as day care, paid pregnancy leaves, affirmative action, etc., are going to cost money. Such costs are going to cut into surplus value and will in this way "destabilize" capitalism. Eisenstein says the "new right" has foreseen these developments, which is why it has produced such a barrage of arguments against women working, centered upon opposition to the Equal Rights Amendment. Other more radical demands some socialist feminists are making include wages for housework and guaranteed annual incomes. What effect these might have on the economy has not been determined.

Some analysts have zeroed in on the extreme differential between men's and women's wages (globally from 1970 to 1990 women's earnings still averaged only 50 to 70 percent that of men's). Some have suggested that this, coupled with the impermanent, unskilled nature of most women's public work, creates a "reserve army of labor" that is functional to capitalism. This is argued in particular by Iris Young (1981), and earlier by Ira Gerstein (1973).[35]

Heidi Hartmann in the article cited considers the wage differential one of the central contributors to women's subjugation. This is because the wage differential derives from the so-called "family wage" (that paid to the man on the assumption that he is using it to support a family). The family wage itself, as Hartmann notes, is "the cornerstone of the present sexual division of labor" (25), the economic cornerstone of the nuclear family, and consequently of women's continued economic dependence on men.

A related topic that has concerned socialist feminists is the question of which class women belong to.[36] Most theorists agree that traditional Marxist distinctions between the bourgeoisie and the proletariat do not work when applied to women, because women have dual class status. They may be identified in terms of the class status of the man on whom they depend financially, but they may also be defined in terms of their own wage status if they work in the public sphere. (Recall that one's class in traditional Marxist analysis depends upon one's relationship to the modes of production.) The problem of where to place the divorced wife of a capitalist may be used to illustrate difficulties in the traditional concepts. For, if she herself does not own capital or the means of production, through divorce she becomes working class or proletariat, and falls even lower if she is unskilled and uneducated. Radical feminists argue that women form a class, or rather a caste, unto themselves (see chapter 6), but socialist feminists continue to stress that class differences do exist among women. A useful analysis of these differences is found in the *Quest* anthology, *Building Feminist Theory* (1981), in the section entitled "Feminist Perspectives on Class."

A final area on which socialist feminist analysis of the household has focused is concentration on the family as the site of ideological socialization, and on the role of the mother therein. Picking up a cue from Eli Zaretsky, Hartmann explores the question of the relationship between the sex-based division of values and capitalism. In particular, Hartmann suggests that the stereotypical behavior expected of men and women is functional to the capitalist system. Such behavior, she implies, is established by ideological socialization.

Hartmann notes that the characteristics typically ascribed to men—competitiveness, rationality, manipulativeness, and a tendency to dominate—are traits needed for proper functioning in the industrial capitalist public world. "Sexist ideology serves the dual purpose of glorifying male characteristics/capitalist values, and denigrating female characteristics/social need" (28). Because capitalism values products that are for exchange more than those for use, its ideology denigrates the use-value realm—the sphere of women—and the characteristics associated with that sphere—emotionality, nurturing, etc. So long as this ideology governs, so long will "the confrontation of capital's priority on exchange value by a demand for use values . . . be avoided" (29).

In a 1981 article, "What is the Real Material Base of Patriarchy and Capital?" Sandra Harding pursues Hartmann's observation on the congruence of male behavioral traits and capitalist values.[37] The reason for this congruence lies in the fact that ideological socialization occurs in the home and is done by women. Indeed, the very division of labor itself, which is materially based, creates that ideology. This is because care is in fact nearly universally provided by women, and because, also nearly universally, women are devalued. The child comes to consciousness in the context of these facts and so learns her or his own gender identity, and gender ideology in the process.

Other socialist feminists have further analyzed this process. For the most part they follow the postwar Frankfurt School of Marxism which attempted to integrate aspects of Freudian theory with Marxism. Most important in this regard was Max Horkheimer's theorizing about the "authoritarian personality"—that workers are ideologically reproduced to be functional in the capitalist work world.[38] Child rearing was thus construed as reproduction of workers with correct ideological imprints. Nancy Chodorow's "Mothering, Male Dominance, and Capitalism" (1979) established many of the central ideas current in this vein of feminist analysis. Following the Zaretsky thesis she notes that capitalism furthered the split between public and private and separated the realm of social production from the home. She continues, "women's work in the home and the maternal role are devalued because they are outside the sphere of monetary exchange and unmeasurable in monetary terms, and because love, though supposedly valued, is valued only within a devalued and powerless realm."[39]

Women as mothers contribute to the reproduction of workers for capitalism, "both physically and in terms of requisite capacities, emotional orientations, and ideological stances" (95). Since the details of her argument rely on Freudian theories of child development, they will be discussed more fully in chapter 4 in conjunction with Chodorow's book *The Reproduction of Mothering*. The gist of her thesis, however, is stated as follows:

> The . . . repressions, denials of affect and attachment, rejection of the world of women and things feminine, appropriation of the world of men, identification with the idealized absent father—all a product of women's mothering—create masculinity and male dominance in the sex-gender system and also create men as participants in the capitalist work world (102).

I might mention here parenthetically a curious lack in Marxist discussions of reproduction which is their failure to focus upon the alienating aspects of biological reproduction, or childbearing labor, as it is now practiced. Juliet Mitchell isolates this in *Woman's Estate* as one of the four structures that define women's oppression—the others being production (women's lack of access to its processes), lack of control over sexuality, and her role as socializer of children.[40] But it is really a non-Marxist, Adrienne Rich, who most thoroughly details the alienation inherent in this kind of labor in *Of Woman Born* (1976).

The final aspects of contemporary theory that derive from Marxist theory, though many of its advocates may not be Marxists, are the concepts of praxis, consciousness-raising, and ideology. In a 1975 article Nancy Hartsock argues that the Marxist idea of praxis is the modus operandi which must distinguish a feminist revolution from any other. "The *practice* of small-group consciousness raising, with its stress on examining and understanding experience and on connecting personal experience to the structures that define our lives, is the clearest example of the method basic to feminism."[41] Citing Marx she notes, "the coincidence of the changing of circumstances and of human activity or self-changing can be conceived and rationally understood only as *revolutionary practice*."[42]

In the same collection Beverly Fisher-Manick (1977) cautions that the so-called c-r group may be a more congenial form to white upper middle-class women than to Third World and working- and lower-class women.[43] This is because the formality of the group discussion process may turn off these women. Moreover, they may see the concept as pretentious: "many black women see it as typical for white people to make a big deal out of something they do (talking) and call it by a fancy name (consciousness raising)" (158). Fisher-Manick seems to be zeroing in on a fundamental issue inherent in the notion of consciousness-raising. This issue in turn points to a basic paradox that is at the heart of the Marxist notion of consciousness and its relationship to revolutionary change.

For, if a consciousness-raising session is just undirected talking, the assumption is that a sharing of (negative) experiences will lead members of the group to see common denominators in that experience and determine the political reasons for that negative experience, for their oppression. This idea is at the heart of a modern Marxist work like Freire's *Pedagogy of the Oppressed.* It assumes that a class or group will more or less spontaneously through critical analysis come to "consciousness," that is come to a political awareness of their condition. Such awareness is necessarily revolutionary, because the group will see who and what is causing its distress. As Carol Ehrlich notes, for women it is a question of gaining "the *consciousness* that they are oppressed as *women,* that they are not inferior, and that patriarchy need not be inevitable."[44] Consciousness-raising thus leads to an awareness of membership in a politically oppressed group: for Marx it was the proletariat; for feminists it is women.

Consciousness-raising is therefore not just undirected talking. It is not a coffee klatch, and this may figure into the resistance Fisher-Manick claims Third World women have to the process. There are certain ground-rules, and often there is an implied and expected analysis. At its worst, hypothetically, consciousness-raising could be a rather dictatorial means of imposing ideology. (I do not believe that this happened to any great extent in the American women's movement, but it is at least theoretically possible.)

The question of whether people's consciousness will rise by itself or whether it needs to be prompted from outside is an old revolutionary problem. For the most part, Marx himself seems to have believed in a revolution rooted in the masses coming to consciousness spontaneously. But, as is well known, Lenin came to believe that a revolutionary elite was necessary both to do the consciousness-raising and to provide leadership for the proletariat. Feminists in theory reject the concept of a party elite. "We cannot support the elitism implicit in the concept of a vanguard party . . . the Leninist model . . . was developed to create a vehicle that could function in the *absence of* . . . political education."[45]

Inherent in the idea of consciousness is the concept of ideology. Ideology is often used in two distinct ways: one, as a "generic term for the processes by which meaning is produced, challenged, reproduced, transformed" (Barrett, 97). The second is more narrowly used to imply a false intellectual system rooted in ruling class interests. In either case, the traditional Marxist view was, as we have seen, that ideology is rooted in a material base, indeed is determined by it.[46] Because of this the Marxist view of consciousness involves a fundamental or "classic paradox"; namely, "that [material] being may determine consciousness but [that] revolutionary transformation of the conditions of being will depend upon raising the level of class-consciousness" (Barrett, 89). There are two ways out of this paradox: if one sticks to a strictly material analysis, one can assume that the conditions of production will lead the members of an economic class to see the nature of their condition dialectically, to identify with other class members and resolve to change things. But even this theory moves beyond a strictly material analysis, for it implies the existence of a reflective, critical consciousness in the workers that is not completely determined by material conditions (whether the logic of the dialectic itself impels workers' minds in a certain direction is another question; if so, then the dialectic itself imposes control, and material determinism still holds).

The other way of resolving the paradox is to allow a leadership or elite that has somehow itself come to consciousness help the proletariat recognize its own interests, or to formulate those interests for them and to lead them (the latter obviously the Leninist solution). These two directions reflect the two epistemological strains inherent in Marxism from the beginning, indeed, from Marx himself. As Catharine A. MacKinnon has remarked (1982): "In the first tendency, all thought, including social analysis is ideological in the sense of being shaped by social being, the conditions of which are external to no theory. . . . In the second tendency, theory is acontextual to the extent that it is correct."[47]

MacKinnon argues that feminist theory may be distinguished from Marxist theory in that feminism must focus on sexuality or gender rather than material conditions as the base for ideological construction. "Sexuality is to feminism what work is to Marxism" (515). And: "as Marxist method is dialectical materialism, feminist method is consciousness raising." Dialectical materialism "posits and refers to a reality outside thought which it considers to have an objective . . . content. [Feminist] consciousness raising, by contrast, inquires . . . into that mixture of thought and materiality which is women's sexuality in the most generic sense" (543). (MacKinnon's own thesis is basically an existentialist elaboration of a radical feminist position and therefore belongs to the tradition discussed in chapters 5 and 6.)

The issue is not a matter of intellectual nit-picking, however, for it entails fundamental questions of revolutionary strategy. At question is really the relationship between consciousness and reality, involving both how consciousness is formed and how it acts upon reality. As noted above, the dominant assumption in contemporary feminist theory is that consciousness-raising is itself a form of praxis that is revolutionary.[48]

In many respects, as Carol Ehrlich notes, this direction is really more correctly labeled anarchist than Marxist. Gloria Steinem has observed that feminist theory has focused on "the integrity of the process of change as part of the change itself. . . . In other words, the end cannot fully justify the means. To a surprising extent, the end *is* the means."[49] A radical black feminist collective states a similar belief in their 1977 manifesto:

> In the practice of our politics we do not believe that the end always justifies the means. Many reactionary and destructive acts have been done in the name of achieving "correct" political goals. As feminists we do not want to mess over people in the name of politics. We believe in collective process.[50]

In this respect Steinem and the black feminists are echoing classic anarchist theory, expressed by Emma Goldman among others (see chapter 2). Ehrlich urges that feminists consciously adopt the anarchist position.

> For anarchists, means and ends must be consistent: freedom cannot be achieved through the paradox of limiting it in the present. People learn the habits of freedom and equality by attempting to practice them in the present, however imperfectly. The primary means of doing this is through building alternative forms of organization alongside the institutions of the larger society (114).

"For social anarchists, then, the revolution is a process, not a point in time" (114). Anarchists come down on the side of ideas controlling material reality, rather than the other way around. "It is *people* who will have to decide to get rid of the state; it will not come about because of changes in the mode of production" (115). Ehrlich points to the continual oppression of women in Marxist states to illustrate that conventional overnight revolutionary transformation of the modes of production does little to change sexist ideology. Such questions (for which there are no Marxist answers, she says) must be asked of them, as:

> Why are there so few women in decision making positions in socialist states? Who does the housework? Why are lesbianism and male homosexuality suppressed? Are children in socialist countries socialized according to sex role stereotypes? Are women equally represented in all occupations? Are their incomes equal to men's? How secure is the woman's freedom of choice in matters of sexuality and reproduction? . . . Who decides these matters—the woman, or the mostly male leadership. . . . In sum, if patriarchy still exists in socialist countries, *why?* (110–11)

Consciousness-raising is not the only form of praxis envisaged by feminists. The concept of praxis also implies the development of alternative arrangements that will themselves provide models for change and will in the process change consciousness. In an article entitled "Staying Alive" Nancy Hartsock urges that since alienated labor remains one of the central modern oppressions, feminists need to develop "a new conception of work itself."[51]

> We know that a feminist restructuring of work must avoid the monotony of jobs with little possibility of becoming more creative and the fragmentation of people through the organization of work into repetitive and unskilled tasks. Although we have some ideas about what such a reorganization of work would look like, *the real redefinition of work can occur only in practice* (115, emphasis added).

She concludes: "a feminist restructuring of work requires creating a situation in which thinking and doing, planning and routine work, are parts of the work each of us does; it requires creating a work situation in which we can both develop ourselves and transform the external world" (118). This is the classic Marxist concept of praxis as unalienated labor.

Praxis also means building alternative institutions. Various women's groups are in the process of doing this today. The establishment of rape crisis and wife-abuse centers, various alternative women's publications, collective small businesses, changes in personal relationships—all are contributing to the growth of an alternative women's culture. Such a culture may be seen as a form of nonviolent revolutionary action and resistance, a form of praxis. Christine Riddiough, following in the tradition of Italian Marxist Antonio Gramsci, sees "gay/lesbian culture" as a model of such a "culture of resistance." "Many aspects," she notes, "of gay/lesbian culture—the bars, women's music, camp—are part of a culture of resistance that has helped gay people survive and fight back against the stereotypes taught by ruling class hegemony."[52]

A women's culture may be seen similarly as a "revolutionary" means of resistance. Two other feminists, Ann Ferguson and Nancy Folbre, urge that what is required is

> the establishment of a self-defined revolutionary *feminist women's culture* which can ideologically and materially support women "outside the patriarchy." Counter-hegemony cultural and material support networks can provide woman-identified substitutes for patriarchal . . . production. . . .[53]

Some contemporary socialist feminists believe that women's culture, women's experience and practice, can provide the basis for a feminist opposition to destructive patriarchal ideologies. Nancy Hartsock, in particular, has developed this thesis in two works published in 1983. She argues for the formulation of a "feminist standpoint," which will enable us to "better understand both why patriarchal institutions and ideologies take such perverse and deadly forms and how both theory and practice can be redirected in more liberatory directions."[54]

The "feminist standpoint" must be rooted in an understanding of "women's perspective," which itself "requires the articulation of an epistemology that grows from women's life-activity" *(Money,* 152). That activity is very different from men's activity. "The position of women is structurally different from that of men, and the lived realities of women's lives are profoundly different from those of men."[55] Just as Marx's vision of the liberated community derived from the experience and practice of unalienated labor and a production for use characteristic of preindustrial work activity, Hartsock's "feminist standpoint" is rooted in the labor experience and practice of traditional women.

In Marxist terms she sees the material basis of women's existence as constituent of women's consciousness. While women also work for wages, their primary institutionalized activities are housework (production of use values) and child rearing. Like certain earlier socialist feminists and other contemporary cultural feminists (see chapter 7) Hartsock concludes that these practices create a consciousness that is relational, contextual, integrative, and life affirming, as opposed to the "abstract masculinity" engendered by men's activities in the capitalist world of commodity exchange. This consciousness forms the basis of a "feminist standpoint" from which to critique patriarchal ideology and practice.

Hartsock's "feminist's standpoint" is derived from women's "experience of continuity and relation with others, with the natural world, of mind with body," an experience that provides

> an ontological basis for developing a non-problematic social synthesis, a social synthesis that need not operate through the denial of the body, the attack on nature, or the death struggle between self and other, a social synthesis that does not depend on any of the forms taken by abstract masculinity. *(Money,* 246).

In other words, it provides intimations of a way out of the impasse discussed at the end of chapter 1.

Hartsock's conclusions correlate fundamentally to those of other contemporary feminists, including those deriving from the Freudian tradition such as Nancy Chodorow; the existentialist tradition, Rosemary Radford Ruether; the radical feminists, Shulamith Firestone and Barbara Starrett; the vision of radical women of color, Cherríe Moraga and Gloria Anzaldúa, and other contemporary cultural feminists like Sara Ruddick and Carol Gilligan. Their views will be presented in succeeding chapters and their collective theory in chapter 7. Further refinements in standpoint theory are discussed in chapter 8.

Hartsock's vision, like theirs, is of a world where "for the first time in human history the possibility of a fully human community, a community structured by a variety of connections rather than separation and opposition" may come to exist *(Money,* 247).

4 Feminism and Freudianism

Our insight into this early, pre-Oedipus phase in the little girl's development comes to us as a surprise, comparable in another field with the effect of the discovery of the Minoan-Mycenaean civilization behind that of Greece.
Sigmund Freud, 1931

Freud was not a feminist. Nevertheless, his perceptions into the organization of human arrangements in the modern world, like those of Marx, offer insights into the nature of women's oppression. For Freud, in his analysis of relations within the family, provided theoretical access to an area held sacrosanct by liberals. His tentative identification of the roles women and men play in the drama of the family, and even more important, his description of the process through which the infant evolves into the socially prescribed roles of adulthood, remain a base upon which an important branch of contemporary feminist theory is built.

As in the discussion of Marxism, it is best to begin with a review of the writings of Freud himself; a discussion of feminist critiques of his basic theory will follow. Then we will consider the second-wave feminist theorists who attempted to reclaim Freud, the most important of whom were Juliet Mitchell, Gayle Rubin, and Nancy Chodorow. Finally we will discuss the "new French feminisms," written under the influence of and often in opposition to the French Freudian theorist, Jacques Lacan.

Freud wrote about women in several important books and articles. *Three Contributions to the Theory of Sex* (1905)[1] is one of Freud's earliest speculations about women and their process of growth. The first "contribution," entitled "The Sexual Aberrations," begins with observations about various psychosexual "inversions," including homosexuality, sadism, and masochism. In general, Freud did not take a judgmental attitude toward homosexuality, although his understanding of lesbianism was limited (see below). In this article he rejects labeling homosexuality "degenerate," especially "where the capacity for working and living do not in general appear markedly impaired" (4). He finds it in most cases to be an acquired orientation rather than an innate one (5); it has a multiplicity of causes (9–12). He stresses that some of the great artists in history have been homosexuals (4, n. 7).

Freud's tolerant attitude toward homosexuality, unusual for its time, is confirmed in other accounts. An anecdote by Helene Deutsch's grandson, an active member of the Boston gay liberation movement, illustrates this attitude.

> This is a story my grandmother told me; she had just begun practicing on her own, under Freud's supervision, in Vienna, and she took on a patient who was a Lesbian. My grandmother was disturbed because, although the analysis finally concluded successfully—the woman could deal with various problems in her life—she was still a Lesbian. My grandmother was rather worried about what Freud would say about this turn of events. When she next saw Freud the first thing he said was, "Congratulations on your great success with Miss X." My grandmother, startled, said, "But she's still a Lesbian." To which Freud replied, "What does it matter so long as she's happy?"[2]

In his 1905 discussion of sadism and masochism Freud associates the former with masculine behavior and the latter with feminine. This is partly because, as he later notes, in psychoanalysis the only "utilizable" definition of masculinity and femininity is where "one uses masculine and feminine . . . in the sense of activity and passivity" (77, n. 8). Freud further suggests that "there is no pure masculinity or femininity" in any one person. "On the contrary every individual person shows a mixture of his [her] own biological sex characteristics with the biological traits of the other sex and a union of activity and passivity" (77, n. 8). Elsewhere he says there is a "bisexual disposition" in all people.[3]

As noted, Freud associates sadism with masculine behavior. "The sexuality of most men shows an admixture of aggression, of a propensity to subdue, the biological significance of which lies in the necessity for overcoming the resistance of the sexual object" (21). "Masochism," on the other hand, "comprises all passive attitudes to the sexual life and to the sexual object; in its most extreme form . . . connected with suffering . . . pain at the hands of the sexual object" (22). The two behaviors are thus rooted in masculine activity and a quest for mastery, and feminine passivity, respectively.

In the second "contribution" Freud develops his celebrated theory of the phases of the child's psychosexual development. The infant begins life in the "pre-genital phase," which is divided into an oral stage where "the sexual aim consists in the incorporation of the object into one's own body" (57) and an "anal-sadistic" stage. This stage, because of its sadistic nature, seems to be a quintessentially masculine phase. As he notes in a later article, the girl has "a comparative weakness of the sadistic component of the sexual instinct."[4]

Following comes the genital phase, which is a period of "object selection," itself divided into three stages. The first occurs while the child is between three and five years old; the second is a latency period that lasts until the third phase, which is puberty. During the latency period, "the psychic forces develop which later act as inhibitions on the sexual life, and narrow its direction like dams. These psychic forces are loathing, shame, and moral and esthetic ideal demands" (39). It is a process of repression and of "sublimation" (40).

In the third "contribution," "The Transformations of Puberty," Freud articulates his first concrete ideas on female psychosexual development. His central notion is that until puberty boys and girls are very much alike but that at puberty "the sharp differentiation of the male and female character originates" (76). In the pregenital phase both have as their first charged object the mother's breast (79). Freud notes that "it would . . . be most natural for the child to select as the sexual object that person whom it has loved since childhood" (82). But during the latency period various societal taboos are erected which enable and/or accompany the resolution of the boy's Oedipus complex; that is, he moves beyond an attraction to the mother and hostility to the father.

Freud is less clear about what happens to the girl during this period. Indeed, much of his subsequent theorizing (and subsequent Freudian theorizing to this day) concerns the question of the girl's relationship to the Oedipus complex, or how she transforms from what Freud sees as essentially a little boy into a "normal" adult woman. He acknowledges, even at this point, that there are strong homosexual pressures inherent in the individuation process, and only "the authoritative inhibition of society" (86) prevents their manifestation (in most cases). Freud indeed seems to feel that men brought up by men (not the norm) might tend to be homosexual, as well as women brought up by women (which is the norm) (86).

The girl, however, must go through a tortuous growing-up process. In the early phases she is psychosexually similar to the boy. "The autoerotic activity . . . is the same in both sexes" (77). In this respect, Freud claims, "the sexuality of the little girl has entirely a male character" (77). (This, by the way, is the sort of arbitrary assumption of male primacy that has enraged feminists. One could assert equally well that the sexuality of the boy is in this stage "feminine," if in fact the sexuality is identical.) Freud continues, "one might advance the opinion that the libido is regularly and lawfully of a masculine character, whether in the man or in the woman; and if we consider its object, this may be either the man or the woman" (77). In this passage it is clear that Freud simply means that the libido is of an active character, following his assumption that masculinity and activity are interchangeable terms.

Freud's final observation about female psychosexual development in this essay is that for the girl puberty involves the "transference of the erogenous excitability from the clitoris to the vagina" (79). For her, therefore, puberty is accompanied by a major process of clitoral repression. "Puberty, which brings to the boy a great advance of libido, distinguishes itself in the girl by a new wave of repression which especially concerns the clitoris sexuality" (78). Freud notes that this process does not often occur gracefully. "It often takes some time for this tranference to be accomplished, during which the young wife remains anesthetic. This anesthesia may become permanent if the clitoris zone refuses to give up its excitability" (78). Contemporary feminists, as noted below, have taken issue with the necessity for this transference, but it must be said that Freud is not necessarily prescribing but describing a socialization process that encourages women to think of their sexuality primarily in terms of male needs and of the wife and mother role.

Freud's next major discussion of female psychology appears in "On Narcissism" (1914).[5] In this essay Freud distinguishes between two kinds of love object: anaclitic and narcissistic. Anaclitic [*Anlehnungstypus* or "leaning-up-against type"] derives from the relationship with the mother or whoever has fed, cared, and protected the child in its earliest stages (68). Narcissistic love has one's self as the love object (69).

Men and women differ in their proclivity toward one or the other of these tendencies. "Complete object-love of the anaclitic type is . . . characteristic of the man" (69). The woman, however, for unspecified reasons,[6] experiences at puberty

> an intensification of the original narcissism, and this is unfavourable to the development of a true object-love with its accompanying sexual over-estimation; there arises in the woman a certain self-sufficiency (especially where there is a ripening into beauty) which compensates her for the social restrictions upon her object-choice. Strictly speaking, such women love only themselves with an intensity comparable to that of the man's love for them. Nor does their need lie in the direction of loving but of being loved; and the man finds favour with them who fulfills this condition (70).

In other words, what Freud seems to be saying is that due to the difficulties inherent in the woman's transference from her original love for the mother to a love for the father (this will be seen to be an essential ingredient in the girl's so-called Oedipus complex, discussed below) the girl's narcissistic tendencies are enhanced to the point where this becomes her primary emotional orientation. One is tempted to point out, although Freud does not, that self-love for the girl is love of a female. It may therefore be a substitute mother love, since the mother is denied her.

Freud's male perspective and indeed a certain misogyny are evident in this essay, despite his protests to the contrary, "No tendency to depreciate woman has any part . . . tendentiousness is alien to me" (70). Nevertheless, his picture of the "cool" (71) self-absorbed beauty who is interested in a suitor only because he pours adulation upon her is hardly flattering. On the other hand, to be fair, many feminists from Wollstonecraft on have isolated a similar image; in their case, however, such "narcissistic" absorption was seen as caused by a society that staked women's economic survival on the issue of attracting a mate.

Opposed to the "feminine" type of narcissistic love, according to Freud, is "the masculine type," which is fundamentally altruistic or other-directed. Some women, however, he admits, do develop this "masculine type" of love. (No wonder Freud was anathema to Charlotte Perkins Gilman.) Even love for a child is often narcissistic. "Parental love . . . is nothing but parental narcissism born again" (72).

Freud refines his analysis of the girl's psychosexual coming of age in two essays published back to back in the 1920s: "The Passing of the Oedipus Complex" (1924) and "Some Psychological Consequences of the Anatomical Distinction Between the Sexes" (1925).[7] In the former essay Freud elaborates his notion of "penis envy," seeing it as a central element in girls' development. The girl, according to Freud, early develops the notion that her clitoris is a deficient organ, that "she has 'come off short,' " and consequently she "takes this fact as ill treatment and as a reason for feeling inferior" (180).

The girl, therefore, accepts her so-called castration "as an established fact . . . whereas the boy dreads [its] possibility" (181). Since the fear of castration (or of being turned into a girl) is one of the most powerful forces in the male psychic development, it serves as a powerful "motive towards forming the super-ego" (181). The girl, however, since supposedly she sees herself as already castrated, has nothing to worry about in this respect and therefore experiences considerably less impetus toward the development of a superego.

The next stage the girl goes through is her attempt to compensate for the lack of a penis by wishing to bear her father a child (181). These two drives, the desire for a penis, called the "masculinity complex," and the desire to bear her father's child "remain powerfully charged with libido in the [adult's] unconscious" (181).

The resolution of the Oedipus complex in the girl should be the renunciation of the desire to have the father's child. How this occurs (or, indeed, *if* any of this occurs) is not well explained by Freud. He acknowledges in fact that "our insight into these processes of development in the girl is unsatisfying, shadowy and incomplete" (181). Somewhat feebly he notes, however, "one has the impression that the Oedipus complex is later gradually abandoned because this [childbearing] wish is never fulfilled" (181). In "Some Psychological Consequences" Freud suggests "the Oedipus complex [in girls] escapes the fate which it meets with in boys: it may be slowly abandoned or got rid of by repression, or its effects may persist far into women's normal mental life" (192–93).

In this article, published in 1925, Freud returns to the question of the Oedipus complex in girls, evidently unhappy with earlier formulations of the topic. Acknowledging that "the mother is the original object" for both girls and boys, Freud finally asks the paramount question, "But how does it happen that girls abandon it [the mother-object] and instead take their father as an object?" (186).

Freud's answer to this question is to urge that psychosexual development in girls and boys is very different: "*Whereas in boys the Oedipus complex succumbs to the castration complex, in girls it is made possible and led to by the castration complex*" (191, Freud's emphasis). In other words, for the boy the fear of castration (by the father) is so great it leads him to develop the necessary moral inhibitions (superego) to reject his primal desire for his mother, thus resolving his Oedipus complex. The girl, however, is already "castrated," i.e., is without a penis, and this leads her to want one and failing that to transfer her penis envy into a desire for a child by the father (thus: "penis-child," 191). At this point "her mother becomes the object of her jealousy" (191). This is the girl's Oedipus complex, but Freud does not explain how the girl moves beyond it.

In this essay Freud also elaborates a point he touched upon earlier, namely that women's superego is weaker than men's, because they experience no castration threat.

> I cannot escape the notion . . . that for women the level of what is ethically normal is different from what it is in men. Their super-ego is never so inexorable, so impersonal, so independent of its emotional origins as we require it to be in men. . . . [Women] show less sense of justice than men, that they are less ready to submit to the great necessities of life, that they are more often influenced in their judgments by feelings of affection or hostility (193).

Whether Freud saw this negatively or not is hard to tell. That he did is suggested by his nervous attempt to counter anticipated feminist criticism in making his point. "We must not allow ourselves to be deflected from such conclusions by the denials of the feminists, who are anxious to force us to regard the two sexes as completely equal in position and worth." (193).

In a later work, *Civilization and Its Discontents* (1930), Freud similarly suggested that women have a somewhat subversive attitude toward civilization. "Women," he claims in speculating about the rise of civilization, "soon come into opposition to civilization and display their retarding and restraining influence."[8] This is because "women represent the interests of the family and of sexual life [while] the work of civilization has become increasingly the business of men" (40), in somewhat circular logic. Because civilization "confronts [men] with ever more difficult tasks [it] compels them to carry out instinctual sublimations of which women are little capable" (40).

The claims of the public world, or "civilization," require the man to make "an expedient distribution of his libido," "since a man does not have unlimited quantities of psychic energy at his disposal" (40). For this reason he "withdraws from women and sexual life" (41). "Thus the woman finds herself forced into the background by the claims of civilization and she adopts a hostile attitude towards it." (41).

As we have seen, Freud believes that men have a more developed superego than women. The superego enforces the rules of civilization by means of primal guilt. In men this guilt comes from "the Oedipus complex and was acquired at the killing of the father by the brothers banded together" (68). (This idea Freud had elaborated in *Totem and Taboo* [1912] which hypothesizes an original prehistoric event in which the sons rose up and killed the father. This triggered original sin, or "primal guilt.") Freud does not say whether women experience primal guilt or not. If they did, it would not presumably be from the killing of the father, but more likely from the rejection and turning away from the mother, which Freud later came to see as the primal event in the girl's development. Also, civilization has much less need to control the sadistic-aggressive drive in women because, as we have noted, it is much less developed; but this is one of its main tasks with men.

Some contemporary theorists have built upon Freud's suggestion of women's subversive moral make-up. Herbert Marcuse and Angela Davis, for example, seized upon the idea in the early 1970s. Elaborating upon Freud's distinction between the reality principle and the pleasure principle in *Beyond the Pleasure Principle* (1920), Marcuse argues that for a series of historical reasons male civilization has come to embody the reality principle carried to an extreme, which he calls the performance principle. This behavioral code expresses the values of male capitalist society: "profitable productivity, assertiveness, efficiency, competitiveness."[9]

Socialism, Marcuse says, "as a *qualitatively* different society, must embody the *antithesis,* the definite negation of the aggressive and repressive needs and values of capitalism as a form of male-dominated culture" (282). It is women who express the values and behavior required by such a society.

> Formulated as the antithesis of the dominating masculine qualities, such feminine qualities would be receptivity, sensitivity, non-violence, tenderness, and so on. These characteristics appear indeed as opposite of domination and exploitation. On the primary psychological level, they would pertain to the domain of Eros, they would express the energy of the life instincts, against the death instinct and destructive energy (283).

In a 1971 paper Angela Davis speaks of "the revolutionary function of the female as antithesis to the Performance Principle."[10] Marcuse elaborates on this idea, urging that feminism must not just call for equality, for "as equals in the economy and politics of capitalism, women must share with men the competitive, aggressive characteristics required to keep a job and to get ahead in the job" (285). Rather, feminists must call for a liberation that "subverts the established hierarchy of needs—a subversion of values and norms which would make way for the emergence of a [new] society" governed by feminine values (285). The liberation of women would thus entail the release of those otherwise repressed feminine characteristics that Marcuse links with the life instincts or Eros, and which are subversive of the performance principle that governs patriarchal capitalist society. In this way Marcuse and Davis have turned Freud's perception of women's subversive attitude toward civilization into a positive virtue, indeed into a revolutionary, redemptive force. Some of the new French feminists have taken a similar position, and their views will be discussed later in this chapter, while further speculation on the differences between women's and men's moral constitutions and value systems will follow in chapter 7.

"Female Sexuality" (1931), the next essay Freud devoted to women, recapitulates and refines Freud's by-then established theory of the girl's maturation process. It is probably the most complete statement of his theory, and the most important from a feminist point of view.[11] In this essay Freud returns to the problem that vexed him in the 1925 article: not only must women "renounce" the clitoris in favor of the vagina; in their passage to adulthood they must also "exchange" the "original mother-object for the father" (194). Here Freud begins to stress the importance of the girl's pre-oedipal attachment to the mother. Indeed, he is coming to see this as one of the most critical aspects of the girl's development: it is "far more important in women than . . . in men" (199). The existence of this powerful "pre-oedipal" phase seems now to Freud a momentous revelation. He compares its discovery to the "discovery of the Minoan-Mycenaean civilization behind that of Greece" (195). This is an interesting analogy because the Minoan-Mycenaean civilization was matriarchal in character;[12] so is the pre-oedipal phase. Although Freud does not say so, this appears to be a case of ontogeny recapitulating phylogeny (or vice versa, if one believes that matriarchal civilization is a projection of theorists' fantasies).

Freud now argues that the bisexual disposition is stronger in the female than the male. This is partly because the woman has two sexual organs: "the vagina, the true female organ, and the clitoris, which is analogous to the male organ" (197). The girl's development involves two phases: the early masculine stage and the later feminine one. "As she changes in sex, so must the sex of her love-object change" (197).

At this point Freud parenthetically rejects the term "Electra Complex" to describe the girl's eventual attachment to the father. The situation of the two sexes is not simply a matter of role reversal. Indeed, the classic triangle of the Oedipal complex is characteristic only of the boy's situation. "It is only in male children that there occurs the fateful simultaneous conjunction of love for the one parent and hatred of the other as a rival" (198).

In the girl's transformation from little boy or little bisexual to adult woman, the crucial event is the rejection of the mother. This rejection is part of the girl's transformation from an active agent (seen in the "masculinity complex") to a passive one, which is the essential occurrence of her maturation, as we have seen.

> The turning-away from the mother is a most important step in the little girl's development: it is more than a mere change of object . . . hand in hand with it [we observe] a marked diminution in the active and an augmentation of the passive sexual impulses (207–8).

Freud continues:

> Frequently with the turning-away from the mother there is a cessation of clitoridal masturbation, and very often when the little girl represses her previous masculinity a considerable part of her general sexual life is permanently injured. The transition to the father-object is accomplished with the assistance of the passive tendencies so far as these have escaped overthrow (208).

In other words, Freud is identifying the girl's early assertive, active phase with a strong maternal bond. That this stage has been analogized to a matriarchal realm is of considerable interest from a feminist point of view. The girl is, however, forced to reject this realm of experience, to repress her "previous masculinity" which results in a permanent injury. Her arrival at the oedipal phase is therefore accomplished at a great expense: she now assumes the passivity that is considered the essence of true femininity. Freud amplifies: "there is an antithesis between the attachment to the father and the masculinity complex—this is the universal antithesis between activity and passivity, masculinity and femininity" (211). Freud is uncertain, however, how "the turning away from the mother-object, originally so vehemently and exclusively loved" is accomplished (200).

An interesting case where this "normal" process of socialization did not occur is described by Freud in "The Psychogenesis of a Case of Homosexuality in a Woman" (1920).[13] Freud's analysis of this individual is compelling, if wrongheaded in certain key respects. It is particularly intriguing for the light it sheds on the phenomenon of "romantic friendship" which by now has been acknowledged as the primary orientation of significant numbers of pre-twentieth-century women.[14]

The woman, "a beautiful and clever girl of eighteen, belonging to a family of good standing" (133) has taken to worshipping an actress. The actress has kept her at some distance and there has been "genital chastity" (139). Freud considers that analysts can rarely cure homosexuality; this case seems particularly unlikely, because the girl has not come to Freud out of a wish to be cured, nor does she have any neurotic symptoms. (Since Freud considers bisexuality to be the norm, the most he says an analyst can do for homosexuals is to restore them "to full bisexual functions. After that it lay with themselves to choose whether they wished to abandon the other way that is banned by society" (137).

Freud notes that in her youth the girl had a "masculinity complex" and was "a spirited girl." What's more she was "a feminist; she felt it to be unjust that girls should not enjoy the same freedom as boys, and rebelled against the lot of woman in general" (156). Her love for the actress was accordingly anaclitic (though Freud does not use the term in this essay): "she . . . assumed the masculine part . . . she displayed the humility and the sublime over-estimation of the sexual object so characteristic of the male lover, the renunciation of all narcissistic satisfaction, and the preference for being lover rather than beloved" (141).

The development of her crush on the actress occurred shortly after her mother had had a baby, when the girl was fifteen. Freud sees the development of the affair as a quest on the part of the girl for a mother-substitute. "The beloved lady was a substitute for—the mother" (143). Freud's arrival at this conclusion is reached somewhat illogically, however. He maintains that the birth of the baby interfered with the girl's Oedipus complex (i.e., she resented the fact that her mother was having her father's child rather than she herself; this triggered her unconscious rivalry with her mother). For this reason, according to Freud, she turned against men. This does not make much sense; if we follow Freud's determination of the genesis of her orientation, it would seem more logical to assume that the arrival of the infant engendered in the girl a sense of the mother's betrayal by giving her up for both the father and the baby), which therefore motivated the girl to seek a mother-substitute, thus generating her passion for the actress.[15] This explanation connects back to the fundamental engagement of the girl with her mother and its necessary dissolution, which Freud saw as the crucial experience of the young girl's evolution.

This survey of Freud's ideas on feminine psychology lays the groundwork for a review of contemporary feminist Freudian theory. However, it should also be noted that most major feminists of the twentieth century—from Charlotte Perkins Gilman, who called Freudianism a revival of "phallic worship," to Germaine Greer—have strongly criticized Freud's theories. Even Freudians themselves, such as Karen Horney and Clara D. Thompson, have challenged key aspects. Other feminists who have joined in this challenge include Viola Klein, Simone de Beauvoir, Betty Friedan, Eva Figes, Shulamith Firestone, Kate Millett, Anne Koedt and Ti-Grace Atkinson. Indeed, a central component of second-wave feminist theory has been its rejection of Freudianism, especially as it had become construed by American "revisionist" Freudians whose doctrine had by the 1940s and 1950s become ideology,[16] and whose practice a brainwashing of women about male supremacy.

One of the central critiques feminists have leveled against Freud and his followers concerns the extent to which they believe that psychosexual development is biologically determined. Obviously, Freud's own comment, "Anatomy is destiny," implies biological determinism.[17] It is clear elsewhere in his writings that Freud did in many instances subscribe to this view. In the 1905 discussion of the sexual aggressiveness of the male, for example, he roots the behavior in the "biological . . . necessity for overcoming the resistance of the sexual object." As Viola Klein points out in *The Feminine Character* (1964), Freud here legitimizes a view of sexual intercourse as rape by establishing it as biologically "normal."[18]

Kate Millett, whose critique in *Sexual Politics* (1970) remains one of the most substantial negative feminist analysis of Freudianism, also zeroes in on what she sees as its inherent biological determinism. Millett provides an amusing example of the lengths to which neo-Freudians have gone to shore up the theory of the biological necessity of male aggressiveness in sexual intercourse. Ransacking the annals of sub-human biology (which, of course, provides a plethora of examples of female aggressivity, such as the spider), theorists discovered the prehistoric cichlid fish. They concluded that "the male cichlids failed to find the courage to mate unless the female of their species responded with 'awe'." As Millett acerbically comments, "how one measures 'awe' in a fish is a question perhaps better left unanswered."[19]

More seriously, Millett charges that the net effect of Freud's message has been to inform "the dispossessed that the circumstances of their deprivation are organic, therefore unalterable" (187). The central concepts of Freudian theory have been used as clubs to keep women submissive. "Should she grow insubordinate, she will invade the larger world . . . [male 'territory'] and seek to 'compete,' thereby threatening men. She may then be convicted of a 'masculinity complex' " (186). Viola Klein similarly rejects the way in which the "masculinity complex" has been used to intimidate women (74). Other feminists concur. Millett continues: "In such cases Freud and his school will do all in their power to convince her of the error of her ways . . . the renegade must adjust or succumb" (186).

> The whole weight of responsibility, and even of guilt, is . . . placed upon any woman unwilling to "stay in her place." The theory of penis envy shifts the blame of her suffering to the female for daring to aspire to a biologically impossible state (189).

Shulamith Firestone in *The Dialectic of Sex* (1970) similarly convicts Freud of a failure to seriously consider the possibility of social genesis of psychic disorders. A feminist view cannot "accept the social context in which repression . . . must develop as immutable."[20]

Another central feminist objection to Freudian ideas about female psychology is the obvious male bias inherent in them. As Millett notes, Freud follows the misogynistic Western philosophical tradition initiated by Aristotle, which sees women as incomplete males (182, n. 66). In 1924 Karen Horney wrote one of the first critiques of Freud's views on women, arguing that they reflect "masculine narcissism."[21] Horney notes that "psychoanalysis is the creation of a male genius, and almost all those who have developed his ideas have been men."[22] "The psychology of women," therefore, "has hitherto been considered only from the point of view of men . . . the psychology of women hitherto actually represents a deposit of the desires and disappointments of men" (5). She urges that what is needed is to free ourselves from "this masculine mode of thought" to determine an authentic description of female psychology (7).

One expression of male bias is the notion of penis envy. As Simone de Beauvoir states (1949) in rejecting the notion, "this outgrowth, this weak little rod of flesh can in itself inspire [girls] only with indifference, or even disgust."[23] Kate Millett urges that it is just as probable that the girl, invested with "childish narcissism," "take her own body as norm" (181).

In any event, Clara Thompson notes, two of Freud's most critical ideas, penis envy and the castration complex "are postulated on the assumption that women are biologically inferior to men."[24] Like most feminists Thompson argues that if there is any validity to the idea of penis envy, it must lie in a female envy of the male *social* status, his power, freedom, and dominance.[25] De Beauvoir similarly argues, "if the little girl feels penis envy, it is only as the symbol of privileges enjoyed by boys" (38). Horney urges that in fact a more important envy may be that of the male for the female's reproductive powers (7), a thesis developed by Azizah al-Hibri (see chapter 7).

Other Freudian concepts feminists believe reflect a male bias include the notion of the libido being masculine, an idea de Beauvoir criticizes (35). Millett ridicules the chauvinistic contortions necessary to produce the theory that the wish to have a child is a form of penis envy. "Freudian logic has succeeded in converting childbirth, an impressive female accomplishment . . . into nothing more than a hunt for the male organ" (185). She notes further: "Woman is thus granted very little validity even within her limited existence and second-rate biological equipment: were she to deliver an entire orphanage of progeny, they would only be so many dildoes" (185).

On the subject of biological determinism there is enough ambiguity in Freud to allow some feminists to reject that aspect of his theory, interpreting his ideas in terms of social-cultural conditioning. Gayle Rubin warns (1975), however, that a considerable tightrope act is required to accomplish the latter interpretation, for one cannot entirely eliminate the biological basis for his theories.[26]

Nevertheless, from Horney on, feminists have argued that if Freud's theories are to be used at all, they must be read as descriptions of socioculturally induced processes. Horney states, for example, that if a "masculinity complex" exists, it is because "a girl is exposed from birth onward to the suggestion . . . of her inferiority" (15). Naturally, she would want to be like that which is supposed to be superior to her. Thus, it is sexist ideology that is at the root of the phenomenon identified by Freud.

Similarly, Kate Millett notes that Freud did not see his patients' dissatisfaction as a "justified" reaction to "the limiting circumstances imposed on them by society, but as symptomatic of an independent and universal feminine tendency . . . 'penis envy' " (179). Freud was blocked, she says, by his assumption of the superiority of male anatomy, which prevented him from locating the source of women's unhappiness in their social situation. Penis envy may no more be taken as a literal expression of female aesthetic values than a black's pre-1960s envy of white skin may be taken as a statement about the aesthetic superiority of whiteness. In each case it reflects envy of privileged status (180).

Firestone suggests that what Freud observed were "symptoms of the power psychology created by the family" (55). The "Oedipus complex" describes the power realities of the Victorian nuclear family: the patriarchal, all-powerful, unloving father; the mother and child united in a bond of oppression (49). De Beauvoir similarly suggests that if there is such a thing as an "Electra complex" (Freud did not use the term)—that is, a transference of the girl's interest to her father from her mother—it simply reflects the power reality of patriarchal civilization, that of "the sovereignty of the father" (38). Viola Klein takes issue with Freud's view of the female superego as defective. This is, she urges, the "traditional view of feminine inferiority" but "clad in a new jargon" (76). Karen Horney similarly argues that the supposed malfunction of women's powers of sublimation (due according to Freud to her "castrated" physiognomy) is more likely due to historical and social pressures that prevented her from "sublimating." "Owing to the hitherto purely masculine character of our civilization, it has been much harder for women to achieve any sublimation . . . for all the ordinary professions have been filled by men" (15).

Another Freudian notion with which contemporary feminists have taken issue is the clitoral-vaginal shift. As Kate Millett notes, the clitoral versus vaginal orgasm issue "has provided careers and put bread on the table for an army of disciples" (198). This is because Freudian theory held that vaginal orgasms were normal and truly feminine and that clitoral were not. Much psychoanalytic practice was devoted to getting women to behave "normally." Anne Koedt's "The Myth of the Vaginal Orgasm" (1968) confronted the issue directly. Following Masters and Johnson, Koedt argues that "there is only one area for [female] sexual climax . . . that area is the clitoris. All orgasms are extensions of sensations from this area."[27]

Freudian therapists have, however, spent much time and effort on misguided attempts to cure female "frigidity" because they have focused on the vaginal orgasm. Koedt notes that one Freudian, Marie Bonaparte, even suggested surgery as a means of encouraging the desired response. Bonaparte explains that in such surgery "the suspensory ligament of the clitoris [is] severed and the clitoris secured to underlying structures" (38). This brutal suggestion parallels the techniques of cliterodectomy practiced in certain parts of the Middle East and Africa.[28] As Koedt points out, such destruction of the clitoris, both physically and through the brainwashing of psychoanalysis, is functional in the perpetration of male supremacist ideology. For, because of the clitoris, the male and the male organ are in fact expendable for female sexual pleasure. Shifting the emphasis to the vagina makes the woman once again sexually dependent upon the man. Ti-Grace Atkinson carried forward Koedt's analysis in "The Institution of Sexual Intercourse" (1970)[29] where she argued that that "institution" is in fact a "political construct" used to keep women in their places (prone).

While feminists thus take issue with certain ideas enunciated by Freud himself, it is really the "revisionist" school of American psychotherapists that is their main target. De Beauvoir suggests that through them Freudianism became a "religion"; Firestone calls it "our modern church." It was a church built upon the principle of female inferiority. Betty Friedan argues that revisionist Freudianism was the philosophical underpinning that sustained the "feminine mystique" through the 1940s and 50s in America. As an illustration of the "pop" Freudianism of the period, Friedan cites Farnham and Lundberg's *Modern Woman* (1947): "Feminism," they claim, "was at its core a deep illness."

> The dominant direction of feminine training and development today . . . discourages just those traits necessary to the attainment of sexual pleasure: receptivity and passivity, a willingness to accept dependence without fear or resentment, with a deep inwardness and readiness for the final goal of sexual life—impregnation. . . .
>
> It is not in the capacity of the female organism to attain feelings of well-being by the route of male achievement. . . .[30]

It is clear from this statement how vaginalism had become an ideology of female subordination. As Friedan notes,

> Because Freud's followers could only see woman in the image defined by Freud . . . with no possibility of happiness unless she adjusted to being man's passive object,—they wanted to help women get rid of their suppressed envy, their neurotic desire to be equal. They wanted to help women find sexual fulfillment as women, by affirming their natural inferiority (119).

Psychoanalysis thus became a central brainwashing device to keep women passive. The catchword of the 50s became "adjustment" which meant, in essence, acceptance of a role with which one is dissatisfied. What Friedan called the "feminine mystique" could equally be called the Freudian mystique. It told women that it was normal to be passive and dependent and abnormal to have intellectual ambitions. "The feminine mystique, elevated by Freudian theory into a scientific religion, sounded a single, overprotective, life-restricting, future-denying note for women" (125).[31]

Shulamith Firestone argues in a similar vein that revisionist Freudianism was a central component of the "counterrevolution," or the ideological backlash, that came in response to the first wave of feminist theory and activity. "Freudian theory, regroomed for its new function of 'social adjustment,' was used to wipe up the feminist revolt" (70). For Freudianism "had a safety catch that feminism didn't—it never questioned the given reality" (70). Firestone acknowledges the validity of basic Freudian perceptions, however, and uses them in constructing her own theory (see chapter 6).

The rejection of Freudian theory by feminists of the early 1970s was challenged by a new vein of feminist inquiry that developed in the late 1970s. It is not necessary to determine which of these views of Freudianism is correct, for each "sees" and focuses on a very different aspect of Freudian theory. As Gayle Rubin rather neatly sums up: "To the extent that it [Freudian theory] is a rationalization of female subordination, [the feminist] critique has been justified. To the extent that it is a description of a process which subordinates women, this critique is a mistake" (197). Her view is that "as a description of how phallic culture domesticates women, and the effects in women of their domestication," psychoanalytic theory is unique (197–98). One may, she suggests, read Freud's essays on women "as descriptions of how a group is prepared, psychologically, at a tender age, to live with its oppression" (196).

Rubin suggests further that because Freudian theory "sees female development based largely on pain and humiliation, . . . it takes some fancy footwork to explain why any one ought to enjoy being a woman" (197). This is why Freudians like Helene Deutsch had to develop the concept of masochism as the key to the feminine character. But, as Rubin points out, why did Freudians—aware as they were of the brutal psychic mutilations necessary to transform the assertive little girl into a passive object—why did they not seek alternative developmental structures instead of trying to legitimate the status quo? (197)

Rubin notes that rather than assuming that women "naturally" enjoy pain and humiliation—the position at which revisionist Freudians had to arrive—one could take an opposite stance, based implicitly on the hypothesis that no one naturally "enjoys" pain and humiliation. This should lead one to "question the entire procedure" of the gender socialization process (197). "The theory of gender acquisition could have been the basis of a critique of sex roles." (184) But the revisionists failed to develop this radical critical perspective.

It is this radical view that Juliet Mitchell, Rubin herself, and Nancy Chodorow have sought to develop. Mitchell's *Psychoanalysis and Feminism* appeared in 1974. It is not a perfect work, but as with all exploratory endeavors, it is best to focus on the new insights it offers, rather than harp on its faults, one of which is a tendency to make rather astonishing generalizations. For example, she notes, "all infants believe that everyone has a penis."[32] One is tempted to echo Millett and suggest that how one determines "belief" in a neonate is a question perhaps better left unanswered.

Nevertheless, Mitchell does offer some interesting ideas. The most important of these are: 1) her recognition of the fact that Freud stressed the importance of the pre-oedipal phase in female psychosexual development, and 2) her attempt to incorporate the structuralist theories of French anthropologist Claude Lévi-Strauss into a theory of women's oppression that is based on the relationship between ideology and the unconscious.

In chapters entitled "Pre-Oedipal Sexuality" and "The Pre-Oedipal Mother and the Oedipal Father," Mitchell accentuates this aspect of Freud's theory, noting that he himself was late in recognizing the importance of the mother attachment, because of his own and his culture's androcentric bias. The implications of this element in Freud's theory, she notes, is that "the father . . . and the men that follow him . . . are only secondary figures, for pride of place as love-object is taken by the mother—in both sexes" (111).

Mitchell picks up on Freud's analogy between the Minoan-Mycenaean civilization (anterior to Greek culture) and the pre-oedipal phase. She suggests that Freud's ontogenetic description parallels Engels' phylogenetic one: both see that "the power of women ('the matriarchy') is pre-civilization, pre-Oedipal" (366). " 'The world historical defeat' of the female takes place with the girl's castration complex and her entry into the resolution of her Oedipus complex—her acceptance of her inferior, feminine place in patriarchal society" (366). Mitchell sees "Greek culture" as masculine and inimical to women.

> For women Greek history represented a massive defeat, and it will be at their peril that their pre-history [the Minoan-Mycenaean phase], though it will be always in evidence, will continue to dominate in their lives. All its values must be abandoned or thoroughly displaced on to the new Oedipal possibilities (110).

It should perhaps be pointed out that in Freudian theory there is implication of biological (or irreversible cultural) determinism, and no less so in this vein of Freudian feminism. For, inherent in Mitchell's thesis is that culture—that is reason, intelligence, critical thinking, all that we revere in the Greek tradition—is male, and that its opposite (necessarily nonthinkingness) is female. The further implications of the idea that women find entry into culture more difficult than men *can be interpreted* to mean that women are culturally predisposed to be incapable of rational thought. Obviously, no feminist could subscribe to such a thesis. I point this up here, because Mitchell (and also certain French feminists—see below) sometimes imply not just an opposition between the pre-oedipal, matriarchal world of the mother and the oedipal world of male culture, but suggest that women somehow *belong* back in the pre-oedipal, nonrational stage. Mitchell's attempt to conflate Engels and Freud, therefore, is fraught with dangerous implications, as is any attempt to equate "pre-oedipal," which necessarily means nonrational, with "matriarchal," which does not. More successful attempts to amplify the significance of the pre-oedipal phase, or the mother, in girls' development are undertaken by Rubin and Chodorow (see below).

The other major thesis Mitchell introduces is her assertion of a relationship between ideology and the unconscious. Borrowing from French theorist Louis Althusser, Mitchell notes, "Understanding the laws of the unconscious . . . amounts to a start in understanding how ideology functions, how we acquire and live the ideas and laws within which we must exist" (403). In other words, "the unconscious . . . [is] the domain of the reproduction of culture or ideology" (413).

The culture or ideology that is reproduced, according to Mitchell, is that described by Lévi-Strauss in his analysis of kinship systems, *The Elementary Structures of Kinship* (1949). In that work he said primitive societies were held together by a system of gift-exchange that formed the primary mode of communication among human groups. Underlying this exchange system was the universal taboo on incest which imposed the necessity of exogamous intercourse. The primary form of exchange was that of women in marriage. Why it was women who were exchanged rather than men is not explained in Lévi-Strauss's theory.

Mitchell argues that "the systematic exchange of women is definitional of human society" (372). Or, as Rubin puts it, Lévi-Strauss argued that "the incest taboo and the exchange of women are the content of the original social contract" (192). In other words, human society, which is patriarchal, is predicated upon the use of women as objects for exchange. And it is this kinship system which determines the patriarchal ideology that is reproduced via the unconscious in each generation of humans. "The controlled exchange of women that defines human culture is reproduced in the patriarchal ideology of every form of society" (Mitchell, 413). "The patriarchal law speaks to and through each person in his unconscious; the reproduction of the ideology . . . is . . . assured in the acquisition of the law by each individual" (413).

The kinship system is therefore "internalized" in the Oedipus complex (374). And while men "enter into the class-dominated structures of history . . . women . . . remain defined by the kinship patterns of organization" (406). Women's identity is therefore determined by *"their cultural utilization as exchange objects"* (Mitchell's emphasis, 408). Because she equates culture and history with the male and preculture with the female, Mitchell is led to assume a radical dualism. She finds that "the economic mode of capitalism and the ideological mode of patriarchy" are "two autonomous areas" (412)—a point which Marxists such as Michèle Barrett and Ann Foreman have criticized.[33]

The task for feminists, according to Mitchell, is to effect "a change in the basic ideology of human society." It must be "a cultural revolution" (414). She concludes that such a revolution must intervene in the reproduction of the ideology of women as exchange-objects that is now seated in the unconscious. "Some other expression of the entry into culture than the implications for the unconscious of the exchange of women will have to be found in a non-patriarchal society" (415). To summarize, Mitchell says the devaluation of women in the kinship system is the governing ideology in patriarchal society. The processes of induction into this ideology are what Freud described.

Gayle Rubin similarly develops a theory based on Freud and Lévi-Strauss (as well as Marx and Lacan). As an anthropologist her understanding of the subtleties of Lévi-Strauss's theory is perhaps greater than Mitchell's. She denies, for example, that the exchange of women is *the* sine qua non of human society, though it is a fundamental factor (177). Like Mitchell she urges that "psychoanalysis . . . is a theory about the reproduction of kinship" (183). And following Lacan she suggests that "psychoanalysis deals with the 'conscription' process by which individuals are initiated into kinship systems and the effects of that process that remain with the individual (188). "The Oedipal crisis occurs when a child learns of the sexual rules embedded" in the kinship system, and his or her relationship to it. "The crisis is resolved when the child accepts [its] place [within kinship] and accedes to it" (189). Through the oedipal crisis the child's "libido and gender identity [are] organized in conformity with the rules of the culture which is domesticating it" (189).

Rubin also asserts that the incest taboo, which is at the heart of the oedipal complex, depends upon an even more basic taboo on homosexuality (180). With this in mind Rubin revises the Freudian theory of female maturation. The oedipal crisis is precipated in both boy and girl by the discovery of the incest taboo, of the difference between the sexes and of a heterosexual imperative. Through the incest and the homosexual taboos the girl learns not only that her mother is off limits (as the boy learns) but that all women are forbidden. For the girl discovers that in order to "properly" love her mother she must possess a "phallus" (194). At this point the "pre-Oedipal lesbian" turns to the father, because it is only from him that she can get the phallus (194). But, of course, she never does. At this point "she 'recognizes her castration,' [and] accedes to the place of a woman in a phallic exchange network" (195).

Rubin urges, therefore, that "feminism must call for a revolution in kinship," through which current systems would be reorganized to eliminate the exchange of women as a basis for the social contract and for the current process by which gender identity is formed (199).

Nancy Chodorow's *The Reproduction of Mothering* (1978) is perhaps the most important and impressive feminist interpretation of Freudian theory. Her central thesis is that gender personality is shaped within the psychodynamics of the family, in particular within the "object-relations" the child forms, especially with the mother. These gender personality traits—independence and relatively affectless behavior in men and interdependency and emotional intensity in women—prepare people for their respective roles in society and the economy. Men's traits enable them to function in the capitalist world of production; women's characteristics prepare them for their place in the world of reproduction, and particularly incline them toward the reproduction of mothering.

As noted in chapter 3, some Marxists have also identified a congruence between gender traits and the sexual division of labor. Like them Chodorow asserts, "the sexual division of labor both produces gender differences and is in turn reproduced by them."[34] This dynamic is not simply a matter of socialization, however; it is rooted in the basic psychodynamics of early childhood, in the processes Freud described. Chodorow assumes that the division of labor, the split between public and private with women relegated to the latter realm, is at the root of women's oppression. The reason this division is perpetuated is the unchanging process of reproduction of gender types that takes place in the family. Another factor that contributes to women's subjugation, also rooted in childhood developmental processes, is the inherent misogyny involved in the boy's resolution of various complexes—the fact that the boy must reject his mother and things female in order to become a man.

Not only does the psychic reproduction process create beings functional to the continuance of capitalism and patriarchy, it also produces creatures—men and women—whose emotional organization is fundamentally incompatible. This leads women to seek other outlets for their emotional needs than men; it impels them, in short, toward motherhood where with their own children they can recreate the emotional bonding that they need. The details of Chodorow's view of the formative processes deserve review here.

Chodorow follows the "object-relations" school of Freudians, who perceive that "the child's social relational experience from earliest infancy is determining for psychological growth and personality formation" (47). Rather than looking to "instinctual determinants" this school stresses the early social world of the infant and child. The most important of these early relationships is with the mother.

Like Freud, Chodorow stresses the paramount significance of the pre-oedipal phase in the girl's psychosexual development. She notes that "prolonged symbiosis and narcissistic overidentification are particularly characteristic of early relationships between mothers and daughters" (104). Because mothers and daughters are the same sex, there is a mutual tendency toward close identification and intense emotional involvement. "Mothers tend to experience their daughters as more like, and continuous with, themselves" (166). This relationship is not rejected at the end of the pre-oedipal phase; it continues on as an important, indeed the most important, component of a woman's emotional life.

Chodorow suggests that mothers treat their sons and daughters differently and tend to kick sons out of the nest earlier; that is, move them out of the pre-oedipal and into the oedipal stage. Because he is of a different sex the son comes to his identity in contradistinction to the mother and to the feminine. He therefore develops a sharper sense of ego boundaries than the girl and must learn to deny or repress his affective inclinations.

The girl, too, must separate herself from the mother but because of the prolonged pre-oedipal stage this separation is blurred and never as precise as that of the boy's. The girl does have to change her love object to the father in order to emerge as a normal heterosexual, but why or how this is accomplished remains as unclear in Chodorow as it is in Freud. (Chodorow explicitly rejects biological explanations for heterosexual inclinations.) At some points Chodorow seems to suggest that for the girl the father or the male represents freedom and independence from the identification and dependency she experiences with the mother, but she does not fully develop this idea (82, 121). In any event, the bond with the mother remains primary, although a secondary bond with the father does form.

The net effect of these processes for personality development is that a woman's sense of ego-boundary separateness and independence remains more fluid than men's, and her emotional orientation more bisexual (or indeed homosexual). Her emotional need for others is also more pronounced. The woman's makeup is thus ideally suited for the role of mother.

> As long as women mother, we can expect that a girl's preoedipal period will be longer than that of a boy and that women, more than men, will be more open to and preoccupied with those very relational issues that go into mothering—feelings of identification, lack of separateness or differentiation, ego and body-ego boundary issues and primary love not under the sway of the reality principle (110).

Thus:

> Girls emerge . . . with a basis for "empathy" built into their primary definition of self in a way that boys do not. Girls emerge with a stronger basis for experiencing another's needs or feelings as one's own . . . girls come to experience themselves as less differentiated than boys, as more continuous with and related to the external object-world (167).

Boys on the contrary "come to define themselves as more separate and distinct, with a greater sense of rigid ego boundaries and differentiation." In short, "the basic feminine sense of self is connected to the world, the basic masculine sense of self is separate" (169). Chodorow concludes therefore, "Women's mothering . . . produces asymmetries in the relational experiences of girls and boys as they grow up, which account for crucial differences in feminine and masculine personality" (169).

Because of these crucial differences the adult woman and man have very different emotional makeups. Men are prepared "to participate in the affect-denying world of alienated work, but not to fulfill women's needs for intimacy and primary relationships" (207). Moreover, both men and women seek a return to a primary relationship with the mother. "Oedipal love for the mother . . . contains . . . a promise of primal unity which love for the father never does. . . . Men cannot provide the kind of return to oneness that women can" (194). Thus a heterosexual woman can achieve that sense of oneness only by identifying with the man who loves her or by identifying with her mother (194). Only a lesbian can herself experience the primary love with another woman that is implanted in the female psyche by the relational processes of early childhood. (Chodorow does not, however, specify this implication.)

Because "an exclusive relationship to a man is not enough" women seek other means to replicate the primal mother love: one way is with other women (200). The other is to have children and rebuild this kind of relationship with one's own child. (This would have to be a daughter, but Chodorow does not specify this.) "By doing so, she recreates for herself the exclusive intense primary unit" (202). Thus is effected "the reproduction of mothering."

Because this process tends to create gender identities that are functional to the perpetuation of the division of the world into private and public (capitalist), Chodorow appears to believe that this division will be ended or considerably changed if we alter the nuclear family child rearing process. The principal way to do this, she suggests, is to have "primary parenting [be] shared between men and women" (215).

The result of shared parenting would be that the emotional asymmetries between men and women would be evened up—they would become "androgynes"—and men would no longer be imprinted with character traits that are functional to the capitalist world of work. Presumably, they too would become a-civilized in the way Freud, Marcuse, and Davis thought women were. Chodorow seems to think that if people become non-functional to the capitalist work structure, it will wither away. As Michèle Barrett said of a similar proposition, capitalism is probably more resilient than the thesis implies. Rather, the conscious challenge to governing ideologies proposed by Marxist advocates of praxis seems a more promising mode of cultural revolution. (Of course, shared parenting can be seen as a form of praxis, but this is not Chodorow's point.)[35]

Chodorow and Freud's descriptions point strongly in another feminist direction that neither chooses to pursue; they indicate that the very powerful mother-daughter bond has been obscured or made marginal in patriarchal society. It is not too great a leap from their premises to suggest that a reassertion of this matriarchal tradition and its value system is what is necessary for a fully feminist revolution. It is in this direction that many French feminists have headed.[36]

In order to understand their theories it is necessary to review the reinterpretation of Freud by French psychoanalyst Jacques Lacan. While Lacan's views are difficult if not impossible to summarize, the gist of his theory is that Freud's hypotheses and observations must be interpreted symbolically. They described what is essentially the "fall" of individuals into consciousness, into language, into the realm of the symbolic, which is a patriarchal state. The fall is out of the blissful state of oneness and nonentity that the neonate enjoys with the pre-oedipal mother. This is the intransitive stage of the Imaginery.[37]

The fall also entails a split within oneself. This notion is similar to Sartre's idea of the dialectic of otherness, an existentialist position to be discussed in chapter 5. In this process the self becomes constituted as an object that is nameable ("me"). Before that one is total subject, or zero. It is through absence or lack that one comes to know one's self as separate from another. Thus develops the transitive stage, which reflects the desire for another or for the mother.

Language is already there, however, and children must use it to express themselves. With language comes the symbolic knowledge that Freud identified in various stages—castration, oedipal, etc. Castration is the awareness of separation. Men try to deny their separation or alienation through their affirmation of phallic means of mastery.

With the fall into consciousness comes an awareness not only of difference as separateness from another but also of the differences between the sexes and their prescribed life courses. "So the man is 'castrated' by not being total, just as the woman is 'castrated' by not being a man." The man's "lack of wholeness" is "projected onto woman's lack of phallus, lack of maleness. Woman is then the figuration of a phallic 'lack'; she is a hole."[38]

One could criticize Lacan from a feminist point of view for equating wholeness with the phallus and alienation with castration. Lacan uses the Freudian term "phallic mother" to describe the pre-oedipal figure which is destroyed by the Name-of-the-Father. Under its influence and in a desire for the mother the girl becomes aware of her lack of a phallus, and the boy learns that he cannot compete with the father.

> The phallus symbolizing unmediated, full *jouissance* must be lacking for any subject to enter the symbolic order, that is to enter language. . . . Human desire, according to Lacanian doctrine, is always mediated by signification. That is our human lot of castration.[39]

The phallus thus "comes to stand for totality, or a state in which all is union and nothing is differentiated." As Richard Wollheim notes, "why the phallus? . . . why does not Lacan think of phallic phantasies as later reworkings of phantasies about the nipple?"[40] Thus, while Lacan like Freud reflects a male bias, in particular a similar penis- or phallus-obsession, the French feminists have seized upon aspects of his theory for their own purposes.

Julia Kristeva and Hélène Cixous, two of the most important French feminists, have offered unique interpretations of Lacan. Kristeva urges: "By *Freudianism* I mean that lever . . . which once again poses the question of sexual difference and of the difference among subjects who themselves are not reducible one to the other."[41] She emphasizes that sexual difference "is translated by and translates a difference in the relationship of subjects to the symbolic contract which *is* the social contract: a difference, then, in the relationship to power, language and meaning" (21). "Feminism has only been but a moment in the . . . process of coming to consciousness about the implacable violence (separation, castration, etc.) which constitutes any symbolic contract" (28). For women "the sociosymbolic contract" has been "a sacrificial contract" (25).

Cixous also stresses the Lacanian emphasis on language as the seat of patriarchal oppression. "For as soon as we exist, we are born into language and language speaks (to) us, dictates its law, a law of death."[42] Cixous picks up the idea Freud broached in *Civilization and Its Discontents* that women are a-civilized.

> For Freud/Lacan woman is said to be "outside the Symbolic" . . . that is outside language, the place of the law, excluded from any relationship with culture and the cultural order. And she is outside the Symbolic because she lacks any relation to the phallus, because she does not enjoy what orders masculinity—the castration complex (46).

These French feminists tend to view the patriarchal symbolic order as fascistic and death-oriented. Women and their realities have been denied and destroyed by this order. Because they exist "outside the Symbolic" on the margins of discourse, they remain in an other, different space. From this zone they remain as subversives, who must "deconstruct" the symbolic order of the phallus. At the same time they must affirm the values and vision of their own *other* realm of experience; while the patriarchal order is death-oriented, theirs is life-affirming. The French feminists thus arrive—via the concept of the dialectic seen in Jacques Derrida's notion of "deconstruction"—at a position not dissimilar to that proposed by Charlotte Perkins Gilman, especially in *His Religion and Hers,* and other cultural feminists (see chapter 2), as well as the position of Herbert Marcuse and Angela Davis noted earlier in this chapter. The specifics of the French theory follow.

Derrida himself accused Lacan of being guilty of "phallogocentrism," a composite of "logocentrism," a rationalistic hubristic outlook associated with Cartesian humanism, and phallocentrism, or what Americans might call male chauvinism. "The composite word," Derrida states, "declares the inextricable collusion of phallocentrism with logocentrism . . . and unites feminism and deconstructive, 'grammatological' philosophy in their opposition to a common enemy."[43] Derrida thus proposes a critique of the Newtonian or Cartesian world-view adumbrated in chapter 1. The French feminists amplify this position. As one unsympathetic critic noted, the opposition drawn is that between "Cartesian-Man" and "Witch-Woman," the witch being the ultimate representative of a marginal, repressed female culture.[44]

In expressing the Derridan idea of feminism's deconstructive or iconoclastic potential, Kristeva says,

> If women have a role to play . . . it is only in assuming a *negative* function: reject everything finite, definite, structured, loaded with meaning, in the existing state of society. Such an attitude places women on the side of the explosion of social codes: with revolutionary moments.[45]

Kristeva notes the dilemma women find themselves in vis-à-vis the Symbolic, however. Either they can enter it and become functional men, or can "flee everything considered 'phallic' to find refuge in the valorization of a silent underwater body, thus abdicating any entry into history" (166).

Xavière Gauthier points to the same problem: on the one hand, women can integrate themselves into the male symbolic order. They can "find 'their' place within the linear, grammatical, linguistic system that orders the symbolic, the superego, the law . . . a system based entirely upon one fundamental signifier: the phallus." In this case they remain schizophrenic: "completely divorced from themselves without knowing it, women were transformed into this Crazy Sex which was named the 'Second Sex'." On the other hand, women have throughout history been silent, mute. But "as long as women remain silent, they will be outside the historical process. But, if they begin to speak and write *as men do*, they will enter history subdued and alienated; it is a history that, logically speaking, their speech should disrupt."[46]

In her article "Castration or Decapitation" Cixous insists that it is political repression that has kept women's potentially deconstructive energy under control. To make her point Cixous relates a Chinese anecdote about a man who was told to turn his 180 wives into soldiers. The women did not comply: they were disobedient, they laughed and chattered until he decapitated the two leaders. Then the others obeyed. "It's a question," Cixous observes, "of submitting feminine disorder, its laughter, its inability to take the drumbeats seriously, to the threat of decapitation" (43). These French feminists thus urge that women affirm their otherness, their differentness as a means of destroying, subverting, or deconstructing the patriarchal order—despite the fact that such an orientation, separatism, may mean perpetual relegation to a marginal world outside history, outside the realm of public discourse.

Since women's differentness is located in their bodies, it is the female body and female sexuality that must be the source of an authentic, disruptive, "feminine Imaginary." In particular, it is the sexual mother, "la mère qui jouit," that has been repressed and who must be resurrected.[47] The French feminists therefore rely upon Freud's notions of the eros-instinct and the death-instinct, seeing the female erotic as redemptive.[48] They see the erotic pre-oedipal mother as a source for a non-repressed feminine Imaginary, which itself may be a vehicle for the transformation of ideology.

Though only Catherine Clément, a Marxist, seems to have specified the consequences of this idea, it remains a question of cultural revolution.[49]

Hélène Cixous has most fully developed these arguments, recently urging, "things are starting to be written, things that will constitute a feminine Imaginary" (52). And, "Writing in the feminine is passing on what is cut out by the Symbolic, the voice of the mother, passing on what is most archaic" (54). Cixous sees as models those women who have operated on the edge of culture; their voice is the most authentic—witches, madwomen, hysterics. "The hysteric is a divine spirit that is always at the edge. . . . She's the unorganizable feminine construct" (47).

"The Laugh of the Medusa" remains the most important elaboration of Cixous's theory. In it she announces, "Now women return from afar, from always: from 'without,' from the heath where witches are kept alive; from below, from beyond 'culture'."[50] Women must write, must speak out of an authentic sense of their own differentness, their own body. "Write your self. Your body must be heard. Only then will the immense resources of the unconscious spring forth" (250). Women must seize the "occasion to speak, hence her shattering entry into history, which has always been based on her suppression. To write and thus forge for herself the antilogos weapon" (250). "Women should break out of the snare of silence. They shouldn't be conned into accepting a domain which is the margin or the harem" (251).

Women's authentic language is organic, erotic, holistic: its source is the pre-oedipal mother. "Even if phallic mystification has generally contaminated good relationships, a woman is never far from 'mother' . . . there is always within her at least a little of that good mother's milk. She writes in white ink" (252). It is the mother within "who nourishes, and who stands up against separation; a force that will not be cut off but will knock the wind out of the codes" (251). Women's reality is fluid, uncatagorizeable, beyond the either-or, sado-masochistic dichotomizing that characterizes phallic logic.[51]

Luce Irigaray also suggests the mother-daughter relationship may be the source of a reenergized authentic feminine Imaginary, a revolutionary feminine ideology. The "desideratum," she specifies, is that "as women become subjects, mothers and daughters may become women, subjects and protagonists of their own reality rather than objects and antagonists in the Father's drama."[52]

These French feminists thus see the Freudian pre-oedipal relationship between mother and daughter as a source for a resurrection, so to speak, of the female Imaginary, of female strength and identity. A vision rooted in this hitherto repressed realm must destroy the phallogocentric order, must project a "countersociety."

> A "female" society is then constituted as a sort of alter ego of the official society, in which all real or fantasized possibilities for *jouissance* take ref-

> uge. Against the sociosymbolic contract, both sacrificial and frustrating, this counter-society is imagined as harmonious, without prohibitions, free and fulfilling.[53]

And, as Françoise d'Eaubonne concludes, such a feminist deconstructive transformation will mean that "the planet in the feminine gender [will] become green again for all."[54]

5 Feminism and Existentialism

The situation of woman is that she—a free and autonomous being like all human creatures—nevertheless finds herself living in a world where men compel her to assume the status of the Other.

Simone de Beauvoir, 1949

Two of the most important works of modern feminist theory—Simone de Beauvoir's *The Second Sex* (1949, published in this country in 1952) and Mary Daly's *Beyond God the Father* (1973)—derive their ideological premise from the twentieth-century philosophical movement, existentialism. This body of ideas was itself rooted in the theoretical constructs of several German philosophers, notably Hegel, Husserl, and Heidegger, but had its most popular formulation in the works of French thinker Jean-Paul Sartre, de Beauvoir's life-long companion.

Before specifying the theories of de Beauvoir and Daly, then, it will be helpful to summarize some basic tenets of existentialism. These ideas found their earliest statement in Hegel's *Phenomenology of Spirit* (1807), but it is in Heidegger's *Being and Time* (1927) and Sartre's *Being and Nothingness* (1943) that they were formulated as the concepts elaborated by Simone de Beauvoir in *The Second Sex*.

Hegel's description of the psyche as "self-alienated spirit" remains the kernel from which subsequent existentialist descriptions of consciousness derive. Hegel saw consciousness presiding in a divided arena: on the one hand is the transcendent or observing ego; on the other, the fixed self, or the observed ego. Sartre was later to call these selves the "pour-soi" and "en-soi"—the for-itself and the in-itself.

The two sides are in a perpetual dialectic; the pour-soi attempting to move beyond the fixed, reified status of the en-soi but at the same time needing the en-soi as an object against which to measure or define itself. A similar dialectic exists between pour-soi and the world or other people. In Hegel's view self-consciousness forever needs or desires other people to prove or validate its existence, if only by the negative proof that it is not the other consciousness. This affirmation-denial, Hegel argues, takes the form of a master-slave relationship: on the one hand there is "the independent consciousness whose essential nature is to be for itself, the other is the dependent consciousness whose essential nature is simply to live or to be for another."[1]

> [The master's] essential nature is to exist only for himself; he is the sheer negative power for whom the thing is nothing. Thus he is the pure, essential action in this relationship, while the action of the bondsman is impure and unessential." (116).

"The unessential consciousness is for the lord the object, which constitutes the *truth* of his certainty of himself" (116).

Heidegger also envisions the self existing in a negative dialectic with the world of others but describes different aspects of this confrontation than does Hegel. For Heidegger the self, called *Dasein,* is in a perpetual tension between an alienated, reified level of existence—existence as an object—and existence as a projective, creative, transcending subject. The object-level of existence Heidegger sees as the level of what he calls "das Man," the masses. It is the level that we would today associate with the stereotypical, ideologically determined, individuality-less figures of mass advertising. To live on this level, according to Heidegger, is to live in an inauthentic mode. It is to conform to the "dictatorship of the 'they'."[2] What is dictated is a kind of averageness that smothers authentic individuality: in the "public 'environment,' " he writes, "every Other is like the next. This Being-with-one-another dissolves one's own Dasein completely into the kind of Being of 'the Others' " (164).

As opposed to this fallen, inauthentic *they-self* is the *authentic Self,* "the Self which has been taken hold of in its own way" (167). It is the self which has particularized itself against the crowd, which has realized itself or found itself via the authentic mode. "As they-self, the particular Dasein has been dispersed into the 'they,' and must first find itself" (167). Finding oneself means being reopened to the possibility of self-authentication or self-realization. In this mode Dasein exhibits "the possibility of Being-free *for* its ownmost potentiality-for-Being" (183) Dasein should be a "self-projective Being towards its ownmost potentiality-for-Being" (236).

Despite this moral imperative to realize oneself—the keystone of existentialist ethics—Dasein is attracted to the inauthentic modality of the public realm. This is because it fears the nothingness it senses at the core of itself. In order to escape from this "non-being" it seeks to turn itself into being, to objectify itself in the world of reified relations. The self tries to flee the feeling of "uncanniness which lies in Dasein" (234). It does this by losing itself in the bourgeois familiarity of the everyday world of prefabricated identity. In this tranquillized condition, however, Dasein "drifts along towards an alienation [*Entfremdung*] in which its own-most potentiality-for-Being is hidden from it" (222). "This alienation *closes off* from Dasein its authenticity and possibility" (222).

In this lost state Dasein begins to feel anxious. This anxiety or dread is another concept fundamental to existentialist ethics; it functions as a kind of barometer warning Dasein that it is not living up to its potential. In other words, anxiety is the expression of existentialist guilt; it is the "voice of conscience" summoning Dasein to a realization of its authentic potential. "Anxiety brings [Dasein] back from its absorption in the 'world.' Everyday familiarity collapses" (233).

> Anxiety individualizes. This individualization beings Dasein back . . . and makes manifest to it that authenticity and inauthenticity are possibilities of its Being (235). The call of conscience has the character of an *appeal* to Dasein by calling it to its ownmost potentiality-for-Being-its-Self; and this is done by way of *summoning* it to its ownmost Being-guilty (314).

"Conscience" for Heidegger "is precisely the disclosure to someone of what he ought to be, of his authentic self."[3]

Heidegger thus conceives the self as torn between two modes, the inauthentic and the authentic. This dilemma expresses a fundamental dialectic between being an object, on the one hand, and being a creature in the process of becoming. Since the latter process is not being per se but becoming, Heidegger calls it non-being.

Sartre picked up on this idea, however problematic it may be,[4] and uses it to form the basis for his great work, *Being and Nothingness*. Like Hegel and Heidegger, Sartre saw the self as existing in two dimensions: the pour-soi (for-itself) is the transcending, creative, future-oriented self; the en-soi (in-itself) is the reified contingent object self that is immanent and ultimately inauthentic. Like Heidegger, Sartre saw the level of the en-soi as that of "being" and the pour-soi as "non-being" or "nothingness."

Sartre elaborated that the pour-soi is reflective consciousness capable of withdrawing from everyday immanence, capable of forming projects. In this capacity it transcends the fixed self which remains mired in immanence with no possibility of change or growth. Like Hegel, Sartre saw the en-soi as an object that was constituted under the reflective eye of the pour-soi or by other consciousnesses. A fixed identity is therefore a reified entity that allows for no authentic change. Such "unity of being" is a false construction, nothing more than the "for-itself hypostasized in the in-itself."[5]

Like Heidegger, Sartre saw this dyad locked in a perpetual dialectic. Pour-soi remains dependent upon en-soi; as a particularized consciousness *of* something, pour-soi remains contingent upon that which it is conscious of (58). At the same time it is a continual process of refusing to be fixed as en-soi or as being, and therefore in a continual process of non-being, nothingness, or becoming.

Sartre's conception of the authentic, or authenticating self, is therefore, like Heidegger's, dynamic. Pour-soi is in a continual process of self-realization, of self-projection, but it is a process which can never be realized lest the pour-soi *be* itself once and for all, which would mean that it would lose its character as pour-soi and become en-soi. It is the potentiality of self-creation involved in this process that constitutes human freedom, or human liberation.

> The being which is what it is can not be free. Freedom is precisely the nothingness which *is* . . . at the heart of man and which forces human-reality to *make itself* instead of *to be* (416).

"Freedom . . . is characterized by a constantly renewed obligation to remake the *Self* which designates the free being" (34–35).

Another aspect of Sartre's discussion in *Being and Nothingness* that is especially relevant to Simone de Beauvoir's theory is his concept of the Other. Sartre appears to have derived his concept in part from Hegel's observations on the self-other dialectic and in part from Heidegger's theory of the inauthentic realm of *das Man*. On one level, Sartre sees the Other as a kind of hypostasized public opinion: it projects a powerful "gaze" that can fix one in an inauthentic pose, that does not allow one to exist as an authentic, independent, separate consciousness. The gaze or opinion of the Other can thus be internalized; it can help to shape the en-soi.

Conversely for the subject-self, for pour-soi, the Other can appear as an object. Thus the same relationship that exists between pour-soi and en-soi can describe the relationship between the self and others, or the Other. In particular, Sartre sees the self-other relationship as being played out along the lines of Hegel's master-slave. In order to constitute itself as a subject, pour-soi must cast the Other as object. "It is by the very fact of being that I exclude the Other. The Other is the one who excludes me by being himself, the one whom I exclude by being myself" (212).

Just as the pour-soi depends on the en-soi, so does the master or subject consciousness depend on the existence of an Other: "the slave is the Truth of the Master" (213). For the pour-soi defines itself by the fact that it is not the Other. "If in general there is an Other, it is necessary above all that I be the one who is not the Other, and it is in this very negation effected by men upon myself that I make myself be and that the Other arises as an Other." "The For-itself which I am simply has to be what it is in the form of a refusal of the Other" (259).

Unlike the en-soi, however, the Other exists also as consciousness attempting to reduce other selves to the level of object in order that it may exist as pour-soi. So, struggle ensues when the self attempts to reduce the other consciousness to an object level, in order itself to become a transcendent free pour-soi.

> Inasmuch as the Other as the-Other-as-a-look . . . the for-itself experiences itself as an object in the Universe beneath the Other's look. But . . . soon . . . the for-itself by surpassing the Other towards its ends makes of him a transcendence-transcended . . . (496).

One thus comes eventually to see the Other as having all the negative qualities that one wishes not to have oneself. "The Other becomes then that which I make myself not-be" (264). It is interesting here to note the similarity of Sartre's position to that of Jacques Lacan who saw the masculine identity constructed on the fact of not being castrated. The congruence is not surprising perhaps, since both Sartre and Lacan were heavily influenced by Alexandre Kojève's lectures on Hegel, presented in Paris from 1933 to 1939.[6]

In other works Sartre developed the idea of the collective Other as scapegoat or repository for the undesired aspects of the dominant group in society. In particular, what is projected onto the Other is physicality and therefore mortality and contingency—attributes Sartre had already associated with the en-soi. In an important feminist critique of Sartre's theory, Margery L. Collins and Christine Pierce point out that to a considerable extent the en-soi represents feminine attributes where the pour-soi is masculine.[7] But Sartre himself does not consciously develop this point in *Being and Nothingness*. It remained for Simone de Beauvoir to fully explain the place of women implied in the existentialist schema.

Sartre did, however, explore the cultural phenomenon of projecting evil onto the Other. In *Saint Genet* he notes that in order to evade responsibility for one's own evil one sees "the evildoer [as] the Other. . . . Never is it more perceptible than in wartime. We know the enemy only by comparison with ourselves; we imagine his intentions according to ours."[8] Sartre explains this as follows:

> The decent man . . . will define himself narrowly by traditions, by obedience . . . and will give the name *temptation* to the live, vague swarming which is still himself, but a himself which is wild, free, outside the limits he has marked out for himself. His own negativity falls outside him, since he denies it with all his might. Substantified, separated from any positive intention, it becomes a pure negation that poses itself for its own sake . . . namely Evil. Evil is . . . what he wants but does not want to want. . . . In short . . . Evil is the Other (35).

Sartre had used this theory earlier to explain anti-Semitism in "Portrait of an Anti-Semite" (1946). Thomas Szasz in *The Manufacture of Madness* (1970) applied the theory to witches, to the insane, and to homosexuals—all marginal people on whom the good, normal folk project their own unorthodox feelings. Szasz remarks the "existential cannibalism" of the phenomenon and wonders if we can learn to overcome this Hegelian dialectic: "Can we create meaning for our lives without demeaning the lives of others?"[9]

A final aspect of Sartre's theory must be discussed and that is his concept of bad faith. Bad faith occurs when the self, instead of choosing to engage in the authenticating porject of self-realization, consents to become an object, to exist as en-soi. One makes this choice out of fear of the nothingness and uncertainty involved in the creative freedom of the pour-soi. One attempts to escape from the anxiety of freedom by losing oneself in the en-soi, or in the everyday, inauthentic other-directed identity. "Thus we flee from anguish by attempting to apprehend ourselves from without as an Other or as a *thing" (Being and Nothingness,* 43). Bad faith is therefore an attempt to "fill up the nothingness which I *am*" (44). In bad faith one slips into a mass-produced identity created by the Other. One takes "toward oneself the point of view of the Other" (504). Erich Fromm characterized bad faith as an "escape from freedom." And existentialist theologian Paul Tillich urged that the decision to live an authentic life is a difficult one that most would prefer to avoid; it requires "the courage to be."[10]

Simone de Beauvoir's contribution to feminist theory was her use of the existentialist vision to explain the cultural and political status of women. For de Beauvoir realized that a dialectic obtains within a culture as well as within the individual: in a patriarchal culture the male or masculine is set up as the positive or the norm, where the female or the feminine is set up as the negative, the unessential, the abnormal, as in short, the Other. The woman is "defined and differentiated with reference to man and not he with reference to her; she is the incidental, the inessential as opposed to the essential. He is the Subject, he is the Absolute—she is the Other."[11]

Following Hegel, de Beauvoir believes that "Otherness is a fundamental category of human thought" (xvii). Indeed, de Beauvoir suggests with Lévi-Strauss, whose pioneer study of early societies (*Elementary Structures of Kinship*) appeared the same year as *The Second Sex,* that the transition to a state of culture is marked by the development of an awareness of binary opposition. This phenomenon de Beauvoir associates with the Hegalian dialectic. "Things become clear, . . . if, following Hegel, we find in consciousness itself a fundamental hostility toward every other consciousness; the subject can be posed only in being opposed—he sets himself up as the essential as opposed to the other, the inessential, the object" (xvii). It is woman who is so defined through the viewpoint of the masculine subject.

Women therefore, who know themselves to be subjects, find themselves "living in a world where men compel her to assume the status of the Other" (xxvii). In the struggle described by Sartre as that between pour-soi and en-soi, women are cast in the role of en-soi, while men take the independent transcending position of the pour-soi. Men "propose to stabilize her as object and to doom her to immanence since her transcendence is to be overshadowed and forever transcended by another ego [the male] . . . which is essential and sovereign" (xxviii). Women, therefore, are caught in a perpetual dilemma, feeling in themselves the impulses of the pour-soi but fixed in the status of the en-soi. De Beauvoir further asserts that the male-female dialectic is one aspect of an endemic cultural manicheism. "Otherness, is the same thing as negation, therefore Evil. To pose the Other is to define a Manichaeism" (73). As an example of the association of evil with women, de Beauvoir gives the following aphorism of Pythagoras: "There is a good principle, which has created order, light and man; and a bad principle, which has created chaos, darkness, and woman" (74). We noted in chapter 1 how the Baconian man of science assumed this dualism in his view of nature and of woman.

De Beauvoir speculates that woman's identity as Other and her fundamental alienation derive in part from her body—especially her reproductive capacity—and in part from the prehistoric division of labor dictated by the child bearing and rearing function. She sees the female body as inherently alienating because it demands so much of women's energy that it saps their potential for engaging in creative pour-soi activity. Childbearing, childbirth, and menstruation are draining physical events that tie women to their bodies and to immanence. The male is not tied down by such inherently physical events (19–29).

While de Beauvoir does not believe that anatomy is destiny (29), she does insist that a person relates to the world through her or his body: "it is the instrument of our grasp upon the world, a limiting factor for our projects" (30). Where the male body facilitates his engagement in free creative activity (because he can engage in sexual activity with impunity and because he is not tied down by menstruation or child bearing), the female body is an impediment (583).

Because of women's reproductive role in prehistory, a corresponding division of labor occurred. The work assigned to women predisposed them toward an en-soi mentality, for their tasks were those of repetitive maintenance. On the other hand, the masculine labor of hunting and fighting involved the use of tools to subdue the world. Woman by the early division of labor was thus condemned to the part of the en-soi or other where the male enjoyed the transcending privileges of the pour-soi. Through his projects "he has subdued Nature and Woman" (60).

Woman's mentality, her cultural outlook, and her religious world view are thus an expression of the fundamental role she has been cast in.

> The religion of woman was bound to the reign of agriculture, the reign of irreducible duration, of contingency, of chance, of waiting, of mystery; the reign of *Homo faber* is the reign of time manageable as space, of necessary consequences, of the project, of action, of reason (70).

De Beauvoir considers that women have continued in this situation to the present day. Housewives are condemned to lives of sterile repetitiveness with no hope of engaging in creative, transcending projects. Their lives are lived vicariously through the projects of their husbands.

Because men and women are cast in the pour-soi/en-soi dialectic, both are tempted to engage in bad faith. This may be understood by considering that de Beauvoir subscribes to the same existentialist ethic as Heidegger and Sartre. Every individual's duty is to engage in self-transcending projects.

> Every time transcendence falls back into immanence, stagnation, there is a degradation of existence into the "en-soi"—the brutish life of subjection to given conditions—and of liberty into constraint and contingence. This downfall represents a moral fault if the subject consents to it (xxviii).

For the man, the idea of woman as en-soi can attract his desire to *be* once and for all, his desire for Being, for losing himself in an absolute immanence. From this posture have evolved various stereotypical views of woman as the apotheosis of Being, such as the Earth Goddess. On the other hand, men can look at woman as physical nature, a being that is contingent and mortal, and he can hate and fear her for this (134–35). From this perspective stem the various stereotypes of woman as evil Other (bitch, witch, etc.). Both of these postures are essentially gestures in bad faith, for they deny the "nothingness" that is at the core of each man, as every individual; they deny the human condition; they are false attempts at transcendence.

Women can also engage in bad faith; usually this comes from denying their potential as freely creative subjects and accepting their role as Other or object. This is the "escape from freedom" phenomenon described previously. "Indeed, along with the ethical urge of each individual to affirm his subjective existence," de Beauvoir notes, "there is also the temptation to forgo liberty and become a thing" (xxi). This is a morally destructive choice but it is often the path of least resistance for women. "It is an easy road; on it one avoids the strain involved in undertaking an authentic existence" (xxi). Perhaps one should suggest that it appears to be an easy road, but such appearances are deceptive, for often the acceptance of otherness leads to severe schizophrenia and despair—a syndrome seen in such women as Marilyn Monroe, Zelda Fitzgerald, and Sylvia Plath. The serious implications of the internalization of otherness will be discussed more fully later in this chapter.

To an extent, de Beauvoir accuses women of collusion in allowing themselves to be defined as Other—a serious question which Michèle Barrett and Mary Daly also address.[12] But de Beauvoir sees the reasons for such collusion as lying in the fact of women's dispersion—that they have never (until recently of course) collectively identified themselves as a subject, as We (xviii). And she suggests further that women are seduced by the obvious advantages that come from accepting the role of protected object—it is much easier than accepting responsibility for one's own life.

> To decline to be the Other, to refuse to be a party to the deal—this would be for women to renounce all the advantages conferred upon them by their alliance with the superior caste. Man-the-sovereign will provide woman-the-liege with material protection and will undertake the moral justification of her existence (xx).

De Beauvoir, however, as a true existentialist, sees women as having a moral choice, one that is nonetheless fraught with anxiety, for it involves an apparent rejection of her femininity. "Woman's independent successes are in contradiction with her femininity, since the 'true woman' is required to make herself object, to be the Other" (246). De Beauvoir urges that women's liberation or fulfillment can only come in the choice to exist as a pour-soi, as a transcending subject who constitutes her own future by means of creative projects. She thus joins Mary Wollstonecraft and other liberal feminists in urging that women strengthen their rational faculties and critical powers in order to achieve transcendence (581).

Whereas de Beauvoir has pointed out an important dimension of women's subjugation, there are aspects to the theory that are disturbing. One is that it is focused primarily on the white bourgeois housewife. It is she that de Beauvoir has in mind when she urges women to shed their lives of otherhood, and to engage in transcending work, a career. For women who are "mired" in immanence by other factors than sexism—by racism and poverty—such exhortations must sound fatuous. We have seen, also, that the question of how alienating or "immanent" the housewife role actually is can be considered open to debate (chapter 3; see further discussion below).

Another question concerns the denigration of immanence, of the "agricultural" level of repetitiveness that de Beauvoir sees as the lot of most women. Similarly one must question the vaunting of the male mode of transcending projects. She herself acknowledges that this mode often involves subduing women and nature. It seems that de Beauvoir and Sartre have succeeded in simply endorsing the Western, Faustian model of active transformation of the world as a proper means to fulfillment or redemption. We now know that this dynamic of Becoming, of perpetual consumption of the resources of one's environment, a perpetual attempt to stamp the materials of reality as one's own and reshape one's environment accordingly, have led to ecological disaster. Might there not be something to be said for the en-soi realm, the level of immanence, of contingency—women's realm, the realm of Being and repetition? Eastern religions suggest this as a positive alternative. In more recent work (see chapter 7) de Beauvoir seems to have come around to a realization that a resurgence of the female perspective, rooted in immanence, may yield more positive results than the denial of the physical implicit in transcendence beyond en-soi.[13]

One feminist in the existentialist tradition who has recently taken a position diametrically opposed to de Beauvoir's is Kathryn Allen Rabuzzi. In *The Sacred and the Feminine: Toward a Theology of Housework* (1982) she argues that we should not denigrate the realm of housework, as de Beauvoir does, but rather see it as the site of a continuing feminine culture. Indeed, in the vein of existentialist theology, which locates transcending reality within the everyday world, she urges that the home can be the site of religious events, where occurs "hierophany," the revelation of the sacred.[14] And the priestess of the "cultic ritual" of housework is the housewife (94). She engages not in the linear, progressive time of the masculine realm of Becoming but participates "in mythic time, ritually returning . . . to the time of origins, the primordial time in which the gods and goddesses originally created order out of chaos" (97).

Rabuzzi argues that the masculine mode of being has typically been that of questing, where the traditionally feminine mode has been that of waiting (143–45). The woman's life does not follow a line of progressive, linear change and "achievement"; rather it is repetitious, cyclical, static. "Women's housebound time is typically characterized by amorphousness or circularity or both . . . above all it is static" (146). Rabuzzi equates women's time with Henri Bergson's "durée" and Eliade's mythic time. It is "timeless" duration, beyond linear historical time (146). Unlike de Beauvoir, who characterizes housework as Sisyphean labor—boring, meaningless, and repetitive—Rabuzzi urges (while acknowledging that it can be a "profane" experience, as de Beauvoir suggests) that it points to a different modality than the typical Western, masculine mode of questing. "Ultimately, waiting appears to name a *via negativa* that so far has been construed as the inenarrable counterpart to questing. As such, it is neither inferior nor superior, but merely different" (181). Her hope for the future is that new modes of being may emerge out of the current women's movement, modes that are "forged from the best of both traditions"—questing and waiting (193).

Mary Daly's *Beyond God the Father* (1973), along with her more recent *Gyn/Ecology* (1978), which will be discussed in chapter 6, are among the most important contributions to feminist theory developed in the second wave of feminism. *Beyond God the Father* is a work written very much within the tradition of existentialist theology. In particular, Daly has been influenced by Paul Tillich and Martin Buber, especially the latter's *I and Thou* (1922), which itself is related to Heidegger's intuitions. Also useful for understanding existentialist theology is Mircea Eliade's *The Sacred and the Profane* (1957).[15]

Basically, existentialist theologians rely on the central contrast between the fixed, reified, "profane" level of existence that Sartre called en-soi, and an intense, charged, "sacred" level of existence and relationship that is fundamentally an experience of being alive and sensing the aliveness of other organic life. The one level evokes an "I-it" relationship, classically that of a scientist dissecting dead nature, according to Buber; the other calls for an "I-Thou" relationship, that of an I to a personal "Thou." Existentialists, especially the "death-of-God" theologians, reject objectified, reified forms of relationship and abstract hypostasized images of the deity; instead, they urge that one see God as an experience of Being in the midst of life, as a Thou. Such a reality is dis-covered or un-covered when fixed, objectified ideas and images are destroyed. Those idols are seen as impeding the revelation of Being.

Mary Daly rejects the idea of God as an "hypostasized transcendence" or a fixed image of a Supreme Male Being. She asks, "Hasn't the naming of 'God' as a noun been an act of murdering that dynamic Verb?"[16] She suggests that we see that what is conventionally labeled God is a "Verb in which we participate" (34). "This Verb—the Verb of Verbs—is intransitive" (34).

The women's movement she sees as a "spiritual revolution." Women's rejection of their status of Otherness will prove redemptive, will lead to the discovery of Becoming, of transcendence, beyond the reified God-the-Father.

> The women's revolution . . . is an ontological, spiritual revolution, pointing beyond the idolatries of sexist society and sparking creative action in and toward transcendence. . . . It has everything to do with the search for ultimate meaning and reality, which some would call God (6).

What is involved is "a *creative political ontophany*" (34)—or revelation of being.

The process through which the discovery/uncovering of God is realized is dialectical. First there occurs a negative phase in which the idols—the reified, oppressive forms of patriarchal society—are destroyed or exorcized. The reason these traditional images of God must be destroyed, exorcised, or passed beyond is that these legitimize the oppressive status quo. "The various theologies that hypostasize transcendence, that is . . . [that] objectify 'God' as a *being* . . . legitimate the existing . . . status quo" (19). For it is this God that has ratified the "phallic morality" (97) of a "rapist culture" (116), a society that engages in "rape, genocide and war"—"the most Unholy Trinity" (114). The power of this evil trinity will be broken, according to Daly, when women assert their own counter-identities. "The casting out of the demonic Trinities *is* female becoming" (122).

The process of women's liberation is thus perceived as redemptive—both for women and society. "The becoming of women in sisterhood is the countercultural phenomenon *par excellence* which can indicate the future course of human spiritual evolution" (11). Daly advocates an anti-establishment course that is in the tradition of the great antinomian women of earlier centuries—Anne Hutchinson and Sarah Grimké. "The movement is smashing images that obstruct the becoming of the image of God. The basic idol-breaking will be done on the level of internalized images of male superiority, on the plane of exorcising them from consciousness and from the cultural institutions that breed them" (29).

The iconoclasm must begin from within. Women must exorcise and reject any sense of Otherness that they have internalized. Daly feels that process will be redemptive for society as a whole, because it will provide new avenues through which Becoming may come to exist. "By refusing to be objectified and by affirming being, the feminist revolution is creating new possibilities of I-Thou" (39). Such a process "makes us aware of the Verb who is infinitely personal, who is nonreifiable. . . . This Verb is the Eternal Thou" (178).

The refusal to be object forces those who would see women as objects toward a recognition of their existence as subjects. Such an experience is radicalizing and forces the dynamics of relationship beyond what Hegel and others called the master-slave dialectic. An "encounter with another subject, an I who refuses to be an It" can lead to a new awareness, a new consciousness (40).

The rebellion of the "object" can lead to a reassertion of what Paul Tillich called "ontological reason" as the ground of academic and scientific inquiry, as opposed to the "technical reason" that now governs such knowledge. Technical reason is confined to the observation of the mechanical processes of a phenomenon and does not deal with ultimate questions such as those concerning purposes and ends.[17] In modern society, Daly believes, "technical controlling knowledge" has become destructive not only of women but also of the natural environment. Women's "creative refusal of victimization by sexual stereotypes" can therefore lead to new modes of seeing and being beyond the destructive and narrow modalities of technical reason. Such "creative refusal" points to a way beyond the destructive scientific consciousness we associated with the Newtonian world view in chapter 1. "This creative refusal involves . . . efforts to develop new life-styles in which I-Thou becomes the dominant motif, replacing insofar as possible the often blind and semi-conscious mechanisms of I-It, which use the Other as object" (39). In the area of knowledge, Daly adds, this "means breaking down the barriers between technical knowledge and that deep realm of intuitive knowledge which some theologians [Tillich] call ontological reason" (39).

As a first step women must shed or exorcise the ideology of otherness they have internalized. Daly recognizes that such a move—a rejection of object status—is not easy. It requires "courage to *see* and to *be* in the face of the nameless anxieties that surface when a woman begins to see through the masks of sexist society and to confront the horrifying fact of her alienation from her authentic self" (4).

Daly recognizes the temptation to live in bad faith, to refuse to authenticate one's life and take responsibility for it. To accept a limited role like that of housewife does help one to "avoid the experience of nothingness [here following Heidegger and Sartre] but she also avoids a fuller participation in being. . . . Submerged in such a role, she cannot achieve a breakthrough to creativity" (23).

Those who do have the courage to refuse their Otherness and who move to reject the false naming, the idolatry of patriarchal society both within and without, are contributing to the revelation of new being. And with that comes new symbolizing and new naming. Rather than being named, women must participate in the naming, they must articulate "new words" (8). One could, of course, question whether new names will not once again reify experience into new objects. But Daly urges that the new consciousness is fundamentally a refusal to objectify. "Our liberation consists in refusing to be 'the Other' and asserting instead 'I am'—without making another 'the Other' " (34).

Given the evil of existing institutions and ideologies the new sisterhood is a radically antinomian phenomenon. It is "anti-Church" and "anti-Christ" and yet moves dialectically beyond these negative positions toward "sisterhood as cosmic convenant," toward the Dionysian discovery of new modes of being and becoming. One weakness in Daly's formulation of the new mode of transcendence is that in this work she tends to equate it with androgyny—an equation she later rejected as too limited in *Gyn/Ecology.* Daly's ultimate perception in *Beyond God the Father* is of a redemptive sisterhood which, through its iconoclastic refusal of the falsities of patriarchy, will mean a "Second Coming" not of Christ "but a new arrival of female presence . . . enchained since the dawn of patriarchy" (96). Such a presence entails the discovery/revelation of Being/Becoming, of Thou in the midst of life.

Another important vein of contemporary feminist existentialism comes from the "liberation" school of theology that emerged in the 1970s. First articulated as a black theology by James Cone in the late 1960s, liberation theology has since been applied to Latin American peasants and other oppressed groups, including women. When the latter, it has been called feminist theology.[18]

Liberation theology is social, political, and revolutionary. It perceives evil in social and political terms, and conversely sees redemption, or the liberation of good, as occurring through the denial, refusal, and destruction of institutional and ideological evils. The process through which redemptive liberation occurs is that of the refusal of Otherness foisted upon oppressed groups by dominant institutions and accompanying ideologies. For example, racism and sexism create feelings of inferiority, incompetence, and powerlessness in the oppressed, which keeps them in a state of inactivity, or on the level of the en-soi. One of the fundamental goals of liberation theology is therefore what Letty Russell calls "humanization": "In society people are so often treated as *things* that they become pawns of social fate, unable to exercise their human ability to shape their own world in community with others."[19]

By affirming the cultural identity of the oppressed group—an identity which includes the awareness of oppression—the adherents of liberation theology believe oppressed groups will reject Otherness, which in effect means they will reject ideological support for continued oppression. Black theology is therefore "a theology of black liberation." "[It] . . . is a theology of 'blackness.' It is the affirmation of black humanity that emancipates black people from white racism, thus providing authentic freedom for both white and black people." (Statement issued by the National Committee of Black Churchmen, June 13, 1969, in Atlanta.[20]) Similarly, other groups who are oppressed, whether women or the poor, must come to a sense of their own group identity; this is an essential dimension of the liberation process. For liberation theologies are specific; the process of liberation must be rooted in the concrete experiences of the oppressed group. As Russell notes in her important contribution to liberation theology, "in every situation, every culture, every subculture, the things *from* which people would be free and the things *for* which they long are different" (26). Oppressed groups are, however, united by their common longing for freedom from oppression, in whatever form it may take (26). In "Black Theology and Feminist Theology: A Comparative View" (1978), Pauli Murray concurs that theologies of liberation are "specific . . . written out of the concrete situations and experiences of particular groups. . . . Their common purpose is to commit Christians to radical political and social change, and to transform society in order to create a new and more humane world."[21]

Liberation occurs through the process of "conscientization" and praxis that we discussed in the chapter on Marxism (chapter 3). The model for this process was derived from Paulo Freire's work with illiterate peasants in Brazil.[22] Russell notes, "illiterates needed first to discover that they were *subjects* . . . and not just objects to be manipulated by fate and unseen powers" (35).

Echoing the exhortations of feminists from Wollstonecraft to de Beauvoir, Russell urges that an essential part of the liberation process must be the development of "critical discernment." Using the biblical term *diakrisis* (I Cor. 12:10), Russell explains her view of the educational process: "The diacritical role [is one] of discernment and critique" of "those parts of the world (including themselves) which deny God's plan and purpose of justice, freedom and peace for humanity" (39). In other words, critical discernment leads one to see the cultural myths that justify subjugation for what they are: myths. It enables one to identify the cultural ideology (sexism, in the case of women) that keeps one oppressed. "Cultural revolution must include an ongoing process of conscientization that attacks the myths as well as the culture that has produced them" (118)—an idea derived from Marxist/anarchist theories of praxis (see chapter 3). Russell acknowledges that for women the diacritical role may be especially difficult because they have been "enculturated to spend time making people 'like them'." To accept such a contrary role may mean "having courage to be a misfit in society; . . . [it] may mean becoming 'marginal persons' " (39).

The liberation process, as envisaged by liberation theologians, is inductive, rooted in the real experience of individuals. "The direction of thought," Russell notes, "flows not only 'downward' from the 'theological experts' but also upward and outward out of the collective experience of action and ministry" (55).

The development of a group identity that is positive and counter to that of Otherness is a central goal in the liberation process of "conscientization," or "consciousness-raising." As Pauli Murray notes,

> Both black theology and feminist theology express the goal of wholeness of the human being, of authentic selfhood, self-esteem, and dignity. They deal with questions of identity, the retrieval of lost history, the destruction of self-depreciation, and liberating self-affirmation (406).

The retrieval of lost history, of what Russell calls the "search for a usable past," becomes an essential part of the liberation process, for as she notes, "an unexamined history operates as fate" (85). Alice Walker's article, "In Search of Our Mothers' Gardens" (1974), which originally appeared in *Ms.* magazine, is included in the collection *Black Theology: A Documentary History* as an example of this important effort. (See further discussion of Walker's article in chapter 6.) Redemptive images that project an identity beyond Otherness must therefore be rooted in the authentic experience of the group, insofar as that experience can be determined. For black women, such images cannot be of white women. The Virgin Mary, for example, is a meaningless symbol for them. Murray rejects Daly's "Second Coming of Women" as an unacceptable vision for one working out of black experience (410).[23]

Liberation theologians reinterpret traditional biblical and theological concepts to reveal the liberation message. Thus, to Russell "salvation" is "a social event" (61). "Salvation is not an escape from fated nature, but rather the power and possibility of transforming the world, restoring creation, and seeking to overcome suffering" (61).

Sin is interpreted as "the opposite of liberation . . . as *oppression,* a situation in which there is no community, no room to live as a whole human being" (62). Russell returns to the root meaning of one word for salvation: *yeshu'ah* (which is "to be broad, or spacious," "to have room"), to explain that sin is "the denial of this space or room in which to live" (112). Sin is, in short, "the dehumanization of others by means of excluding their perspectives from the meaning of human reality and wholeness" (113). Sin is therefore the projection of Otherness effected by various ideologies. Murray says sin is "seen as a social, historical fact and is evident in oppressive institutional structures, in human exploitation, and in the domination of peoples, races and classes" (400). Evil is therefore located in the institutions that promulgate and perpetuate such behavior. "Racism and sexism illustrate corporate evils which are built into the structures of the United States" (410). Rosemary Ruether and James Cone have equated "corporate evil with [St. Paul's] . . . 'Powers and Principalities' " (400).[24]

The biblical injunction to resist evil means therefore to prepare the way for a new life, a new being. It is consequently a matter of combating corporate powers and cultural ideologies that impede the arrival of the new world. Various modes of praxis anticipate new being. Russell uses another biblical term, "prolepsis," which means anticipation of a new world, to describe such experiments. "By living out new life-styles of partnership . . . [people] can become proleptic signs" (47). Ruether also calls for the development of new social forms—praxis—as a means to the promised end. "We need to build a new cooperative social order but beyond the principles of hierarchy, rule and competitiveness."[25] Her feminist theology is principally developed in *New Woman, New Earth* (1974) and *Sexism and God-Talk* (1983). Here I focus on the former.

Ruether elaborates on de Beauvoir's thesis that the masculine is associated with the pour-soi or the transcendent rational aspect of a person, while the feminine is identified with en-soi, the immanent, material side. But Ruether takes the view that a continual cultural attempt to transcend the feminine is what has led to an ecological and moral crisis. She argues that all the destructive antinomies that govern the present organization of society are rooted in the self-other model of consciousness. Such dualism describes "the hierarchical concept of society, the relation of humanity and nature, and of God and creation" (3). In each case a transcendent aspect is held superior to its counter, as the masculine is held superior to the feminine. Certain French feminists, especially those who expand upon the theories of Jacques Derrida, similarly see "the metaphysical logic of dichotomous oppositions" as a "totalitarian principle" which must be dislocated or "deconstructed." In an article on Luce Irigaray's *Speculum de l'autre femme* (1974), Shoshana Felman says that the logic of such oppositions as "Presence/Absence, Being/Nothingness, Truth/Error, Same/Other, Identity/Difference . . . is, in fact, a subtle mechanism of hierarchization which assures the unique valorization of the 'positive' pole . . . and, consequently, the repressive subordination of all 'negativity,' the mastery of difference as such."[26]

Ruether sees the self-other, masculine-feminine model emerging early in human history; she associates it with the development of patriarchal religions, which, she stipulates, entailed a repression and denial of the Mother-goddess figure. Patriarchal religions correlate to the historical emergence of ego-consciousness that arose in opposition to nature, which was seen as feminine. Sexism is therefore rooted in this early " 'war against the mother,' the struggle of the transcendent ego to free itself from bondage to nature" (25). One may note the similarity here with Freudian theory which sees the rejection of the mother not as a phylogenetic but as an ontogenetic phenomenon. But, as Freudians would perhaps acknowledge, it may be a question of ontogeny recapitulating phylogeny.

Ruether theorizes that the struggle against the mother or the feminine, which represented nature or the physical aspects of being, took place in three phases. She deduces them from observing the changing "ideology or symbolization of the 'feminine' " (5) in Western myth and religion. The first stage she calls "the conquest of the mother"; the second, "the negation of the mother," and the third, "the sublimation of the mother."

The conquest of the mother is exemplified in an event in the Akkadian creation story, the *Enuma Elish*. Marduk, the god-king, defeats the primal mother, Tiamat, and splits her body into heaven and earth (12). Thus commences the dualism between the transcendent and the material, with the latter perceived as inferior.

> Patriarchal religion split the dialectical unities of mother religion into absolute dualism, elevating a male-identified consciousness to transcendent apriority. Fundamentally this is rooted in an effort to deny one's own mortality, to identify essential (male) humanity with a transcendent divine sphere beyond the matrix of coming-to-be-and-passing-away (194–95).

Women as Other were identified with the mortal matrix and thus with death. On its most profound level, sexist dualism enables men to deny their contingency, so it is a primary example of what Sartre called "bad faith."

The second phase, the negation of the mother, carried out the process begun in phase one. Much of the history of Christian theology may be located in this stage. A transcendent, immortal male deity was projected into the heavens far from the corrupt feminine world of nature; but the transcendent deity remained master of that subservient world. Here "men seek to master nature . . . by subordinating it and linking their essential selves with a transcendent principle beyond nature which is pictured as intellectual and male."

In patriarchal myth,

> creation is seen as initiated by a fiat from above, from an immaterial principle beyond visible reality. Nature, which once encompassed all reality, is now subjugated and made into the lower side of a new dualism. . . . The primal matrix of life . . . is debased as mere "matter" (a word which means "mother"). . . . Maleness is identified with intellectuality and spirituality; femaleness . . . with lower material nature. This also defines the female as ontologically dependent and morally inferior to maleness (14).

Ruether sees the identification of women with nature and the derogation of both, as at the root of Western destructiveness, similar to Merchant in *The Death of Nature* (see chapter 1). "The Achilles' heel of human civilization, which today has reached global genocidal and ecocidal proportions, resides in this false development of maleness through repression of the female" (11). This thesis has become a central tenet of second-wave cultural feminism and ecofeminism (see further discussion, chapters 7 and 8).

The third phase, the sublimation of the mother, is exemplified in the cult of the Virgin Mary, which Ruether suggests is a further false attempt to transcend material reality, the real world of women. Ruether, like Merchant, associates the witch-hunts with this phase of Western ideology. It culminated in the Victorian "cult of true womanood" which similarly posited an incorruptible female reality, wholly divorced from physical nature. In the southern United States, Ruether notes, this cult resulted in a racist dualism which projected physicality and sexuality onto the black woman, leaving the virginal white woman on a pedestal (21).

Ruether also correlates the split between public and private morality with the sexist dualism that sustains the cult of true womanhood. As seen in chapter 1, morality becomes

> lodged in the private sphere. . . . The real world of public man is the realm of competitive egotism, where it is "unrealistic" to speak of morality. Religion and morality are privatized and sentimentalized, so as to lose all serious public power. Morality and religion become the realm of the home, of women (23).

Ruether contends that "we must dissolve the false dichotomy between a pacified morality and the public world of technological rationality which renders the message of the Church 'effete' while the masters of war go about their 'manly' activities" (82).

For, the second aspect of phase three—the unchecked behavior of the rational transcendent ego of the male in the public sphere—has led to "the destruction of the earth" (195). Ruether explains how the premises of science and those of progress derive from the notion of rational transcendence and combine to result in disastrous exploitation.

> Males, identifying their egos with transcendent "spirit," made technology the project of progressive incarnation of transcendent "spirit" into "nature." The eschatological god became a historical project [namely "progress"] (194).

Thus, "patriarchal religion ends . . . with a perception of the finite cosmos itself as evil in its intractibility" to technological progress (195). The natural earth must be destroyed, transformed into a "rational," planned, subdued order. So, marshlands must be transformed into shopping malls, grasslands into concrete highways, wildlife into furs, the wilderness into skyscrapers.

The fundamental defect in "the male ideology of transcendent dualism" is that its only mode is conquest.

> Its view of what is over against itself is not that of the conversation of two subjects, but of the conquest of an alien object. The intractibility of the other side of the dualism to its demands does not suggest that the "other"

> has a "nature" of her own that needs to be respected and with which one must enter into conversation. Rather, this intractibility is seen as that of disobedient rebellion (195–96).

Like the radical feminists (see chapter 6) Ruether sees "a repressive view of the alien female" not just at the root of the exploitation of nature, but as "the model for the inferiorization of other subjugated groups, lower classes, and conquered races" (4). Such groups are seen by the dominant group as having "feminine" attributes because like women they are repositories of "repressed bodiliness" (4).

As Susan Griffin suggests in *Pornography and Silence* (1981), such "repressed bodiliness" is the root cause of pornography, which is similarly a masculine attempt to subdue nature.

> The bodies of women in pornography, mastered, bound, silenced, beaten, and even murdered, are symbols for natural feeling and the power of nature, which the pornographic mind hates and fears . . . "the woman" in pornography, like "the Jew" in anti-Semitism and "the black" in racism, is simply . . . that region of being the pornographic or racist mind would forget and deny.[27]

Ruether urges that if we are to find a way beyond the destructive pornographic behavior that characterizes patriarchal civilization, it must lie in a resolution of the basic sexist dualism of masculine self versus feminine other. She concludes,

> The project of human life must cease to be seen as one of "domination of nature," or exploitation of . . . bodily reality. . . . Rather, we have to find a new language of ecological responsiveness, a reciprocity between consciousness and the world systems in which we live and move and have our being (83).

Two other aspects of feminist existential theory must now be discussed. The first concerns the internalization of Otherness that colonized groups experience; and the second, the phenomenological reconstruction of reality that is essential to the liberation process. Internalization of Otherness means that one has come to identify oneself through the eyes of the dominant group in society. One becomes fixed on the level of an object that exists for and is constituted by the dominant group. In the case of blacks it is to accept the white racist definition of the black as Other; in the case of women it is to accept the male sexist view of women as Other. To accept such a role, as de Beauvoir and the existentialists have pointed out, is to accept being an object; it is to deny the subject-self that is autonomous and creative. To become an object means ultimately to risk madness and schizophrenia; the denial of the subject-self necessarily means a fundamental falseness. It means engaging in a perpetual lie.

In an important second-wave article that appeared in 1970, Meredith Tax described the colonized mentality women exhibit in their everyday lives. To survive they must keep aware of the eye of the male Other. Women have "to be tuned in to the nuances of social behavior so that they can please those whom it is essential to please."[28] "You must be prepared to return the right kind of smile to passing Prince Charmings" (10). This is because they have the power, they hold the key to one's future—a point decried by feminists from Wollstonecraft on. Moreover, Tax says, women have to be "hyper-aware of their surroundings" for protective reasons.

> Walk down a city street without being tuned in and you're in real danger; our society is one in which men rape, mug, and murder women . . . every day. You'd better keep track of what car is slowing down, and of who is walking up behind you (10).

Tax says the everyday occurrence of catcalling or whistling illustrates women's colonized status.

> What [catcallers] do is *impinge* on her. They will demand that her thoughts be focused on them. They will use her body with their eyes. They will evaluate her market price. They will comment on her defects, or compare them to those of other passers-by. They will make her a participant in their fantasies without asking if she is willing. They will make her feel ridiculous, or grotesquely sexual, or hideously ugly. Above all, they will make her feel like a *thing* (12).

In this situation women are forced to a fundamentally schizophrenic response, one that is emblematic of the choice allowed them in society at large.

> Either she remains sensitive and vulnerable to the pain; or she shuts it out by saying, "It's only my body they are talking about. It doesn't affect me. They know nothing about me." Whatever the process, the solution is a split between the mind and body. . . . One may hate the body and consider the mind the real "self." One may glorify the body . . . by becoming an instrument to satisfy the desires of others; in this case the body becomes a thing, and the mind a puppeteer to manipulate it (12).

Citing British psychiatrist R. D. Laing, Tax notes that the woman is left with the problem of not being acknowledged as a subject and therefore seeking to legitimate herself by being an object; clearly, a schizophrenic response. The schizophrenic, Laing says, can only establish a conviction of being real is "by feeling himself to be an object . . . in the world of someone else" (13). Furthermore, since being an object means to be highly visible and therefore uncamouflaged and vulnerable, "the obvious defense against such a danger is to make oneself invisible in one way or another" (13). The result is an extreme split in personality: on the one hand there is the object-self seen by the male world; on the other hand is the withdrawn, invisible self—invisible at times even to oneself. Such is the psychic alienation created by an internalization of Otherness.

Sandra Bartky has also analyzed this phenomenon in an article entitled "On Psychological Oppression" (1979). Using Franz Fanon's analysis of the oppressed mentality seen in Third World colonized peoples—especially as stated in his *Black Skin, White Masks* (1952)—Bartky shows how "the terrible messages of inferiority" are also internalized by women.[29] Bartky also focuses on the catcalling event as illustrative of the entire phenomenon of sexual objectification.

> It is a fine, spring day, and with an utter lack of self-consciousness I am bouncing down the street. Suddenly I hear men's voices. Catcalls and whistles fill the air. . . . I freeze. As Sartre would say, I have been petrified by the gaze of the Other. . . . I have been made into an object (37).

Bartky calls such an episode "a ritual of subjugation" (37).

When women come to see their identity as that of an object, they become obsessed with their physical selves—their bodies—and consequently with making those bodies conform to male-defined notions of beauty. Several feminists have analyzed this dimension of women's psychic oppression. A classic second-wave article on the subject is Dana Densmore's "On the Temptation to Be A Beautiful Object" (1968).[30] Densmore notes that the myth of feminine beauty is essential to the cultural definition of women. An ugly woman is seen as being not truly feminine, not truly womanly. Instead, it is the female imperative to put on a pretty face.

Such a face, Densmore notes, is really an object mask. It is created by means of cosmetics. Densmore describes the ritual of putting on makeup prior to a "date": the desired end is to create a beautiful object of oneself. The cosmetic face is "just an object, a work of art, to look at, not to know, total appearance, bearing no personality or will" (205). Densmore sees women as bombarded with advertising-brainwashing to accept the fundamental equation that to be a woman means to be a beautiful object.

Again women as conscious selves have but two schizoprenic alternatives: We either distance ourselves from the mask, retire within, keep our true self invisible, and see the mask as "artificial and unnatural" (207). Or, "we slip into the schizophrenic world of play-acting and narcissism. . . . And then we will be imprisoned within the walls of the object we created in the minds of others and in our own minds" (208). The latter is exemplified in figures such as Monroe, Fitzgerald, and Plath. Plath's description of the oppressive "bell jar" gives a good idea of the sensation of being entrapped within a culturally defined object-self.[31]

In an important article, "Narcissism, Femininity and Alienation" (1982), Bartky attempts to combine a Marxist and existentialist explanation by naming the Other who perpetuates women's identification with a false object-self, "the fashion-beauty complex." This multi-billion dollar industry has an obvious stake in selling cosmetics to women. Bartky suggests that while it may resemble the "military-industrial complex" in corporate magnitude, it functions in a manner analogous to the Catholic Church. Like the church the fashion-beauty complex creates profound anxieties in the individual about whether she is measuring up to objectively determined standards. Like the church "it then presents itself as the only instrument able . . . to take away the very guilt and shame it has itself produced." "Body care rituals are like sacraments; at best, they put a woman who would be lost and abandoned without them into what may feel to her like a state of grace; at worst, they exhibit the typical obsessive-compulsive features of much religious behavior."[32]

Bartky concludes that in Western society the Other that is internalized in many women is a concoction of the fashion-beauty complex (12). It is internalized through the cultural brainwashing effected by mass media, especially advertising. "We are presented everywhere with images of perfect female beauty—at the drugstore cosmetics display, the supermarket magazine counter, on television" (12). And it is against these male-determined standards of beauty that women learn to measure themselves. Such false standards are internalized; they become part of women's self-opinion.

> I must cream my body with a thousand creams, each designed to act against a different deficiency, oil it, pumice it, powder it, shave it, pluck it, depilate it, ooze it into just the right foundation, reduce it overall through Spartan dieting or else pump it up with silicon (13).

While there may be a commercial motive in exploiting women's colonized mentality and promoting their sexual objectification—both sell products—it is not enough to explain the phenomenon as a creation of capitalism. Rather, as de Beauvoir notes, such objectification is a wide-spread cross-cultural phenomenon, functional to the perpetuation of male supremacy. Cosmetics and fashion serve to encase women in their Otherness; they prevent her from attempting transcendence. In *The Second Sex* she notes, "Costumes and styles are often devoted to cutting off the feminine body from any possible transcendence." She cites as examples Chinese foot-bindings, the Hollywood star's extended fingernails, "which deprive her of her hands; high heels, corsets, panniers, farthingales, crinolines," as well as "makeup and jewelry [which] . . . further women's petrification" (147). Like Wollstonecraft, Sarah Grimké, and others de Beauvoir protests that a woman is "required by society to make herself an erotic object." For, "the purpose of the fashions to which she is enslaved is . . . to cut her off from her transcendence in order to offer her as prey to male desires" (498).[33]

A final aspect of the internalization of Otherness must be discussed, and that is the fundamental lying it requires. Susan Griffin contends that as women have no authentic tradition of reality on which to draw, they have only false selves to emulate.

> And who is this false self? She is the pornographic idea of the female [woman as sex object]. We have learned to impersonate her. Like the men and women living in the institution of slavery we have become talented at seeming to be what we are not (202).

As de Beauvoir notes, "like all the oppressed, woman deliberately dissembles . . . all [who] depend on the caprices of a master, have learned to turn toward him a changeless smile or an enigmatic impassivity; their real sentiments, their actual behavior, are carefully hidden." Women thus learn "to lie to men, to scheme, to be wily"; to put on "an artificial expression"; to be "cautious, hypocritical," to play-act (243).

In a powerful article entitled "Women and Honor: Some Notes on Lying" (1975), Adrienne Rich warns that like all "powerless people" who are forced to lie to survive, women run the risk of forgetting that they are lying or when they are lying. While women have learned to lie to their masters, they may continue to lie to those who are also powerless. They may lie to other women. Rich urges that it is imperative for women to learn to tell the truth about themselves, so as to break the hold of the patriarchal falsehoods that keep women ideologically subjugated.

> Women have been driven mad, "gaslighted," for centuries by the refutation of our experience and our instincts in a culture which validates only male experience. The truth of our bodies and our minds has been mystified to us. We therefore have a primary obligation to each other; not to undermine each others' sense of reality for the sake of expediency; not to gaslight each other.[34]

Like Rich, Mary Daly, and others treated in this book, most feminists believe there is a great urgency to create counter-traditions whereby women's "new words" and new truths may be heard and validated. For, as Rabuzzi notes in the tradition of Paulo Freire and other theorists of *conscientização,*

> to internalize otherness is almost definitionally to be unable to speak in the language of the self. . . . Not only have women been named by men, women have been defined, told exactly what they were to be, with an implicit "or else" menacing them. . . . To experience being an Other is often

> to feel so schizophrenically torn, that not even a clandestinely authentic "I" dares to speak (176).

In order for women to dare to speak their own truths, they must receive validation from other women, from other feminists. For, the "social construction of reality" requires a collective effort. The validation of one's reality, of one's truths, "requires ongoing interaction with others who co-inhabit this same socially constructed world."[35]

Bartky suggests that the way by which the internalized Other may be countered is for another social witness to express its view. Such a witness, born of the authentic collective testimony of women, can provide an alternative Other. "As part of our practise, we must create a new witness, a collective significant Other, integrated into the self but nourished and strengthened from without, from a revolutionary feminist community."[36] Thus, feminist existentialist theory merges at this point with the feminist theories of praxis treated in chapter 3. At the center of the theory remains the concept of consciousness-raising, as Catharine A. MacKinnon points out in the article (1982) cited in chapter 3. For, since the world, since reality is defined from a masculine point of view, women must deconstruct and re-constitute the world. This can only be done through a collective effort of "re-vision."[37]

6 Radical Feminism

Feminism must be asserted by women . . . as the basis of revolutionary social change.
Roxanne Dunbar, 1968

Radical feminist theory was developed by a group of ex-"movement women" in the late 1960s and early 1970s, primarily in New York and Boston. "Movement women" were those who had participated in the political activities of the civil rights and antiwar campaigns of the 1960s. Much as nineteenth-century feminists became aware of their own oppression through the treatment they received from their male cohorts in the abolition movement, so twentieth-century radical feminists came to their consciousness in reaction to the contemptuous treatment they received from male radicals in the "New Left." That treatment was exemplified at the 1969 anti-inauguration demonstration in Washington. When feminists attempted to present their position at the rally, "men in the audience booed, laughed, catcalled and yelled enlightened remarks like 'Take her off the stage and fuck her.' "[1] A description of similar experiences may be found in Marge Piercy's article, "The Grand Coolie Damn" (1969).[2]

Much of radical feminist theory was therefore forged in reaction against the theories, organizational structures, and personal styles of the male "New Left." Having themselves experienced continual "second class" treatment within male radical organizations and because of the *machismo* radical style, women were concerned that their organizations express internal democracy and allow for an authentic women's style (or, at least allow for such a style to emerge). In terms of theory radical feminists became determined to establish that their own personal "subjective" issues had an importance and legitimacy equal to those great issues being dealt with by the New Left—issues of social justice and peace. Eventually radical feminists came to believe that all these issues were interrelated, that male supremacy and the subjugation of women was indeed the root and model oppression in society and that feminism had to be the basis for any truly revolutionary change.

Other central theses of radical feminism, developed at the same time and in the same process, included the idea that the personal is political; that patriarchy, or male-domination—not capitalism—is at the root of women's oppression; that women should identify themselves as a subjugated class or caste and put their primary energies in a movement with other women to combat their oppressors—men; that men and women are fundamentally different, have different styles and cultures, and that the women's mode must be the basis of any future society.[3]

An early article which articulated many of these ideas was Roxanne Dunbar's "Female Liberation as a Basis for Social Revolution" (1968). Dunbar urged women not to work in mixed groups like SDS (Students for a Democratic Society), but to form an independent women's movement.[4] Women's grievances, she contends, are not "petty or personal, but rather constitute a widespread, deeply rooted social disease." Indeed, all people live "under an international caste system, at the top of which is the Western white male ruling class, at the very bottom of which is the female of the non-white colonized world" (49). Western imperialism is rooted in sexism. "The Western nation-states, which have perfected colonialism, were developed as an extension of male dominance over females and the land" (49). Finally, Dunbar asserts that women *are* different from men, that they have been conditioned to have certain "maternal traits," such as caring for others, flexibility, non-competitiveness, and cooperativeness. Women have "the consciousness of the oppressed" (53). Such traits and awarenesses are essentially humane and must be the moral basis for a new society.

> By destroying the present society, and building a society based on feminist principles, men will be forced to live in the human community on terms very different from the present. For that to happen, feminism must be asserted by women, as the basis of revolutionary social change (53).

Dana Densmore, another member of the Boston women's movement, also made major contributions to the development of radical feminist theory. "Independence from the Sexual Revolution" (1971) made the important point that women's liberation and sexual liberation were not synonymous. Densmore urges that women not consider sexual freedom the be-all and end-all of liberation. "Spiritual freedom, intellectual freedom, freedom from invasions of privacy and the insults of degrading stereotypes"—these are more important.[5] In fact, so-called sexual liberation is another ploy to keep women subjugated. Sex (and, as other radical feminists urged, love) is sold as a magical experience that is supposed to justify otherwise dreary lives.

Instead it functions as an opiate keeping women from thinking about their overall condition.

The New York radical feminist groups, formed in 1967 and 1968, developed the main body of radical feminist theory. The first major radical feminist publication, *Notes from the First Year,* appeared in June 1968, followed by *Notes from the Second Year* (1970), and *Notes from the Third Year* (1971). These included the most important early articulations of radical feminist theory.

The Feminists, a group formed by Ti-Grace Atkinson after she resigned as president of the New York chapter of NOW in October 1968 (the group had originally been called "the October 17 Movement" after the date of Atkinson's resignation), issued a series of position papers in the summer of 1969. In these, important aspects of radical feminist theory were formulated. A cardinal thesis that emerged was that the politically oppressive male-female role system is the first and original model of all oppression.[6] The Feminists also held that since marriage is "a primary formalization of the persecution of women," "we consider the rejection of this institution both in theory *and in practice* a primary work of the radical feminist" (116). To this end the Feminists established a membership quota whereby no more than a third of the members could be living with a man.

The Feminists also attacked love as an "institution" that "promotes vulnerability, dependence, possessiveness, susceptibility to pain, and prevents the full development of woman's human potential" (117). This critique was made by Shulamith Firestone in *The Dialectic of Sex* and repeated by Atkinson in other articles (see below). The Feminists also called for the elimination of marriage and the family, "the institution of heterosexual sex," and urged the development of "extra-uterine means of reproduction" (117).[7] These ideas were amplified in articles by Atkinson, including her celebrated "The Institution of Sexual Intercourse" (1970), mentioned in chapter 5. Since Atkinson's main bone of contention with NOW had been that it replicated the hierarchical power structure of male organizations,[8] the Feminists were determined to be a non-hierarchical, fundamentally democratic organization. Lots were drawn, for example, to determine who did the "shitwork" or uncreative work, as well as who would serve as chair, secretary, and treasurer for the month.

Another group, the New York Radical Feminists, formed in December 1969 by Shulamith Firestone, Anne Koedt, Diane Crothers, and Cellestine Ware, issued a manifesto entitled "The Politics of the Ego." This statement, prepared by Koedt, was one of the first to articulate another central radical feminist thesis—that women's oppression is rooted primarily in psychological, not economic, factors.

> We believe that the purpose of male chauvinism is primarily to obtain psychological ego satisfaction, and that only secondarily does this manifest itself in economic relationships. For this reason we do not believe

> that capitalism, or any economic system, is the cause of female oppression, nor do we believe that female oppression will disappear as a result of a purely economic revolution.[9]

The manifesto continues: "The political oppression of women has its own class dynamic; and that dynamic must be understood in terms previously called 'non-political'—namely the politics of the ego." (124). Further, "man establishes his 'manhood' in direct proportion to his ability to have his ego override woman's, and derives his strength and self-esteem through this process" (124). The stress on the psychological basis of oppression was also made in Carol Hanisch's important essay "The Personal Is Political" (in *Notes from the Second Year,* pp. 76–78), and it forms the basis for Kate Millett's theory of sexual politics (discussed below).

Another important early radical feminist essay was "The Fourth World Manifesto" (1971) by Barbara Burris and others. Burris argues that around the world women form a caste that is "colonized" by male "imperialism." As with all colonized peoples, women's culture has been suppressed. However, Burris insists, women cannot ally themselves with other anti-imperialist movements because they are male-dominated. Using the Algerian struggle for independence from French colonial rule as an example, Burris cites a remark by Franz Fanon to illustrate how male "liberators" perceive women's proper place. Fanon had urged in *A Dying Colonialism* that the veil symbolizes ethnic Arab culture. Burris says Fanon has confused male culture with ethnic culture; the veil in fact symbolizes female oppression. Because Fanon failed to recognize that oppression, the revolution he envisaged did not entail any change for women, only a liberation of the suppressed male national culture.

Women must therefore organize, as women, in order that their own culture be liberated. Women must "raise the banner of the female principle." "We are proud of the female culture of emotion, intuition, love, personal relationships, etc." "It is only by asserting the long suppressed and ridiculed female principle that a truly human society will come about." "We identify with all women of all races, classes and countries all over the world. The female culture is the Fourth World."[10]

Radical feminist theory found its fullest articulation in two primary texts that appeared in 1970: Kate Millett's *Sexual Politics* and Shulamith Firestone's *The Dialectic of Sex: The Case for Feminist Revolution.* Two important later works were Ti-Grace Atkinson's *Amazon Odyssey* (1974) and Mary Daly's *Gyn/Ecology: The Metaethics of Radical Feminism* (1978). Each will be discussed here, while the separate and somewhat different analyses developed by radical women of color and by radical lesbians will also be treated, separately.

The germ of Millett's *Sexual Politics* was presented in "a manifesto for revolution" the winter of 1968, in connection with the organization of a women's group at Columbia University where Millett was a doctoral student in English and comparative literature. Indeed, *Sexual Politics* was a revised version of her doctoral dissertation.

> When one group rules another, the relationship between the two is political. When such an arrangement is carried out over a long period of time it develops an ideology (feudalism, racism, etc.). All historical civilizations are patriarchies: their ideology is male supremacy.[11]

So opens the 1968 manifesto. Millett proceeds to state her theory of how patriarchy or male-rule is maintained.

> Government is upheld by power, which is supported through consent (social opinion), or imposed by violence. Conditioning to an ideology amounts to the former. But there may be a resort to the latter at any moment when consent is withdrawn—rape, attack, sequestration, beatings, murder. Sexual politics obtains consent through the "socialization" of both sexes to patriarchal policies (111).

Here Millett's theory is not dissimilar to those of the Marxists Louis Althusser and Antonio Gramsci.[12] The state maintains its rule through force, but also through ideological hegemony. Patriarchal ideology is that of male supremacy, which conditions women to exhibit male-serving behavior and to accept male-serving roles. Millett argues that this ideology permeates every aspect of culture and touches every aspect of our lives—even the most personal. Like other radical feminists Millett sees women, therefore, as programmed to a "castelike status"[13] that is maintained through force or ideological conditioning. The force exerted to keep women in their proper place includes such exotic atrocities as footbinding, the veil, and cliterodectomies (which Daly elaborates in *Gyn/Ecology*), but also rape, sadistic or what Millett calls "perverse heterosexuality," the ideological violence inflicted by literature, and at its extreme, pornography.

Sexual Politics opens with a catalog of "instances of sexual politics" drawn from modern literature. These exempla are grotesque descriptions of sexual abuse of women seen in the works of such then chic male authors as D. H. Lawrence, Henry Miller, and Norman Mailer. They serve to provide another powerful illustration of the ideological attitudes—canonized in literature and accepted as "normal"—against which radical feminists were rebelling. Millett uses these descriptions of relationships in which women are humiliated and abused to emphasize that politics obtains in the personal realm of sexual intimacy. Hence the concept "sexual politics."

Millett sees the family as the main source of ideological indoctrination. It socializes "the young . . . into patriarchal ideology's prescribed attitudes toward the categories of role, temperament, and status" (35). Just as many Marxists see the family as essential to the ideological "reproduction" of capitalism, so Millett and the radical feminists believe it necessary to the reproduction of patriarchy.

The use of rape as a political device to keep women terrorized was a thesis developed further by other radical feminists. Barbara Mehrhof and Pamela Kearon urged in a 1971 article, "Rape: An Act of Terror," that rape be considered a political crime, a terrorist act that keeps women subordinate. It is "an effective political device . . . not an arbitrary act of violence by one individual on another; it is a political act of *oppression* . . . exercised by members of a powerful class on members of the powerless class."[14]

Susan Brownmiller advanced this thesis in her comprehensive study of rape, *Against Our Will: Men, Women, and Rape* (1975). Calling it a "masculine ideology," she argues that "men who commit rape have served in effect as front-line masculine shock troops, terrorist guerrillas in the longest sustained battle the world has ever known."[15] Like Millett, Brownmiller believes sexual violence against women is not only culturally condoned and pervasive, but also that rape is culturally perceived as a primary means by which men establish their "manhood" (see especially Brownmiller's chapter, "The Myth of the Heroic Rapist").

Brownmiller points out how pornography and prostitution, because they promote an ideology that degrades and abuses the female body, contribute to the rape phenomenon. "The case against pornography and the case against toleration of prostitution are central to the fight against rape," Brownmiller argues (390).

> Perpetuation of the concept that "the powerful male impulse" must be satisfied with immediacy by a cooperative class of women . . . is part and parcel of the mass psychology of rape. Indeed, until the day is reached when prostitution is totally eliminated . . . the false perception of sexual access as an adjunct of male power and privilege will continue to fuel the rapist mentality (393).

"Pornography is the undiluted essence of anti-female propaganda" (393). In pornography women's bodies are "stripped, exposed and contorted for the purpose of ridicule to bolster that 'masculine esteem' which gets its kick and sense of power from viewing females as anonymous, panting playthings, adult toys, dehumanized objects to be used, abused, broken and discarded" (393). "This," Brownmiller notes, "is also the philosophy of rape" (394).[16]

Shulamith Firestone's *Dialectic of Sex* is a revolutionary document that deserves a place next to the works of Mary Wollstonecraft, Sarah Grimké, and Charlotte Perkins Gilman. Like them, it was written hastily; it is impelled by a sense of urgency, and is full of brilliant insights. But perhaps more than its predecessors, it can be faulted for rash overstatements, inaccuracies, and sometimes wild projections. As a reading experience it remains closer to Margaret Fuller's tract, for the reader must often go more than half way in grasping ideas that are only sketchily developed. Despite its faults, the *Dialectic* outlines a coherent radical feminist theory and projects a vision for the future that remains a challenge.

Departing from classic Marxist theory, Firestone argues that the material base for women's oppression lies not in economics but in biology. The female reproductive function is the reason for the gender division of labor upon which patriarchy and its ruling ideology, sexism, are constructed. "The natural reproductive difference between the sexes led directly to the first division of labor at the origins of class, as well as furnishing the paradigm of caste."[17] Without clearly articulating it, Firestone implies that there is a causal relation between the material biological base and the ideology of female subjugation. This ideology, which she calls "psychosexual" reality (5), is connected to the Oedipus complex, the political situation that governs the nuclear family. Thus, Firestone like Millett hints at a thesis developed in more sophisticated fashion by Marxist feminists (see chapter 3)—that the nuclear family is the primary site for ideological imprintation or "reproduction." As a radical feminist, however, Firestone insists it is the biological division of labor that is the material basis for the sexual political ideology of female subjugation.

Like other radical feminists Firestone believes a primary goal of a feminist revolution must be to end "the tyranny of the biological family" (11). Such a result will end a host of other evils as well, namely the compartmentalization of the emotional and the erotic which Firestone, in the tradition of Marcuse, sees as a primary factor in the unbridled technological imperialism of the present.

The main means by which a feminist revolution will be accomplished, according to Firestone, is by seizing the means of *re*production, that is by using technology to release women from their biological destiny. Specifically, Firestone calls not just for birth control but new means of reproduction using artificial devices like test-tube fertilization and artificial placentas (197–98). This would mean that "barbaric" pregnancy could be by-passed and that men too could have children (11, 197). Such artificial systems would end the gender role divisions attached to child bearing and rearing.

Firestone further urges that the break-up of oedipal family situations should be accompanied by the end of the incest taboo. This would mean "humanity could finally revert to its natural polymorphous sexuality—all forms of sexuality would be allowed and indulged" (209). "Polymorphous sexuality" is a concept borrowed from Freud and elaborated by neo-Freudians like Marcuse and Norman O. Brown to mean a diffusion of the erotic from the genitals throughout the body and into society at large.

Firestone argues that the incest taboo forces upon the male child a "compartmentalization" of the personality that splits off sexual from emotional responses. This sexual schizophrenia works to the disadvantage of women, because it sets up in the male the dichotomy in his perception of women between good, sexless but emotional types—his mother—and bad, sexual types—most other women (59). Firestone sees the separation of "sex from

emotion" as a disease that is "at the very foundations of Western culture and civilization."

> If early sexual repression is the basic mechanism by which character structures supporting political, ideological, and economic serfdom are produced, an end to the incest taboo, through the abolition of the family, would have profound effects: sexuality would be released from its strait-jacket to eroticize our whole culture, changing its very definition (60).

Like Nancy Chodorow, but without the sophistication of her analysis, Firestone concludes that the very different psychosexual makeup of men and women contributes to women's oppression. Citing Freud, Firestone notes that while men learn to sublimate their "libido"—their sexual, emotional needs—into creative work projects, women do not. Thus, "he displaces his need for love into a need for recognition. This process does not occur as much in the female: most women never stop seeking direct warmth and approval" (127). Women are therefore at a disadvantage in the sexual political game, for while men can disconnect their sexual and emotional needs, women cannot. Women therefore continue to depend on men for emotional sustenance in a way that is not reciprocated. Men's independence gives them an obvious political edge, which helps to perpetuate the various social structures that contribute to women's oppression. "Men were thinking, writing, and creating, because women were pouring their energy into these men; women are not creating culture because they are preoccupied with love" (126).

Firestone argues that romantic love is a means by which a man can idealize "one woman over the rest in order to justify his descent to a lower caste" (131). But such "love" is but a facade to mask his primary interest, which is sexual. Because of their psychic makeups, Firestone asserts, somewhat similarly to Chodorow, men are "emotional invalids." Women conversely cling to men and to love because of their political situation of dependency (a point made as early as Wollstonecraft). Women love, Firestone concludes, in exchange for security (139).

The ideology of romance, according to Firestone, is an opiate that keeps women drugged. "*Romanticism develops in proportion to the liberation of women from their biology*" (146). It promotes the idea that women should live for men and for romance/sex. It equates political redemption with sex (147). It identifies women as "love" objects or sex objects, thus contributing to their devaluation as a class, and through such media as mass advertising, analyzed in chapter 5, it establishes a "beauty ideal" through which women are led to believe they will achieve happiness—that is, a man, romance, and sex.

Firestone concludes her work with a general but suggestive theory she calls the "dialectics" of cultural history." Positing two cultures, a male and a female, she notes that where male culture reflects the psychoemotional invalidism of the male, women's culture has been repressed and confined to the private sphere; it has also been used as fuel and as subject matter for the male creator.

> Men of culture were emotionally warped by the sublimation process; they converted life to art, thus could not live it. But women, and those men who were excluded from culture, remained in direct contact with their experience—fit subject matter (156).

Firestone extends her analysis to argue that the two psychological modes, female and male, may be appropriate to two cultural modalities, the aesthetic and the technological, by defining culture as *"the attempt . . . to realize the conceivable in the possible"* (172). The aesthetic mode is the "search for the ideal, realized by means of an artificial medium," where the technological response operates so that "the contingencies of reality are overcome, not through the creation of an alternative reality, but through the mastery of reality's own workings" (174).

> The aesthetic response corresponds with "female" behavior. The same terminology can be applied to either: subjective, intuitive, introverted, wishful, dreamy or fantastic, concerned with the subconscious (the *id),* emotional, even temperamental (hysterical). Correspondingly, the technological response is the masculine response: objective, logical, extroverted, realistic, concerned with the conscious mind (the ego), rational, mechanical, pragmatic and down-to-earth, stable (175).

Thus the biologically-based sex division extends to this cultural division. Firestone's utopian goal is that these two cultural modes will synthesize, the "conceivable will be realized in the actual" and the aesthetic ideal will become the real by means of technology. At this point both cultural modes will disappear, along with "culture" itself, which Firestone sees as a product of sublimation that keeps us from the "real." Firestone envisages an "anticulture revolution" in which a "matter-antimatter explosion" will occur "ending with a poof! culture itself" (190). People will then be free to experience reality directly, no longer impeded by artificial restrictions on emotion and eros. Through this process the personal will be reintegrated with the public, "the subjective with the objective, the emotional with the rational—the female principle with the male" (210). The "female principle" will no longer be privatized but rediffused throughout society (211).

More specifically, Firestone proposes "limited contract households" to replace the traditional nuclear family (231). These households would include approximately ten people, one-third of whom would be children, not necessarily biologically related to others in the unit (they may have been artificially reproduced or adopted). Responsibility for early child rearing "would be evenly diffused among all members of the household" (232). But such early training must be minimal, because Firestone believes children are overly repressed by current practices. Housework will rotate among unit members, and cybernation will eventually eliminate the need for housework entirely—indeed it will eliminate all alienated labor (234–35). City planning will be modified accordingly (reminiscent of the material feminists of the nineteenth century), and people will be free to pursue their own authentic interests in "noncompulsory 'learning centers' " (236).

Thus Firestone's vision mixes the neo-Freudian perception of a liberation of eros, effected through the end of sublimation and culture, with comparatively practical concern for the organization of this post-cultural society. Women would no longer be subjugated in such a world because "men" and "women," as defined by current gender traits and role responsibilities, would no longer exist.

There are obvious criticisms to be made of Firestone's theory. One might find her reliance on technology—for example, artificial means of reproduction—not a humanistic prospect. One might question the effect ending the incest taboo would have on human behavior and psychic makeup; such fundamental tampering seems risky. And one could argue that her theories on incest could lead to exploitation of children.

Recent feminists, particularly those with a Marxist orientation, have criticized her stress on biology as a universal. Michèle Barrett suggests that Firestone falls into the trap of biologism or biological determinism, and fails to see that women's condition is culturally and historically variable. Zillah Eisenstein makes a similar point and argues that since technology is controlled by the male ruling class, it is unlikely that it will be used to liberate women from their biology.[18] Heidi Hartmann says Firestone's analysis suffers from an "overemphasis on biology and reproduction. What we need to understand is how sex (a biological fact) becomes gender (a social phenomenon)."[19]

Ti-Grace Atkinson's *Amazon Odyssey* (1974) is a collection of twenty-four articles and speeches presented between 1967 and 1972. An eccentric but pioneer work, like Firestone's, it presents important ideas that are not fully developed. It is a work that reflects the intense energy, the "unlimited hopes," and the emotional agonies of the early years of the movement.[20]

Atkinson helps forge the radical feminist position that "the oppression of women is . . . the beginning of the class system and women [were] the first exploited class" (30). "Every culture or institution or value developed since that time contains that oppression as a major foundational ingredient." She contends that the very definition of women, and therefore their inherited identities, are functional to the perpetuation of male supremacist society. As she puts it bluntly to a group of college women, "Your definition *is* that you're a woman and your function is either to get knocked up or to get laid" (29). In other words women are defined in terms of the functions they fulfill in an androcentric society: reproduction.

> What separates out a particular individual from other individuals as a "woman"? . . . This separation has two aspects, "sociological" and "biological." The term for the sociological function is "woman" (wifman); the term for the biological function is "female" (to suckle). Both terms are descriptive of functions in the interests of someone other than the possessor (52).

Atkinson moves beyond Firestone's biological analysis to insist that the important question is "how did this biological classification become a political classification?" (52). For, by Atkinson's definition, political classes are those people who are grouped together in terms of the function they play in serving another group (53). Such predefinition of a person as a member of a class obviates the possibility of that person developing as a free individual (53). "By class definition, women are not individual or free but rather extensions of other human beings" (106). It is this sex-class identification, or sex role, that must be destroyed (55).

One of Atkinson's imperatives is therefore that women must develop new identity concepts apart from their political class identity. "A major cultural reversal" is necessary "to radically change the source of identity from outer-directed to inner-directed" (111). Atkinson argues that at present our identities are built "from the outside. . . . But what if identity were built from inside?" (80). Atkinson thus arrives at a position similar to that developed by Elizabeth Cady Stanton in "Solitude of Self," and to a certain extent, that of the feminist existentialists.

Atkinson targets male-female relationships as examples of the pathology of other-directed identity formation. Indeed, like other radical feminists, she roots the cause of male subjugation of women in the psychology of male identity. Borrowing from the existentialists, Atkinson says masculine identity is achieved by means of "metaphysical cannibalism." Suggesting that humans feel incomplete and abbreviated from the inside and that they see others as complete and autonomous (which recalls the existentialist idea of pour-soi and en-soi), Atkinson says that men appropriate the substance of their underclass, women, to palliate their anxieties. Thus, the psychic security of males is established at the expense of women. Atkinson roots the origin of this phenomenon in prehistory. "Men invaded the being of those individuals now defined as functions, or 'females,' appropriated their human characteristic [their constructive imagination], and occupied their bodies" (60). Women thus became a means of self-justification for men; women provided them with a way to deny their own imperfections, their own mortality (79). Atkinson therefore urges the development of new concepts of identity for men, too. Oppression, she argues, relies on the "proposition that life is not self-justifying" (79). The oppressor must psychologically cannibalize the oppressed, in order to feel complete. All existing institutions, she claims, are based on this premise: that individual life is not free, independent, and self-justifying, but is rather based on mutual, pathological dependency.

> Our society is based on dependency as a given, guaranteed by a rigid institutional structure. What would happen to the family if each individual life were independent and *self*-justifying? And what would happen to love? (80)

Atkinson's most radical and intriguing discussions revolve around the idea of love as a pathology rooted in the maimed, incomplete identities of men and women. "The phenomenon of love," she argues, "is the psychological pivot in the persecution of women" (43). Women develop love as a psychological means of dealing with hopeless oppression. Isolated from one another, prey to their oppressor, and denied any hope of aid, they come to "exist in a special psychopathological state of fantasy both in reference to themselves and to their manner of relating to their counterclass. This pathological condition . . . is what we know as the phenomenon of love" (43–44). Atkinson theorizes that love is a psychological mechanism women use to absorb some of men's power into themselves. It is a matter of seeking wholeness by merging one's inadequate self with another perceived to be more powerful and substantial. Through love "the woman is instinctively trying to recoup her definitional and political losses by fusing with the enemy. 'Love' is the woman's pitiful deluded attempt to attain the human: by fusing she hopes to blur the male/female role dichotomy" (44).

> The combination of his power, her self-hatred, and the hope for a life that is self-justifying—the goal of all living creatures—results in a yearning for her stolen life—her Self—that is the delusion and poignancy of love (62).

"If we were free," Atkinson concludes, "would we *need* love?" (93).

Consistent with Atkinson's theory of the independent, self-justifying self as the ideal identity is her thesis that we should not wait for the revolution to happen at some future date but should live it today. In this she is consonant with the anarchists' and others' idea of the revolution as praxis. "Each of us," Atkinson urges, "is *the* revolution" (118). From this is derived the ethical imperative of Atkinson's feminist revolutionary. Not surprisingly, given her theory of individual responsibility, it is, she acknowledges, a reworking of Kant's categorical imperative. That moral directive, as stated by Kant, was that one should never act "otherwise than so that [one] could also will that [one's] maxim should become a univeral law."[21] Atkinson's variation is, "the revolutionary is one who acts as it thinks everyone must act in a good and just society" (119).

Like *Amazon Odyssey,* Mary Daly's *Gyn/Ecology: The Metaethics of Radical Feminism* is constructed upon the myth of the Amazon voyager. But Daly's voyage takes one beyond earlier radical feminist statements and beyond (as she herself put it) *Beyond God the Father.* Despite its originality, the work belongs very much in the tradition of twentieth-century intellectual history. In particular it derives its fundamental ontology from Heidegger's Gnostic existentialism. Daly's basic methodological premise is Heideggerean: by negating the "public" reality that surrounds us, which she like Heidegger sees as a lie perpetrated by the world's powers (in her case by the patriarchs), one allows the truth to be revealed. Heidegger used the Greek *alethea,* which means "the uncovered" or "the unconcealed," to identify his concept of truth. "Truth is the unconcealment and revealment of what-is."[22] Conversely, "the untruth is the veiling of Being . . . the presence of the covering is the presence of the 'public.' "[23] Mary Daly similarly sees women as cast in a false, veiled realm which must be destroyed in order for the truth of women's being to emerge. "Radical feminist consciousness spirals in all directions, discovering the past, creating/dis-closing the present/future."[24]

Since reality is constructed through language, it is through a radical destruction or "deconstruction" of language that Daly makes her way. It is, as she puts it, a voyage of "new words" (the book includes a special index which lists nearly two hundred such entries from "A-mazing process" to "witch"). These new words constitute a "gynomorphic" language that attempts to create new awarenesses, a sense of a new female reality, even as it destroys the false reified images of patriarchal society.

Daly therefore uses a modernist, or, more correctly, a postmodernist style, which intends to shock the reader, to force new awarenesses by means of puns, neologisms, and an inversion of the traditional definition of certain words, particularly negative terms used for women, such as hag, crone, spinster, lesbian, harpie, and fury. These historically negative images of marginal and denigrated women become, in Daly's handling, positive prototypes for the "woman-identified woman," the woman who has refused to capitulate to masculine hegemony. These witch-women are Daly's heroes, and she calls upon all women to discover the hag/crone/spinster/lesbian in themselves, to join her on this Amazon voyage.

Daly also builds her gyn/ecological vision on metaphors taken from women's traditional cultural activities, such as spinning. Spinning becomes a metaphor for the deconstructive/constructive voyage she is taking. Spinning knowledge is not fixed, it continues in a state of change, of fluidity, it forms threads between hitherto unlinked sections of reality, it forms new webs, new connections imperceptible in traditional scholarly modes. "Since Gyn/Ecology Spins around, past, and through the established fields, opening the coffers/coffins in which 'knowledge' has been stored, re-stored, re-covered, its meaning will be hidden from the Grave Keepers of tradition" (xiv).

As opposed to the false knowledge perpetrated by patriarchal powers, Daly offers a new knowledge, a gnosis, that is available only to initiates through the magical "new words." In this sense Daly belongs in the tradition of gnostic alchemy (as does Heidegger),[25] which also used a reversal of commonly accepted definitions to reveal a new truth. Daly herself acknowledges that what is involved is "a process of alchemy. We transmute the base metals of man-made myth by becoming unmute, calling forth from our Selves and each other the courage to name the unnameable" (34).

Radical feminism is therefore, according to Daly, a process or voyage of "women becoming" (1). It is "very much an Otherworld Journey. It is both discovery and creation of a world other than patriarchy" (1). Daly structures her otherworld journey upon the Gnostic myth of the soul's redemptive passage. In this myth the soul must say the correct or magical words at each stage of the journey in order to pass the hostile gatekeepers.[26] In Daly's feminist version of the myth the gatekeepers are "the demonic powers of patriarchy. . . . Women who are able to name our Selves are thereby empowered to name the demons at each Passage" (29). The power of naming the "new words" thereby effects the women's passage out of the netherworld of patriarchy (this world) into the new world of women's being. The magical substance that propels "women's becoming" in Daly's vision is "gynergy," or women's energy (34).

Women's journeys are patterned upon a movement from an inauthentic false realm into a realm of truth. This trajectory recalls Heidegger's vision of the movement of Dasein out of the inauthentic public world into the authentic realm. According to Heidegger, when the self is engaged in this redemptive trajectory, it is in *"primordial and authentic temporality,"* as opposed to the fallen time of just existing "in which the ecstatical character of primordial temporality has been leveled off" *(Being and Time,* 337–78). The process is therefore one of moving "outside-of" one's conventional self, of entering an "ec-static" mode.

Similarly, Daly sees the authenticating process as one of exorcism, or casting off the demonic powers, and ecstasy. "Concomitant with the a-mazing struggle, which is exorcism, is the ecstatic process of Spinsters dis-covering the labyrinth of our own unfolding/becoming" (32). On the one hand, voyagers must exorcise patriarchal names (as proposed in *Beyond God the Father*); on the other, they will find that such negations of negatives yield a positive. That positive is a movement *out of* the previous patriarchally defined self and world, beyond patriarchal space into new worlds of being or becoming. This positive process is "ecstasy."

The book is therefore structured upon the passages a woman must make in the "ec-statical" voyage of becoming. The first passage (pp. 35–105) involves undoing the lies, mystifications and false namings of patriarchy, which Daly sees as a "necrophiliac" civilization.

The second passage (pp. 107–312) engages in the idea that "Goddess murder" is the primordial event in the establishment and perpetuation of patriarchy. Daly opens this section with the description of the dismemberment of the goddess Tiamat seen in the Babylonian *Enuma Elish* (similar to Ruether, see chapter 5). In this section, the longest of the book, Daly describes in gruesome detail "a number of barbarous rituals, ancient and modern, in order to unmask the very real, existential meaning of Goddess murder in the concrete lives of women" (111). The atrocious rites she focuses on are the

Indian suttee (where widows had to fling themselves on the funeral pyres of their husbands), Chinese foot binding, African female genital mutilation, European witch burning, and American gynecology. In this passage "Crone-ographers who have survived dis-covering the various manifestations of Goddess-murder on this patriarchal planet have become aware of the deep and universal intent to destroy the divine spark in women" (315).

The third passage (pp. 313–424) is that of "Spinning: New Time/Space" and thereby creating "a new, woman-identified environment. It is the becoming of Gyn/Ecology" (313). The section is divided into three parts: "Spooking, Sparking, and Spinning."

"Spooking" means turning spooking back on perpetrators who terrorize women. "This Spinster-Spooking is also re-calling/re-membering/re-claiming our Witches' power to cast spells" (318). "Sparking" is "speaking with tongues of fire. Sparking is igniting the divine Spark in women" (319). It also means sparking the "Fire of Female Friendship" (354). "Sparking means building the fires of gynergetic communication" (320). The final phase, spinning, means "spirit spiraling, whirling . . . into our own world. Gyn/Ecology is weaving the way past the dead past and the dry places, weaving our world tapestry out of genesis and demise" (320).

Like any Gnostic and magical solution, Mary Daly's thesis may be faulted for its "metaethical" premise. The monolithic reduction of existing reality to a lie perpetrated by patriarchal powers denies the variety of human life and the degrees of good and evil that exist. Any presumption of being beyond ethics, beyond an obligation to this human world as it exists, is dangerous. Daly's work is nevertheless a dazzling construction; it is not without profound insights into the very real mind- and body-binding oppressions that women universally endure.

The remaining section of this chapter will be devoted to a discussion of the second-wave theory developed by radical women of color and lesbians. Black women and other minority women in the United States face a "double jeopardy," as Frances Beale pointed out in 1968.[27] On the one hand, like all women they endure oppression on account of their sex; on the other hand, they along with black and other minority men experience oppression due to their race. Compounding the problem is the fact that black women meet sexism in political groups organized to combat racial injustice and racism in white feminist organizations.

Like white feminists, many black women came to feminism through an awareness that they were being treated as second-class citizens within the civil rights movement of the 60s. As the Combahee River Collective, a black feminist group, explained in 1977: "It was our experience and disillusionment within these liberation movements, as well as experience on the periphery of the white male left, that led to the need to develop a politics that was antiracist, unlike those of white women, and antisexist, unlike those of Black and white men."[28] Bell Hooks amplifies, "black women felt they were asked to choose between a black movement that primarily served the interests of black male patriarchs and a women's movement which primarily served the interests of racist white women."[29]

Women of color have a different cultural history and continue to have a different cultural experience than do white women, especially middle-class white women who dominate feminist organizations. Blacks and other women of color are concerned that these differences not be ignored or rendered invisible, for this would deny the reality and validity of their identity. At issue, as Gloria Joseph points out, is Sojourner Truth's question writ large. For, "Ain't I A Woman?" is really not a question but a statement that black women with their divergent experience are nevertheless women, too.[30] White women's ignorance of other women's experience is one of the primary forms of racism that women of color decry in the women's movement.

Cherríe Moraga dramatizes the difference in the black and white experience in a piece entitled "I Transfer and Go Underground" (1980). Moraga transforms a routine Boston transit ride into a symbolic journey between the white and black worlds. Leaving the white suburb of Watertown, she transfers at Harvard Square to the "T," which carries her underground to Roxbury, the black ghetto in the heart of Boston. It is a journey the white feminists of Watertown do not take. Like the other contributors to *This Bridge Called My Back: Writings by Radical Women of Color* (which Moraga and Gloria Anzaldúa edited), Moraga is concerned to establish a feminism that does not deny the realities of race, ethnic, and class differences and to develop an analysis where race and class are integral with sex in explaining the multiple oppressions of women of color.[31]

Many black feminists point to specific differences in the history of black and white women's experiences. One is that black women have rarely experienced the leisure-class white women's problem of being denied access to productive work. On the contrary, "most black women have [had] to work to help house, feed, and clothe their families. Black women make up a substantial percentage of the black working force and this is true for the poorest black family as well as the so-called 'middle-class' family" (Beale, 342). Beale further points out the unique horrors black women have had to endure.

> Her physical image has been maliciously maligned; she has been sexually assaulted and abused by the white colonizer; she has suffered the worst kind of economic exploitation, having been forced to serve as the white woman's maid and wet nurse for white offspring while her own children were starving and neglected. It is the depth of degradation to be socially manipulated, physically raped, used to undermine your own household—and to be powerless to reverse this syndrome (343).

Pauli Murray, writing in 1964, points to the difference in the black and white woman's economic and social situation. The black woman "remains single more often, bears more children, is in the labor market longer, has less education, earns less, is widowed earlier and carries a heavier economic burden as a family head than her white sister."[32]

On the plantation, as noted in chapter 1 and after, black women stood side by side with men in performing heavy field labor. Alice Walker recalls her own mother: "during the 'working' day, she labored beside—not behind—my father in the fields."[33] But black feminists reject the stereotype of the super-strong matriarchal black woman as one of the grossest distortions of black women's experience. As Angela Davis notes, "The designation of the black woman as a matriarch is a cruel misnomer. It is a misnomer because it implies stable kinship structures within which the mother exercises decisive authority. It is cruel because it ignores the profound traumas the black woman must have experienced when she had to surrender her child-bearing to alien and predatory economic interests."[34] Davis explains that the concept of matriarchy itself implies a power that black women could have never possessed (4).

In particular, black feminists railed against the codification of the matriarchy myth seen in Daniel Moynihan's 1965 report *The Negro Family: The Case for National Action.* In this analysis Moynihan asserted that since a fourth of black families were headed by single women, black society was a matriarchy. This situation undermined the confidence and "manhood" of black men, and therefore prevented their competing successfully in the white work world. As Bell Hooks points out, Moynihan's view can be seen as one more version of American neo-Freudian revisionism where women who evidenced the slightest degree of independence were perceived as "castrating" threats to the male identity (180–81). Unfortunately, Hooks continues, many black men "absorbed" the Moynihan ideology, and this misogyny itself became absorbed into the black freedom movement. "Black men were able to use the matriarchy myth as a psychological weapon to justify their demands that black women assume a more passive subservient role in the home" (79). Freedom came to be seen by some macho black militants as a liberation from the oppression caused by black women (181–87).

Black women have had to contend with a variety of other stereotypes. The black stereotypes are different from the white but they nevertheless connote what is "Other" in a white patriarchal society. "Merely naming the perjorative stereotypes attributed to Black women (e.g., mammy, matriarch, Sapphire, whore, bulldagger), let alone cataloguing the cruel, often murderous, treatment we receive, indicates how little value had been placed upon our lives during four centuries of bondage in the Western hemisphere."[35] In its 1973 organizing statement of purpose the National Black Feminist Organization similarly called for a rejection of "the myriad of distorted images that have portrayed us as grinning Beulahs, castrating Sapphires, and pancake-box Jemimas." "We, not white men or black men, must define our own self-image as black women."[36]

Despite the differences between black and white feminists, many black feminists have urged that the two groups attempt to negotiate these differences and find common cause. Black poet Audre Lorde claimed, "Without community, there is no liberation. . . . But community must not mean a shedding of our differences, nor the pathetic pretence that these differences do not exist." She continued,

> Those of us who stand outside the circle of this society's definition of acceptable women; those of us who have been forged in the crucibles of difference; those of us who are poor, who are lesbians, who are black, who are older, know that *survival is not an academic skill.* It is learning how to stand alone, unpopular and sometimes reviled, and how to make common cause with those others identified as outside the structures, in order to define and seek a world in which we can all flourish. It is learning how to take our differences and make them strengths.[37]

Because they are united with black men on issues of race, most black feminists reject a separatist feminist position. They have noted, for example, that where white women got the vote in 1920 black women and men were prevented from exercising the franchise in the South until the 1965 Voting Rights Act (and the voter registration drives of the 1960s).[38] Gloria Joseph insists, "the Black woman's fate . . . is inexorably bound with that of the Black male."[39] In their 1977 manifesto the Combahee River Collective states:

> Although we are feminists and lesbians, we feel solidarity with progressive Black men and do not advocate the fractionalization that white women who are separatists demand. . . . We struggle together with Black men against racism, while we struggle with Black men about sexism (16).

Certain black feminists zeroed in on specific aspects of radical feminist theory developed by white feminists. Audre Lorde, for example, in "An Open Letter to Mary Daly" in 1981, expressed dismay that Daly had not included examples from "African myth/legend/religion" in her search for sources of "old female power."[40] "Why are her goddess-images only white, western-european, judeo-christian? Where was Afrakete, Yemanje, Oyo and Mawulisa?" (94) Lorde further criticizes the fact that materials from African-American history and culture seem clustered in one negative section, that devoted to female genital mutilation, thus implying that "non-white women and our herstories are noteworthy only as decorations, or as examples of female victimization" (96). And Angela Davis has criticized aspects of Shulamith Firestone's and Susan Brownmiller's theories in *Women, Race and Class* (1981).[41]

Another important aspect of the feminism articulated by radical women of color is their concern to retain their racial and ethnic roots. In many cases this concern is manifested as a desire to preserve authentic women's traditions, to preserve the history and culture of their mothers.[42] A series of statements by black, Latina, and Native American feminists strongly expresses a concern that the mother's culture remain alive and that its moral vision be at the foundation of any feminist change. As noted above, this is an important aspect of earlier radical feminist theory; it is a central tenet of lesbian separatist theory, and, as we shall see in chapter 7, it may well become the dominant feminist theory of the future.

Alice Walker's already classic article, "In Search of Our Mothers' Gardens" (1974), is one of the first to urge that feminists look at their mothers' experience in a new light. Walker starts with Jean Toomer's observation that black women in the South in the 1920s exhibited a spirituality "so intense, so deep, so *unconscious,* that they were themselves unaware of the richness they held" (64). Yet this spiritual energy had no outlet, for black women had neither the time nor the means to put that energy to creative use, to make art.

> For these grandmothers and mothers of ours were . . . Artists; driven to a numb and bleeding madness by the springs of creativity in them for which there was no release. They were Creators, who lived lives of spiritual waste, because they were so rich in spirituality—which is the basis of Art—that the strain of enduring their unused and unwanted talent drove them insane (66).

Nevertheless, black women did manage to create, and their cultural traditions may be found in unlikely places. Walker's own mother, for example, despite an onerous work schedule, expressed herself through her garden, "a garden so brilliant with colors, so original in its design, so magnificent with life and creativity, that to this day people drive by our house in Georgia . . . and ask to stand or walk among my mother's art" (105).

Retaining connections with the mothers' culture means reclaiming "our female-identified cultural tradition," as Moraga and Anzaldúa put it in *This Bridge Called My Back* (106). Moraga, a poet, acknowledges an ambivalence that many of the contributors to her collection feel. They speak of being torn between two worlds; one brown, one white: one that of the mothers, the other patriarchal.

> I have, in many ways, denied the voice of my brown mother—the brown in me. I have acclimated to the sound of a white language which, as my father represents it, does not speak to the emotions in my poems—emotions which stem from the love of my mother (31).

Naomi Littlebear similarly speaks of wishing to express in her life the "voice of my mothers" (157).

In an article entitled "It's In My Blood, My Face—My Mother's Voice, The Way I Sweat," Anita Valerio points to some of the difficulties involved in unselfconsciously retaining ties with one's ethnic culture, however. She describes participating in a tribal ceremonial, aspects of which she found "weird," then realizing, " 'weird' only a non-Indian would say that" (42). Through exposure to white culture she has developed a critical consciousness toward her own customs, one that cannot be erased.

A Puerto Rican woman, Aurora Levins Morales, also stresses the difficulties inherent in a mother-daughter relationship where the mothers are trained in patriarchal ways. In her culture, she notes, mothers give their daughters a double message. Men, they say, are disgusting, but you have to "catch" one to survive (53). "You've got to learn how to hold on 'em just enough to get what you want . . . lie down and grit your teeth and bear it, because there's no escape" (53). Gloria Joseph notes a similar contradictory message in advice black women give their daughters.[43] Morales sees that resolving this contradiction must be at the heart of any feminist change. "The relationship between mother and daughter stands at the center of what I fear most in our culture. Heal that wound and we change the world" (56). An Asian-Pacific American woman, Mitsuye Yamada, says succinctly that the ethnic woman's identity must be integral with the history of her mother's culture: "I . . . have come to know who I am through understanding the nature of my mother's experience" (74).

Lesbian feminism also evolved in the course of 1970s from an initial period in which the anti-lesbian attitudes of "straight" feminists were challenged, to an articulation of theory that reflected lesbians' own unique life-situations. By the late 1970s and early 1980s, lesbians were arguing that the root of women's oppression was the institution of "heterosexism." This section will trace the evolution of second-wave lesbian theory.

Like women of color, lesbians are victims of "double jeopardy": oppressed not only for being women, but also for being homosexual. Similarly, lesbians found themselves uncomfortable in both the women's movement and the gay liberation movement. In the former they had to deal with what has come to be called "homophobia," or fear of homosexuality; in the latter with male chauvinism.[44]

The "Radicalesbians," a New York group, prepared the first major statement of lesbian feminist theory, "The Woman Identified Woman," published in *Notes from the Third Year* in 1971. (Significantly, there had been nothing on lesbianism in *Notes from the Second Year,* 1970). This piece developed one of the most important theoretical concepts introduced by second-wave radical feminism—one I have already used in this book—that of the woman-identified woman.

Trying to get away from the concept of lesbianism as a strictly sexual identity, the Radicalesbians argue that the lesbian is really a natural, "unconscious" feminist, a woman who devotes her energies to other women, who refuses to be identified in terms of a man.

> What is a lesbian? A lesbian is the rage of all women condensed to the point of explosion. She is the woman who, often beginning at an ex-

> tremely early age, acts in accordance with her inner compulsion to be a more complete and freer human being than her society . . . cares to allow her (81).

The document notes that such early assertiveness often brings the young woman "into painful conflict with people, situations, the accepted ways of thinking, feeling and behaving, until she is in a state of continual war with everything around her, and usually with her self" (81). The lesbian "may not be fully conscious of the political implications of what for her began as personal necessity," but her gesture of revolt is really against "the limitations and oppression laid on her by . . . the female role" (81).

The term "lesbian," the authors maintain, is indeed a scare word designed the keep the assertive, independent woman in her place. "Lesbian is a label invented by the Man to throw at any woman who dares to be his equal, who dares to challenge his prerogatives (including that of all women as part of the exchange medium among men), who dares to assert the primacy of her own needs" (82). By definition an independent woman cannot be a "real woman"—"she must be a dyke" (82). As the Radicalesbians point out, this means that the cultural definition of a "real woman" "when you strip off all the packaging . . . is to get fucked by men" (82). To be "feminine" or to be a "real woman" in our society means to be "the [sexual] property of some man whose name we bear" (83). Conversely, to reject such an identification, "to be a woman who belongs to no man is to be invisible, pathetic, inauthentic, unreal" (83).

The Radicalesbians advocate that women refuse to accept identities that are conceived only in terms of a man's "power," "ego," or "status" (82). This means a refusal to be "male-identified." The concept of male-identification was further elaborated by Kathleen Barry in 1979, as follows. It means

> internalizing the values of the colonizer and actively participating in carrying out the colonization of one's self and one's sex. . . . Male identification is the act whereby women place men above women, including themselves, in credibility, status, and importance. . . . Interaction with women is seen as a lesser form of relating on every level.[45]

Rather, the Radicalesbians urge, women should forge their identities in terms of one another, in terms of their own needs, experiences and perceptions. And in words that echo Margaret Fuller's call for female separatism, the Radicalesbians insist that "only women can give to each other a new sense of self. That identity we have to develop with reference to ourselves, and not in relation to men" (83). Such new women will therefore be "woman identified."

Another influential article on lesbian feminism also appeared in *Notes from the Third Year*. In "Loving Another Woman," Anne Koedt interviewed a feminist who had recently discovered her lesbian potential, about her relationship with another woman. In this discussion lesbianism was presented as a very human experience: "all of a sudden I became very, very aware. I was flooded with a tremendous attraction for her. And I wanted to tell her, I wanted to sleep with her, I wanted to let her know what I was feeling. At the same time I was totally bewildered" (26). The woman continues, "when I did bring it up in an oblique way and told her that I was attracted to her, she replied somewhat generally that she felt the same way. You see, she was as scared as I was, but I didn't know it" (26). This article, perhaps more than any other, helped dispel the myth of the lesbian as a diseased freak.

In articles published in 1969 and 1970, Martha Shelley urged further that the lesbian should be seen as a model of the independent woman. "I have never met a Lesbian who was not a feminist. . . . I have never met a Lesbian who believed that she was innately less rational or capable than a man; who swallowed one word of the 'woman's role' horseshit." Shelley concludes, "in a male-dominated society, Lesbianism is a sign of mental health."[46] In a later article she urges that lesbianism is really "the heart of the Women's Liberation Movement." For, "in order to throw off the oppression of the male caste, women must unite—we must learn to love ourselves and each other, we must grow strong and independent of men so that we can deal with them from a position of strength."[47]

The positive image of the lesbian as a woman of strength and independence continued as a central thesis of lesbian feminist theory. As Elsa Gidlow, an elderly lesbian poet, put it in 1977:

> The lesbian personality manifests itself in independence of spirit, in willingness to take responsibility for oneself, to think for oneself, not to take 'authorities' and their dictum on trust. It usually includes erotic attraction to women, although we know there have been many women of lesbian personality who never had sexual relations with one another. . . . What is strongly a part of the lesbian personality is loyalty and love of other women. . . .

Gidlow concludes that since the lesbian "has freed herself from the external and internal dominance of the male," the "lesbian personality" is unusually "creative."[48]

Adrienne Rich had urged a similar idea in a 1976 presentation in which she argued that the strong, creative side of every woman is her lesbian self.

> It is the lesbian in every woman who is compelled by female energy, who gravitates toward strong women, who seeks a literature that will express that energy and strength. . . . It is the lesbian in us who is creative, for the dutiful daughter of the fathers in us is only a hack.[49]

Similarly broad definitions of lesbianism have come to dominate feminist revisionist scholarship. In 1977, for example, Blanche Wiesen Cook offered this definition: "Women who love women, who choose women to nurture and support and to create a living environment in which to work creatively and independently, are lesbians."[50] Using similar categories, historians have discovered that such woman-identified relationships were pervasive in past societies. Carroll Smith-Rosenberg found intense relationships between women to be a widespread pattern among nineteenth-century American women, and Lillian Faderman has traced such friendships back to the Renaissance.[51]

Another aspect of lesbian feminist theory that became established early in the 1970s was the idea that because woman-to-woman relationships need not involve sex roles, they can become model egalitarian bonds. In a 1971 article Sydney Abbott and Barbara Love urged that feminists "consider lesbianism a total life style that is valued in itself, not simply a matter of sexual union."[52] That life-style derived from the fact that most lesbians live apart from men, and therefore have relationships that are free from role expectations. "In the absence of roles there is no prescribed way of thinking or acting. Everything is open for new consideration, from who will wash the dishes, to who will aggress in love, to who will relocate for whom" (449).

By the mid-1970s lesbian theorists were maintaining that heterosexuality, as Charlotte Bunch put it, was "a cornerstone of male supremacy."[53] Lesbian theory must go beyond "an analysis of sexual politics to an analysis of sexuality itself" (68). As "institution and ideology," heterosexuality is a primary factor in the oppression of women (68). What is the ideology of heterosexuality? "Basically, [it] means men first. . . . It assumes that . . . every woman is defined by and is the property of men. Her body, her services, her children belong to men. If you don't accept that definition, you're a queer—no matter who you sleep with" (69).

Drawing upon socialist feminist theory Bunch notes that the organization of labor, and in particular the so-called family wage, depends on heterosexual assumptions—that it is the man who works and that women are supported by the working man. If a woman works, it is considered marginal and secondary. Such conventional assumptions, Bunch points out, ignore the existence of lesbian workers.

Bunch urges further that lesbians are accorded fundamentally different treatment than "straight" women because the latter may take advantage of "heterosexual privilege." Through her association with men this woman "receives some of the benefits of male privilege indirectly and is thus given a stake in continuing those privileges and maintaining their source—male supremacy" (70). Bunch suggests that if "straight" women doubt the existence of "heterosexual privilege" they should try "being a queer for a week. Do not walk out on the street with men; walk only with women, especially at night, for example. For a whole week, experience life as if you were a lesbian, and I think you will know what heterosexual privilege is very quickly" (70).

Lucia Valeska extends Bunch's analysis. "Heterosexuality is far more than a private matter between a woman and a man; it is, in fact, a mandate that all women be forever divided against each other through a compelling allegiance to one man at home and all men outside the home."[54] The logical response to the analysis developed by Bunch, Valeska, and others is lesbian separatism. For, if male domination is sustained by heterosexuality, which creates a situation where individual women are tied socially, economically, and emotionally to individual men, it follows that women should break the heterosexual bonds and ally with other women in order to fight against male dominion. This is the logic of female separatism. It is an important vein in lesbian feminist theory that can be seen to operate on several levels. If interpreted in psychological terms, it implies that women must break their "psychological and emotional addiction to male power," as Valeska puts it (29). Or, it can mean "the development of strictly lesbian feminist living and working collectives" (28). It can mean the development of an alternative culture, authentically woman-identified art, music and literature. It can mean the development of alternative life-styles. All these possibilities are happening, and all reflect a "base opposition to heterosexual hegemony and its role in maintaining male supremacy" (28).

Adrienne Rich furthered discussion initiated by Bunch and others in an important 1980 article, "Compulsory Heterosexuality and Lesbian Existence." In this essay Rich suggests that "compulsory heterosexuality" is a "*political institution*" (637) that guarantees women's continued subordination, because it requires "male identification" on the part of most women: this means, as we have seen, putting men's needs, issues, and perspectives first, and denying the existence or potential of woman-identification. Citing numerous studies—especially Nancy Chodorow's, which was discussed in chapter 4—that see the mother-bond as primary, Rich asks why theorists have not questioned the violent wrenching required for the girl to switch her affections to a man (Freud himself seriously considered this issue, as we have seen; so did Gayle Rubin). Rich suggests that it is the ideology and institution of "compulsory heterosexuality" that forces women to make this transferral. It is not, she maintains, a natural or innate choice; rather it is forced upon the woman by her political environment.

Rich cities Catharine A. MacKinnon's study of sexual harassment at work to point up how pervasive the heterosexual imperative is and how it may be seen as a root cause of such continuing and seemingly surface problems as job discrimination. MacKinnon pointed to the fact that "male employers often do not hire qualified women even when they could pay them less than men" because those women resist the inherent "sexualization" of the position—that it requires the woman to "market sexual attractiveness to men."[55] Thus, for most women getting and keeping a job depends on acting like a "real" woman, which means "dressing and playing the feminine, deferential [male-flattering] role" (642).

Because women are relatively powerless and economically disadvantaged, most are willing to play the double role mandated by such a system. Rich argues that a central component of all women's lives—past and present—is this having to live a *"double life"*; expressing on the one hand, an "apparent acquiescence to an institution founded on male interest and prerogative" (654), and on the other, experiencing the strong pulls that draw her toward other women and a woman-identified experience.

One of the central ways in which "compulsory heterosexuality" is perpetuated is through rendering the woman-identified or lesbian experience invisible (647). Rich urges that researchers and scholars open their eyes to the extensive continuum of lesbian experience in the past and present, so that women in the future will realize that male-identification is not the only option (648–49). As we begin to explore lesbian culture we will come to realize, Rich believes, that it is, "like motherhood, a profoundly *female* experience" (650), and that it is a pervasive one. An awareness of the continued and widespread reality of woman-identified commitments will show that compulsory heterosexuality is a "lie" that has been forced upon women as a means of sustaining male dominion (657).

When Rich states that she believes the lesbian cultural experience is a profoundly female one, she is asserting another of the central premises of lesbian cultural separatism: that women are fundamentally different from men and that their cultural behavior, experience, history, and value system are also at odds with the dominant patriarchal culture. In the 1970s cultural separatists developed important theoretical intuitions, which are summarized in the final section of this chapter.[56]

In a suggestive article entitled "Rosy Rightbrain's Exorcism/Invocation" (1975), Gina Covina articulates the separatist dream of a "woman-centered culture"—a conception that is similar to that formulated by such nineteenth-century cultural feminists as Charlotte Perkins Gilman.

> In the coming women's culture, that fantasy of fantasies, when the left hand moves everywhere openly, when the full moon shines bright as the sun on our days, when every particle $\frac{\text{white}}{\text{black}} = \frac{\text{right}}{\text{left}} = \frac{\text{male}}{\text{female}} = \frac{\text{good}}{\text{bad}}$ has been burned out of all our genes by a growing insistance on multiplicity (yes-and) rather than duplicity (either/or), when we as a planet live cooperatively without the patriarchal tools of war, money, governments, racism, family and religious systems, etc.[57]

Covina here expresses a number of cultural feminist themes: one is the reliance on symbols traditionally associated with the feminine, such as the moon and the left; another is a concern about establishing a holistic vision; another is her anti-militarist, anarchist position.

Like Shulamith Firestone, Covina imagines a women's utopia as one in which "there will be no art" (91). Rather, we will live art. "In the old matriarchal cultures, aesthetic, spiritual, sensual and practical ways of perceiving the world has not yet been separated and labeled so it was possible for a visit to the community spring, for example, to be a daily chore, a social event, an aesthetic and sensual pleasure, and an experience of spiritual affirmation, all at once" (92). Like Firestone and like Audre Lorde in "Uses of the Erotic: the Erotic as Power" (1979), Covina rejects the compartmentalization of the erotic off from ordinary life, urging that it be integrated with all activities as an energizing force. Rich, following Lorde, made a similar point in "Compulsory Heterosexuality": "as we delineate a lesbian continuum we begin to discover the erotic in female terms: as that which is unconfined to any single part of the body or solely to the body itself, as an energy not only diffuse but . . . omnipresent" (650).

Covina describes the assimilation of the erotic and the aesthetic into daily life as she imagines the feelings of the matriarchal woman at the community spring: "Everything I come in contact with is alive . . . I feel strong familiar communication with this clay and all the spirits of this place. Energy flows freely through my body, down my legs grounding me in the earth, and sparks out my fingertips, making a dance with the half-formed clay bowl" (92).

Covina grounds her theory of women's differentness in two factors: one, similar to Gilman's position in *His Religion and Hers,* is that women's and men's prehistories were different because of their different tasks. Women "raised children, planted and tended the crops, decided the cycles of the community, sang the prayers. Men did not create life and had no noticeable cycles. . . . Men hunted—killing was easier for them, distanced as they were from the processes of life" (94–95). The second contributing factor is the different brain lateralization in men and women (hence the title, Rosy Rightbrain). Covina cites still controversial studies which indicate that women are more "rightbrained" than men. This theory relies on the fact that the brain is lateralized into left and right hemispheres, each of which is specialized; the left to analytic, sequential thinking, the right, according to Covina, "deals with experience in a diffuse non-sequential way, assimilating many different phenomena simultaneously, finding connections between separate bits of information. . . . Awareness of our bodies, recognition of faces, understanding of art and music, dreams and 'extra-sensory' perception are all based in the right hemisphere" (96).

Left-brained thinking Covina sees as characteristically masculine; it is "focused narrowly enough to squeeze out human or emotional considerations, [enabling] men to kill (people, animals, plants, natural processes) with free consciences" (96). This kind of thinking allowed "men to ignore the principles of morality inherent in all the earth's systems" and to impose their own propositions, one of which was the system of hierarchy (96). The patriarchal, left-brained and right-handed world has universally categorized as deviant right-brained and left-handed modalities. It has branded them as Other. Like many of the French feminists, Covina sees the patriarchal left-brained modus operandi as destructive and death-oriented. Only a holistic vision rooted in the multiple perspectives allowed by the right brain can lead the world in a life-affirmative direction. Such a holism would be characteristic of a women's culture.

Another important essay that developed cultural separatist theory further was Barbara Starrett's "I Dream in Female: The Metaphors of Evolution" (1975). Starrett similarly rejects binary, either-or thought, and proposes that women "have the ability . . . to think in ways that negate dualities."[58] The reason dualistic thinking is so repugnant to thinkers like Starrett is that they believe the compartmentalization required is the basis for destructive male behavior. The separation of the subject from the object, the rigid identification of the subject with the good and the object with evil enables the rapist mentality which separatists see as the governing modality of male behavior. "Male society has made rape the prototypical expression of its patterns. Domination of the other by force: of nature and land and resources, of 'inferior' nations and groups, of women, of money and markets and material goods" (107). Women, however, have the ability to remain in touch with what is outside them, "to move between and amid opposites, to feel gradations and complexities" (114)—a contention confirmed by Carol Gilligan's recent studies (see chapter 7). Women, Starrett maintains, do not cut off their feelings, and this allows for a more integral response, one that respects the reality of the other.

Starrett urges that the female sensitivity and value system must be ratified by a new set of symbols. She suggests that these be rooted in reinterpreted myths of the past, for example "the Demeter-Kore myth, in the semi-mythical history of the Amazons, in witchcraft, in the occult" (117). These sources will provide new cultural symbols for the value transformation that a women's culture will entail. Such myths

> will change or reverse the male-centered structures. Many of them concern the replacement, by the Mother, of the father and the associated images of patriarchy. When this replacement occurs . . . what results is . . . a shifting of thought and emotions, and a redirection of our present values (117).

The new symbols of the female will express typically female responses: "intuition, subjectivity and extra-rational processes; our nourishing and sympathetic qualities; our personal and empathic relationships with nature and the earth, our involvement in the processes of life" (118). Such resymbolization will transcend the dualisms of patriarchal culture.

> The image of the Mother does not lose its old connotations of earth, intuition, nature, the body, the emotions, the unconscious, etc. But it also lays claim to many of the connotations previously attributed to the father symbol: beauty, light, goodness, authority, activity, etc. (118)

Many separatists have looked to a semimythical matriarchal past for the new symbols and images, as Starrett suggests. Indeed, an important quest was begun for more information about matriarchies and about the Great Goddess worshiped in prepatriarchal times. Elizabeth Gould Davis's *The First Sex* (1971), although highly speculative, is a fascinating compendium of information on what hints exist of this obscure matriarchal past. A special 1978 issue of *Heresies* magazine on "The Great Goddess" provides a useful introduction to this direction in cultural separatist theory.[59]

Cultural separatists see a women's culture as pacifist and ecologically holistic, unlike men's culture, which is seen as rooted in the prehistoric experience of hunting and meat eating. Many cultural feminists, therefore, include vegetarianism as an important aspect of women's culture. Carol Adams articulated this idea in an article entitled "The Oedible Complex: Feminism and Vegetarianism" (1975). Adams argues that there are many connections between sexism and carnivorism. "Acts of aggression against women and animals are on the same continuum."[60] The ethos of hunting is a quintessentially masculine activity that has obvious connections with war, as well as rape. "Perhaps," Adams suggests, "the sympathy many women feel towards animals is recognition of the mutual victimization of both women and animals by men" (149). Adams associates meat eating with the dawn of patriarchy and theorizes that in matriarchal days women were pacifist vegetarians (151).

In *This Bridge Called My Back,* Gloria Anzaldúa summarizes the future envisaged by cultural feminist theory.

> I see . . . [a] left-handed world coming into being. For centuries now, ever since the industrial age or maybe even before, it has always been a world of the intellect, reasoning, the machine. Here women were stuck with having tremendous powers of intuition experiencing other levels of reality and other realities yet they had to sit on it because men would say, well, you're crazy. All of a sudden there's a reemergence of the intuitive energies—and they're very powerful (223).

Anzaldúa and Moraga project a left-handed world, El Mundo Zurdo, where all who have been branded as Other will "feel at home": "the colored, the queer, the poor, the female, the physically challenged. From our blood and spirit connections with these groups, we women at the bottom throughout the world can form an international feminism" (196).

> Together we form a vision which spans from the self-love of our colored skins, to the respect of our foremothers who kept the embers of revolution burning, to our reverence for the trees—the final reminder of our rightful place on this planet (196).

7 The Moral Vision of Twentieth-Century Cultural Feminism

But it is obvious that the values of women differ very often from the values which have been made by the other sex . . .
Virginia Woolf, 1929

Many second-wave feminists believed that a feminist political ethic could be derived from women's traditional culture, practice, and experience. They therefore join other contemporary theorists, from certain French feminists to American radical women of color and ecofeminists, who propose that feminism be seen not merely as a prescription for granting rights to women but as a far broader vision.

The social reform tendency in cultural feminist theory was not new. An earlier expression of it is described in chapter 2. Yet, second-wave political cultural feminists differed from their predecessors in that they had the history of the earlier movement to remind them that women do not automatically "purify" politics as they assume public positions of power. They also had new theoretical bases for their vision. This chapter indicates what some of these bases are so as to identify the feminist theoretical synthesis and moral paradigm that emerged in the 1980s.

In 1973 Susan Sontag asserted, "Virginia Woolf was altogether correct when she declared . . . that the fight to liberate women is a fight against fascism."[1] This is because, as Jane Addams brilliantly perceived, women are subjectively the victims of masculine behavior that is objectively destructive. There is, in other words, as she urged, a congruence between women's subjective experience of oppression and the objective realities of war, imperialism, and the technological destruction of the environment. Second-wave theorists held that this is because masculine destructiveness correlates to a denial of the feminine side of life.

Radical feminists claimed that destructive masculine behavior, which they call pornographic (Griffin) and rapist (Daly), is rooted in male attitudes toward women. Simone de Beauvoir and other French feminists identified masculine rejection of the feminine with the phenomenon of Otherness. Freudian feminists have seen the turning away from the mother as fundamental to the male maturation process and to the establishment of patriarchal civilization. All perceive masculine psychology as a primary factor in female subjugation and the destructive military imperialism that dominates world politics.

In order to counter this masculine ideology, these feminists believe that women must turn their "left-handed" world into a subject, into a cultural ideological source. For such an ideological transvaluation to occur, however it is necessary to establish a clear theoretical idea of what constitutes women's "left-handed" world, its culture and values, and how it relates to women's historical material base. As noted, Nancy Hartsock has done important work in this direction (see chapter 3). Despite the accusations of "essentialism" that this project has engendered, I believe it must remain a major effort in feminist studies.

For it is now apparent that there are certain patterns that occur nearly universally in women's historical cultural experience. These appear to obtain in nearly all racial, ethnic, and cultural groups and classes, providing a common denominator for the group experience of women. Second, it appears probable that these historical structures have contributed to the formation of a particularly female epistemology and ethic. Finally, this chapter on the moral vision of second-wave cultural feminism, which is based on these premises, concludes with an earlier but visionary work: Virginia Woolf's *Three Guineas,* which was first published in 1938.

Historical and anthropological studies—many of which have been cited in this book—reveal a number of determinant structures of experience under which women, unlike men, have nearly universally existed. First and foremost, women have experienced political oppression. While isolated examples to the contrary may be cited, by and large women have not had substantial political power in society, and have not been in control of the realities that have shaped their lives.

Second, nearly everywhere and in nearly every period, women have been assigned to the domestic sphere and to caring labor. Although it is true that in preindustrial societies the division between public and private labor may not have been so rigid as in industrialized nations, women have nevertheless been consigned to the domestic sphere and to domestic duties—including child rearing or mothering—throughout recorded history.

Third, women's historical economic function has been production for use, not production for exchange. Production for use, as noted in chapter 3, means creation of material consumed by the immediate family such as food, clothing, not goods sold off or exchanged, so it is therefore not valued for its abstract or exchange worth but for itself—for its immediate physical worth.

Fourth, women experience significant physical events that are different from men's. The most important of these are menstruation, which nearly all women at one time or another experience, childbirth and breastfeeding, which many women experience. In addition, it appears that, as the Freudians have pointed out, the child-maturation process in the nuclear family is very different for men and women.

Fifth, women have been and continue to be victims of male violence—rape, sexual harassment, physical abuse—world wide. It remains the fact that, as American philosopher Richard Rorty succinctly put it, "the people with the slightly larger muscles have been bullying the people with the slightly smaller muscles for a very long time."[2]

The cultural feminist hypothesis is that the experience of living under these different conditions has led to the formation of what one may call a women's standpoint, reflecting the particular consciousness, epistemology, ethic, and aesthetic that emerged under the above-noted conditions. In what follows I focus primarily on women's epistemology and the ethic that derives from it. While much of this theorizing is based on the experience of Western women, it may well prove to be relevant to the experience of women worldwide.

A substantial body of evidence has been produced that suggests that women's judgments are based on a fundamental respect for the contingent order, for the environmental context, for the concrete, everyday world. Women more than men appear to be willing to adopt a passive mode of accepting the diversity of environmental "voices" and the validity of their realities. Women appear less willing to wrench that context apart or to impose upon it alien abstractions or to use implements that subdue it intellectually or physically. Such an epistemology provides the basis for an ethic that is non-imperialistic, that is life-affirming, and that reverences the concrete details of life. Such an ethic has been articulated by British philosopher and novelist Iris Murdoch and will be introduced later in this chapter.

Considering the structures of experience outlined above, it is not difficult to hypothesize how women may have developed an environmentally aware, or holistic, vision. The primary condition of powerlessness has necessarily meant that women have had to be aware of their environment to survive, for that environment—insofar as it is patriarchal—has continually impinged upon them. As Meredith Tax pointed out in the article cited previously: "Women are hyper-aware of their surroundings. They have to be. Walk down a city street without being tuned in and you're in real danger."[3]

In the domestic sphere, while women have been able to carve out a separate space of their own and to sustain separate cultural traditions, they nevertheless even there were continually at their masters' beck and call. The fundamental "interruptibility" of women's projects may also have contributed to women's sense of personal vulnerability to environmental influence, fostering a sense of being bound to chance, to circumstance, of not being in control of one's world.[4] The resulting consciousness would be one of flexibility, of relativity, of contingency.

Similarly, both the monthly experience of menstruation and the fact that until recently, with the advent of relatively effective methods of birth control, women could not have sexual intercourse with men without having to risk pregnancy, would have contributed to a feeling of being tied to physical realities that impinge upon one's projects. A woman could not have ignored this physical context; it was *there;* it was a part of her life.

Women's experience in the domestic sphere may be analyzed in terms of its three primary aspects—housekeeping, child rearing and economic production for use—which seem to have further contributed to the construction of a female epistemology. A provocative work that suggests ways in which housework may have contributed to the development of a feminine world view is Kathryn Allen Rabuzzi's *The Sacred and the Feminine: Toward A Theology of Housework* (1982), aspects of which are discussed in chapter 5. Rabuzzi finds that women's fundamental experience in the domestic sphere is one of repetition and waiting. Unlike the traditional male experience of linear historical time through the quest, the quintessential accomplishment for Western males, the home-bound woman experiences time as a stasis—either as a perpetual repetition or "eternal return" (to use Eliade's term), or as a pattern of passive waiting. From the point of view of the Western male questor stasis is a negative experience, but Rabuzzi urges that it be reconsidered. The static waiting pattern may be seen as "simply another mode of being." "It may imply rootedness of a positive . . . sort."[5]

Rabuzzi suggests that out of this women's mode has emerged a sensibility that is a positive alternative to the masculine mode of questing and conquering. This sensibility involves an adaptation to contingency, a kind of serendipitous passivity where one flows with the waves. "Responding in this way to the whim of the moment is markedly different from imposing your will on time . . . The passivity so induced is that of a light object thrown into the water; it is not the object that determines its direction, but the movement of the water" (153). This is different "from the assertive striving more typical of the masculine temporal mode, questing" (153). While both modes when carried to extremes can be destructive, the women's mode can provide a model for a new way of being, according to Rabuzzi.

It is the experience of child rearing or mothering that Sara Ruddick sees as constituent of a woman's epistemology and moral vision in her important article, "Maternal Thinking" (1980). Like Rabuzzi, Ruddick focuses upon the different but positive modes that have emerged from women's domestic experience, and in particular from the maternal role; Ruddick proposes that these modes must become the basis of a new public ethic.

Like other women, mothers are forced into an intense awareness of their environment; in their case it is by the reality of a child. (Ruddick does not confine "mothering" to biological parenting but to all forms of maternal, caretaker roles; teaching, for example, can be so experienced.) "Maternal thinking," Ruddick urges, grows out of "maternal practice," which requires responding to the reality of the child, an other who demands preservation and growth.[6] Because so many of the factors involved in this process are beyond her control, and because she realizes that excessive control may defeat the purpose of growth, the mother must adopt a relatively passive attitude, the attitude Rabuzzi described as a waiting mode. Ruddick calls it a "holding" attitude, one that "is governed by the priority of keeping over acquiring, of conserving the fragile, of maintaining whatever is at hand and necessary to the child's life" (350). Ruddick contrasts this maternal attitude to that of scientific thought in a way analogous to Rabuzzi's distinction between feminine waiting and masculine questing. "The recognition of the priority of holding over acquiring . . . distinguishes maternal from scientific thought, as well as from the instrumentalism of technocratic capitalism" (350). "To recognize excessive control as a *liability* sharply distinguishes maternal from scientific practice" (350).

A similar distinction is drawn by Evelyn Fox Keller in her article "Feminism and Science" (1982). Keller contrasts contemporary scientist Barbara McClintock's attitude with the aggressive manipulation of nature proposed by Francis Bacon (see chapter 1). McClintock evinces a feminine mode when she talks of "letting the material speak to you" or of allowing it to "tell you what to do next." McClintock does not believe that scientists should "impose an answer" upon their material; rather they should respond to it and retain an emphathetic respect for it.[7] Keller suggests that the feminine modality points to "a science less restrained by the impulse to dominate"—a direction she sees as positive (601).

"Maternal thinking" according to Ruddick is characterized by a "humility" that stems from a realization that much is beyond one's control—"damage and death, but also the facts of the independent and uncontrollable, developing and increasingly separate existences of the lives it seeks to preserve" (351). The inevitable fact that the child changes in the process of growth further contributes to the maternal sense of humility, of resigned patience. Finally, the mother's concern for the child fosters the development of "attentive love, the training to ask, 'What are you going through?' " (359). Maternal thinking therefore involves a reverential respect for an immediate, daily, other reality to which one accedes an independent validity, on which one does not attempt to impose total control.

Another factor which appears to have contributed to the development of a female epistemology is the historical economic function women have held of production for use. Items which were to be used within the family retained a more personal, "sacred" quality than goods valued for their abstract exchange worth, or those which had been mass produced, exhibited. Women's products therefore constituted an immediate concrete environment that was and is valued for its own sake and not for its abstract potential. Once again, it is not difficult to hypothesize that such an economics impinged upon women; it constituted a cultural environment that remained intimate and a part of herself, rather than being a separate and profane "it," emotionally expendable.[8]

Certain psychological testing confirms that women exhibit perceptual habits consistent with the above-described *episteme*. Tests such as the Witkin's Embedded Figures Test (EFT) and Rod and Frame Test (RFT), which measure "spatial decontextualization," show that women tend to see the context of a phenomenon more readily than men, who are more prone to lift a figure out of its context and to "see" it and consider it separately.[9] Women's perceptual habit is usually described pejoratively as "field dependency."

While these tests may be problematic in some respects (especially insofar as they reflect socialization and education levels), the perceptual trait is one that earlier feminists noted. Some like Wollstonecraft decried it as an inability to see the forest for the trees. She saw it as a liability that impeded women's ability to think abstractly. Margaret Fuller, however, saw it positively. Woman, she wrote, "excels not so easily in classification, or recreation, as in an instinctive seizure of causes, and a simple breathing out of what she receives, that has the singleness of life, rather than the selecting and energizing of art."[10] Such a perceptual attitude resists rearranging the context in accordance with an imposed idea; rather it pays attention to the reality *as it is*, inductively. This allows for a more synthetic, holistic vision.

The most recent and perhaps the most persuasive observations about the different functioning of women's and men's psyches are those developed by Carol Gilligan at Harvard. In a series of psychological profiles developed from in-depth interviews, Gilligan determined that moral reasoning in men and women is different. Consistent with the description of the female epistemology presented above, Gilligan discovered that women's moral processing is contextually based and oriented toward relationship.

In her book, *In A Different Voice* (1982), Gilligan selects an episode from Chekhov's play *The Cherry Orchard* to illustrate the difference she noticed between men's and women's judgments. Lopahin, a capitalist entrepreneur, wants to cut down a cherry orchard in order to build profitmaking summer cottages. The owner of the orchard, Madame Ranevskaya, refuses because she is attached to the orchard and because she does not accept his imperialistic philosophy that it is human destiny to "develop" nature.[11] Gilligan uses the episode to set the stage for her thesis that men's and women's moral reasoning is different.

Indeed, the results of several studies she conducted indicate that women's moral reasoning tends to exhibit awareness of "conflicting responsibilities rather than from competing rights." Such a perception "requires for its resolution a mode of thinking that is contextual and narrative rather than formal and abstract" (19).[12] The women's "conception of morality" is "concerned with the activity of care," and it centers "moral development around the understanding of responsibility and relationships," where the men's "conception of morality as fairness ties moral development to the understanding of rights and rules" (19). Gilligan calls the feminine conception a "morality of responsibility," as opposed to the masculine "morality of rights" which is based upon an "emphasis on separation rather than connection," and on a "consideration of the individual rather than the relationship as primary" (19). In analyzing one woman's characteristic response Gilligan notes that in her view "morality and the preservation of life are contingent on sustaining connection, seeing the consequences of action by keeping the web of relationships intact" (59). She concludes, "the logic underlying an ethic of care is a psychological logic of relationships, which contrasts with the formal logic of fairness that informs the justice approach" (73).

The difference between women's and men's approaches to moral problems is apparent quite early in life. Gilligan cites studies by Jane Lever and Jean Piaget which indicate that in childhood games girls tend to be less bound by abstract rules and more able to play it as it lays, so to speak. Girls are more tolerant of intruding realities, more accommodating to the contingencies of play, more willing to innovate, and less concerned with abstract codification. Indeed, according to Lever, girls would rather end the game than quarrel over the rules. "Rather than elaborating a system of rules for resolving disputes, girls subordinated the continuation of the game to the continuation of relationships" (10).

In analyzing two responses to the same hypothetical moral problem Gilligan notes that the male sees "the dilemma [as] a math problem with humans" where the female considers the hypothetical as "a narrative of relationships that extends over time" (28). Amy, the girl, perceives "a world comprised of relationships rather than of people standing alone, a world that coheres through human connection rather than through systems of rules" (29).

Where the boy engages in a quantitative, mechanical balancing of conflicting rights based upon a hierarchy of values, the girl assumes a "network of connection, a web of relationships that is sustained by a process of communication" (32). These "contrasting images of hierarchy and network" (33) represent the basic differences in the male and female "structure of knowing."[13] Their divergent perspectives also help to explain the childrens' different views of themselves.

> Describing himself as distinct by locating his particular position in the world, Jake sets himself apart from that world by his abilities, his beliefs, and his height. . . . Amy . . . locates herself in relation to the world, de-

> scribing herself through actions that bring her into connection with others, elaborating ties through her ability to provide help (35).

Gilligan further contrasts the masculine and feminine conception of morality by comparing two biblical stories, that of Abraham and of the mother who came before Solomon. Abraham is willing to sacrifice his son in the name of an abstraction, where the woman whose child is at stake is willing to sacrifice the truth rather than see the child killed (104). Her primary value is the immediate living reality of the child.

A final aspect of the differing structures that shape men's and women's experiences, at least in Western cultures, is that analyzed by the Freudians, in particular by Nancy Chodorow. Her theory, discussed in chapter 4, proposes that because of the emotional transferences required in the nuclear child-maturation process, girls remain more interpersonally connected, with more fluid ego-boundaries, where boys, because they must reject their mothers to resolve the oedipal complex, develop more discrete, separate identities. Gilligan relies on this theory in part to explain the results she discovered of the male tendency to see less in terms of interpersonal network connections and more in terms of a self in competition with other separate selves (7–9).

We have also noted previously the tendency of Freud and contemporary Freudians to see women as inherently "subversive" because their maturation process does not involve the sublimation of the maternal erotic bond, which is necessary to patriarchal civilization. According to this theory, women do not take as seriously the imperatives of civilization—unless like the women in the Chinese parable they do so under threat of death. As Simone de Beauvoir observed in 1976 (somewhat modifying her earlier position), "women always retain a little nook of humor, a little distance between themselves and the hierarchy. . . . And irony, a sense of the concrete, because women are more strongly rooted in everyday life."[14]

It must also be noted that the resolution of the oedipal complex for the boy involves an inherent misogyny: he must reject the feminine in order to become a man. As noted in chapter 5, Rosemary Radford Ruether sees the rejection of the mother as the primary element in the emergence of patriarchy. Ruether's analysis, unlike the Freudians, is phylogenetic rather than ontogenetic; she sees the struggle against the feminine as an historical process that occurred over centuries. It is at the core of the Western identity, for the denial of the feminine established the basic dualism between transcendent ego and material body—the latter mortal and inferior; the former with illusions of immortality. Ruether noted that this process "fundamentally . . . is rooted in an effort to deny one's own mortality, to identify essential (male) humanity with a transcendent divine sphere beyond the matrix of coming-to-be-and-passing-away."[15] Ruether, like Carolyn Merchant and contemporary feminists, concludes, "the Achilles' heel of human civilization, which today has reached global genocidal and ecocidal proportions, resides in this false development of maleness through repression of the female" (11).

Evelyn Fox Keller uses feminist Freudian theory to explain the origins of the ideal of objectivity inherent in the scientific world-view identified in chapter 1. In "Gender and Science" (1978) she states that for the child the earliest experience of merging are associated with the mother, and those of "delineation and separation" with "not-mother."[16] "It is the father who comes to stand for individuation and differentiation—for objective reality itself" (197).

> Thus . . . our earliest experiences incline us to associate the affective and cognitive posture of objectification with masculine, while all processes which involve a blurring of the boundary between subject and object tend to be associated with the feminine (197).

Thus, the scientist, who historically has been male, has like all other men in the Freudian view had to reject the feminine in order to establish his maculine identity. This has entailed a rejection of non-binary thinking and an endorsement of either-or objectivity, hallmarks of the Newtonian world view.

In a fascinating article (1981) Azizah al-Hibri has articulated a theory somewhat along the lines of Ruether's explaining male misogyny, which she too sees at the root of patriarchal destructiveness. Al-Hibri hypothesizes that prehistoric men came to envy women's reproductive powers and the magical phenomenon of menstruation ("that females can bleed suddenly and heavily without dying").[17] Men saw these physical processes as a means to immortality that they did not share. "Not only did she constantly recover from her bouts with bleeding, but more significantly, she constantly reproduced herself—she had the key to immortality and he did not" (172). The male thus saw the woman originally as Other but superior, for he was "excluded and cut off from the cycle of ever-regenerating life" (172).

In order to establish his own sense of superiority and to lay out his own avenue to immortality or transcendence, the male, al-Hibri suggests, turned to production. "Production became an imitation of reproduction" (174). The male channeled his energy (or sublimated it) into technology, into transforming his world; this gave him a sense of power and enabled him to sense that he was transcending his condition. Like Ruether and other existentialists, al-Hibri sees that the establishment of the transcendental male self meant the domination of an Other, the female and a feminized nature. Following Hegel she suggests that the male could establish his own transcendence, his own mastery only by subduing an Other.

Al-Hibri says that not only must women and other "Others"—"black, red, Jew, Arab, native, etc." (179)—rebel in order that a feminist, humanist revolution be accomplished. But also "the male has to come to terms with his own being"—which means that he must face the fact that his obsessive technological imperialism is rooted in a fear and denial of the feminine, which itself is rooted in a sense of masculine inadequacy.

> Underlying the entirety of this [historical] movement is the male's severe feelings of inadequacy, and hence his need for recognition and affirmation of self-worth. Since the solution to such feelings of inadequacy can never come from the outside, the male is doomed to continue experimenting with different modes of domination until the roots of the problem are finally recognized and faced (181).

The Newtonian or scientific world view discussed in chapter 1 is rooted in the binary masculine psychology of discrete self versus dominated Other. However, developments in twentieth-century science, such as Heisenberg's Principle of Indeterminacy (1927) and Einstein's Special and General Theories of Relativity (1905, 1916), have challenged the validity of the Newtonian paradigm. The new vision of the universe that is emerging is no longer of an Other that operates in predictable, mechanical fashion, but of a contextual network in which every discrete entity is defined relative to its environment and subject to the positional relativity of the observer. Under this perspective black and white, I-it dualism is no longer appropriate. It may be therefore, as Robin Morgan suggests in *The Anatomy of Freedom* (1982), that there is a congruence between the cultural feminist vision and the new physics (see further discussion below).

The emergence of an anti-Newtonian "feminine" modality may also be traced in modern philosophy, particularly in the works of Ludwig Wittgenstein, Simone Weil, and Iris Murdoch. Wittgenstein came to the conclusion in the *Tractatus* (1911) that symbolic forms imposed upon reality are "arbitrary" and tell "*nothing* about the world."[18] In particular he questions the imposition of scientific mathematical "laws" upon reality. Is there not another reality beyond the ken of rational forms, one that resists categorization and abstraction, that is ultimately inarticulable? This is the thesis Wittgenstein develops in the *Tractatus*.

Wittgenstein argues that the scientific world view establishes a series of objective propositions that are true and consistent within themselves, but do not reach beyond their tautological network.

> But the network is *purely* geometrical, and all its properties can be given a priori.
>
> Laws, like the law of causation, etc. treat of the network and not of what the network described (6.35).

In other words, the Newtonian paradigm is an order imposed upon the world that is consistent within itself but does not tell us anything about what lies between the holes of its grid, so to speak.

To attempt to order the world, to see the world through this paradigm is to remain imprisoned, according to Wittgenstein, within an epistemological net that prevents access to other kinds of knowledge, or of beings and reality that do not fit into the Newtonian world scheme. But there is another reality, a subjective reality which one does know and which exists apart from Newtonian or other symbolic forms: the I. "The I, the I is the deeply mysterious!" (5.18.16). For, "the I is not an object" (7.8.16). "I objectively confront every object. But not the I" (11.8.16). The "I" therefore remains a mysterious source of "Thou" knowledge that is not objective or scientific but rather intuitive, mystical.

Wittgenstein argues finally that any sense of meaning must come not from subduing the world intellectually with abstract forms but from turning into that vast, marginal silence that exists beyond the scope of the Newtonian paradigm. For "the world is independent of my will" (6.373). It cannot be subdued and forced to yield meaning, as Francis Bacon advocated. Elsewhere Wittgenstein concluded, "I cannot bend the happenings of the world to my will: I am completely powerless."[19] Yet beyond the world seized by Newtonian physics is another source of meaning: "There is indeed the inexpressible. This shows itself; it is the mystical" (6.522). The celebrated concluding line of the *Tractatus* counsels a philosophy of abnegation, of passive resignation: "of what one cannot speak one must remain silent." (Wovon man nicht sprechen kann, darüber müss man schweigen" [7]). If arrogant imposition of one's meaning upon reality is a masculine posture, then Wittgenstein's closing wisdom may be seen as feminine.

The moral implications of Wittgenstein's thesis were developed by two women philosophers, Simone Weil and Iris Murdoch. They suggest that people use such conceptual schemes as the Newtonian paradigm to promote their own feelings of significance. Such paradigms enable one to deny the randomness, the incoherence, the contingency of the world, and thereby enable one to deny one's own mortality. Thus, the rationalist hypothesis enabled men to feel "lords of creation" superior by dint of their reason to other nonrational creatures (including women) and other organic life. As we have seen, such false attempts at transcendence have led to the arrogant assumption that only oneself or one's kind—whatever fits into the rationalist paradigm—is real and has a right to exist. All else is relegated to the category of the non-real, of it-ness, of Otherness. What is in that category is therefore subject to the imposition of alien forms by the rationalist "lords."

Unlike Wittgenstein, who tended to see such psychic mechanisms as inherent in human epistemology, Weil and (to a greater extent) Murdoch believed that in the social world people tend to resort to the use of commonplace paradigms (or stereotypes) out of moral weakness.[20] Murdoch proposes that the way out of this epistemological trap, this conceptual net, is by a moral effort—a redirection of the will and attention: to *see* what is other than oneself. Such a redirection can lead to a moral knowledge of the Other, and of the real and the good. Rosemary Ruether similarly calls for a renewed "ecological consciousness" (*New Woman,* 83), an ability to enter into reciprocity with the Other—to acknowledge the validity, the reality, the "Thouness" of the Other's being (194–95).

Murdoch's first novel, *Under the Net* (1954), illustrates how this may occur. Jake, the protagonist, is a good example of a person who has fallen into the habit of projecting his own order, his own conceptual ideas, upon an alien world. In particular, he attempts to impose various self-serving paradigms upon his would-be girl-friend, Anna. Anna herself has, by contrast, developed a philosophy of silence. (Murdoch consciously modeled Anna in this respect upon Wittgenstein.) She seems to feel that at this stage in our moral development it is only through silence (only by "knowing the void" in Weil's term) that we can begin to see the world as it *really* is and each other as we *really* are. Only in this way can we overcome the tendency to impose self-justifying theories on the world and on others, can we come to accept and receive knowledge of reality, the mystery and the diversity of worlds beyond the self. At the end of the novel Jake has made some progress to this end. "It seemed," he reflected, "as if, for the first time, Anna really existed now as a separate being, and not as part of myself."[21]

In numerous books and articles, Murdoch further developed the view that it is through a redirection of the attention and a reverential regard for the existence of worlds and persons who may be different from oneself that the destructive impositions of false orders may be halted.

> The direction of attention . . . [must be] away from self which reduces all to a false unity, toward the great surprising variety of the world, and the ability to so direct attention is love.[22]

> The more the separateness and differentness of other people is realized, and the fact seen that another . . . has needs and wishes as demanding as one's own, the harder it becomes to treat a person as a thing (66).

Murdoch labels love the reverential attention to what is not oneself, to what is other to one's order. "Love is the extremely difficult realisation that something other than oneself is real. Love, and so art and morals, is the discovery of reality."[23] The implications of Murdoch's theory are that the I-it view of Newtonian science must give way to a more comprehensive vision that accepts the "thou-ness" of life beyond the self and accepts the importance and reality of dimensions beyond the rational.

Robin Morgan proposes in *The Anatomy of Freedom* that the cultural feminist moral vision is in many ways analogous to the vision of reality offered by the new physics. Feminism, Morgan proposes, is "crucial to the continuation of sentient life on this planet"; it is "the key to our survival and transformation."[24] The reason for this is that women have over the centuries developed an ethic that is appropriate to the world view that is emerging out of the new physics: they see in terms of relationships and in terms of environmental contexts. Moreover, women have been the custodians of humane values for centuries; their primary value is a reverence for life (12, 282–84). This ethic must become the governing morality in the modern world, she believes.

Morgan sees several aspects of the new cosmic vision as especially congruent with a feminine world view: the principle of indeterminancy has dissolved the Newtonian view of discrete objects operating according to abstract laws; quantum theory has posited a contextual, discontinuous image of subatomic behavior that is affected by the observer; and the theories of relativity have proposed that all reality is bound up in an integrated space-time continuum where no one item may be defined apart from its relationship to others.

Where Newtonian physics posits the world "as constituted of entities which are outside of each other" (185), quantum theory and in particular the principle of indeterminancy "has . . . demolished the classical concepts of solid objects and of strictly deterministic laws of nature" (174). Moreover, "the classical ideal of an objective description of nature is no longer valid," for the observer necessarily affects what is being observed (174).[25] And, as physicist David Böhm explains, "Entities, such as electrons, can show different properties . . . depending on the environmental context within which they exist and are subject to observation" (190). Under such conditions the old dualism—either-or, I-it, subject-object—are no longer operative: what is needed is a holistic, contextual, both-and approach to reality (310–15). Such is the approach proposed in the cultural feminist moral vision.

It is fitting that we conclude this chapter with Virginia Woolf's *Three Guineas* (1938), for it was in that great work that she posed feminism as most fundamentally a struggle against patriarchal fascism. Anticipating the direction taken by contemporary cultural feminists, Woolf saw women as custodians of a feminine value system, one that is inherently antifascist. Like them, too, Woolf saw fascism as a sexism that depends upon the derogation of women.

Three Guineas is structured as a response to three letters Woolf has received: one from a man who has suggested that she help to prevent war by contributing to his pacifist society; the second from a woman soliciting funds for the rebuilding of a women's college; the third requesting money for a society dedicated to helping women to enter the professions. Woolf decides that the three causes are interrelated—all might help to prevent war and to eradicate fascism—so she will give a guinea to each but only on condition. The college must teach a women's ethic; the women entering the professions must remain true to that ethic, and, while she will support a pacifist organization, she will not join. Rather, she urges that women must form their own feminist pacifist Outsiders' Society.

The book centers upon the question of how women may help to prevent war. In building her case Woolf assumes a fundamental differentness between men and women, their psychologies, culture, and value systems.

First, she notes, women have never made war. "Scarcely a human being in the course of history has fallen to a woman's rifle; the vast majority of birds and beasts have been killed by you, not us."[26]

Second, Woolf develops the thesis that women see the world "through different eyes" (18). Women are "a different sex"; they have "a different tradition, a different education, and . . . different values" (113). Women's differentness stems from their condition of being outsiders; their perspective on patriarchal ways is necessarily subversive and unrespectful. It enables women to ask fundamental questions about the institutions of power; such questions as "Where in short is it leading us, the procession of the sons of educated men?" (63).

Women's distance from the trappings of power enables them to see that those trappings—military parade dress, for example—contribute to the psychology of the heroic male ego that is at the heart of militarism and fascism. "Obviously the connection between dress and war is not far to seek; your finest clothes are those that you wear as soldiers" (21).

As she pointed out in an earlier treatise, *A Room of One's Own* (1929), such male posturing, inherent in fascism, is based upon the denigration of women. Without having women to look down on, against which to measure its heroic stature, the male ego would shrink proportionately. For "women have served all these centuries as looking-glasses possessing the magic and delicious power of reflecting the figure of man at twice its natural size. . . . That is why Napoleon and Mussolini both insist so emphatically upon the inferiority of women, for if they were not inferior, they would cease to enlarge."[27]

In *Three Guineas* Woolf compares dictatorial statements by a contemporary British bureaucrat and those by Adolf Hitler to show that fascist sexist attitudes toward women are pervasive (53). Feminism, she urges, has always been a fight against tyranny. The nineteenth-century feminists "were fighting the tyranny of the patriarchal state" just as today one fights against "the tyranny of the Fascist state" (102).

The first means of preventing war, that is, of combating fascism, that Woolf proposes is the construction of a college that teaches the tenets of a women's value system. Unlike the great patriarchal universities that contribute to war, both by colluding in the construction of weapons and by encouraging ruthlessly competitive attitudes in students, this college will do no war-related research and will promulgate a humanistic ethic based upon a feminine epistemology.

> The poor college must teach only the arts that can be taught cheaply and practised by poor people; such as medicine, mathematics, music, painting and literature. It should teach the arts of human intercourse; the art of understanding other people's lives and minds, and the little arts of talk, of dress, of cookery that are allied with them. The aim of the new college . . . should be not to segregate and specialize, but to combine. It

> should explore the ways in which mind and body can be made to co-operate; discover what new combinations make good wholes in human life.[28]

The second direction must be to have women enter positions of power, but these women must remain faithful to the tenets of a feminine value system, so that the institutions will themselves be changed accordingly. That value system Woolf sees as deriving from what she calls "the four great teachers of the daughters of educated men—poverty, chastity, derision and freedom from unreal loyalties" (79). (One could argue that nearly all women are subject to these "teachers," not just the educated class.)

By remaining faithful to the experiences learned from these four great teachers one should live according to the following ethic. Poverty teaches that one must not amass riches, as one becomes successful, but hold just enough to live independently and to fully develop one's body and one's mind. "But no more" (80). Chastity teaches that "you must refuse to sell your brain for the sake of money" (80), or commit what Woolf calls "adultery of the brain" (93). Derision urges, "you must refuse all methods of advertising merit and hold that ridicule, obscurity and censure are preferable, for psychological reasons, to fame and praise. Directly badges, orders, or degrees are offered you, fling them back in the giver's face" (80). Freedom from unreal loyalties means refusing to support what are ultimately fascist causes—nationalism, racial chauvinism, etc. (80). Such is Woolf's subversive feminist ethic: it is dedicated to the destruction of fascist psychology.

Finally, Woolf proposes the establishment of an Outsiders' Society or separatist cultural institutions that will preserve a subversive women's culture and will encourage the development of a women's ethic that is holistic, antimilitaristic, and life affirming. Such an ethic, Woolf and other cultural feminists urge, must become the basis for a new public morality, for the constitution of El Mundo Zurdo, a left-handed world. The urgency of the case is argued in this poignant meditation by a native American woman, Chrystos:

> I will be sad to see the trees & birds on fire   Surely they are innocent as none of us has been
>
> With their songs, they know the sacred   I am in a circle with that soft, enduring word
>
> In it is the wisdom of all peoples   Without a deep, deep understanding of the sacredness of life, the fragility of each breath, we are lost   The holocaust has already occurred   What follows is only the burning brush   How my heart aches & cries to write these words   I am not as calmly indifferent as I sound
>
> I will be screaming no no no more destruction in that last blinding light[29]

8 *Into the Twenty-first Century*

How sisterhood became powerful while women were powerless will take its place among the classic alchemies of political history. How did *they do that? students will be encouraged to wonder.*
Catharine A. MacKinnon, 1987

Resistance to the tyranny of monolithic concepts became the central concern in feminist theory at the end of the twentieth century. Spurred on by the stress on difference in postmodernist and multiculturalist theory, feminist theory has become more specific, paying more attention to the differences among women—particularly those of race, class, ethnic background, and sexuality.

But the fundamental divergence within feminist theory continues to be between those who assert that women form a separate cultural group with its own values and practices and, on the other hand, those who resist this assumption. In the past, the latter were mainly feminists who subscribed to liberal Enlightenment premises, but now they include postmodernists who in the main reject the assertion of any coherent political identity. The former, labeled cultural feminists (see chapters 2 and 7), include those socialist feminists who propose what are now called "standpoint epistemologies" (see chapter 3, p. 102). One theorist has suggested that we label this direction gynocentric feminism; that is, theory which pays attention to the particularities of women's shared experiences. It holds that "women's oppression consists . . . [in] the denial and devaluation of specifically feminine virtues and activities by an overly instrumentalized and authoritarian masculine culture."[1] Most of the feminist debates of the 1980s and 1990s can be seen as clashes between liberal humanist theory on the one hand and cultural feminist or gynocentric theory on the other.

A major vein in recent feminist theory has been a continuing refinement of critiques of liberalism from a gynocentric perspective, especially of the constitution, practices, and ideology of modern science, while central contentions in contemporary feminist jurisprudence or legal theory revolve around liberal versus cultural or radical feminist approaches to the law. In my discussion I will concentrate particularly on the antipornography legislation, and the issue of equality versus difference (largely a rehash of the old protectionism debate; see chapter 2, p. 75), with a focus on the maternity-leave issue. Other debates within feminism as well have centered around deviation from a traditional liberal position toward one seen as more reflective of women's experience and practice. The "caring debate" over Carol Gilligan's assertion of an ethic of responsibility versus one based on rights may be seen in this light. And the articulation of the specificities of the oppressions of women of color, of lesbians, of older women, and of the disabled constitute a protest against unitary liberal theory that would ignore those differences.

Probably the most important theoretical development of the 1980s was the impact of poststructuralist, or postmodernist, theories upon feminism. The premises and assertions of poststructuralism will therefore be treated at length below. Finally, probably the most important theoretical movement in the 1990s has been in the area of ecofeminism, or feminist theory concerned with ecology and the connections between male-domination and the contemporary despoliation of the natural world. The chapter will conclude with a discussion of the major elements of ecofeminism.

Several theorists have in recent years developed major and profound critiques of the premises of liberal theory. These include Carole Pateman, Genevieve Lloyd, Susan Bordo, and Iris Young. In a far-reaching discussion of social contract theory, Pateman argues in *The Sexual Contract* (1988), for example, that women were never conceived by liberal theorists as persons or citizens with rights in the public sphere because a tacit sexual contract precedes the so-called social contract by which people consent to being governed. Most Enlightenment theorists, including Locke (see chapter 1, p. 20), relied on social contract theory—the idea that people agree to government, relinquishing their "natural" freedom in exchange for protection from the dangers of the natural state and for various civil rights. But "women are not party to the original contract through which men transform their natural freedom into the security of civil freedom. Women are the subject of the contract. The (sexual) contract is the vehicle through which men transform their natural right over women into the security of civil patriarchal right."[2]

In other words, Pateman contends, in a patriarchy the laws reflect the basic patriarchal principle that males have sexual rights to women; this is the sexual contract. Thus, marriage contracts and the law of coverture (see chapter 1, pp. 19, 22) guaranteed husbands' control over their wives and the latter's subordination. Even today some legal jurisdictions do not accept the concept of marital rape because of sexual contract premises (7).

The legal division between the public and the private spheres, with the latter domain still largely ruled by kinship rather than citizenship rights, means that in many cases women/wives still have a prescribed place within patriarchal law. Pateman argues indeed that "in an exploration of contract and patriarchal right, the fact that women are *women* is more relevant than the differences between them. For example, the social and legal meaning of what it is to be a 'wife' stretches across class and racial differences" (18). By definition, *wife* means "to provide certain services for and at the command of a man (husband)" (128). The parties to the marriage contract cannot legally alter its terms of a "relation of protection and obedience" (165); for example, a husband cannot legally pay a wife for her services.[3] In other words, the marriage contract is not one freely determined by free agents; rather, its terms are prescribed by the state. Not surprisingly, beginning in the nineteenth century several feminists have called for the abolition of marriage as a state-certified institution.[4]

As we shall see, the public–private division and the traditional ascription of women to certain functional roles within the private sphere remain at the heart of current debates in feminist jurisprudence. Since liberal theory focused exclusively on the public sphere and on individual citizens and their rights, feminist critiques of liberalism continue to point up the fundamental contradictions the elision of the private sphere entails. In short, it is becoming clear that traditional liberal theory—upon which American jurisprudence is largely based—simply does not work when you try to add women and stir, for it is based upon prior assumptions about the division between public and private and roles assigned to women in the latter sphere.

Susan Moller Okin, a contemporary liberal feminist, attempts, in *Justice, Gender, and the Family* (1989), to challenge liberal theory from within. She does so by extending liberal John Rawls' theories to women and the domestic sphere. In *A Theory of Justice* (1971) Rawls argued that the principles of justice that should operate in a society may be arrived at through this hypothetical: individuals placed in an "original position" and operating through a "veil of ignorance" (i.e., not knowing what class, race, sex, nationality, etc. they are going to be in life) would establish principles that would be fair to all, regardless of the specifics of their situation, because if one could end up as one of the less well-off, one would want to ensure that in this capacity one were treated fairly.

Okin applies Rawls' theory of justice to the family or domestic sphere, arguing that the same principles of justice that are stipulated for the public sphere should also govern in the home. In other words, labor such as parenting should be equally shared. Currently, Okin writes, "marriage and the family . . . are unjust institutions. They constitute the pivot of a societal system of gender that renders women vulnerable to dependency, exploitation, and abuse."[5] "[W]hat has not been recognized as an equal opportunity problem . . . is the disparity *within* the family, the fact that its gender structure is itself a major obstacle to equality of opportunity" (16). Okin emphasizes that we must "dispense with the traditional labor assumptions about public versus domestic, political versus nonpolitical" if we are to "use Rawls's theory as a tool with which to think about how to achieve justice between the sexes both within the family and in society at large" (109). She also urges attendant social changes in order to ensure "egalitarian families" (184) in which the burden of domestic labor is shared equally: these include flex time and adequate day care (with government subsidies for lower income parents).

In a collection aptly entitled *Feminist Challenges* (1986), edited by Carole Pateman and Elizabeth Gross, several contributors urge that not just liberal political theory but much of Western philosophy is predicated upon the subordination of women. As the editors remark in their introduction,

> recent investigations have [uncovered] how the understanding of "theory" is dependent on an opposition to women and all that is symbolized by the feminine and women's bodies, and why. Traditionally, women's intuition and deficiency in rationality have been presented as the antithesis of the logic, order and reason required of theorists.[6]

Political theory has traditionally concerned itself only with the public sphere, but the theorists fail to "acknowledge that the public sphere gains its meaning and significance only in contrast with, and in opposition to, the private world of particularity, natural subjection, inequality, emotion, love, partiality—and women and femininity" (6). The editors specify the inadequacies of liberal feminist theory:

> Since the seventeenth century, one of the major feminist arguments has been that women possess the same capacities and abilities as men, and, if only educated properly, can do everything that men can do. The argument is admirable, as far as it goes. What it glosses over is that there is a womanly capacity that men do not possess, and thus it implicitly denies that birth, women's bodies and the feminine passions inseparable from their bodies and bodily processes have any political relevance (7).

In other words, "Existing patriarchal theory has no place for women as *women;* at best, women can be incorporated as pale reflections of men" (8). Thus, many "gender-neutral" laws have failed to benefit women because they neglect the contingencies of most women's social situations. The editors urge, finally, that new feminist theory be constructed which begins from a recognition of difference, from an acceptance "that individuals are feminine and masculine, that individuality is not a unitary abstraction but . . . embodied and sexually differentiated" (9).

A similar point is made by Merle Thornton in an article entitled "Sex Equality Is Not Enough." Rather, she suggests we must "explore new societal forms which build on the distinctive gender characteristics of women." "We must," she concludes, "look beyond equality to liberation" (98). Elizabeth Gross calls for a theoretical separatism to develop new theory, "a new *discursive space* . . . where women can write, read and think *as women*" (204)—an idea reminiscent of Margaret Fuller's similar proposal over 150 years ago (see chapter 2, p. 49).

As an illustration of the way in which liberal theoretical conceptions are constructed in masculine terms, Genevieve Lloyd shows how the idea of the citizen is identified with military service, still largely a masculine preserve. War involves the ultimate repression of attachment to local, particular loves—of oneself and one's close connections—upon which the idea of public citizenship is predicated. Service to abstract universals replaces private attachments.

> The masculinity of war is what it is precisely by leaving the feminine behind. It consists in the capacity to rise above what femaleness symbolically represents: attachment to private concerns, to "mere life." In leaving all that behind, the soldier becomes a real man, but he also emerges into the glories of selfhood, citizenship and truly ethical, universal concerns. Womankind is constructed so as to be what has to be transcended to be a citizen (75).[7]

In her book *The Man of Reason* (1984) Lloyd shows how much of Western philosophy, particularly its rationalist ideals, calls for "transcendence" of realms of experience deemed feminine (pejoratively). A similar "flight from the feminine" is identified in Cartesian thought by Susan Bordo.[8]

In the same vein, Iris Young notes the identification of public citizenship with the ethical ideal of impartial rationality or normative reason. The public/private division "corresponds to an opposition between reason, on the one hand, and the body, affectivity and desire on the other."[9] Thus, public discourse requires the exclusion of femininity and women; it also means that "since man as citizen expresses the universal and impartial point of view of reason . . . someone has to care for his particular desires and feelings" (59). That someone is usually a woman.

In a critique that recalls an earlier, more extended analysis of Enlightenment thinking, Max Horkheimer and Theodor W. Adorno's *Dialectic of Enlightenment* (1944)[10]—a work of the Frankfurt School of Marxism—Young notes that its requirements of impartiality and universality enforce a "logic of identity" (Adorno's term) that eliminates and denies differences and particularities (61). Instead, we need a new conception of "public and private that does not correlate with an opposition between reason and affectivity and desire, or universal and particular," toward what she calls "a heterogeneous public life." (73)[11]

Kathy Ferguson recognizes that the modern social form which the Enlightenment "logic of identity" has taken is bureaucracy. In *The Feminist Case against Bureaucracy* (1984) Ferguson argues, following French theorist Michel Foucault, that bureaucracy, the principal modern social organization of public space, is a totalitarian system. From educational institutions to hospitals to prisons to the military, bureaucracy relies upon disciplinary assumptions that force clients into regimented slots. "Seen in the light of the ubiquity and intensity of their control mechanisms, bureaucracies are much like explicitly authoritarian political systems. They share a common goal of regimentation and rationalized manipulation of human life for purposes of rendering it predictable and directing it toward behavior that supports, or at least fails actively to challenge, the established authority structures."[12] Women and other marginalized groups, she argues, "are less embedded in the linguistic and institutional structures of bureaucratic society" and therefore less indoctrinated in its practices. Such groups have "subjugated knowledges" (Foucault's term) that can prove subversive (23);[13] thus Ferguson develops a "standpoint" theory to critique what is probably the most pervasive modern form of dominance: bureaucracy.

Like other radical critics of liberal thinking, Ferguson argues that "theories of legal equality and contract-based rights . . . mask the coercive dimensions of administrative [bureaucratic] society, [what Foucault calls] the 'closely linked grid of disciplinary coercions' that enforce inequality, normalcy, and control" (38).[14] It is not surprising, Ferguson notes, following Foucault, that "prisons resemble factories, schools, barracks, hospitals, which all resemble prisons" (40).[15] These "service bureaucracies," which dominate the public sphere, "operate on the basis of rules, which [purport to be] neutral, objective, and scientific, while clients are seen as operating on the basis of values, which are personal, subjective, and biased" (137). Thus, the voices of the subject-clients are twisted to conform to the dominant normative discipline; whether it be in the university or the clinic, their voices are simply not heard or are dismissed as deviant. In this way, the monolithic discourses of such Enlightenment epistemologies as modern science and medicine are seen as totalitarian forms of dominance and control over women and their deviant "feminine" views. Ferguson joins Foucault in calling for *"an insurrection of subjugated knowledges"* (155), leading toward the construction of nonbureaucratic, nondominative forms of social arrangement.[16]

Feminist critiques of science have proliferated in recent years. Criticisms have ranged from the low numbers of women in the field to its collusion with military-industrialism. Some have targeted its dualist objectifying epistemology, which they see as inherently derogating the physical, natural world—the world of the body, expressing especial concern about developments in biotechnology and genetic engineering. Others have criticized its rejection of traditional folk healing methodologies and craft-based epistemologies. And all have rejected the sexist and racist distortions evident in much scientific practice, such as formulation of hypotheses, methods, observation, and interpretation of results, as well as in the theoretical fallacies of much research in sex differences and sociobiology.[17]

In a useful overview of the issues, *The Science Question in Feminism* (1986), Sandra Harding suggests that feminist critiques generally fall into three theoretical categories: empiricist, standpoint, and postmodernist.[18] The empiricist position rests on liberal feminist premises; it holds that the problems that science poses for a feminist are a result of faulty practice or "bad science." Evidence is not properly observed, or is not accurately interpreted; if sexist and racist biases were removed, a truly objective science would emerge.

The standpoint theories question more deeply the validity of the mathematizing and objectifying epistemology of science. They suggest that a holistic epistemology—one that does not reify the material world as *other*—would create a less destructive, less elitist, and more humane body of scientific knowledge. As standpoint theorists, these critics claim that women's traditional labor, which inherently involves respectful and caring interaction with the physical world on a daily basis (women's domestic practices, for example), provides a foundation for an epistemology that is less dominative and more interactive.

Hilary Rose, a leading standpoint critic of science, argues, for example, that "a feminist epistemology derived from women's [caring] labour . . . represent[s] a more complete materialism, a truer knowledge. It transcends dichotomies, insists on the scientific validity of the subjective, on the need to unite cognitive and affective domains; it emphasizes holism, harmony, and complexity rather than reductionism, domination and linearity."[19] In a somewhat parallel gesture Ruth Berman returns to a Marxist concept of dialectical materialism as her model for a new dialogical, interactive scientific epistemology. Like many other feminist critics of science, Berman sees the work of Nobel Prize–winning biologist Barbara McClintock as exemplary (see chapter 7, p. 187).[20]

The postmodernist critics of science are resistant to its unitary claims, reflecting their fear that any generalizing theory necessarily represses or ignores contradictory evidence. In this vein Jane Flax, speaking as a postmodernist, muses: "perhaps reality can have 'a' structure only from the falsely universalizing perspective of the dominant group."[21] Sandra Harding makes a similar point when she notes, "it is the scientific subject's voice that speaks with general and abstract authority; the objects of inquiry 'speak' only in response to what scientists ask them, and they speak in the particular voice of their historically specific conditions and locations."[22] All feminist critics of science would agree, I think, that this is the underlying problem science presents for a feminist. Postmodernists, however, turn their criticism to feminist theories, as well. As Flax remarks, "within feminist theory a search for a defining theme of the whole or a feminist viewpoint may require the suppression of the important and discomforting voices of persons with experiences unlike our own. The suppression of these voices seems to be a necessary condition for the (apparent) authority, coherence, and universality of our own."[23] While postmodernist proposals for alternative epistemologies are somewhat incoherent, generally their idea is that our "dream" should "not be of a common language [the title of Adrienne Rich's 1978 collection[24]], but of a powerful infidel heteroglossia," as put by Donna Haraway, a major postmodernist critic.[25] (Further discussion of postmodernism will be found later in this chapter.)

As Catharine MacKinnon proposes, Anglo-American jurisprudence "aspires" to the condition of science: "To the immanent generalization subsuming the emergent particularity, to prediction and control of social regularities and regulations, preferably codified. The formulaic 'tests' of 'doctrine' aspire to mechanism, classification to taxonomy."[26] As with science, the law therefore tends to overlook the substantive particularities of women's situation. Most seriously, its presumption that neutrality and impartiality assure fairness ignores the substantive inequalities that exist by virtue of social, economic, and ideological factors. As MacKinnon remarks, "the problem with neutrality as the definition of principle in constitutional adjudication is that it equates substantive powerlessness with substantive power and calls treating these the same, 'equality.' "[27] In other words, as Simone de Beauvoir pointed out (see chapter 5), standards of the norm reflect men's lives; women and the structure of their lives are seen as deviant by the law as by society at large.

> Men's physiology defines most sports, their health needs largely define insurance coverage, their socially designed biographies defined workplace expectations and successful career patterns, their perspectives and concerns define quality in scholarship, their experiences and obsessions define merit, their military service defines citizenship, their presence defines family, their inability to get along with each other—their wars and rulerships—defines history, their image defines god, and their genitals define sex. These are the standards that are presented as gender neutral.[28]

Most successful legal reforms of the past several years have, as Robin West points out, "been won by characterizing women's injuries as analogous to . . . injuries men suffer." Instead, West proposes, in gynocentric fashion, that new legal theory needs to be developed that has its "origin in women's distinctive existential and material shape of being."[29] In order to do this we need to change ideology; "we need to flood the market with our own stories" (65). For example, the law should come to reflect "the importance of love to a well-led public life. . . . We need to show that a community and a judiciary that relies on nurturant, caring, loving, empathic values rather than exclusively on the rule of reason will not melt into a murky quagmire, or sharpen into the dreaded specter of totalitarianism" (65). "We need to show that community, nurturance, responsibility, and the ethic of care are values at least as worthy of protection as autonomy, self-reliance, and individualism" (66).

Meanwhile, a number of interesting feminist challenges to constitutional doctrine have been formulated in the past several years. Most of these point up the difficulties involved in attempts to use and/or modify existing legal standards to provide remedies for the injuries and injustices suffered by women. One example of this is the antipornography legislation drafted by MacKinnon and Andrea Dworkin and its relationship to the First Amendment. On December 30, 1983, the Minneapolis City Council declared that pornography was a form of sex discrimination and therefore a violation of Title VII of the 1964 Civil Rights Act. This ordinance was vetoed by the mayor on the grounds that it violated the free speech clause of the First Amendment. A similar ordinance was later passed by the Indianapolis City Council; its constitutionality was challenged in *American Booksellers v. Hudnet.* In 1986 the Supreme Court upheld the Court of Appeals decision that the Indianapolis ordinance violated the First Amendment. That decision conceded that pornography was a form of sex discrimination and did therefore constitute harm to women but that it was superseded by the right to free speech.[30]

A number of interesting issues are raised here. One stems from the theoretical assumption behind the First Amendment that, as MacKinnon points out, speech is already free. Congress is enjoined against abridging what already in theory exists—free speech. However, "this tends to presuppose that whole segments of the population are not systematically silenced *socially,* prior to government action." Pornography, she argues, effectively silences women.[31] Once again, in other words, liberal legal assumptions—in this case, an absolutist interpretation of the First Amendment—ignore the substantive political reality of women's subordination.

One area, however, where feminists have successfully extended women's redress potential under existing laws is sexual harassment. In 1986 the Supreme Court upheld the theory that sexual harassment is a form of sex discrimination under Title VII of the 1964 Civil Rights Act and therefore illegal.[32]

An underlying debate among feminist legal theorists is over whether to identify women as a special group that needs special legal (sometimes called preferential) treatment or whether women can be accorded remedies by applying existing standards fairly and equally. Sometimes this is referred to in shorthand as the "equality versus difference" debate. Two areas where this issue has been central are the self-defense plea for battered women who kill their victimizers, and pregnancy/maternity leave. In the former cases it has been argued that battered women are a special group who behave in particular ways because of their experiences, and that in order to fairly judge their behavior those experiences must be taken into consideration, sometimes seen as exonerating. In other words, "it violates a woman's right to equal treatment to assess her situation in male terms."[33] On the other hand, some feminists fear that institutionalizing "difference" will only ratify the status quo or indeed intensify existing differences; moreover, while the self-defense plea may save an individual woman from prison, it does little to stop wife abuse.[34]

The pregnancy leave issue poses the following question for feminists: "which rule better serves the goals of equality and freedom for women: one that requires employers to provide for pregnancy and maternity leaves or one that requires employers to provide the same treatment for women and men, pregnant and nonpregnant employees?"[35] In 1987, in *California Savings and Loan v. Guerra,* the Supreme Court held constitutional a California law that requires employers to grant up to four months unpaid leave to women "disabled" by pregnancy and childbirth, even if similar leaves are not granted for other disabilities. Pregnant women are therefore singled out as a special group for preferential treatment.

In arguing the majority opinion, Thurgood Marshall denied that the California law was comparable to protective labor legislation (see chapter 2), stating rather that it promoted "equal employment opportunity" because it "allows women as well as men, to have families without losing their jobs."[36] The California law was thus held to be in compliance with a 1978 federal act that forbade discrimination against pregnant women, seeing it as a form of sex discrimination.

In short, while feminists have criticized the terms of the decision (NOW as well as the ACLU opposed preferential treatment, arguing that all disabled employees should be treated equally[37]), it addresses a fundamental problem created by a difference between men and women, that only women get pregnant. How then to accommodate this fact without on the one hand harming women in their pursuit of equal job opportunities (by denying them pregnancy leaves) but on the other hand institutionalizing preferential treatment, which historically has stigmatized women as the "weaker" sex, requiring paternalistic accommodation, thus contributing to the ideological construction of women as inferior?[38]

The "equality versus difference" approaches clashed most dramatically in the *EEOC v. Sears* case (1979), a sex discrimination suit in which feminist lawyers were engaged by both sides. Sears argued that " 'fundamental differences'—the result of culture or long-standing patterns of socialization—led to women's presumed lack of interest in commission sales jobs."[39] EEOC argued that Sears' hiring practices, which, according to the statistics, favored men, were discriminatory. The presiding judge ruled in Sears' favor, agreeing that some sort of "natural" preference expressed by women explained why there were more men in certain jobs, that Sears itself had not discriminated. The problem here, once again, is that the social context is ignored: If women do in fact choose certain (lower-paying) jobs, why? In other words, if women are ideologically prepared for subordination, equal opportunities are meaningless. Moreover, even if women are not so prepared, their prescribed labor of pregnancy, childbirth, and child care, as seen above, necessitates differential treatment if they are to be able to proceed in the workplace on equal terms.

There is a way out of this dilemma, it seems, and that is to integrate what it means to be female into what it means to be human. In other words, if women get pregnant, then people get pregnant, and for the law to treat all people equally it must provide for the fact that pregnancy is a human experience. Humans have children; therefore, the law must accommodate itself to the fact that humans have to care for them. Indeed, as West and others have pointed out, the law and society in general have to integrate into the notion of the public sphere the vast range of caring labor that women perform (usually unpaid) in private.[40] As MacKinnon argues, "To one-sidedly measure one group's standards against a standard set by the other incarnates partial standards. The moment when one's particular qualities become part of the standard by which humanity is measured is a millennial moment."[41]

The idea that women are inclined toward an ethic of caring was first developed by Carol Gilligan in her influential *In a Different Voice* (1982). Since then a number of works have followed in this vein, including *Caring* (1984) by Nel Noddings, *Women's Ways of Knowing* (1987) by Mary Belenky et al., and *Maternal Thinking* (1989) by Sara Ruddick.[42] Criticism, refinement, and application of the Gilligan hypothesis has become a major area of feminist theory. (Indeed, the Robin West critique above of American jurisprudence is explicitly based on Gilligan's theory.) A useful survey of developments in this field may be found in the introduction to *Women and Moral Theory* (1987), a collection of essays that refine and critique aspects of Gilligan's theory.[43]

The caring debate (primarily between Gilligan and her supporters and Lawrence Kohlberg) is, once again, between the liberal "justice tradition" with its emphasis on autonomous individuals and a rights-based ethic that is neutral and universalizable, and, on the other hand, what Caroline Whitbeck calls a feminist relational ontology, in which the individual is viewed in contextual relationship and ethics are construed in terms of relationship responsibilities.[44] According to this view, the ethical decision made or seen in a particular context may not be universalizable but contingent to that context.

The justice tradition is embedded in social contract theory and thus relationships are construed largely in terms of contractual theory.[45] But, as Carole Pateman has pointed out (in terms that are congruent with Catharine MacKinnon's critique of liberalism's elision of substantive political inequalities), "the modern contract . . . typically takes the form of the exchange of obedience for protection" (31); it thus effects social relationships of subordination while pretending to ensure equal treatment based on the neutral abstraction of individual rights (7, 58). Once again, the substantive differences among people are ignored; it is assumed that all people are reasonable, educated, white, and male.

Seyla Benhabib calls this fictional figure the "generalized other" (seen in Rawls' theory, noted above): "the standpoint of the generalized other requires us to view each and every individual as a rational being entitled to the same rights and duties we want to ascribe to ourselves. In assuming this standpoint, we abstract from the individuality and concrete identity of the other."[46] "The standpoint of the concrete other, by contrast, requires us to view each . . . [person] as an individual with a concrete history, identity, and affective-emotional constitution" (164). The narrative context—the individual's life story—is considered a relevant ethical factor. An awareness of the moral identity of the "concrete other" engenders a caring ethic rooted in a relational sense of responsibility.[47]

In a significant article, Gilligan contextualizes her own theory by analyzing Susan Glaspell's celebrated story "A Jury of Her Peers" (1917).[48] In it, two women understand the personal history of emotional abuse that has motivated a neighbor woman to kill her husband; their piecing together of the contextual details of the event enables them to apply a standard of fairness that could not operate if universalizable, "neutral" ethical standards were invoked. Gilligan argues, as well, that the real crime here was "detachment"; that is, the woman's abandonment by kin and community. The women adjudge themselves guilty of a failure of relational responsibility—in not caring for the woman earlier, in not recognizing the desperate emotional isolation she was enduring. By thus focusing on the narrative context of the issue, the women make an ethical decision (to exonerate the woman) that would not be possible under absolute principles of justice (*all* murder is wrong).

In other words, a caring ethic requires an awareness of contingencies of a situation. Power differentials—differences rooted in class, race, sexuality, and ethnicity—as well as personal histories are not ignored, or silenced. Rather they are factored into the ethical/political decision-making process and given appropriate weight. Understandably, critics argue that such a situationist ethic could degenerate into anarchy, with no ethical standards possible, or into concern about only one's immediate community and disregard for larger social evils; or it could end up revalidating prejudicial preferences according to gender, race, class, and so forth.[49] Further refinement of this theory is needed, but it is emerging as such a major alternative to the liberal political, ethical tradition that one senses the makings of a major paradigm shift.

Theories about women's difference have in the past often relied upon versions of Freudian theory, especially that of the object relations school (see chapter 4). In recent years, however, socialist feminists, developing a vein of Marxist theory, have looked to women's traditional labor or praxis as a basis for what they see as a different epistemology in women. The principal initiator of this so-called standpoint theory was Nancy Hartsock (see chapter 3, pp. 102–3). We have already noted above how standpoint theories have been used to critique modern science. Dorothy Smith has effectively used standpoint theory to critique the social sciences.[50]

The initiator of this vein of thought in Marxism was Hungarian theorist Georg Lukács. (See his *History and Class Consciousness: Studies in Marxist Dialectics* [1922; Cambridge: MIT Press, 1971], especially the section "Reification and the Consciousness of the Proletariat.") Lukács, of course, focuses on the proletariat as the oppressed group that evinces a privileged or standpoint epistemology. This is, in Lukács' view, largely because of its commodification in the production process (167–68); however, implicit in this idea is that the memory or ideal of craft-based, use-value production is at the root of the proletariat's critical consciousness.

It is the latter vein that feminist standpoint theorists have pursued; however, it is apparent that women are objectified or commodified in specifically sexual ways—a phenomenon that transcends historical modes of production—in which the proletariat is not. This may also contribute to the development of a critical awareness. Feminists in the existentialist tradition have analyzed this aspect of women's oppression (see chapter 5) which dovetails with Marxist theories of alienation/reification.

While one of the criticisms of standpoint theory is that it "essentializes" particular groups, the real problem, in my opinion, remains that of whether a revolutionary vanguard—feminists—is necessary to identify the standpoint epistemology or whether women as a group "automatically" express it. Since it is apparent that the latter is not the case, either some sort of consciousness-raising process is necessary or a feminist leadership must encourage women as a class toward a critical awakening.[51] Hartsock is aware of this issue (see chapter 3, pp. 98–99); however, today feminist theorists are using standpoint theory, more on the grounds that women's standpoint is potentially rather than actually subversive, as a means of critiquing and changing ideology. This is a different tactic than that seen in Lukács and traditional Marxism. (For an interesting discussion of the feminist appropriation of Lukács' standpoint theory, see Fredric Jameson, "History and Class Consciousness as an Unfinished Project" [1988]).[52]

On the other hand, for feminism to be successful as a mass political movement, it is important that large numbers of women come to see their standpoint as critical, as subversive. That "awakening" process is described by Linda Alcoff as follows: "When women become feminists the crucial thing that has occurred is . . . that they have come to view . . . facts from a different position, from their own position as subjects. When colonial subjects begin to be critical of the formerly imitative attitude they had toward the colonists, what is happening is that they begin to identify with the colonized rather than the colonizer."[53]

In view of recent confusions on the issue of identity (see further discussion below), it seems important to stress at this point that the standpoint is a feminist construction developed as a political analysis. A distinction needs to be made between a natural (or deep social) identity, such as gender and race, which one is "thrown into" (to use Heidegger's phrase), and political identities such as feminism. One cannot choose one's gender (of course, sex-change surgery is a possibility, but generally people remain the gender they were born), but one can choose how to interpret it and how to act upon it.

Feminism is a political interpretation of the condition of being a woman and it urges the recognition of that condition as the basis for political identity.[54]

Unlike traditional Marxist analysis, some feminist theorizing has attempted to integrate the emotional as one of the components of a standpoint epistemology. Hilary Rose, for example, adds "heart" to "hand" and "brain" as factors to be integrated in a holistic science—the "heart" representing caring labor.[55] Alison Jaggar suggests that the emotional responses of oppressed people, especially women, help to constitute the "epistemological privilege" accorded the oppressed in standpoint theory.[56] And, in *Eros and Power* (1986), Haunani-Kay Trask, redeploying Herbert Marcuse's theorizing about the erotic (see chapter 4, pp. 111–12), suggests that "women's relationship to the sphere of social reproduction gives rise to privileged access to the memory of instinctual gratification. This access, in turn, fosters a critical consciousness . . . of . . . patriarchy . . . [as] a dominating, repressive civilization."[57] In other words, women's traditional reproductive (in the Marxist sense) labor keeps them in closer touch with the sensual, the erotic. Women "are less subjugated by the performance principle, closer to the sources of pleasure" (91). Trask thus sees women's potentially subversive standpoint as deriving from their connection to eros, which in turn derives from their traditional praxis: "the material grounding and epistemological source of the feminist Eros are found in women's social practice as caretakers" (174).

In "The Social Construction of Black Feminist Thought" Patricia Hill Collins argues that African-American women "have a self-defined standpoint on their own oppression."[58] And black feminist theory, she asserts, must be anchored in this standpoint, "an Afrocentric feminist epistemology," which itself is rooted in the real material conditions of black women's lives (770). "The unpaid and paid work that Black women perform, the types of communities in which they live, and the kinds of relationships they have . . . suggest that African-American women, as a group, experience a different world than those who are not Black and female . . . [and] these experiences stimulate a distinctive Black feminist consciousness concerning that material reality" (747–48). Similarly, in *Lesbian Ethics* (1988) Sarah Hoagland argues in effect that lesbians have a distinctive standpoint.[59]

In his article on standpoint theory Fredric Jameson suggests that there may be multiple standpoints, reflecting the culture and tradition of each particular oppressed group. For example, he discusses the contours of a Jewish standpoint. Unlike classical Marxist, Lukácsian standpoint theory, future theorizing in this vein should, according to Jameson, acknowledge "that each form of privation [produces] its own specific view from below, and its own specific and distinctive truth claim" (71). Although such diversification risks dispersion into ineffective pluralism, there are undoubtedly considerable overlaps among these standpoints (Collins points out the commonalities between Afrocentric and feminist standpoints [756–57]), and such groups are united by the fact that they are marginalized and subordinated by the same dominant epistemology.[60]

While poststructuralism, or postmodernism, has been developing for decades as an intellectual movement in Europe (its principal origins go back to Heidegger and Nietzsche), its impact in the United States was felt mainly in the late 1970s and 1980s.[61] We discussed one vein of poststructuralism in chapter 4—Jacques Derrida's "deconstruction" of "phallogocentrism"—in connection with recent French feminism (see p. 127).

Like feminism, postmodernism is both a manifestation of and a contributor to what Jürgen Habermas has called the "legitimation crisis" in Western culture.[62] It challenges what Jean-François Lyotard identifies as the "grands récits," the "grand narratives of legitimation," or the "metanarratives" of Western civilization.[63] These include particularly the Enlightenment faith in an historically progressive science. Such narratives, as Craig Owens points out, are really "narratives of mastery, of man seeking his telos in the conquest of nature." They legitimize "Western man's self-appointed mission of transforming the entire planet in his own image."[64] Insofar as postmodernism has worked to destabilize these master narratives, it would seem an ally of feminist interests.

Jane Flax effectively makes this case in her "Postmodernism and Gender Relations in Feminist Theory" (1987)—along with Donna Haraway's "Manifesto for Cyborgs" (1985) (see above, p. 206), the most important statements of feminist postmodernism. Flax argues that feminists have common cause with postmodernists in casting "radical doubt" upon such central tenets of Enlightenment theory as the belief in a "stable, coherent self" anchored in rationality; faith in reason and science as transcendental methodologies that yield objective and universal truths; and the idea of language as "transparent" and representative. "[F]eminists," she notes, "like other postmodernists, have begun to suspect that all such transcendental claims reflect and reify the experience of a few persons—mostly white, Western males."[65]

In addition to attacking metanarratives, postmodernists, particularly Foucault, critique and resist the grand institutions of Western civilization that are also seen as reifying disciplinary practices which are dominative. As noted (see p. 204), Foucault sees a homology between modern bureaucratic institutions such as schools, which are usually considered liberatory, and prisons and the military: all rely on regimentational subordination.

As opposed to these metanarratives and grand institutions, which are considered, in effect, new forms of tyranny, postmodernists favor shifting the epistemological ground for such theories and institutions so as to allow local, ad hoc, and historically contextual truths and practices to emerge or be heard.[66] Such truths—repressed and/or marginalized by metanarratives—provide new, if fragmentary, bases for legitimation. "[I]n the postmodern ear legitimation becomes plural, local, and immanent" (23). Theory will "look more like a tapestry composed of threads of many different hues than one woven in a single color" (35).

While such directions would seem to favor the empowerment of women and other dispossessed, and therefore be congruent with feminist interests, there is much that is problematic in postmodernism from a feminist point of view. The first and perhaps most important difficulty is that postmodernists have attacked feminist theory itself as a metanarrative. In particular, the radical feminism of Shulamith Firestone, Mary Daly, Adrienne Rich, and Catharine MacKinnon (whose theories, it must be said, differ considerably among themselves), the feminist-Freudian theory of Nancy Chodorow, Carol Gilligan's theories, and standpoint theory have all been critiqued as "essentialist" and "monocausal."[67]

In short, postmodernism rejects all theory and all generalization indiscriminately. The reductio ad absurdum, therefore, of the postmodernist critique is an extreme nominalism: only individual particulars have legitimacy. Any theory or generic statement is suspect and rejected, because it elides particular differences.

There are two major problems with this premise. One is that postmodernism offers no way to choose among theories; all are equally "essentialist" and "monocausal" and therefore equally suspect. As a political theory, therefore, it offers only a relativist pluralism. Second, it blocks the possibility of generic political identity. Since political assertion depends upon the cohesion of a group identity, such as women, and upon the articulation of an agenda of needs by that group, this aspect of postmodernism seems most problematic from a feminist point of view because it negates the possibility of political action.

As Terry Eagleton notes, poststructuralism is really a kind of "cultic pluralism," a "liberalism without the subject." It ensures that "political quietism and compromise are preserved . . . by a dispersal of the subject so radical as to render it impotent as any kind of agent at all, least of all a revolutionary one."[68] Mary E. Hawkesworth warns, "Should postmodernism's seductive text gain ascendancy, it will not be an accident that power remains in the hands of the white males who currently possess it. In a world of radical inequality, relativist resignation reinforces the status quo."[69]

Like liberalism, postmodernism fails to recognize that the world is one of "radical inequality," that it is not the same to deconstruct or destabilize the master narratives of Western culture and the feminist theories of, say, Carol Gilligan. The one subtends the world view of the dominant power in society; the other reveals the partial perspective of an oppressed group.

As Sandra Harding remarks,

> the articulation of relativism . . . emerges historically only as an attempt to dissolve challenges to the legitimacy of purportedly universal beliefs and ways of life. It is an objective problem, or a solution to a problem, only from the perspective of the dominating groups. Reality may indeed appear to have many different structures from the perspectives of our different locations in social relations, but some of those appearances are

> ideologies . . . they are not only false and "interested" beliefs but also ones that are used to structure social relations for the rest of us. For subjugated groups, a relativist stance expresses a false consciousness.[70]

Harding recognizes that the political world is not just a free-floating plurality of ideologically neutral perspectives, but rather is politically charged. Some perspectives weigh more than others: some are dominant, some are subordinate. As Catharine MacKinnon remarks, gender distinctions are not simply a matter of a neutral play of differences but rather are embedded within a political hierarchy: the male gender is dominant, the female subordinate.[71]

Some feminists find it suspicious that postmodernism was embraced in the most prestigious academic institutions at the very moment when feminism was reaching the high tide of its second wave, noting that it has served to destabilize and disorient the political coherence of the movement. Elizabeth Gross suggests that "the call for the extermination of all possibility of group resistance to oppression [is] a significant countermove at precisely the first moment in Western history when women as an (international) group are agitating for the right to construct an identity for and self-representations of women."[72]

In a powerful refutation of central tenets of feminist postmodernism, Susan Bardo acknowledges that abstract categories such as gender are never neat and are always open to modification by race, class, and other variables; however, she has noted that in a classroom "there are many junctures at which, for example, women of color and white women discover profound *commonalities* in their experience, as well as differences."[73] When carried to an extreme, she points out, the "inflections that modify experiences are endless, and *some* item of difference can always be produced which will shatter any proposed generalizations. . . . What remains is a universe composed entirely of counterexamples" (150–51). In such a postmodernist universe any cultural generalizations about group experience—whether it be that of gender, race, or class—must be rejected.

Like Hawkesworth, Gross, and many other feminists, Bordo sees postmodernism as curiously serving ruling-group interests by preventing the formulation of oppositional consciousness in subordinate groups. "It is no accident," she suggests, "that feminists are questioning the integrity of the notion of 'female reality' just as we begin to get a foothold in those professions which could be most radically transformed by our (historically developed) Otherness. . . . Could feminist gender-skepticism . . . now be operating in the service of the reproduction of white, male knowledge/power?" (151). Barbara Christian goes farther to suggest in "The Race for Theory" (1987) that "some of our most daring and potentially radical critics (and by *our* I mean black, women, Third World) have been influenced, even co-opted, into speaking a language and defining their discussion in terms alien to and opposed to our needs and orientation." Christian says, "the language it creates

. . . mystifies rather than clarifies our condition, making it possible for a few people who know that particular language to control the critical scene."[74] In other words, such critical discourse has become a tool of power rather than of knowledge.

There are signs, however, that the debate between the postmodernist feminists and gynocentric feminists is moderating; indeed, it appears in general that the influence of postmodernism is waning. Postmodernist feminists now acknowledge that we need not "forswear . . . largely historical narratives nor analyses of societal macrostructures" (Fraser and Nicholson, 34). In other words, we need not forswear feminist theory. On the other hand, postmodernists insist that such theory be responsive to historical and contextual specificities, as well as to variations and differences due to class, race, sexuality, and so forth. Feminist theorizing in the past decade has in fact become more sensitive to diversity, thus responding to the critiques offered by postmodernism, as well as by multiculturalism. In this it has undoubtedly been strengthened.

Although this book is principally about U.S. feminism, with the new "global marketplace" it becomes increasingly apparent that U.S. women's lives are implicated in women's lives elsewhere. And while the subject can only be touched upon here, it is by no means an exaggeration to claim that the "new" global economy is being built largely upon the backs of women worldwide. The exploitation of women in developing nations, as well as what Marilyn Waring has called the "universal servitude" of millions of housewives who provide unpaid domestic labor throughout the world generate the capital and profit margin ("surplus value") for international corporations.[75] To the extent that U.S. and European women benefit from the global economy they are participating in the exploitation of their sisters in southern latitudes and Asian countries. Ending the concomitant and escalating international traffic in women and tourist prostitution must remain high on any feminist agenda.[76]

In addition, the complex question of nationalist cultural traditions that are injurious to women must continue to be addressed by feminists worldwide. As Uma Narayan remarks in her comments on the difficulty of relating to "motherlands [that are] spaces where fathers still have most of the privileges and power," reconceptualizations are needed that "may require us to rethink notions of what it is to 'be at home' in a culture, and to redefine notions of cultural loyalty, betrayal, and respect in ways that do not privilege the experiences of men."[77] And to the extent that Western feminism has become identified with the negative aspects of Western capitalism and materialism (in the "Jihad versus McWorld" confrontation), U.S. feminists must work to ensure that it be understood that feminism in its cultural feminist wing includes a strong spiritual component, that socialist feminism offers a critique of capitalism, and that ecofeminism similarly provides a powerful comdemnation of the Western global exploitation of nature and women.

The term *ecofeminism* was coined by French feminist Françoise d'Eaubonne in 1974 (see chapter 4, p. 130). While it implies a merging of ecology and feminist theory, it is largely an outgrowth of radical and cultural feminist theory, as outlined above (see pp. 181–82 and chapter 7), with a more directed focus on ecological matters. Influences from "deep ecology" theory and the Goddess spirituality movement are also evident. In recent years, ecofeminism has extended its focus to include the "global marketplace," considering the linkages between the capitalist exploitation of the natural world in non–Western countries and the global exploitation of women noted above.

Nineteenth-century feminists did not dwell to any extent upon ecological problems (largely because, comparatively speaking, there were none), but many were aware of what today we would call animal rights issues, which is a major concern of one branch of contemporary ecofeminism. Charlotte Perkins Gilman, for example, condemned the use of furs as well as of feathers to decorate women's hats.[78] And other feminists from Wollstonecraft and Fuller to Stanton and Anthony indicated concern about animal welfare and/or interest in vegetarianism.[79] In particular, there was a congruence between feminists and antivivisectionists, who sought an end to laboratory experimentation on living animals—a practice that continues today. In her useful book on the subject, *The Old Brown Dog* (1985), Coral Lansbury suggests that English suffragists, many of whom had been subjected to torturous forced feeding during hunger strikes in prison, identified with vivisected animals through that experience. "Every dog or cat strapped down for the vivisector's knife reminded them of their own condition." "[T]he image of the vivisected dog blurred and became one with the militant suffragette being forced fed in Brixton Prison."[80]

A negative identification between women and animals is a deep theme in Western civilization, extending back at least as far as Aristotle, who excluded both from serious consideration as moral entities. A positive identification of women with nature is a major premise of the current ecofeminist movement. While many earlier feminists resisted this identification (Simone de Beauvoir, for example, urged that we transcend the *en-soi,* the "immanence" of the natural world—see chapter 5, p. 139), contemporary ecofeminists are suggesting that it is such "transcendence" that has legitimated Western exploitation of nature. Rosemary Radford Ruether, for example, has identified "the male ideology of transcendant dualism" as a major source of ecological destructiveness (see pp. 146–49).

In *Beyond Power* (1985), Marilyn French makes domination of nature and animals central to her definition of patriarchy and therefore central to feminist theory:

> [P]atriarchy is an ideology founded on the assumption that man is distinct from the animals and superior to it. The basis for this superiority is man's contact with a higher power/knowledge called god, reason, or

> control. The reason for man's existence is to shed all animal residue and realize fully his "divine" nature, the part that *seems* unlike any part owned by animals—mind, spirit, or control.[81]

Ynestra King, a major ecofeminist theorist, argues that we should "*choose* not to sever the woman nature connection. . . . Rather, we can use it as a vantage point for creating a different kind of culture and politics."[82] King thus invokes standpoint theory, using here as the basis for women's privileged perspective their link with nature. Elsewhere she reiterates this position: the woman-nature connection, she argues, provides a "vantage point of *critical otherness*. The ecology question weights the historic feminist debate in the direction of traditional female values over the overly rationalized combative male way of being in the world."[83]

As a practical matter, some women, especially in the Third World, are positioned with nature because of economic necessity. The surrounding natural world provides them with their livelihood or is essential to their traditional practices. This is the case in the celebrated Chipko movement in India, where organized groups of women blocked development projects that entailed destruction of woodlands; they did this by using Gandhian tactics of nonviolent resistance, hugging the trees in the face of loggers' saws. In a compelling ecofeminist analysis of this movement, Indian ecofeminist Vandana Shiva notes: "The violence of nature, which seems intrinsic to the dominant development model, is also associated with violence to women who depend on nature for drawing sustenance for themselves, their families, their societies." The Chipko women "have challenged the western concept of nature as an object of exploitation and have protected her as Prakriti, the living force that supports life. They have challenged the western concept of economics as production of profits and capital accumulation with their own concept of economics as production of sustenance and needs satisfaction."[84]

Although probably the most influential ecologist in history was a woman, Rachel Carson, a feminist approach to the issue was not really developed until the late 1970s and 1980s. Influential early works include Rosemary Radford Ruether's *New Woman/New Earth* (1975), Susan Griffin's *Woman and Nature* (1978), Carolyn Merchant's *Death of Nature* (1980), articles by Ynestra King, and Mary Daly's *Gyn/Ecology* (1978). Indeed, two recent feminist animal rights books originated under the latter's aegis.[85]

The main tenet of ecofeminist theory is that the domination of women and the domination of nature are integral. As Marti Kheel points out, "for deep ecologists, it is the anthropocentric worldview that is foremost to blame" for our current ecological crisis, whereas "ecofeminists . . . argue that it is the androcentric worldview that deserves primary blame. For ecofeminists, it is not just 'humans' but men and the masculinist worldview that must be dismantled from their privileged place."[86]

Hierarchical, dualistic thinking is the aspect of the "masculine worldview" that ecofeminists have especially targeted. As Karen Warren notes, "such patriarchal value-hierarchical thinking gives rise to a *logic of domination,* i.e., a . . . way of thinking which explains, justifies, and maintains the subordination of an 'inferior' group by a 'superior' group."[87] Thus, new terms have been coined: *naturism,* which means the ideology that legitimates subordination of nature to humans, and *speciesism,* which legitimates the subordination of animals to humans (both are based upon an analogy to sexism and racism).

One of the main theoretical projects of ecofeminism is to construct new ways of thinking about the relationship between humans and nature, including animals, replacing the dualistic, objectifying mode characteristic of Western science (see chapter 1, pp. 44–45). As yet this project is incomplete, but interesting tentative proposals have been advanced. Ruether, for example, in *Sexism and God-Talk* (1983) suggests that human consciousness should not be seen as different from other life-forms but rather as continuous with the "biomorphic" spirit inherent in them.

> Our intelligence is a special, intense form of . . . radial energy, but it is not without continuity with other forms; it is the self-conscious or "thinking dimension" of the radial energy of matter. We must respond to a "thouness" in all beings. This is not romanticism or an anthropocentric animism that sees "dryads in trees," although there is truth in the animist view. . . . We respond not just as "I to it," but as "I to thou," to the spirit, the life energy that lies in every being in its own form of existence.[88]

In *The Sacred Hoop* (1986) Paula Gunn Allen, a Laguna Pueblo-Sioux, suggests that we turn to American Indian traditions for conceptualizations about nature that are different from the alienation and dominance inherent in Western epistemologies. God and the spiritual are seen not as transcendent from life but rather as immanent in all life-forms. All creatures are considered to be deserving of fundamental respect. "When I was small," Allen recalls, "my mother often told me that animals, insects, and plants are to be treated with the kind of respect one customarily accords to high-status adults." Nature, in her culture, is seen "not as blind and mechanical, but as aware and organic." There is a "seamless web" between "human and non-human life."[89] Feminist goddess spirituality also stresses that the sacred is inherent or "immanent in the living world," as Starhawk explains in "Feminist, Earth-based Spirituality and Ecofeminism" (1989), which means that the natural world has an organic aliveness that must be revered.[90]

While, in general, ecofeminists agree on these basic principles, there are some theoretical divergences within the movement. Chief among these is that between animal rights feminists and ecofeminists whose position remains closer to "deep ecology" theory, a radical vein of environmental theory that developed largely from Aldo Leopold's articulation of the "land ethic" in *A Sand County Almanac* (1949).

As opposed to traditional conservationists, who wanted to preserve nature for human use and interests, Leopold argued for a "biotic right," that the earth had a right to exist in and of itself, apart from human interests. Leopold viewed nature as a "biotic community," where the interests in individual creatures, including humans, are subsumed to the survival and integrity of the whole community.[91]

Certain aspects of deep ecology theory have been criticized by feminists, such as an uncritical use of sexist language, and a view of the wilderness as a masculine preserve where men may realize themselves apart from women.[92] But the most serious critique has been framed by animal rights feminists, who part company with deep ecologists on their willingness to subsume the individual in the whole, discounting the suffering of individuals, whether they be humans or animals. (Tom Regan, a leading animal rights theorist has labeled Leopold's ecoholism "environmental fascism."[93])

In "Ecofeminism and Deep Ecology" (1990) Marti Kheel attacks the reverence for hunting in deep ecology theory in which killing of animals is seen as necessary to masculine self-realization. In another article Kheel goes to the heart of deep ecology theory, suggesting that it is not really holistic but rather a new version of hierarchical thinking. "Many holists will protest that theirs is a nonhierarchical paradigm in that everything is viewed as an integral part of an interconnected web. However, holists such as Aldo Leopold . . . clearly indicate that the interconnected web does, indeed, contain its own system of ranking. . . . [I]ndividuals are valued on the basis of the relative contribution to the good of the whole (i.e., the biotic community)."[94] Thus, J. Baird Callicott, a contemporary follower of Leopold, ranks rare, endangered species higher than companion animals, for example, invoking a hierarchical paradigm. On the other hand, feminist animal rights theorists have also criticized the liberal theoretical assumptions of animal rights theorists Tom Regan and Peter Singer on grounds similar to other feminist objections to rights-based theory.[95]

Ecofeminism remains one of the most vital veins of feminist theory and with its new global emphasis seems likely to remain thus in coming years. Meanwhile, it seems appropriate to end this discussion of current feminist theory by citing an ecofeminist manifesto: it serves to characterize the direction in which feminist theory is heading—away from the traditional conceptualizations of liberal, atomistic theory toward a more comprehensive view that recognizes the interrelationships among all living beings, and the right of all to exist.

Moving beyond its model, the Declaration of Independence, beyond even the feminist Declaration of Sentiments, this ecofeminist manifesto is labeled "A Declaration of Interdependence." "When in the course of human events," the preamble begins, "it becomes necessary to create a new bond among peoples of the earth, connecting each to the other, undertaking equal responsibilities under the laws of nature, a decent respect for the welfare of human kind and all life on earth requires us to Declare our Interdependence. We recognize," it concludes, "that humankind has not woven the web of life; we are but one thread within it. Whatever we do to the web, we do to ourselves. Whatever befalls the earth befalls also the family of the earth."[96]

Notes

Chapter 1
Enlightenment Liberal Feminism

1. The Murray article and the Adams Letter are in Alice S. Rossi, ed., *The Feminist Papers* (1973; New York: Bantam, 1974), pp. 18–24 and pp. 10–11, respectively. There were, in addition, a number of pre-eighteenth-century feminist tracts. These included: Christine de Pisan, *l'Epistre au dieu d'amours* (1399), and *l'Epistre sur le roman de la rose* (1400); Jane Anger, *Her Protection for Women* (1589); Marie de Gournay, *l'Egalité des hommes et des femmes* (1604); Anna van Schurman, *De ingenii muliebris ad doctrinam et meliores litteras aptitudine* (1641); Poulain de la Barre, *De l'egalité des deux sexes* (1673); Bathsua Makin, *An Essay to Revive the Ancient Education of Gentlewomen* (1673); Mary Astell, *A Serious Proposal to Ladies for the Advancement of their True and Greatest Interest* (1694). See also Hilda L. Smith, *Reason's Disciples* (Urbana: University of Illinois Press, 1982).

2. Mary Wollstonecraft, *A Vindication of the Rights of Woman* (1792; Baltimore: Penguin, 1975), p. 88. Further references to this edition follow in the text. See also Rossi, *Feminist Papers*, p. 29. On feminism in the French Revolution see Elizabeth Racz, "The Women's Rights Movement in the French Revolution," *Science and Society* 16, no. 2 (Spring 1952): 151–74.

3. On the natural rights premises of the Declaration see Carl L. Becker, *The Declaration of Independence: A Study in the History of Political Ideas* (1922; New York: Random House, 1942), especially chap. 2.

4. Ernst Cassirer, *The Myth of the State* (New Haven: Yale University Press, 1946), pp. 163–75. Further references to this work follow in the text.

5. René Descartes, *Les Passions de l'âme* (1649; Paris: Edition de Geneviève Rodis-Lewis, 1955).

6. Marxists attribute this split to the rise of industrial capitalism. See Eli Zaretsky, *Capitalism, the Family and Personal Life* (New York: Harper, 1976), discussed in chap. 3. See also Lawrence Stone, *The Family, Sex and Marriage in England 1500–1800* (New York: Harper, 1977).

7. Susan Moller Okin, *Women in Western Political Thought* (Princeton: Princeton University Press, 1979), p. 249. Further references follow in the text. While challenged early on by first-wave feminists, the concept of coverture was not officially laid to rest until 1992 when the Supreme Court held in *Planned Parenthood of Southeastern Pennsylvania v. Casey* that "the common-law principle that 'a woman had no legal existence separable from her husband' . . . [is] no longer consistent with our understanding of the family, the individual, or the Constitution" (as cited in Linda Kerber, "A Constitutional Right to Be Treated like American Ladies," in *U. S. History as Women's History: New Feminist Essays,* ed. Linda Kerber, Alice Kessler-Harris, and Kathryn Kish Sklar (Chapel Hill: University of North Carolina Press, 1995), p. 355, n. 56.

8. As cited in Okin, *Women in Western Political Thought,* p. 249.

9. John Locke, *An Essay Concerning the True Original, Extent and End of Civil Government,* in *The English Philosophers from Bacon to Mill,* ed. Edwin A. Burtt (New York: Random House, 1939), p. 405. Further references to this edition follow in the text.

10. See Lorenne M. G. Clark, "Women and Locke: Who Owns the Apples in the Garden of Eden," in *The Sexism of Social and Political Theory,* ed. Lorenne M. G. Clark and Lydia Lange (Toronto: University of Toronto Press, 1979), pp. 33–34.

11. Teresa Brennan and Carole Pateman, " 'Mere Auxiliaries to the Commonwealth': Women and the Origins of Liberalism," *Political Studies* 27, no. 2 (June 1979): 195. Further references to this article follow in the text. See also Susan Moller Okin, *Justice, Gender, and the Family* (New York: Basic, 1989), discussed further in chap. 8.

12. Two standards are used to determine whether laws are in violation of these Fourteenth Amendment guarantees. Legislation is subjected to "the most rigid scrutiny" where fundamental rights are concerned, or where the classification used in the statute is "inherently suspect" (for example, race or national origin). See Okin, *Women in Western Political Thought,* p. 254.

In *Frontiero v. Richardson* (1973) a plurality of the Supreme Court stated that "classifications based upon sex, like classifications based upon race, or national origin are inherently suspect." See Lizbeth Hasse, "Legalizing Gender-Specific Values," in *Women and Moral Theory,* ed. Eva Feder Kittay and Diana T. Meyers (Totowa, N.J.: Rowman & Littlefield, 1987), pp. 284–87, and Okin, *Women in Western Political Thought,* p. 268.

13. William L. O'Neill, "Feminism as a Radical Ideology," in *Dissent, Explorations in the History of American Radicalism,* ed. Alfred F. Young (Dekalb, Ill.: Northern Illinois University Press, 1968), p. 279.

14. Elizabeth Cady Stanton, Susan B. Anthony and Matilda Joslyn Gage, eds. *The History of Woman Suffrage,* 3 vols. (Rochester: Charles Mann, 1881–86), 1:70–73 (emphasis added). The *History* eventually comprised six volumes; further references to vols. 1 and 2 will follow in the text. The Declaration of Sentiments and Seneca Falls Resolutions may also be found in Rossi, *Feminist Papers,* pp. 413–21.

15. The distinction between liberal and radical feminism drawn by Zillah Eisenstein, *The Radical Future of Liberal Feminism* (New York: Longman, 1981), is useful here. Eisenstein states that a radical analysis must see women as a "sex-class" that is subjugated by men. She criticizes Wollstonecraft for having failed to develop this thesis (p. 95), but lauds Stanton who did (p. 162). In this work I use the term "radical feminist" to refer to an analysis that assumes the "sex-class" identity (see chap. 6).

16. Frances Wright, *Course of Popular Lectures* (1834) in Frances Wright D'Arusmont, *Life, Letters and Lectures, 1834/1844* (New York: Arno, 1972), p. 10. Further references to this edition follow in the text.

17. Maria W. Stewart, "What if I Am a Woman?" in *Black Woman in White America,* ed. Gerda Lerner (New York: Pantheon, 1972), p. 564.

18. Sarah M. Grimké, *Letters on the Equality of the Sexes and the Condition of Woman* (1838; New York: Burt Franklin, 1970), p. 3. Further references to this edition follow in the text.

19. See Sydney E. Ahlstrom, *A Religious History of the American People* (New Haven: Yale University Press, 1972), pp. 418–27; 642–44. See also Rossi, *Feminist Papers,* pp. 241–81.

20. See Barbara Welter, "The Cult of True Womanhood: 1820–1860," *American Quarterly* 18, no. 2, pt. 1 (Summer 1966): 151–74.

21. Susan B. Anthony and Ida Husted Harper, *The History of Woman Suffrage,* vol. 4 (Indianapolis: Hollenbeck Press, 1902), p. 189. Further references to this address follow in the text.

22. This conclusion is not included in *The History of Woman Suffrage;* it is taken from a pamphlet issued by Stanton's daughter Harriot Stanton Blatch, as cited in *Feminism,* ed. Miriam Schneir (New York: Vintage, 1972), p. 159.

23. See n. 12 above. For a full discussion see Okin, *Women in Western Political Thought,* pp. 247–73. In *Minor v. Happersett* (1874) the Court said that while women were persons, even citizens, the Constitution does not specify that one of the privileges of citizenship is the right to vote. Thanks to Pam Elam for drawing my attention to this case.

24. For a further discussion of the relationship between the abolition and women's rights movements see Catharine Stimpson, " 'Thy Neighbor's Wife, Thy Neighbor's Servants': Women's Liberation and Black Civil Rights," in *Woman in Sexist Society,* ed. Vivian Gornick and Barbara K. Moran (New York: Basic, 1971), pp. 453–79. For a modern use of the analogy between women's status and that of minority groups, see Helen Mayer Hacker, "Women as a Minority Group" (Indianapolis: Bobbs-Merrill reprint, 1951).

25. Bell Hooks, *Ain't I a Woman* (Boston: South End Press, 1981), p. 4. Further references to this work follow in the text.

26. This passage is usually presented in dialect, which I find demeaning and have therefore changed.

27. Angela Davis, "Reflections on the Black Woman's Role in the Community of Slaves," *Black Scholar* 3, no. 4 (Dec. 1971): 7.

28. See Angela Y. Davis, *Women, Race and Class* (New York: Random, 1981), pp. 70–86; and Adrienne Rich, "Disloyal to Civilization: Feminism, Racism, Gynephobia" (1978) in *On Lies, Secrets, and Silence* (New York: Norton, 1979), pp. 275–310. Also Aileen S. Kraditor, *The Ideas of the Woman Suffrage Movement 1890–1920* (1965; New York: Anchor, 1971), pp. 138–84.

29. Frances Ellen Watkins Harper, "Woman's Political Future" (1893), in *Black Women in Nineteenth-Century American Life,* ed. Bert James Loewenberg and Ruth Bogin (University Park, Pa.: Penn State Press, 1976), p. 246, and Anna Julia Cooper, "The Higher Education of Women," in Loewenberg and Bogin, pp. 318–31. See also Fannie Barrier Williams, "The Intellectual Progress of the Colored Woman of the United States Since the Emancipation Proclamation," in Loewenberg and Bogin, pp. 270–79; Hooks, pp. 159–72; and Eleanor Flexner, *Century of Struggle* (1959: New York: Atheneum, 1972), pp. 187–92. On the anti-lynching movement, see Jacquelyn Dowd Hall, "The Mind That

Burns in Each Body: Women, Rape, and Racial Violence," in *Powers of Desire,* ed. Ann Snitow et al. (New York: Monthly Review, 1983), pp. 328–49.

30. John Stuart Mill and Harriet Taylor Mill, *Essays on Sex Equality,* ed. Alice S. Rossi (Chicago: University of Chicago Press, 1970). Further references to this edition follow in the text.

31. See also Lois W. Banner, *Elizabeth Cady Stanton: A Radical for Women's Rights* (Boston: Little, Brown, 1980), pp. 81–84.

32. See also Judith Papachristou, ed., *Women Together* (New York: Knopf, 1976), pp. 39–40.

33. Aileen S. Kraditor, ed., *Up From the Pedestal* (Chicago: Quadrangle, 1968), p. 364.

34. See Okin, *Women in Western Political Thought,* pp. 228–30 and Eisenstein, pp. 127–39.

35. Papachristou, p. 203.

36. Eisenstein, *Radical Future,* p. 95. See also below, pp. 201–2, for Susan Moller Okins' recent challenge to traditional liberal theory.

37. Daniel Donno, Introduction, *The Prince and Selected Discourses: Machiavelli* (New York: Bantam, 1966), pp. 6–7. Further references to this edition of *The Prince* follow in the text.

38. Carolyn Merchant, *The Death of Nature* (New York: Harper, 1980), p. 127. Further references to Merchant follow in the text.

39. I am arguing that even though the scientific method relies on induction, and therefore a passive observation of the repetitions of nature, most scientific experiments in fact manipulate nature so that it exhibits the desired regularity. Merchant calls such manipulation "torture" (p. 174), as noted below. See also Popper's thesis, n. 41 below.

40. Merchant relies in part on Sherry Ortner's much-discussed article "Is Female to Male as Nature is to Culture?" in *Women, Culture and Society,* ed. Michelle Z. Rosaldo and Louise Lamphere (Stanford: Stanford University Press, 1974), pp. 67–87. See also Shulamith Firestone's ascription of a division between the aesthetic and the technological to the gender divisions (the former being feminine, the latter masculine) in *The Dialectic of Sex* (1970; New York: Bantam, 1971), pp. 172–81, discussed further in chap. 6.

41. The theoretical flaw in the premise of the scientific (inductive) method was first pointed out by David Hume in *Enquiry Concerning Human Understanding* (1748); he noted that the repetition of events does not "prove" a basic law; it only indicates its probability. Scientific laws are

always "synthetic" propositions, to use Kant's terms, never achieving the certainty of "analytical" mathematical propositions. See also Ludwig Wittgenstein's *Tractatus Logico-Philosophicus* (1911), discussed in chap. 7.

Karl Popper has argued, however, that the function of experiments in science is only to disprove hypotheses. See his *Logic of Scientific Discovery* (1935). Still, this approach relies on induction, even if negatively, to confirm the hypothesis, which is essentially imposed upon the matter being studied. For a further feminist critique of science, see chaps. 7 and 8.

42. See especially Robert Paul Wolff, "There's Nobody Here but Us Persons," in *Women and Philosophy,* ed. Carol C. Gould and Marx W. Warshofsky (New York: Putnam's, 1976), pp. 128–44. Jean Bethke Elshtain, *Public Man, Private Woman* (Princeton: Princeton University Press, 1981), also deals with this issue. Marxists such as Eli Zaretsky also decry the public-private split. Their theories are treated in chap. 3.

Of course, the public-private presumption in liberal theory has worked to the advantage of women in some cases. The 1973 Supreme Court abortion decision, *Roe v. Wade* (410 U.S. 113 [1973]), was based on the concept of the right to privacy. For further discussion of the privacy issue, see Catharine A. MacKinnon, "Feminism, Marxism, Method, and the State," *SIGNS* 8, no. 4 (Summer 1983): 655–57; Catharine A. MacKinnon, *Feminism Unmodified* (Cambridge: Harvard University Press, 1987), pp. 96–102, 155, 210; and Anita L. Allen, "Women and Their Privacy: What Is at Stake?" in *Beyond Domination,* ed. Carol C. Gould (Totowa, N.J.: Rowman & Allanheld, 1983), pp. 233–49.

Chapter 2
Nineteenth-Century Cultural Feminism

1. See Kraditor, *Ideas of the Woman Suffrage Movement,* pp. 38–57.

2. Not all "cultural feminists" embrace all these positions explicitly. Nor can one label all nineteenth-century feminists either "liberal" or "cultural." Stanton and Anthony, for example, expressed each type of theory at different times. Nor can one date a transition from one to the other, though the latter was more prevalent by the turn of the century. Yet the classifications are a useful means of organizing first-wave feminist theory. The term "cultural feminism" was first used, I believe, by Brooke in an article, "The Retreat to Cultural Feminism," in Redstockings, *Feminist Revolution* (New Paltz, N.Y.: 1975), pp. 65–68. She used the term negatively and applied it only to the contemporary movement. I use it positively and see it as the second major tradition of nineteenth-century feminist theory.

3. See Josephine Donovan, *New England Local Color Literature: A Women's Tradition* (New York: Ungar, 1983).

4. Nancy Sahli remarks on such disintegration in "Smashing: Women's Relationships Before the Fall," *Chrysalis* 8 (Summer 1979): 17–27. Theodore Roszak points to the intensification of militarism and "bully boy" Social Darwinist rhetoric at the end of the century as an antifeminist backlash in "The Hard and the Soft: The Force of Feminism in Modern Times," in *Masculine/Feminine,* ed. Betty and Theodore Roszak (New York: Harper, 1969), pp. 87–104. See also Josephine Donovan, *After the Fall: The Demeter-Persephone Myth in Wharton, Cather, and Glasgow* (University Park, Pa.: Pennsylvania State University Press, 1989), chap. 1, and Carroll Smith-Rosenberg, *Disorderly Conduct: Visions of Gender in Victorian America* (New York: Knopf, 1985).

5. Margaret Fuller, *Woman in the Nineteenth Century* (1845; New York: Norton, 1971), p. 36. Further references to this edition follow in the text.

6. Fuller was one of the first to concern herself with Native American conditions. Her *Summer on the Lakes in 1843* (1844) includes information on Indian women. Other women theorists of the nineteenth century who wrote about Native American oppression were: Lydia Maria Child, Caroline Kirkland, Mary Eastman, Helen Hunt Jackson, and Matilda Joslyn Gage. See also Sally Roesch Wagner, *The Untold Story of the Iroquois Influence on Early Feminists* (Aberdeen, S.D.: Sky Carrier Press, 1996).

7. Like many other nineteenth-century feminists Fuller advocated substituting "pulse [beans] for animal food" (113), in other words, vegetarianism. This diet was also followed by the Grimké sisters, Lucy Stone, Amelia Bloomer, Victoria Woodhull, Anthony, and Stanton. See Peter Singer, *Animal Liberation: A New Ethics for Our Treatment of Animals* (1975; New York: Avon, 1977), p. 234, and Carol Adams, "The Oedible Complex: Feminism and Vegetarianism," *The Lesbian Reader,* ed. Gina Covina and Laurel Galana (Oakland, Calif.: Amazon Press, 1975), pp. 146–47. Wollstonecraft advocated teaching children humane treatment of animals in her *Vindication* and wrote a children's book on the subject (Singer, p. 234). Other nineteenth-century feminists who espoused "animal rights" were Harriet Beecher Stowe, "Rights of Dumb Animals," *Hearth and Home* 1, no. 2 (2 Jan. 1869): 24; and Elizabeth Stuart Phelps Ward, who wrote antivivisectionist fiction, notably *Though Life Do Us Part* (1908) and " 'Tammyshanty' " in *The Oath of Allegiance and Other Stories* (1909). See also Josephine Donovan, "Animal Rights and Feminist Theory," in *Beyond Animal Rights: A Feminist Caring Ethic for the Treatment of Animals,* ed. Donovan and Carol J. Adams (New York: Continuum, 1996).

8. See Papachristou, pp. 61–63. Anthony's 1875 speech on prostitution, "Social Purity," may be found in Kraditor, *Up from the Pedestal,* pp. 159–67.

9. Fuller, pp. 132, 148. See also Marie Mitchell Olesen Urbanski, *Margaret Fuller's Woman in the Nineteenth Century: A Literary Study of Form and Content, of Sources and Influence* (Westport, Conn.: Greenwood, 1980), p. 77, n. 18. Later important articles on prostitution were written by Emma Goldman and Jane Addams (see below, including Matilda Joslyn Gage's analysis).

10. See Philip S. Foner, *Women and the American Labor Movement: From Colonial Times to the Eve of World War I* (New York: Free Press, 1979), pp. 129–55, on this unhappy alliance. For further information on the relationship between American socialism and feminism see Mari Jo Buhle, *Women and American Socialism 1870–1920* (Urbana: University of Illinois Press, 1981).

11. Elizabeth Cady Stanton, *The Woman's Bible,* 2 vols. (1895 and 1898; New York: Arno, 1972), 1:127. Further references to this edition follow in the text.

12. See Elizabeth Fee, "The Sexual Politics of Victorian Social Anthropology," in *Clio's Consciousness Raised,* ed. Mary Hartman and Lois W. Banner (New York: Harper, 1974), pp. 86–102; Paula Webster, "Matriarchy: A Vision of Power," in *Towards an Anthropology of Women,* ed. Rayna R. Reiter (New York: Monthly Review, 1975), pp. 141–56. See also Adrienne Rich, *Of Woman Born* (New York: Norton, 1976), pp. 84–109 and Gerda Lerner, *The Creation of Patriarchy* (New York: Oxford University Press, 1986).

    Many of the nineteenth-century feminist theorists knew about Iroquois history and culture from firsthand discussions with natives in New York State. See Wagner, *Untold Story* (n. 6, above).

13. Stanton, "The Matriarchate" (1891), in Kraditor, *Up from the Pedestal,* pp. 140–41. Further references to this article follow in the text.

14. Banner, pp. 86–87.

15. See also her 1869 Address to the Washington Woman's Rights Convention, in *History of Woman Suffrage* 2:351–53.

16. Matilda Joslyn Gage, *Woman, Church and State* (1893; Watertown, Mass.: Persephone, 1980), pp. 209–10. Further references to this edition follow in the text.

17. Gage, Address to Convention (1884), in Kraditor, *Up from the Pedestal,* p. 138.

18. See Margaret Murray, *The Witch-Cult in Western Europe: A Study in Anthropology* (Oxford: Clarendon Press, 1921) for an elaboration of this still controversial thesis.

19. Earlier women theorists who posited a feminine physics were Anne Finch, Lady Conway; and Margaret Cavendish, the Duchess of Newcastle. For an introduction to their theories see Merchant, chap. 11. Robin Morgan sees in quantum physics aspects of a "feminine" nature in her *Anatomy of Freedom* (1982), discussed below in chapter 7.

20. See Elaine Pagels, *The Gnostic Gospels* (New York: Random House, 1979), and Josephine Donovan, "Women and Female Symbolism in the Ancient Heresies" (unpub. article, 1975).

21. Charles Darwin, *The Origin of Species* (1859) in *Man and Universe: The Philosophers of Science*, ed. Saxe Cummins and Robert N. Linscott (New York: Washington Square, 1954), p. 254.

22. Herbert Spencer, *Principles of Sociology*, as cited in Carlton J. Hayes, *A Generation of Materialism, 1871–1900* (1941; New York: Harper, 1963), p. 11. Gilman refuted this thesis in *The Man-Made World* (1911; New York: Johnson Reprint, 1971), p. 215, where she argued that war "eliminates the fit, and leaves the unfit to perpetuate the race!" Jane Addams felt similarly compelled to reject this aspect of Social Darwinism in *Peace and Bread in Time of War* (New York: Macmillan, 1922). Another feminist work that dealt with the implications of Social Darwinism was Olive Schreiner's *Women and Labor* (1911).

23. Richard Hofstadter, *Social Darwinism in American Thought* (1944; rev. ed. New York: Braziller, 1955), p. 45.

24. Jacques Barzun, *Darwin, Marx, Wagner: Critique of a Heritage* (1941; rev. 2d ed. Garden City: Doubleday, 1958), p. 92. Further references to Barzun follow in the text.

25. See Hofstadter, pp. 42–43. Gilman was also influenced by Lester Ward, in particular his *Pure Sociology*. She met him at the 1896 woman's rights convention. See Mary A. Hill, *Charlotte Perkins Gilman: The Making of a Radical Feminist 1860–1896* (Philadelphia: Temple University Press, 1980), pp. 263–70.

26. Charlotte Perkins Gilman, *Women and Economics* (1898; New York: Harper, 1966), p. 5. Further references to this edition follow in the text. Another feminist work in the 1890s that attempted to refute Darwin, especially the doctrine of male superiority seen in *The Descent of Man*, was Eliza Burt Gamble, *The Evolution of Woman: An Inquiry into the Dogma of Her Inferiority to Man* (New York: G. P. Putnam's, 1893). See also Antoinette Brown Blackwell, *The Sexes Throughout Nature* (1875), in Rossi, *Feminist Papers*, pp. 356–77. A contemporary view is offered by Ruth Hubbard, "Have Only Men Evolved?" in *Discovering Reality*, ed. Sandra Harding and Merrill B. Hintikka (Dordrecht, Holland: Reidel, 1983), pp. 45–69.

27. Charlotte Perkins Gilman, *His Religion and Hers* (1923; Westport, Conn.: Hyperion, 1976). Further references to this edition follow in the text. It seems likely that Gilman may have read Freud's *Beyond the Pleasure Principle* (1920) by the time she wrote this; in that work Freud elaborated his theory of the eros and death instincts which Gilman seems to use here.

28. Charlotte Perkins Gilman, *Herland* (1915; New York: Harper, 1979), pp. 57–59.

29. Charlotte Perkins Gilman, *The Home* (1903; Urbana: University of Illinois Press, 1972), p. 38. Further references to this edition follow in the text.

30. Delores Hayden, *The Grand Domestic Revolution* (Cambridge: MIT Press, 1981), p. 3.

31. Gilman was also influenced by her two other Beecher great-aunts, Harriet Beecher Stowe and Isabella Beecher Hooker, with whose work she was familiar. The latter espoused a strongly matriarchal kind of feminism where Stowe for the most part remained within the natural rights tradition. See Josephine Donovan, "Harriet Beecher Stowe's Feminism," *American Transcendental Quarterly* 48–49 (Summer 1982): 141–57.

32. See Fuller, *Woman in the Nineteenth Century,* pp. 123, 175; on Stanton, see Hayden, p. 51.

33. *Woodhull & Claflin's Weekly,* ed. Arlene Kisner (Washington, N.J.: Times Change, 1972), p. 52.

34. See especially her "Afterword" and "There is No Communism in Russia," in *Red Emma Speaks,* ed. Alix Kates Shulman (New York: Vintage, 1972), pp. 337–74. Further references to *Red Emma Speaks* follow in the text.

35. Kathy E. Ferguson, "Liberalism and Oppression: Emma Goldman and the Anarchist Feminist Alternative," in *Liberalism and the Modern Polity: Essays in Contemporary Political Theory,* ed. Michael J. Gargas McGrath (New York: Dekker, 1978), p. 109.

36. Emma Goldman, "Woman Suffrage," in *Female Liberation,* ed. Roberta Salper (New York: Knopf, 1972), p. 129.

37. Rossi, *Feminist Papers,* p. 533; see pp. 517–36 for a summary of Sanger's position.

38. Goldman also makes the by-then usual equation of prostitution and marriage, seeing both as forms of economic exploitation. Goldman may have written her article in response to Jane Addams, "A New Con-

science and an Ancient Evil" (1910), in *The Social Thoughts of Jane Addams*, ed. Christopher Lasch (Indianapolis: Bobbs-Merrill, 1965), pp. 131–51. Goldman made the further point that women's ignorance about sex made them easy prey for pimps, etc. Further references to the Lasch edition follow in the text.

39. See Emma Goldman, "The Unjust Treatment of Homosexuals," in *Gay American History*, ed. Jonathan Katz (1976; New York: Avon, 1978), pp. 567–74. For Goldman's personal ambivalence about lesbianism, however, see Blanche Wiesen Cook, "Female Support Networks and Political Activism: Lillian Wald, Crystal Eastman, Emma Goldman," *Chrysalis* 3 (1977): 43–61. The only other lesbian theory of the period (to my knowledge) was that developed in Germany. See Lillian Faderman and Brigitte Eriksson, *Lesbian-Feminism in Turn-of-the-Century Germany* (Weatherby Lake, Mo.: Naiad, 1980).

40. See William R. Taylor and Christopher Lasch, "Two 'Kindred Spirits': Sorority and Family in New England, 1839–1846," *New England Quarterly* 36, no. 1 (March 1963): 23–41; Carroll Smith-Rosenberg, "The Female World of Love and Ritual: Relations between Women in Nineteenth-Century America," *SIGNS* 1, no. 1 (Autumn 1975): 1–29; and Lillian Faderman, *Surpassing the Love of Men* (New York: Morrow, 1981). For an overview of contemporary romantic friendships see Esther D. Rothblum and Kathleen A. Brehony, eds., *Boston Marriages: Romantic but Asexual Relationships among Contemporary Lesbians* (Amherst: University of Massachusetts Press, 1993).

41. Bell Gale Chevigny, *The Woman and the Myth: Margaret Fuller's Life and Writings* (Old Westbury, N.Y.: Feminist Press, 1976), pp. 112–13.

42. On Anthony see Katz, *Gay American History*, pp. 972–74, n. 9; the Gilman quote is in Hill, p. 189; on Addams, Wald and Eastman, see Cook, "Female Support Networks."

43. Kraditor, *Ideas of the Woman Suffrage Movement*, pp. 53–57; Lasch, *Social Thought of Jane Addams*, p. 152; and, to a lesser extent, Jill Conway, "Jane Addams: An American Heroine," in *The Woman in America*, ed. Robert Jay Lifton (Boston: Beacon, 1967), pp. 247–66, express an essentially liberal and, in the case of Lasch and Kraditor, negative reaction to Addams' ideas. Some of these Progressive Era feminists were influenced by—and influenced—the philosophical movement of pragmatism. See Charlene Haddock Siegfried, *Pragmatism and Feminism: Reweaving the Social Fabric* (Chicago: University of Chicago Press, 1996) and the special issue of *Hypatia* 8, no. 2 (Spring 1993) edited by Siegfried.

44. Lasch, *Social Thought of Jane Addams*, p. 36. Addams does not identify the source of the quote, which is slightly inaccurate. For the correct version, see text, p. 40.

45. The first two are in Lasch, pp. 143–50 and 151–62, respectively; "Women, War and Suffrage" is in *The Survey* 35, no. 6 (6 Nov. 1915): 148–50; "Women and Internationalism" is in Jane Addams, Emily Greene Balch, Alice Hamilton, *Women at the Hague* (New York: Macmillan, 1915), pp. 124–41. Further references to these articles follow in the text. See also Rossi, *Feminist Papers*, pp. 604–12. Arguments similar to Addams' are presented in Olive Schreiner, *Women and Labor* (1911; New York: Johnson Reprint, 1972), especially chap. 4, "Women and War."

46. See *Ideas of the Woman Suffrage Movement*, pp. 38–57. Kraditor's thesis is also misleading, because it sets Stanton up as the exemplar of the natural rights position when in fact she presented arguments that women's entrance into political life would effect a reign of peace as early as 1869. See *History of Woman Suffrage* 2: 351–53.

47. *Crystal Eastman on Women and Revolution*, ed. Blanche Wiesen Cook (New York: Oxford, 1978), p. 54. Eastman had elaborated on the idea that women need "un-personal sources of joy" in an earlier unpublished paper where she asserted that since personal relationships can come and go, women need to have "an absorbing interest in life which is not bound up with any particular person" (43). Further references to this edition of Eastman follow in the text.

48. As cited in Mercedes M. Randall, *Improper Bostonian: Emily Greene Balch* (New York: Twayne, 1964), p. 140. For a detailed account of the first-wave international movement, see Leila J. Rupp, *Worlds of Women: The Making of an International Women's Movement* (Princeton: Princeton University Press, 1997).

49. *Women at the Hague*, p. 154.

50. Randall, pp. 267–68.

51. *Women at the Hague*, p. 156.

52. Ibid., p. 150. On the Hague conference see also Randall, chaps. 6–9.

53. Robert Gottlieb, *Forcing the Spring: The Transformation of the American Environmental Movement* (Washington, D.C.: Island Press, 1993), chap. 2.

54. Linda Gordon, *Heroes of Their Own Lives: The Politics and History of Family Violence* (New York: Viking, 1988), p. 297, as cited in Robyn Muncy, *Creating a Female Dominion in American Reform, 1890–1935* (New York: Oxford, 1991), p. 167, n. 5. See also Paula Baker, "The Domestication of Politics: Women and American Political Society, 1780–1920," in *Unequal Sisters*, ed. Vicki L. Ruiz and Ellen Carol DuBois, 2d. ed. (New York: Routledge, 1994); William H. Chafe, "Women's History

and Political History: Some Thoughts on Progressivism and the New Deal," in *Visible Women: New Essays on American Activism,* ed. Nancy A. Hewitt and Suzanne Lebsock (Urbana: University of Illinois Press, 1993); Estelle B. Friedman, "Separatism Revisited: Women's Institutions, Social Reform, and the Career of Miriam Van Waters," Linda Gordon, "Putting Children First: Women, Maternalism, and Welfare in the Early Twentieth Century," and Alice Kessler-Harris, "Designing Women and Old Fools: The Construction of the Social Security Amendments of 1939," all in *U.S. History as Women's History,* ed. Kerber et al.; Theda Skocpol, *Protecting Soldiers and Mothers: The Political Origins of Social Policy in the United States* (Cambridge: Harvard University Press, 1992), especially part 3; and Seth Koven and Sonya Michel, *Mothers of a New World: Maternalist Politics and the Origins of the Welfare State* (New York: Routledge, 1993).

55. Muncy, *Creating a Female Dominion,* p. xii.

56. J. Stanley Lemons, *The Woman Citizen: Social Feminism in the 1920s* (Urbana: University of Illinois Press, 1973), p. ix. Further references follow in the text. On feminism in the 1930s see Susan Ware, *Holding Their Own: American Women in the 1930s* (Boston: Twayne, 1982), Susan Ware, *Beyond Suffrage: Women in the New Deal* (Cambridge: Harvard University Press, 1981), and Nancy Cott, *The Grounding of Modern Feminism* (New Haven: Yale University Press, 1987). If there was an eclipse of feminism, it occurred in the 1940s and 1950s, largely as a result of the national preoccupation with World War II and its aftermath. But see Leila Rupp and Verta Taylor, *Survival in the Doldrums: The American Women's Rights Movement, 1945 to the 1960s* (New York: Oxford, 1987).

57. See Foner, p. 304; Papachristou, pp. 204–12; and the statement of Rose Schneiderman, President of the NWTUL, before the Senate Judiciary subcommittee (1931), in Kraditor, *Up from the Pedestal,* pp. 296–99. For more on the Trade Union League, see Nancy Schrom Dye, *As Equals and As Sisters: Feminism, the Labor Movement, and the Women's Trade Union League* (Columbia: University of Missouri Press, 1980), and Robin Miller Jacoby, "The Women's Trade Union League and American Feminism," *Feminist Studies* 3, no. 1–2 (Fall 1975): 126–40.

58. In *Equal Rights,* 15 Mar. 1924, in *Crystal Eastman on Women and Revolution,* pp. 156–59.

59. See Gloria Steinem, "Women Voters Can't Be Trusted," *Ms.* 1, no. 1 (July 1972) and Jane Sharron DeHart, "Rights and Representations: Women, Politics, and Power in the Contemporary United States," in *U.S. History as Women's History,* ed. Kerber et al.

60. Some contemporary feminists advocate separatism, an essentially apolitical cultivation of women's culture that may be seen as a form of

praxis (see chaps. 3 and 6). It was this cultural separatism that Brooke criticized in her 1975 article. However, no feminist today supports the idea of women remaining confined in domestic, nuclear arrangements and assigned to traditional roles.

61. See Sara Ruddick, "Pacifying the Forces: Drafting Women in the Interests of Peace," *SIGNS* 8, no. 3 (Spring 1983): 471–89, and Sara Ruddick, "Preservative Love and Military Destruction, Some Reflections on Mothering and Peace," in *Mothering: Essays in Feminist Theory,* ed. Joyce Treblicot (Totowa, N.J.: Rowman & Allanheld, 1983), pp. 231–62. Also see Cynthia Enloe, *Does Khaki Become You?* (Boston: South End, 1983).

62. In *State v. Wanrow,* Wash., 559 P.2d 548 (1977) the Supreme Court of Washington ruled that a woman's right to equal protection was violated because the jury was not instructed to consider "her actions in light of her own perceptions of the situation, including those which were the product of our nation's 'long and unfortunate history of sex discrimination.' " Women's actions, the Court noted, must be understood "in light of the individual physical handicaps which are the product of sex discrimination." The woman in question was a Native American who had killed a white man. For a further discussion of this case see Catharine A. MacKinnon, "Toward Feminist Jurisprudence," *Stanford Law Review* 34 (Feb. 1982): 703–37, and Elizabeth M. Schneider, "The Dialectic of Rights and Politics: Perspectives from the Women's Movement," in *At the Boundaries of the Law: Feminism and Legal Theory,* ed. Martha Albertson Fineman and Nancy Sweet Thomadsen (New York: Routledge, 1991), pp. 301–19. Also Catharine A. MacKinnon, "Feminism, Marxism, Method" (1983): 635–58. Thanks to Karen Crist for bringing this case to my attention. For further discussion of the pregnancy leave issue, see below, chap. 8.

Chapter 3
Feminism and Marxism

1. Karl Marx and Frederick Engels, *Manifesto of the Communist Party* (1848; New York: International, 1948), p. 6. Further references to this edition will be indicated by *Manifesto* in the text.

2. *Karl Marx: Selected Writings,* ed. David McLellan (Oxford: Oxford University Press, 1977), p. 389. Further references to this work will be indicated by *Writings* in the text. A useful if brief summary of Marx and Engels' feminism is Hal Draper, "Marx and Engels on Women's Liberation," in Salper, *Female Liberation,* pp. 83–107.

3. David McLellan, *The Thought of Karl Marx: An Introduction* (New York: Harper, 1971), p. 152. Further references to this work will be indicated by *Thought* in the text.

4. Marx, "The Eighteenth Brumaire of Louis Bonaparte," as cited in McLellan, *Thought*, p. 156.

5. John Plamenatz, *Man and Society: A Critical Examination of Some Important Social and Political Theories from Machiavelli to Marx*, 2 vols. (New York: Longman, 1963), 2: 307–30.

6. Marx, "The German Ideology," as cited in McLellan, *Thought*, p. 199.

7. A useful history of the concept of alienation is Albert William Levi, "Existentialism and the Alienation of Man," in *Phenomenology and Existentialism*, ed. Edward N. Lee and Maurice Mandalbaum (Baltimore: Johns Hopkins, 1967), pp. 243–65. Also helpful is Erich Fromm, Introduction to the *Economic and Philosophical Manuscripts* (1844) in *Marx's Concept of Man* (New York: Ungar, 1961), pp. 1–83. Further references to this edition will be indicated by *Manuscripts* in the text.

8. Edmund Wilson, *To The Finland Station: A Study in the Writing and Acting of History* (Garden City: Doubleday, 1940), p. 291.

9. Fromm, Introduction to *Manuscripts*, p. 44.

10. See Gajo Petrović, *Marx in Mid-Twentieth Century* (Garden City: Doubleday, 1967), pp. 171–98, for a good discussion of praxis from the point of view of a Yugoslav Marxist. Further references to this work follow in the text.

11. See Mircea Eliade, *The Sacred and the Profane: The Nature of Religion* (1957; New York: Harper, 1961).

12. See McLellan, *Thought*, pp. 77–79.

13. See Judith K. Brown, "Iroquois Women: An Ethnohistoric Note," in Reiter, *Anthropology*, pp. 235–51.

14. Friedrich Engels, *The Origin of the Family, Private Property, and the State* (1884; New York: International, 1942), p. 43. Further references to this edition follow in the text.

15. Kathleen Gough, "The Origin of the Family" and Karen Sacks, "Engels Revisited: Women, the Organization of Production, and Private Property," in Reiter, *Anthropology*, pp. 51–76 and 211–34, respectively. Further references to Sacks follow in the text. For another critique of Engels' theory, see Jane Flax, "Do Feminists Need Marxism?" in *Building Feminist Theory*, ed. The *Quest* Staff (New York: Longman, 1981), pp. 174–85. On the correlation between the domestication of animals and the subjugation of women see Jim Mason, *An Unnatural Order: Uncovering the Roots of Our Domination of Nature and Each Other* (New York: Simon & Schuster, 1993).

16. Bebel, *Woman and Socialism*, in Rossi, *Feminist Papers*, p. 502.

17. Lenin's views may be found in *The Emancipation of Women* (New York: International, 1972), which includes the interview by Clara Zetkin, "Lenin on the Woman Question." For an interesting discussion of Russian feminism before and after the Revolution see Richard Stites, *The Women's Liberation Movement in Russia* (Princeton: Princeton University Press, 1978). See also Bernice Glatzer Rosenthal, "Love on the Tractor: Women in the Russian Revolution and After," in *Becoming Visible*, ed. Renate Bridenthal and Claudia Koontz (Boston: Houghton Mifflin, 1977), pp. 370–99. Also useful is *Socialist Women*, ed. Marilyn Boxer and Jean Quataert (New York: Elsevier, 1978). Stites, Rosenthal, and *Socialist Women* have considerable information on Alexandra Kollontai, the most important Bolshevik feminist.

18. Margaret Benston, "The Political Economy of Women's Liberation," *Monthly Review* 21, no. 4 (Sept. 1969): 15. Further references to this article follow in the text.

19. Lise Vogel, "The Earthly Family," *Radical America* 7, nos. 4 and 5 (July–Oct. 1973): 26. Further references to this article follow in the text.

20. See further discussion below, in chaps. 3, 6, and 7.

21. Angela Davis, "Reflections on the Black Woman's Role in the Community of Slaves," *The Black Scholar* 3, no. 4 (Dec. 1971): 7.

22. Susan Sontag, "The Third World of Women," *Partisan Review* 60, no. 2 (1973): 201. Further references to this article follow in the text.

23. Eli Zaretsky, *Capitalism, the Family and Personal Life* (New York: Harper, 1976). Further references to this work follow in the text. See also Rosemary Radford Ruether, "Home and Work: Women's Roles and the Transformation of Values," *Theological Studies* 36 (Dec. 1975): 647–59.

24. Ann Foreman, *Femininity as Alienation* (London: Pluto, 1977).

25. Zillah Eisenstein, "Developing a Theory of Capitalist Patriarchy and Socialist Feminism," in *Capitalist Patriarchy and the Case for Socialist Feminism*, ed. Eisenstein (New York: Monthly Review, 1979), p. 11.

26. Mariarosa Dalla Costa, "Women and the Subversion of Community," *Radical America* 6, no. 1 (Jan.–Feb. 1972): 77. Further references to this article follow in the text.

27. Peggy Morton, "A Woman's Work Is Never Done," (1971), in *From Feminism to Liberation*, ed. Edith Hoshimo Altbach, 2d. rev. ed. (Cambridge: Schenkman, 1980), p. 247. For a complete list of the articles that contributed to the domestic labor debate see Heidi Hartmann, "The Unhappy Marriage of Marxism and Feminism: Towards a More Progressive Union," in *Women and Revolution*, ed. Lydia Sargent (Boston:

South End Press, 1981), pp. 34–35, n. 10. Also: Paul Smith, "Domestic Labour and Marx's Theory of Value," in *Feminism and Materialism,* ed. Annette Kuhn and AnnMarie Wolpe (London: Routledge & Kegan Paul, 1978), pp. 198–219.

28. Gayle Rubin, "The Traffic in Women: Notes on the 'Political Economy' of Sex," in Reiter, *Anthropology,* p. 162. Further references to this article follow in the text.

29. See Ira Gerstein, "Domestic Work and Capitalism," *Radical America* 7, no. 4–5 (July–Oct. 1973): 101–28.

30. Michèle Barrett, *Women's Oppression Today* (London: Verso, 1980), p. 50. Further references to this work follow in the text.

31. Christine Delphy, *The Main Enemy,* as paraphrased in Barrett, p. 18.

32. Heidi Hartmann, "The Unhappy Marriage of Marxism and Feminism," in Sargent, *Women and Revolution,* p. 15. Further references to this article follow in the text.

33. Juliet Mitchell, *Woman's Estate* (Baltimore: Penguin, 1971). For critiques see Vogel, pp. 10–22, and Hartmann, p. 11.

34. Zillah Eisenstein, "The Sexual Politics of the New Right: Understanding the 'Crisis of Liberalism' for the 1980s," *SIGNS* 7, no. 3 (Spring 1982): 569. See also her *The Radical Future of Liberal Feminism* (1981).

35. Iris Young, "Beyond the Unhappy Marriage: A Critique of the Dual Systems Theory," in Sargent, *Women and Revolution,* pp. 43–69; for Gerstein, see n. 29 above. The wage information is reported in a 1991 UN report, *The World's Women 1976–1990* (New York: United Nations Publications, 1991), as cited in the *New York Times,* 16 June 1991.

36. See Jackie West, "Women, Sex and Class," in Kuhn and Wolpe, *Feminism and Materialism,* pp. 220–53.

37. Sandra Harding, "What Is the Real Material Base of Patriarchy and Capitalism?" in Sargent, *Women and Revolution,* pp. 151–52.

38. See Max Horkheimer, "Authority and the Family," in *Critical Theory* (1936; New York: Herder & Herder, 1972).

39. Nancy Chodorow, "Mothering, Male Dominance, and Capitalism," in Eisenstein, *Capitalist Patriarchy,* p. 89. Further references to this article follow in the text.

40. Mitchell, *Woman's Estate,* pp. 101–22.

41. Nancy Hartsock, "Fundamental Feminism: Process and Perspective," in *Building Feminist Theory,* p. 35. My emphasis added. Several radical feminist articles were devoted to the concept of consciousness-raising. See especially Carol Hanisch, "The Personal Is Political"; Kathie Sara-

child, "A Program for Feminist 'Consciousness Raising' "; Irene Peslikis, "Resistances to Consciousness"; Jennifer Gardner, "False Consciousness," and Pamela Kearon, "Man-Hating," all in *Notes from the Second Year,* ed. Shulamith Firestone and Anne Koedt (New York: Radical Feminism, 1970), pp. 76–86.

42. Hartsock, "Fundamental Feminism," p. 37. The Marx passage is from "Theses on Feuerbach" (1845).

43. Beverly Fisher-Manick, "Race and Class: Beyond Personal Politics," in *Building Feminist Theory,* p. 158. Further references to this article follow in the text.

44. Carol Ehrlich, "The Unhappy Marriage of Marxism and Feminism: Can It Be Saved?" in Sargent, *Women and Revolution,* p. 124. Further references to this article follow in the text.

45. Hartsock, "Fundamental Feminism," p. 40. Patricia Hill Collins, however, emphasizes the role of intellectuals in the formation of a standpoint in "Defining Black Feminist Thought," in *The Second Wave,* ed. Linda Nicholson (New York: Routledge, 1997), pp. 241–59.

46. Some contemporary Marxists have moved beyond this narrow materialism. See especially Louis Althusser, "Ideology and State Apparatuses (Notes towards an Investigation)," in *Lenin and Philosophy and Other Essays* (New York: Monthly Review, 1971). Also Antonio Gramsci, *Selections from the Prison Notebooks* (New York: International, 1971).

47. Catharine A. MacKinnon, "Feminism, Marxism, Method and the State: An Agenda for Theory," *SIGNS* 7, no. 3 (Spring 1982): 527, n. 23. Further references to this article follow in the text.

48. See also Sandra G. Harding, "Feminism: Reform or Revolution?" in Gould and Wartofsky, *Women and Philosophy,* pp. 217–84.

49. Gloria Steinem, Forward to *Building Feminist Theory,* p. xii. Other articles on anarchism and feminism include those by Peggy Kornegger, especially "Anarchism: The Feminist Connection," *Second Wave* 4, no. 1 (Spring 1975): 26–37.

50. The Combahee River Collective, "A Black Feminist Statement," in *But Some of Us Are Brave,* ed. Gloria T. Hull, Patricia Bell Scott, and Barbara Smith (Old Westbury, N.Y.: Feminist Press, 1982), p. 21.

51. Nancy Hartsock, "Staying Alive," in *Building Feminist Theory,* p. 112. Further references to this article follow in the text.

52. Christine Riddiough, "Socialism, Feminism and Gay/Lesbian Liberation," in Sargent, *Women and Revolution,* p. 86. See also her "Culture and Politics," in *Pink Triangles: Radical Perspectives on Gay Liberation,* ed. Pam Mitchell (Boston: Alyson, 1980), pp. 14–33.

53. Ann Ferguson and Nancy Folbre, "The Unhappy Marriage of Patriarchy and Capitalism," in Sargent, *Women and Revolution*, p. 330.

54. Nancy C. M. Hartsock, *Money, Sex and Power: Toward a Feminist Historical Materialism* (New York: Longman, 1983), p. 231. Further references follow in the text.

    Another socialist feminist work that attempts to ground feminist theory in women's consciousness is Mary O'Brien, *The Politics of Reproduction* (Boston: Routledge & Kegan Paul, 1981). O'Brien argues that the difference in men's and women's consciousness lies in their different relationship to the reproductive process. Women have a unity of experience from conception through pregnancy to the arrival of an infant, while "male reproductive consciousness is a consciousness of discontinuity . . . [because] the alienation of his seed separates him from natural genetic continuity" (53). "Female time . . . is continuous, while male time is discontinuous" (61).

    Rooted in the "female reproductive consciousness," "feminist philosophy will be a philosophy of birth and regeneration" (200). "In very general terms, the problem is to move from the war against nature and against life to policies of integration with nature and with life" (201). Also, see below, chap. 7, n. 17.

55. Nancy C. M. Hartsock, "The Feminist Standpoint: Developing the Ground for a Specifically Feminist Historical Materialism," in *Discovering Reality*, ed. Harding and Hintikka, p. 284. Further references follow in the text.

Chapter 4
Feminism and Freudianism

1. Sigmund Freud, *Three Contributions to the Theory of Sex*, 4th ed. (1930; New York: Johnson Reprint, 1970). Further references to this edition follow in the text. For an introduction to Freud, see his *Outline of Psychoanalysis* (1940). In this work I have chosen to focus on Freud rather than his epigones such as Jung. For feminist use of the latter's theories, see Naomi R. Goldenberg, *Changing of the Gods* (Boston: Beacon, 1979). Also of interest: Esther Harding, *Woman's Mysteries: Ancient and Modern* (New York: Pantheon, 1955) and C. Kerényi, *Eleusis: Archetypal Image of Mother and Daughter* (New York: Pantheon, 1967).

2. Interview with Jonathan Katz, 1974, in *Gay American History*, p. 247.

3. Sigmund Freud, "Some Psychological Consequences of the Anatomical Distinction Between the Sexes" (1925), in Freud, *Sexuality and the Psychology of Love*, ed. Philip Rieff (New York: Collier, 1963), p. 193.

4. Sigmund Freud, "The Passing of the Oedipus Complex" (1924) in *Sexuality and the Psychology of Love*, p. 181.

5. Sigmund Freud, "On Narcissism: An Introduction" (1914), in Freud, *General Psychological Theory,* ed. Rieff (New York: Collier, 1963), pp. 56–82. Further references to this article follow in the text.

6. In a later essay, "Femininity" (1932), in *The Standard Edition of the Complete Works of Sigmund Freud,* ed. James Strachey (London: Hogarth, 1964), p. 132, Freud suggests that penis-envy is the cause of female narcissism, "for [women] are bound to value their charms more highly as a late compensation for their original sexual inferiority."

7. Both in Freud, *Sexuality and the Psychology of Love,* ed. Rieff pp. 176–82 and 183–93, respectively. Further references follow in the text.

8. Freud, *Civilization and Its Discontents,* rev. and ed. by James Strachey (London: Hogarth, 1963), p. 46. Further references to this edition follow in the text.

9. Herbert Marcuse, "Marxism and Feminism," *Women's Studies* 2, no. 3 (1974): 282. Further references to this article follow in the text.

10. As noted in ibid., p. 284.

11. Freud, "Female Sexuality" (1931), in *Sexuality and the Psychology of Love,* pp. 194–211. Further references to this article follow in the text. Freud wrote one more article on the subject, "Femininity" (1932). See above, n. 6. It adds little, however, to his previous discussions of the subject.

12. See Ruby Rohrlich-Leavitt, "Women in Transition: Crete and Sumer," in Bridenthal and Koontz, *Becoming Visible,* pp. 35–59.

13. Freud, "The Psychogenesis of a Case of Homosexuality in a Woman," in *Sexuality and the Psychology of Love,* pp. 133–59. Further references to this article follow in the text.

14. See chap. 2, n. 40 for works on this subject.

15. Freud offers another interesting explanation. The mother was young and narcissistic in her attitude toward men; she had rejected the girl and perhaps saw her as a rival. The girl may therefore have "retired in favour of" the men in the competition for her mother's affection—seeking instead another object (145). Madelon Sprengnether in *The Spectral Mother: Freud, Feminism, and Psychoanalysis* (Ithaca: Cornell University Press, 1990) argues that throughout his writing Freud ignores or minimizes the importance of the mother.

16. Herbert Marcuse's epilogue to *Eros and Civilization: A Philosophical Inquiry into Freud* (1955; New York: Vintage, 1962), "Critique of Neo-Freudian Revisionism," pp. 217–51, is especially useful here.

In recent years an additional vein of feminist criticism of Freud has grown up around his problematic interpretation of "Dora"'s case,

"Fragment of an Analysis of a Case of Hysteria" (1905). See especially *In Dora's Case: Freud-Hysteria-Feminism,* ed. Charles Bernheimer and Clare Kahane (New York: Columbia University Press, 1985).

In addition, there has been some serious questioning of Freud's conclusion that the childhood seduction/abuse narratives patients told him were fantasies. Jeffrey Moussaieff Masson in *The Assault on Truth: Freud's Suppression of Seduction* (New York, Farrar Straus & Giroux, 1984) argues that the stories were true but Freud used them to establish his repressed fantasy theory, in particular the oedipus complex, as the basis for psychoanalysis.

A useful survey of the history of Freudian theory in relation to feminism in the U.S. is Mari Jo Buhle, *Feminism and Its Discontents* (Cambridge: Harvard University Press, 1998).

17. See Freud, "The Passing of the Oedipus Complex," in *Sexuality and the Psychology of Love,* p. 181.

18. Viola Klein, *The Feminine Character* (1964; 2d ed. London: Routledge and Kegan Paul, 1971), p. 77. Further references to this work follow in the text.

19. Kate Millett, *Sexual Politics* (1970; New York: Avon, 1971), p. 109. Further references to this work follow in the text.

20. Shulamith Firestone, *The Dialectic of Sex,* p. 61. Further references to this work follow in the text.

21. "On the Genesis of the Castration Complex in Women" (1924), as cited in Klein, p. 79. For an overall account of Horney's work see Marcia Wescott, *The Feminist Legacy of Karen Horney* (New Haven: Yale University Press, 1986).

22. Karen Horney, "The Flight from Womanhood" (1926), in *Psychoanalysis and Women,* ed. Jean Baker Miller (New York: Bruner/Mazel, 1973), p. 3. Further references to this article follow in the text.

23. Simone de Beauvoir, *The Second Sex* (1949; New York: Bantam, 1961), p. 37. Further references to this work follow in the text.

24. *Psychoanalysis: Evolution and Development* (1950), as cited in Betty Friedan, *The Feminine Mystique* (New York: Norton, 1963), p. 115.

25. Clara Thompson, "Penis Envy in Women" (1943), in Miller, *Psychoanalysis and Women,* pp. 43–48.

26. Gayle Rubin, "The Traffic in Women," in Reiter, *Anthropology,* p. 190 n. Further references to this article follow in the text.

27. Anne Koedt, "The Myth of the Vaginal Orgasm," *Notes from the Second Year* (1970), p. 37. See William H. Masters and Virginia E. Johnson, *Human Sexual Response* (Boston: Little Brown, 1966) and *Human Sexual Inadequacy* (Boston: Little Brown, 1970). Also see Jill Johnston,

"The Myth of the Myth of the Vaginal Orgasm," in *Lesbian Nation* (New York: Simon and Schuster, 1973), pp. 164–73.

28. See Mary Daly, *Gyn/Ecology* (Boston: Beacon, 1978), pp. 153–77, for more on this gruesome custom. See also Robin Morgan and Gloria Steinem, "The International Crime of Genital Mutilation," *Ms.* 8, no. 9 (March 1980).

29. Ti-Grace Atkinson, "The Institution of Sexual Intercourse," *Notes from the Second Year* (1970), pp. 42–47.

30. Friedan, *The Feminine Mystique,* p. 120. Further references to Friedan follow in the text.

31. Further examples of the damaging effects of Freudian therapy on women may be found in Naomi Weisstein, "Psychology Constructs the Female," in Gornick and Moran, *Woman in Sexist Society,* pp. 133–46, and Phyllis Chesler, *Women and Madness* (Garden City: Doubleday, 1972).

32. Juliet Mitchell, *Psychoanalysis and Feminism* (1974; New York: Vintage, 1975), p. 95. Further references to this work follow in the text.

33. Barrett, p. 61; Foreman, p. 49.

34. Nancy Chodorow, *The Reproduction of Mothering* (Berkeley: University of California Press, 1978), p. 38. Further references to this work follow in the text. A somewhat similar work is Dorothy Dinnerstein's *The Mermaid and the Minotaur: Sexual Arrangements and Human Malaise* (New York: Harper, 1976). See also Jane Flax, "The Conflict Between Nurturance and Autonomy in Mother-Daughter Relationships and Within Feminism," *Feminist Studies* 4 (June 1978): 171–89; Jane Flax, *Thinking Fragments* (Berkeley: University of California Press, 1990), and Jessica Benjamin, *The Bonds of Love* (New York: Pantheon, 1988).

35. For other critiques of Chodorow see Adrienne Rich, "Compulsory Heterosexuality and Lesbian Existence," *SIGNS* 5, no. 4 (Summer 1980): 631–37; Iris Marion Young "Is Male Gender Identity the Cause of Male Domination?" and Pauline Bart, "Review of Chodorow's *Reproduction of Mothering* in Treblicot, ed., *Mothering: Essays in Feminist Theory,* pp. 129–46 and 147–52, respectively.

36. Some French feminists see this direction as anti-intellectual. See the cautionary note sounded in *New French Feminisms,* ed. Elaine Marks and Isabelle de Courtivron (1980; New York: Schocken, 1981), pp. 212–30. See also Elaine Marks, "Women and Literature in France," *SIGNS* 3, no. 4 (Summer 1978): 837–38. For a critique in particular of the theories of Luce Irigaray, a French theorist, see Monique Plaza, " 'Phallomorphic Power' and the Psychology of 'Woman,' " *Ideology and Consciousness* 4 (1978): 4–36. An interesting American feminist article that

correlates with Lacanian French feminist theory is Peggy Allegro, "The Strange and the Familiar: The Evolutionary Potential of Lesbianism," in Covina and Galana, *The Lesbian Reader,* pp. 167–84. Unless otherwise indicated my summary of this branch of French feminism is derived from *New French Feminisms.* I use the shorthand term *French feminists* in this section, but it must be noted that not all French feminists subscribe to these ideas.

37. This summary of Lacanian theory is derived from: Jan Miel, "Jacques Lacan and the Structure of the Unconscious," and Jacques Lacan, "The Insistance of the Letter in the Unconscious," both in *Yale French Studies,* no. 36–37 (1966): 104–11 and 112–47, respectively; Jacques Lacan, *The Language of the Self: The Function of Language in Psychoanalysis,* trans. with a commentary, "Lacan and the Discourse of the Other," by Anthony Wilden (Baltimore: Johns Hopkins, 1968); Richard Wollheim, "The Cabinet of Dr. Lacan," *New York Review of Books,* 25 Jan. 1979, pp. 36–45; and Serge LeClair, "Sexuality: A Fact of Discourse" in *Homosexualities and French Literature: Cultural Contexts/Critical Texts,* ed. George Stambolian and Elaine Marks (Ithaca: Cornell, 1979), pp. 42–55; as well as the Introductions to *New French Feminisms.*

38. Jane Gallop, *The Daughter's Seduction, Feminism and Psychoanalysis* (Ithaca: Cornell, 1982), p. 22.

39. Ibid., pp. 95–96.

40. Wollheim, p. 43, n. 12.

41. Julia Kristeva, "Women's Time," *SIGNS* 7, no. 1 (Autumn 1981): 20. Further references to this article follow in the text.

42. Hélène Cixous, "Castration or Decapitation?" *SIGNS* 7, no. 1 (Autumn 1981): 45. Further references to this article follow in the text.

43. Jacques Derrida, "The Purveyor of Truth" (1975), as cited in Jane Gallop, "The Ladies' Man," *Diacritics* 6, no. 4 (Winter 1976): 30.

44. Editorial Collective of Questions Féministes "Variations on Common Themes," *New French Feminisms,* p. 220.

45. Kristeva, "Oscillation between Power and Denial" (1974), in *New French Feminisms,* p. 166.

46. Gauthier, "Is There Such a Thing as Women's Writing?" (1974), in *New French Feminisms,* pp. 162–63.

47. Marks and de Courtivron, "Introduction III," *New French Feminisms,* p. 36.

48. Theorists Herbert Marcuse and Norman O. Brown similarly valorized eros. See especially Marcuse, *Eros and Civilization,* and Brown, *Life Against Death: The Psychoanalytical Meaning of History* (Middletown, Conn.: Wesleyan University Press, 1959) and *Love's Body* (New York:

Vintage, 1966). Brown urged a "body mysticism" as a means of transcending contemporary death-oriented culture.

49. Catherine Clément, "Enslaved Enclave" (1975), in *New French Feminisms,* p. 131.

50. Cixous, "The Laugh of the Medusa" (1976), in *New French Feminisms,* p. 247. Further references follow in the text.

51. See Kristeva, "Women's Time," pp. 35–36.

52. Hélène Vivienne Wenzel, "Introduction to Luce Irigaray's 'And the One Doesn't Stir Without the Other.' " *SIGNS* 7, no. 1 (Autumn 1981): 59; see also Irigaray, "And the One Doesn't Stir Without the Other," *SIGNS* 7, no. 1 (Autumn 1981); "Women's Exile," *Ideology and Consciousness* 1 (1977):62–76; and "The Bodily Encounter with the Mother," in Luce Irigaray, *The Irigaray Reader,* ed. Margaret Whitford (Oxford: Blackwell, 1991), pp. 35–46.

53. Kristeva, "Women's Time," p. 27.

54. Françoise d'Eaubonne, "Feminism or Death," in *New French Feminisms,* p. 236.

Chapter 5
Feminism and Existentialism

1. G. W. F. Hegel, *Phenomenology of Spirit* (1807; Oxford: Clarendon Press, 1977), p. 115. Further references to this edition follow in the text.

2. Martin Heidegger, *Being and Time* (1927; New York: Harper, 1962), p. 164. Further references to this edition follow in the text.

3. John MacQuarrie, *Martin Heidegger* (London: Lutterworth, 1968), p. 32.

4. In "The Existentialist Recovery of Hegel and Marx," in Lee and Mandalbaum, *Phenomenology and Existentialism,* p. 129, George L. Kline argues that Sartre and others have confused "nonactuality with nonbeing: possibilities are obviously not actual, therefore they are not. Expressed positively what is merely possible is nothing, a nothingness."

5. Jean-Paul Sartre, *Being and Nothingness: An Essay in Phenomenological Ontology* (1943; New York: Citadel Press, 1966), p. 142. Further references to this edition follow in the text.

6. See Alexandre Kojève, *Introduction à la lecture de Hegel,* ed. Raymond Queneau (Paris: Gallimard, 1947).

7. Margery Collins and Christine Pierce, "Holes and Slime: Sexism in Sartre's Psychoanalysis," in Gould and Warshofsky, *Women and Philosophy,* pp. 112–27.

8. Jean-Paul Sartre, *Saint Genet: Actor and Martyr* (1952; New York: Mentor, 1964), p. 40. Further references to this work follow in the text.
9. Thomas S. Szasz, *The Manufacture of Madness* (New York: Delta, 1970), p. 287.
10. See Erich Fromm, *Escape From Freedom* (New York: Farrar & Rinehart, 1941) and Paul Tillich, *The Courage to Be* (New Haven: Yale University Press, 1952).
11. Simone de Beauvoir, *The Second Sex*, p. xvi. Further references follow in the text.
12. Daly in *Beyond God the Father* (Boston: Beacon, 1973), p. 49, attributes collusion to the intensive conditioning or brainwashing women receive. Barrett, pp. 85, 110, mainly suggests that the problem deserves further study, but she rejects the Marxist idea that it is simply a matter of "false consciousness."
13. The fundamental problem here lies in an unwarranted equation between the en-soi as "it," as object, and en-soi as physical, organic reality. The two entities ought not be confused. Insofar as otherness means reduction to an object, de Beauvoir's theory holds. But not, however, if one sees otherness as physical, organic nature (as drawn in opposition to reason and rational thinking). For a further critique see Catriona Mackenzie, "Simone de Beauvoir: Philosophy and/or the Female Body," in *Feminist Challenges*, ed. Carole Pateman and Elizabeth Gross (1986; Boston: Northeastern, 1987), pp. 144–56, and Iris Marion Young, "Humanism, Gynocentrism, and Feminist Politics" (1985), in *Throwing Like a Girl* (Bloomington: Indiana University Press, 1990), pp. 73–91.
14. Kathryn Allen Rabuzzi, *The Sacred and the Feminine* (New York: Seabury, 1982), p. 96. Further references to this work follow in the text. Another article that draws somewhat similar distinctions about a feminine time is Julia Kristeva's "Women's Time" (1981).
15. Other than Buber, *I and Thou* (1922; New York: Scribners, 1970), and Eliade, *The Sacred and the Profane*, the following works provide a useful introduction to Existentialist theology; from them this summary is derived: Martin Heidegger, "On the Essence of Truth," in *Existence and Being*, ed. Werner Brock, 2d. ed. (South Bend, Ind.: Regnery/Gateway, 1979), pp. 292–324; John A. T. Robinson, *Honest to God* (Philadelphia: Westminster, 1963); and *Towards a New Christianity: Readings in the Death of God Theology*, ed. Thomas J. J. Altizer (New York: Harcourt, Brace & World, 1967).
16. Mary Daly, *Beyond God the Father*, p. 33. Further references to this work follow in the text.
17. For a further discussion of "technical reason" see Paul Tillich, *The World Situation* (1945; Philadelphia: Fortress Press, 1965).

18. Major liberation theology texts include the following: James Cone, *Black Theology and Black Power* (New York: Seabury, 1969); Gustavo Gutiérrez, *A Theology of Liberation* (Maryknoll, N.Y.: Orbis, 1972); Frederick Herzog, *Liberation Theology* (New York: Seabury, 1972); Rosemary Ruether, *Liberation Theology* (New York: Paulist, 1973); and J. Deotis Roberts, *Liberation and Reconciliation: A Black Theology* (Philadelphia: Westminster, 1971). Also useful is *Black Theology: A Documentary History, 1966–1979,* ed. Gayraud S. Wilmore and James H. Cone (Maryknoll, N.Y.: Orbis, 1979). For an indication of feminist analysis of the Judaic tradition see Susannah Henschel, ed., *On Being a Jewish Feminist* (New York: Schocken, 1983). Other useful collections of feminist interpretations of both the Christian and Jewish traditions are *Religion and Sexism,* ed. Rosemary Radford Ruether (New York: Simon & Schuster, 1974); *Womanspirit Rising,* ed. Carol P. Christ and Judith Plaskow (San Francisco: Harper, 1979); and Naomi Goldenberg, *Changing of the Gods.*

19. Letty M. Russell, *Human Liberation in a Feminist Perspective—A Theology* (Philadelphia: Westminster, 1974), p. 63. Further references to this work follow in the text.

20. In *Black Theology: A Documentary History,* p. 101.

21. Ibid., p. 398. Further references to Murray follow in the text.

22. See Paulo Freire, *Pedagogy of the Oppressed* (1970; New York: Herder and Herder) and *Education for Critical Consciousness* (New York: Seabury, 1973).

23. Rosemary Radford Ruether also calls racist what she sees as Daly's use of the Virgin Mary as a liberation symbol, in *New Woman, New Earth* (New York: Seabury, 1975), p. 121. Further references to Ruether follow in the text.

24. Ruether in *Liberation Theology* (1973) and Cone in *Black Theology and Black Power* (1969).

25. Ruether, *Liberation Theology,* p. 124, as cited in Russell, p. 62. For a fuller elaboration of Ruether's theory see *Sexism and God-Talk* (Boston: Beacon, 1983).

26. Shoshana Felman, "Women and Madness: The Critical Phallacy," *Diacritics* 5, no. 4 (Winter 1975): 3.

27. Susan Griffin, *Pornography and Silence* (New York: Harper, 1981), p. 2. Further references follow in the text. See also Andrea Dworkin, *Pornography* (New York: Putnam, 1981), and Catharine A. MacKinnon, *Only Words* (Cambridge: Harvard University Press, 1993).

28. Meredith Tax, "Woman and Her Mind: The Story of an Everyday Life," *Notes from the Second Year* (1970), p. 10. Further references to this article follow in the text.

29. Sandra Lee Bartky, "On Psychological Oppression," in *Philosophy and Women*, ed. Sharon Bishop and Marjorie Weinzweig (Belmont, Calif.: Wadsworth, 1979), p. 34. Further references to this article follow in the text.

30. Dana Densmore, "On the Temptation to Be a Beautiful Object," in Salper, *Female Liberation*, pp. 203–8. In addition to other articles on the subject cited below see Una Stannard, "The Mask of Beauty," in Gornick and Moran, *Woman in Sexist Society*, pp. 118–30, and "No More Miss America! Ten Points of Protest," in *Sisterhood Is Powerful*, ed. Robin Morgan (New York: Vintage, 1970), pp. 521–24.

31. On Monroe, see Susan Griffin, *Pornography and Silence*, pp. 204 ff.; on Fitzgerald, see Nancy Milford, *Zelda* (1970; New York: Avon, 1971); on Plath, see her novel, *The Bell Jar* (1963; New York: Harper, 1971). Also see Chesler, *Women and Madness*.

32. Sandra Bartky, "Narcissism, Femininity and Alienation," *Social Theory and Practice* 8, no. 2 (Summer 1982); 137. Further references to this article follow in the text.

33. The degree to which the objectification or commoditization of women's bodies is endemic in the culture may be seen if one considers simply reversing the sexes and attempting to objectify or commodify male bodies. It does not work. Male bodies are simply not perceived as erotic objects (except in a homosexual context) because the controlling viewpoint is the male subject (see Barrett, p. 92).

34. Adrienne Rich, "Women and Honor: Some Notes on Lying" (1975) in *On Lies, Secrets, and Silence*, p. 190. Rich is referring to the classic film *Gaslight* (1944) in which Ingrid Bergman is driven mad by the denials of her husband, Charles Boyer.

35. Peter Berger and Hansfried Keller, "Marriage and the Construction of Reality," *Diogenes* 46 (1964): 4. Also see Peter L. Berger and Thomas Luckman, *The Social Construction of Reality: A Treatise in the Sociology of Knowledge* (1966; Garden City: Anchor, 1967).

36. Bartky, "Narcissism, Femininity and Alienation," p. 19. See also Sandra Bartky, "Toward a Phenomenology of Feminist Consciousness," in *Feminism and Philosophy*, ed. Mary Vetterling-Braggin, Frederick A. Elliston and Jane English (Totowa, N.J.: Littlefield, Adams, 1977), pp. 23–24.

37. As Adrienne Rich put it in "As We Dead Awaken: Writing as Re-Vision," (1971), in *On Lies, Secrets, and Silence*, pp. 33–49.

Chapter 6
Radical Feminism

1. Ellen Willis, "Women and the Left," *Notes from the Second Year* (1970), p. 56.

2. Marge Piercy, "The Grand Coolie Damn," in Morgan, *Sisterhood,* pp. 421–38. See also Anne Koedt, "Women and the Radical Movement" (1968), in *Radical Feminism,* ed. Koedt, Ellen Levine and Anita Rapone (New York: Quadrangle, 1973), pp. 318–21; and Robin Morgan, "Goodbye to All That," in *Going Too Far* (New York: Random, 1977), pp. 121–30.

3. In this chapter I am using "Radical Feminism" to refer to a specific theory that was developed in the late 1960s. Various other feminist theses may be labeled "radical," of course, and not all women who call themselves radical subscribe to what is here labeled "radical feminism." Socialist feminists, for example, espouse various radical positions but may reject aspects of "radical feminism." Similarly, certain radical women of color have objected to various aspects of "radical feminism" (see below).

4. Roxanne Dunbar, "Female Liberation As A Basis for Social Revolution," *Notes from the Second Year* (1970), p. 48. Further references to this article follow in the text. This is the 1970 version of Dunbar's article, which also appears in Morgan, *Sisterhood,* pp. 477–92.

   Dunbar was not the first to call for an independent women's movement or to articulate women's dissatisfaction with their treatment in the antiwar and civil rights movements. Black activist Ruby Doris Smith Robinson led a group of women in developing a critique of women's roles in SNCC (Student Nonviolent Coordinating Committee) that was delivered in November 1964. Shortly thereafter Casey Hayden and Mary King, two SNCC organizers, wrote a memo to "Women in the Peace and Freedom Movements" (1965). In 1967 Joreen Freeman organized an independent women's group in Chicago, which issued its theoretical statement on 13 November 1967. That group formed in response to a Conference on New Politics held earlier that year in Chicago at which feminist issues were ignored or ridiculed. Women who later became leading radical feminists—Ti-Grace Atkinson, Florynce Kennedy, Shulamith Firestone, and Pam Allen—also protested the (mis)treatment of women's issues at that conference. In 1968 Beverly Jones and Judith Brown issued "Towards a Female Liberation Movement," which also called for a separate women's movement. On Robinson see Sara Evans, *Personal Politics* (New York: Knopf, 1979), pp. 84–86. The SNCC statement and the Hayden-King memo are in Evans, pp. 233–38. The Freeman manifesto is in Papachristou, *Women Together,* pp. 228–29 (so is the Hayden-King memo, pp. 227–28). The Jones-Brown paper is excerpted in Papachristou, pp. 230–31. See also Alice Echols, *Daring to Be Bad* (Minneapolis: University of Minnesota Press, 1989) for details on the early history of radical feminism.

5. Dana Densmore, "Independence from the Sexual Revolution," in *Notes from the Third Year: Women's Liberation,* ed. Anne Koedt and Shulamith Firestone (New York: Notes from the Third Year, 1971), pp. 56–61; also in *Radical Feminism,* pp. 107–118.

6. "The Feminists: A Political Organization to Annihilate Sex Roles," *Notes from the Second Year* (1970), p. 114. Further references to this manifesto follow in the text.

7. Even more extreme was Valarie Solanis's SCUM (Society for Cutting Up Men) Manifesto issued in 1968. She called for, among other things, the development of parthenogenetic means of reproduction. See Morgan, *Sisterhood,* pp. 514–19. The idea was further explored in Laurel Galana, "Radical Reproduction: X Without Y," in Covina and Galana, *The Lesbian Reader,* pp. 122–37.

8. See Ti-Grace Atkinson, "Resignation from N.O.W.," *Amazon Odyssey* (New York: Links Books, 1974), pp. 9–11. See also Atkinson, "The Equality Issue," *Amazon Odyssey,* pp. 65–75.

9. "Politics of the Ego: A Manifesto for N.Y. Radical Feminists," *Notes from the Second Year* (1970), p. 124. Further references to this manifesto follow in the text.

10. Barbara Burris, "The Fourth World Manifesto," *Notes from the Third Year* (1971), p. 118. This article is also in *Radical Feminism,* pp. 322–57.

11. Kate Millett, "Sexual Politics: A Manifesto for Revolution," *Notes from the Second Year* (1970), p. 111. Further references to this manifesto follow in the text. It is also in *Radical Feminism,* pp. 365–67.

12. See chap. 3, n. 46.

13. Kate Millett, *Sexual Politics,* p. 36. Further references to this work follow in the text.

14. Barbara Mehrhof and Pamela Kearon, "Rape: An Act of Terror," in *Notes from the Third Year* (1971), p. 80; the article is also in *Radical Feminism,* pp. 228–33. For further feminist analyses of rape, see Susan Griffin, "Rape: The All-American Crime" (1971) and other articles on rape in Vetterling-Braggin et al., *Feminism and Philosophy,* pp. 308–76.

15. Susan Brownmiller, *Against Our Will* (New York: Simon and Schuster, 1975), p. 209. Further references to this work follow in the text.

16. For further radical feminist analyses of pornography see Susan Griffin, *Women and Pornography,* and *Take Back the Night,* ed. Laura Lederer

(New York: Morrow, 1980); for a further analysis of prostitution see Pamela Kearon and Barbara Mehrhof, "Prostitution," in *Notes from the Third Year* (1971), pp. 71–75.

17. Shulamith Firestone, *The Dialectic of Sex,* p. 9. Further references to this work follow in the text.

18. Zillah Eisenstein, "Developing a Theory of Capitalist Patriarchy and Socialist Feminism," in Eisenstein, *Capitalist Patriarchy,* pp. 19–20.

19. Heidi Hartmann, "The Unhappy Marriage," in Sargent, *Women and Revolution,* p. 12.

20. Atkinson characterized the period 1968–69 as one of "unlimited hopes," *Amazon Odyssey,* p. ccliv. Further references to this work follow in the text.

21. Kant, "The Fundamental Principles of the Metaphysic of Morals," in *Kant Selections,* ed. Theodore M. Greene (New York: Scribners, 1957), p. 281.

22. Heidegger, "On the Essence of Truth," in Brock, *Existence and Being,* p. 309.

23. Susan A. Taubes, "The Gnostic Foundations of Heidegger's Nihilism," *Journal of Religion* 34, no. 3 (July 1954): 170.

24. Mary Daly, *Gyn/Ecology,* p. 1. Further references to this work follow in the text.

25. On Gnosticism as a pervasive modern tendency, see Josephine Donovan, *Gnosticism in Modern Literature* (New York: Garland, 1990). For specific analyses of Heidegger's Gnosticism see, in addition to Taubes, "Gnostic Foundations," Hans Jonas, "Gnosticism, Existentialism, and Nihilism," *The Gnostic Religion,* 2d. ed. (Boston: Beacon, 1963), pp. 320–40.

26. Daly does not identify the myth as Gnostic; however, it is. A good example of an ancient Gnostic version is in the Coptic "Gospel of Mary," in *Gnosticism: A Source Book of Heretical Writings from the Early Christian Period* (New York: Harper, 1961), p. 67. The myth was particularly strong in Jewish Gnosticism. See Gershom G. Scholem, *Major Trends in Jewish Mysticism,* rev. ed. (New York: Schocken, 1941), p. 50. Kafka's "Parable of the Law" in *The Trial* may be seen as another version. See Donovan, *Gnosticism in Modern Literature,* pp. 171–73.

27. Frances M. Beale, "Double Jeopardy: To Be Black and Female" (1969) in Morgan, *Sisterhood,* pp. 340–53. Recently, Deborah H. King has suggested that "multiple jeopardy" is a more accurate term. See "Multiple Jeopardy: Multiple Consciousness—The Context of a Black Feminist Ideology," *SIGNS* 14, no. 1 (Autumn 1988): 42–72.

28. The Combahee River Collective, "A Black Feminist Statement," in Hall, Scott and Smith, *But Some of Us Are Brave,* p. 14.

29. Bell Hooks, *Ain't I a Woman,* p. 9. Further references to this work follow in the text. On sexism in the black movement see Michele Wallace, *Black Macho and the Myth of the Super Woman* (New York: Dial, 1978).

30. Gloria I. Joseph and Jill Lewis, *Common Differences* (Garden City: Anchor, 1981), p. 27.

31. Cherríe Moraga, Preface to *This Bridge Called My Back,* eds. Cherríe Moraga and Gloria Anzaldúa (Watertown, Mass.: Persephone Press, 1981), pp. xiii–xix. Further references to this work follow in the text.

32. Pauli Murray, "Jim Crow and Jane Crow," in Lerner, *Black Woman in White America,* p. 597.

33. Alice Walker, "In Search of Our Mothers' Gardens," *Ms.* 2, no. 11 (May 1974): 70. Further references to this article follow in the text. Also available in *In Search of Our Mothers' Gardens* (New York: Harcourt, Brace, Jovonovich, 1983).

34. Davis, "Reflections on the Black Woman's Role," p. 5. Further references to this article follow in the text.

35. Combahee River Collective, "Statement," pp. 15–16.

36. National Black Feminist Organization, "Statement of Purpose," *Ms.* 2, no. 11 (May 1974): 99.

37. Audre Lorde, "The Master's Tools Will Never Dismantle the Master's House," in Moraga and Anzaldúa, *This Bridge Called My Back,* p. 99.

38. See Renée Ferguson, "Women's Liberation Has a Different Meaning for Blacks," in Lerner, *Black Woman in White America,* pp. 589–90.

39. Joseph and Lewis, p. 38. See also pp. 178–230.

40. Audre Lorde, "An Open Letter to Mary Daly," in Moraga and Anzaldúa, *This Bridge Called My Back,* p. 94. Further references follow in the text.

41. Davis, *Women, Race and Class,* pp. 172–201.

42. Gloria Joseph asserts that black women's retention of very strong ties with their mothers is one of the characteristics of black society; see *Common Differences,* pp. 75–148.

43. Ibid., pp. 112, 121. Adrienne Rich has suggested that the mother-daughter relationship remains the "great unwritten story" in *Of Woman Born,* p. 219. See her chap. 9 for a start.

44. Useful early works on lesbianism and the lesbian movement include: Del Martin and Phyllis Lyon, *Lesbian/Woman* (New York: Bantam,

1972); Sidney Abbott and Barbara Love, *Sappho Was a Right-On Woman* (New York: Stein and Day, 1972); Sasha Gregory Lewis, *Sunday's Women, Lesbian Life Today* (Boston: Beacon, 1979); Delores Klaitch, *Woman Plus Woman, Attitudes toward Lesbianism* (New York: Simon and Schuster, 1974); Jonathan Katz, *Gay American History;* and Lillian Faderman, *Surpassing the Love of Men.* More recent works include: Sarah Lucia Hoagland, *Lesbian Ethics* (Palo Alto, Calif.: Institute of Lesbian Studies, 1988) and *Lesbian Philosophies and Cultures,* ed. Jeffner Allen (Albany: State University of New York Press, 1990).

45. Kathleen Barry, *Female Sexual Slavery* (Englewood Cliffs, N.J.: Prentice-Hall, 1979), p. 172, as cited in Adrienne Rich, "Compulsory Heterosexuality and Lesbian Existence," p. 646. Further references to the Rich article follow in the text.

46. Martha Shelley, "Notes of a Radical Lesbian," in Morgan, *Sisterhood,* p. 308.

47. Martha Shelley, "Lesbianism and the Women's Liberation Movement," in *Women's Liberation,* ed. Sookie Stambler (New York: Ace, 1970), p. 127.

48. Elsa Gidlow, "Lesbianism as a Liberating Force" (1977), as cited in Faderman, *Surpassing the Love of Men,* p. 385.

49. Adrienne Rich, "It is the Lesbian in Us . . ." (1976), in *On Lies, Secrets, and Silence,* pp. 200–201.

50. Blanche Wiesen Cook, "Female Support Networks," p. 48. See also her " 'Women Alone Stir My Imagination': Lesbianism and the Cultural Tradition," *SIGNS* 4, no. 4 (Summer 1979): 718–39.

51. See chap. 2, n. 40. Also useful is Jeannette Foster, *Sex Variant Women in Literature* (1945; 2d ed. Baltimore: Diana Press, 1975); *Frontiers* 4, no. 3 (Fall 1979), "Lesbian History Issue"; and Rich, "Compulsory Heterosexuality," pp. 648–60.

52. Sidney Abbott and Barbara Love, "Is Women's Liberation a Lesbian Plot?" in Gornick and Moran, *Woman in Sexist Society,* p. 447. Further references to this article follow in the text.

53. Charlotte Bunch, "Not for Lesbians Only" (1975), in *Building Feminist Theory,* p. 68. Further references to this article follow in the text. See also *Lesbianism and the Women's Movement,* ed. Nancy Myron and Charlotte Bunch (Baltimore: Diana Press, 1975).

54. Lucia Valeska, "The Future of Female Separatism," in *Building Feminist Theory,* p. 28. Further references to this article follow in the text.

55. Catharine A. MacKinnon, *Sexual Harassment of Working Women: A Case of Discrimination* (New Haven: Yale University Press, 1979), pp. 15–16, as cited in Rich, "Compulsory Heterosexuality," p. 64.

56. I use the term cultural separatist here not simply as a theory that posits a *separate* women's culture, history, and value system, but one that advocates the continuing separateness of that culture. It is a cultural feminism, but a generally apolitical one—as opposed to the social reform tendency in nineteenth century and contemporary cultural feminism (see chap. 7). It has strong links to the Goddess spirituality movement (see n. 59 below) and to what is now called ecofeminism (see chap. 8).

57. Gina Covina, "Rosy Rightbrain's Exorcism/Invocation," in Covina and Galana, *The Lesbian Reader,* p. 91. Further references to this article follow in the text.

58. Barbara Starrett, "I Dream in Female: The Metaphors of Evolution," in *The Lesbian Reader,* p. 113. Further references to this article follow in the text.

59. Elizabeth Gould Davis, *The First Sex* (1971; Baltimore: Penguin, 1972); *Heresies* 2, no. 1 (Spring 1978). See especially the articles by Merlin Stone, Carol P. Christ, and Gloria Feman Orenstein in this "Great Goddess" issue. See also Merlin Stone, *When God Was a Woman* (New York: Dial, 1976), and Starhawk, *The Spiral Dance* (New York: Harper, 1979). A useful collection in feminist spirituality is *Weaving the Visions,* ed. Judith Plaskow and Carol P. Christ (New York: Harper, 1989). Also see chap. 5, n. 18.

60. Adams, "The Oedible Complex," in *The Lesbian Reader,* p. 147. Further references to this article follow in the text. See also Carol J. Adams, *The Sexual Politics of Meat* (New York: Continuum, 1990) and Andrée Collard, with Joyce Contrucci, *Rape of the Wild* (Bloomington: Indiana University Press, 1988).

Chapter 7
The Moral Vision of Twentieth-Century Cultural Feminism

1. Sontag, "The Third World of Women," p. 192.

2. Richard Rorty, "Feminism, Ideology and Deconstruction: A Pragmatist View," *Hypatia* 8, no. 3 (Spring 1993):101. See also Marilyn French, *The War against Women* (New York: Ballantine, 1993).

3. Tax, "Woman and Her Mind," *Notes from the Second Year* (1970), p. 10.

4. See Michelle Cliff, "The Resonance of Interruption," *Chrysalis* 8 (Summer 1979): 29–37.

5. Rabuzzi, *The Sacred and the Feminine,* p. 151. Further references follow in the text.

6. Sara Ruddick, "Maternal Thinking," *Feminist Studies* 6, no. 2 (Summer 1980): 348. Further references follow in the text. An expanded analysis appears in Sara Ruddick, *Maternal Thinking* (Boston: Beacon, 1989).

7. Evelyn Fox Keller, "Feminism and Science," *SIGNS* 7, no. 3 (Spring 1982): 599. A further reference follows in the text. Keller stresses that the two modes may be expressed by women or men; however, because historians themselves, as well as scientists, have seen through the focals of masculinist ideology, they have selected the manipulative mode as the dominant one. The implication in her article is nevertheless that the manipulative mode is masculine, while the more passive mode is feminine.

8. See also the socialist feminists' discussion of use-value production and ideological socialization in chap. 3.

9. See Joanna Bunker Rohrbach, *Women: Psychology's Puzzle* (New York: Basic, 1979), p. 72. See also David McClelland, "Wanted: A New Self-Image for Women," in *Dialogue on Women* (Indianapolis: Bobbs-Merrill, 1967), pp. 33–55; and Eleanor E. Maccoby and Carol N. Jacklin, *The Psychology of Sex Differences* (Stanford: Stanford University Press, 1974). According to Paula J. Caplan et al., *Gender Differences in Human Cognition* (New York: Oxford University Press, 1997), gender differences in spatial cognition continue to be registered in psychological tests such as the EFT and RFT, but the authors suggest that subjects' belief in such differences may be an important factor in their performance (p. 112; see also pp. 16–20). Another interesting theory about women's different *episteme* is Robert Jay Lifton, "Woman as Knower: Some Psychohistorical Perspectives," in *The Woman in America,* ed. Lifton (Boston: Beacon, 1967), pp. 27–51.

10. Fuller, *Woman in the Nineteenth Century,* p. 115.

11. Carol Gilligan, *In a Different Voice* (Cambridge: Harvard University Press, 1982), p. 5. Further references to this work follow in the text. I have emphasized Chekhov's scene somewhat differently than Gilligan, and it must be stated that in the play the dialectic is primarily one of class. Lopahin is an upstart peasant entrepreneur; Madame, the last of a dying race of aristocrats.

12. In an earlier version of this chapter Gilligan had used the term "inductive" instead of "narrative," which helps explain that by narrative she means, tied to contextual events. See Gilligan, "Woman's Place in Man's Life Cycle," *Harvard Educational Review* 49, no. 4 (1979): 442.

13. A term used by Georgia Sassen, "Success Anxiety in Women: A Constructivist Interpretation of Its Source and Its Significance," *Harvard Educational Review* 50, no. 1 (1980): 17; following its use by Robert

Kegan, "Ego and Truth: Personality and the Piaget Paradigm" (Ph.D. diss. Harvard University, 1977), p. 99.

14. Simone de Beauvoir, Interview, October 1976, in *New French Feminisms,* pp. 152–53.

15. Ruether, *New Woman, New Earth,* pp. 194–95. Further references follow in the text. See also Jean Bethke Elshtain, *Public Man, Private Woman,* pp. 51, 118–19, 142–43, on the male suppression of the feminine as a major source of contemporary difficulties. Elshtain sees the masculine public world as constructed, indeed, as a defense "against the private sphere in which [feminine] desire, conceived as uncontrollable and arbitrary, is held to rank supreme" (118–19).

16. Keller, "Gender and Science," in Hintikka and Harding, *Discovering Reality,* p. 197. Further references follow in the text.

17. Azizah al-Hibri, "Capitalism Is an Advanced Stage of Patriarchy: But Marxism Is Not Feminism," in Sargent, *Women and Revolution,* p. 171. Further references follow in the text. See also Mary O'Brien, who argues in *The Politics of Reproduction* that because the male experience of reproduction is discontinuous (his sperm is "lost" or alienated in the process), men had to establish "artificial modes of continuity" (53). This required a denigration of the female reproductive process and a valorization of idealist, intellectual (male) reproduction (132).

18. Ludwig Wittgenstein, *Tractatus Logico-Philosophicus* (1911; London; Routledge & Kegan Paul, 1962): 6.341. Further references follow in the text.

19. Ludwig Wittgenstein, *Notebooks 1914–16* (Oxford: Blackwell, 1961), p. 73.

20. Murdoch did not identify these mechanisms with gender behavior; however, cultural feminists make that connection. Sara Ruddick for example, sees Murdoch's moral vision as congruent with maternal thinking (pp. 350–51).
The material in this section is developed more fully in Josephine Donovan, "Ecofeminist Literary Criticism: Reading the Orange," *Hypatia* 11, no. 2 (Spring 1996):161–84; Donovan, "Beyond the Net: Feminist Criticism as a Moral Criticism," *Denver Quarterly* 17, no. 4 (Winter 1983):40–57; and Donovan, "Attention to Suffering: Sympathy as a Basis for Ethical Treatment of Animals," in *Beyond Animal Rights,* ed. Donovan and Adams, pp. 147–69.

21. Iris Murdoch, *Under the Net* (New York: Viking, 1954), p. 261.

22. Iris Murdoch, "On 'God' and 'Good,' " in *The Sovereignty of Good* (New York: Schocken, 1971), p. 66. A further reference to this work follows in

the text. See also her *Metaphysics as a Guide to Morals* (New York: Viking Penguin, 1993).

23. Iris Murdoch, "The Sublime and the Good," *Chicago Review* 13 (Autumn 1959): 51.

24. Robin Morgan, *The Anatomy of Freedom* (Garden City: Doubleday, 1982), pp. xiii, 283. Further references follow in the text.

25. The above citations are statements made by two physicists, David Böhm and Fritjof Capra, quoted by Morgan.

26. Virginia Woolf, *Three Guineas* (1938; New York: Harcourt, Brace & World, 1963), p. 6. Further references to this edition follow in the text.

27. Virginia Woolf, *A Room of One's Own*, pp. 35–36.

28. See also Adrienne Rich, "Toward a Woman-Centered University" (1973–74), in *On Lies, Secrets, and Silence*, pp. 125–55.

29. Chrystos, "No Rock Scorns Me as Whore," in Moraga and Anzaldúa, *This Bridge Called My Back*, p. 245.

Chapter 8
Into the Twenty-first Century

1. Iris Marion Young, "Humanism, Gynocentrism, and Feminist Politics," in *Throwing Like a Girl*, p. 79.

2. Carole Pateman, *The Sexual Contract* (Stanford: Stanford University Press, 1988), p. 6. Further references follow in the text. African-American history differs here from Anglo-American because of slavery, a very different sort of "contract." See Pateman, pp. 60–76; also Patricia T. Williams, "On Being an Object of Property," *SIGNS* 14, no. 1 (Autumn 1988): 5–24.

   For a seventeenth-century feminist critique of contract theory and other liberal tenets, see Ruth Perry, "Mary Astell and the Feminist Critique of Possessive Individualism," *Eighteenth-Century Studies* 23, no. 4 (Summer 1990): 444–57.

3. For a further discussion of the complexities of contract law vis-à-vis the private sphere, see Clare Dalton, "An Essay in the Deconstruction of Contract Doctrine" (1985), in *Interpreting Law and Literature: A Hermeneutic Reader*, ed. Sanford Levinson and Steven Mailloux (Evanston, Ill.: Northwestern University Press, 1988), pp. 285–318. See also Williams, "On Being an Object."

4. For a recent articulation of this position see Carol C. Gould, "Private Right and Public Virtues: Women, the Family, and Democracy," in *Beyond Domination*, pp. 12–13. Earlier advocates included Victoria

Woodhull, Harriet Taylor, Emma Goldman, and several radical feminists.

5. Susan Moller Okin, *Justice, Gender, and the Family* (New York: Basic, 1989), pp. 135–36. Further references follow in the text.

6. Carole Pateman and Elizabeth Gross, *Feminist Challenges* (1986; Boston: Northeastern University Press, 1987), p. 3. Further references follow in the text.

7. See also Nancy C. M. Hartsock, "Masculinity, Heroism, and the Making of War," in *Rocking the Ship of State*, ed. Adrienne Harris and Ynestra King (Boulder, Colo.: Westview, 1989), pp. 133–52. Other useful discussions of women's connection with the military include Cynthia Enloe, *Does Khaki Become You?* (Boston: South End, 1983) and Enloe, *The Morning After: Sexual Politics at the End of the Cold War* (Berkeley: University of California Press, 1993).

8. Genevieve Lloyd, *The Man of Reason* (Minneapolis: University of Minnesota Press, 1984); Susan Bordo, *The Flight to Objectivity* (Albany: State University of New York Press, 1987), and Susan Bordo, "The Cartesian Masculinization of Thought," *SIGNS* 11, no. 3 (Spring 1986): 439–56. See also the articles by Janna Thompson and Catriona MacKenzie in *Feminist Challenges*, ed. Pateman and Gross, pp. 99–111 and 144–56. Another useful collection is *Feminist Interpretations and Political Theory*, ed. Mary Lyndon Shanley and Carole Pateman (University Park, Pa.: Pennsylvania State University Press, 1991).

9. Iris Young, "Impartiality and the Civic Public," in *Feminism as Critique*, ed. Seyla Benhabib and Drucilla Cornell (Minneapolis: University of Minnesota Press, 1987), p. 59. Further references follow in the text.

10. Max Horkheimer and Theodor W. Adorno, *Dialectic of Enlightenment* (1944; New York: Herder and Herder, 1972).

11. The practical means by which such a change might occur include, Young proposes, a model of communicative interaction or dialog that does not ignore the emotional components of speech and that looks to consensus as a means of resolving disputes (pp. 73–76). Other feminist theorists have seen as models for new political organization certain separatist women's groups such as the pacifist encampments at Greenham Common in England and at Seneca, New York, which protested nuclear militarism. These groups have evolved a consensus praxis that might provide a new basis for national political decision-making. See Gwyn Kirk, "Our Greenham Common: Not Just a Place but a Movement," and Ynestra King, "Afterword," in *Rocking the Ship*, pp. 263–80 and 281–98. Also of interest is Charlene Eldridge Wheeler and Peggy L. Chinn, *Peace & Power: A Handbook of Feminist Process* (Buffalo, N.Y.: Margaret-

daughter, 1984), and Robin Leidner, "Stretching the Boundaries of Liberalism: Democratic Innovation in a Feminist Organization," *SIGNS* 16, no. 2 (Winter 1991): 263–89.

Perhaps the most radical recent proposal for changing the current political scene is that made by M. E. Hawkesworth in *Beyond Oppression* (New York: Continuum, 1990). She urges the adoption of "a constitutional principle mandating that women hold 50 percent of all elective, appointive, and bureaucratic offices" (p. 181).

12. Kathy E. Ferguson, *The Feminist Case against Bureaucracy* (Philadelphia: Temple University Press, 1984), p. 17. Further references follow in the text.

13. Michel Foucault, *Power/Knowledge: Selected Inverviews and Other Writings* (New York: Pantheon, 1982), pp. 81–82.

14. Ibid., p. 106.

15. Michel Foucault, *Discipline and Punish: The Birth of the Prison* (New York: Vintage, 1979), p. 228.

16. Foucault, *Power/Knowledge,* p. 81.

17. See *Feminist Approaches to Science,* ed. Ruth Bleier (New York: Pergamon, 1986); *Sex and Scientific Inquiry,* ed. Sandra Harding and Jean F. O'Barr (Chicago: University of Chicago Press, 1987); Helen E. Longino and Evelynn Hammonds, "Conflicts and Tensions in the Feminist Study of Gender and Science," in *Conflicts in Feminism,* ed. Marianne Hirsch and Evelyn Fox Keller (New York: Routledge, 1990), pp. 164–83. For analysis of some of the specific issues see Lynda Birke, *Women, Feminism and Biology* (New York: Methuen, 1986); Josephine Donovan, "Animal Rights and Feminist Theory," *SIGNS* 15, no. 2 (Winter 1990): 350–75; Marti Kheel, "From Healing Herbs to Deadly Drugs: Western Medicine's War on the Natural World," in *Healing the Wounds,* ed. Judith Plant (Philadelphia: New Society, 1989), pp. 96–111; and Vandana Shiva and Ingunn Moser, eds. *Biopolitics* (London: Zed, 1995).

18. Sandra Harding, *The Science Question in Feminism* (Ithaca: Cornell University Press, 1986), pp. 24–28. See also her "Instability of the Analytical Categories of Feminist Theory," *SIGNS* 11, no. 4 (1986): 645–64, and "Feminism, Science, and the Anti-Enlightenment Critiques," in *Feminism/Postmodernism,* ed. Linda J. Nicholson (New York: Routledge, 1990), pp. 83–106.

19. Hilary Rose, "Beyond Masculinist Realities: A Feminist Epistemology for the Sciences," in *Feminist Approaches to Science,* ed. Bleier, p. 72. See her "Hand, Brain, and Heart: A Feminist Epistemology for the Natural Sciences," *SIGNS* 9, no. 1 (1983): 73–90, for a fuller exposition of her theory.

20. Ruth Berman, "From Aristotle's Dualism to Materialist Dialectics: Feminist Transformation of Science and Society," in *Gender/Body/Knowledge,* ed. Alison M. Jaggar and Susan R. Bordo (New Brunswick, N.J.: Rutgers University Press, 1989), pp. 224–55. See also Evelyn Fox Keller's biography of Barbara McClintock, *A Feeling for the Organism* (New York: W. H. Freeman, 1983).

    Other useful discussions of feminist epistemology include Lorraine Code, *What Can She Know?* (Ithaca: Cornell University Press, 1991); Jane Duran, *Toward a Feminist Epistemology* (Savage, Md.: Rowman & Littlefield, 1991); Lynn Hankinson Nelson, *Who Knows: From Quine to a Feminist Empiricism* (Philadelphia: Temple University Press, 1990); and Sandra Harding, *Is Science Multicultural?* (Bloomington: Indiana University Press, 1998).

21. Jane Flax, "Postmodernism and Gender Relations in Feminist Theory," *SIGNS* 12, no. 4 (Summer 1987): 634.

22. Harding, *Science Question,* p. 124.

23. Flax, "Postmodernism," p. 633.

24. Adrienne Rich, *The Dream of a Common Language: Poems 1974–1977* (New York: Norton, 1978).

25. Donna Haraway, "A Manifesto for Cyborgs" (1985), in *Feminism/Postmodernism,* ed. Nicholson, p. 223.

26. MacKinnon, "Feminism, Marxism, Method" (1983), p. 655.

27. MacKinnon, *Feminism Unmodified,* p. 165. Further references follow in the text.

28. Catharine A. MacKinnon, *Toward a Feminist Theory of the State* (Cambridge: Harvard University Press, 1989), p. 224.

29. Robin West, "Jurisprudence and Gender," *University of Chicago Law Review* 55, no. 1 (Winter 1988): 61. Further references follow in the text. See also West's *Caring for Justice* (New York: New York University Press, 1997).

30. See MacKinnon, *Feminism Unmodified,* p. 210. For a thoughtful evaluation of the issues raised here, see the articles by Rosemarie Tong and Ann Ferguson in *Women's Review of Books,* May 1986, pp. 7–9 and 11–13, and Martha Minow, "Adjudicating Differences: Conflicts among Feminist Lawyers," in *Conflicts in Feminism,* ed. Hirsch and Keller, pp. 156–60.

    Prior to but connected with the pornography debate was the so-called "sex wars" debate. A useful introduction to this is Ann Ferguson, "Sex Wars: The Debate between Radical and Libertarian Feminists," *SIGNS* 10, no. 1 (Autumn 1984): 106–12. Background material includes *Plea-*

sure and Danger: Exploring Female Sexuality, ed. Carole S. Vance (Boston: Routledge, 1984) and *The Powers of Desire: The Politics of Sexuality,* ed. Ann Snitow et al. (New York: Monthly Review, 1983).

31. MacKinnon, *Feminism Unmodified,* p. 210.

32. See MacKinnon, *Feminism Unmodified,* pp. 103–16 and 231, n. 7. It was MacKinnon who developed this line of argument in *Sexual Harassment* (1979) (see chap. 6, no. 55, above). MacKinnon was co-counsel in the landmark 1986 sexual harassment case, *Meritor Savings Bank v. Vinson.* Of course, the celebrated Anita Hill-Clarence Thomas confrontation during Thomas' confirmation hearings for nomination to the U.S. Supreme Court in 1991 gave national attention to the issue.

33. MacKinnon, "Toward Feminist Jurisprudence" (1982): 730. See also above chap. 2, n. 62.

34. See Hasse, "Legalizing Gender-Specific Values," in *Women and Moral Theory,* ed. Kittay and Meyers, pp. 289–94.

35. Minow, "Adjudicating Differences," in *Conflicts in Feminism,* p. 149. See also Minow's *Making All the Difference: Inclusion, Exclusion, and American Law* (Ithaca: Cornell University Press, 1990).

36. *New York Times,* 14 January 1987, p. A1.

37. Whether pregnancy leaves should be considered a disability is another question; while some women may be "disabled" by the condition, many are not. Maternity leave is needed not so much because the women are unable to work but because they have to care for their infants. Thus, the usage of a male or gender-neutral term to argue the case obscures the real nature of the women's need. It also serves as an illustration of a gender-specific condition being characterized in gender-neutral terms (see Robin West above, n. 29).

38. See MacKinnon, *Toward a Feminist Theory of the State,* pp. 156–66, and *Feminism Unmodified,* pp. 37–39. See also Wendy W. Williams, "The Equality Crisis: Some Reflections on Culture, Courts, and Feminism," in *Second Wave,* ed. Linda Nicholson, pp. 71–91.

39. Joan W. Scott, "Deconstructing Equality-Versus-Difference; or, The Uses of Poststructuralist Theory for Feminism," in *Conflicts in Feminism,* ed. Hirsch and Keller, p. 139. See also Minow, "Adjudicating Differences," in *Conflicts,* p. 153; Alice Kessler-Harris, "Equal Opportunity Commission vs. Sears, Roebuck and Company: A Personal Account," in *Unequal Sisters,* ed. Ruiz and DuBois, pp. 545–59; and Joan Hoff, "The Pernicious Effect of Post-structuralism on Women's History," in *Radically Speaking: Feminism Reclaimed,* ed. Diane Bell and Renate Klein (North Melbourne, Australia: Spinifex, 1996), pp. 393–412.

40. If women are prepared ideologically for this kind of labor, then one has to ask, is this fair? If not, then equal treatment begins on a much deeper level than the law. Nevertheless, regardless of the reasons women may choose such work, the value of the work should not be demeaned because it thereby is viewed as women's work. The comparable worth and wages for housework movements are promising responses to this problem. On comparable worth see Joan Acker, *Doing Comparable Worth: Gender Class and Pay Equity* (Philadelphia: Temple University Press, 1989). On wages for housework, see MacKinnon, *Toward a Feminist Theory of the State,* pp. 63–80. See also Rosemarie Putnam Tong, *Feminist Thought,* 2d ed. (Boulder, Colo.: Westview Press, 1998), pp. 108–14.

41. MacKinnon, *Feminism Unmodified,* p. 44. For a specific suggestion as to how group differences may be integrated into public policy, see Iris Young's notion of "special rights" in "Polity and Group Difference" in *Throwing Like a Girl,* pp. 114–37 (see further discussion below).

42. Nel Noddings, *Caring* (Berkeley: University of California Press, 1984), Mary Belenky et al., *Women's Ways of Knowing* (New York: Basic, 1987), and Sara Ruddick, *Maternal Thinking* (Boston: Beacon, 1989).

43. See chap. 1, no. 12. For an interesting application of Gilligan's theories to the jurisprudence of Supreme Court Justice Sandra Day O'Connor see Suzanna Sherry, "Civic Virtue and Feminine Voice in Constitutional Adjudication," *Virginia Law Review* 72 (1986):543–616.

44. Caroline Whitbeck, "A Different Reality: Feminist Ontology," in *Beyond Domination,* ed. Gould, pp. 76–82. Also useful is Marilyn Friedman, "Care and Context in Moral Reasoning," in *Women and Moral Theory,* pp. 190–204.

45. Nancy Fraser notes that several socialist-feminist critics follow Nancy Hartsock in seeing that the "dominant moral and political vocabularies," which see people as "relational, self-interested monads who transact with one another in transient, utility-maximizing encounters," reflects the standpoint of exchange; that is, a capitalist ethic. "Toward a Discourse Ethic of Solidarity," *Praxis International* 5, no. 4 (January 1986); 425.

46. Seyla Benhabib, "The Generalized and the Concrete Other: The Kohlberg-Gilligan Controversy and Moral Theory" in *Women and Moral Theory,* ed. Kittay and Meyers, p. 163. Further references follow in the text.

47. Benhabib proceeds to develop a dialogical theory, based in part on Jürgen Habermas's "communicative model of need interpretations," pp. 168–71. For a further elaboration in this vein, see Fraser, "Toward a Discourse Ethic," in which she argues that "an ethic of solidarity elab-

orated from the standpoint of the collective concrete other is more appropriate than an ethic of care for a feminist ethic" (429).

48. Carol Gilligan, "Moral Orientation and Moral Development" in *Women and Moral Theory,* ed. Kittay and Meyers, pp. 29–32. My discussion elaborates Gilligan's points somewhat.

49. See Virginia Held's critique of Noddings, *Women and Moral Theory,* pp. 119–20, and Benhabib, "Generalized and Concrete Other," p. 168.

50. Dorothy E. Smith, *The Everyday World as Problematic: A Feminist Sociology* (Boston: Northeastern Unviersity Press, 1987). For further elaborations of standpoint theory see Alison M. Jaggar, *Feminist Politics and Human Nature* (Totowa, N.J.: Rowman & Allanheld, 1983), pp. 369–89; Susan Hekman, "Truth and Method: Feminist Standpoint Theory Revisited," *SIGNS* 22, no. 2 (Winter 1997):341–65; Nancy C. M. Hartsock et al., Comments on "Hekman's 'Truth and Method,' " *SIGNS* 22, no. 2 (Winter 1997):367–402; and Nancy C. M. Hartsock, *The Feminist Standpoint Revisited and Other Essays* (Boulder, Colo.: Westview Press, 1998).

51. On the importance of consciousness-raising see MacKinnon, *Toward a Feminist Theory of the State,* pp. 83–105; some current feminist groups have developed consciousness-raising sessions that explore differences rather than shared commonalities. See Iris Young, Introduction to *Throwing Like a Girl,* p. 8. But unless the ultimate goal is to unify around a common sense of oppression, consciousness-raising will not serve to develop a standpoint epistemology.
See also Patricia Hill Collins, *Black Feminist Thought* (Boston: Unwin Hyman, 1990), pp. 33–37.

52. Fredric Jameson, "History and Class Consciousness as an Unfinished Project," *Rethinking Marxism* 1, no. 1 (Spring 1988): 49–72. Further references follow in the text.

53. Linda Alcoff, "Cultural Feminism Versus Post-Structuralism: The Identity Crisis in Feminist Theory," *SIGNS* 13, no. 3 (Spring 1988): 434.

54. A useful discussion of this issue is in Young, "Polity and Group Differences," in *Throwing Like a Girl,* pp. 121–24.

55. Rose, "Hand, Brain, and Heart."

56. Alison M. Jaggar, "Love and Knowledge: Emotion in Feminist Epistemology," in *Gender/Body/Knowledge,* ed. Jaggar and Bordo, p. 162.

57. Haunani-Kay Trask, *Eros and Power* (Philadelphia: University of Pennsylvania Press, 1986), p. 90. Further references follow in the text.

58. Patricia Hill Collins, "The Social Construction of Black Feminist Thought," *SIGNS* 14, no. 4 (Summer 1989): 747. Further references follow. See also her *Black Feminist Thought,* pp. 21–40 and 201–20.

59. Sarah Lucia Hoagland, *Lesbian Ethics* (Palo Alto, Calif.: Institute of Lesbian Studies, 1988), p. 6.

60. The norms of the dominant viewpoint also marginalize and stigmatize other "deviancies," such as age and disability. On ageism as it affects women see Barbara Macdonald with Cynthia Rich, *Look Me in the Eye: Old Women, Aging and Ageism* (San Francisco: Spinsters Ink, 1983), and *Women and Aging,* ed. Jo Alexander et al. (Corvallis, Oreg.: Calyx Books, 1986). Simone de Beauvoir's *The Coming of Age* (1970) is useful, but it does not focus specifically on women. On disabled women see *With the Power of Each Breath: A Disabled Women's Anthology,* ed. Susan Browne et al. (Pittsburgh: Cleis, 1985).

61. The term *poststructuralism* refers to developments in critical theory that emerged after and in some senses in rebellion against *structuralism.* Sometimes it is used interchangeably with *postmodernism,* but the latter term is more accurately used as the movement in the arts that succeeded *modernism. Deconstructionism* is a form of poststructuralism practiced in literary theory. Since most feminist poststructuralists or postmodernists favor the latter term, I use it here.

62. Jürgen Habermas, *Legitimation Crisis* (Boston: Beacon, 1975).

63. Nancy Fraser and Linda J. Nicholson, "Social Criticism Without Philosophy: An Encounter Between Feminism and Postmodernism," in *Feminism/Postmodernism,* ed. Nicholson, pp. 21–22; Jean-François Lyotard, *The Postmodern Condition: A Report on Knowledge* (Minneapolis: University of Minnesota Press, 1984). See also Susan J. Hekman, *Gender and Knowledge* (Boston: Northeastern University Press, 1990), p. 13, and Seyla Benhabib, "Epistemologies of Postmodernism: A Rejoinder to Jean-François Lyotard," in *Feminism/Postmodernism,* p. 108.

64. Craig Owens, "The Discourse of Others: Feminists and Postmodernism," in *The Anti-Aesthetic: Essays on Postmodern Culture,* ed. Hal Foster (Port Townsend, Wash.: Bay Press, 1983), 65–66.

65. Flax, "Postmodernism," pp. 624–25.

66. Fraser and Nicholson, "Social Criticism," p. 21. Further references follow in the text.

67. Fraser and Nicholson, "Social Criticism," pp. 27–33. See also Elizabeth V. Spelman, *Inessential Woman* (Boston: Beacon, 1988). In "Upping the Anti (sic) in Feminist Theory" (in *Conflicts in Feminism,* ed. Hirsch and Keller, p. 255), Teresa de Lauretis acknowledges that the term *essentialist* has become a kind of buzzword, used as a club rather than for enlightenment. She faults it for its reductiveness, "its self-righteous tone of superiority, its contempt for 'them' "—characteristics that have unfortunately marred much feminist postmodernist rhetoric.

68. Terry Eagleton, *Walter Benjamin; or, Towards a Revolutionary Criticism* (London: Verso, 1981), pp. 74, 138.

69. Mary E. Hawkesworth, "Knower, Knowing, Known: Feminist Theory and the Claims of Truth," *SIGNS* 14, no. 3 (Spring 1989): 557.

70. Harding, "Instability of Analytical Categories," p. 657.

71. MacKinnon, *Feminism Unmodified,* p. 3.

72. Elizabeth Gross, "Philosophy, Subjectivity and the Body," in *Feminist Challenges,* ed. Pateman and Gross, p. 133. For a powerful orthodox Marxist-feminist critique of postmodern feminism, see Teresa L. Ebert, *Ludic Feminism and After* (Ann Arbor: University of Michigan Press, 1996).

A spin-off of postmodernist feminism has been "queer theory," which focuses mainly on destabilizing sexual identities as a way of countering cultural prejudice against homosexuals and other sexual minorities. The *loci classici* of queer theory are Eva Kosofsky Sedgwick, *Epistemology of the Closet* (Berkeley: University of California Press, 1990) and Judith Butler, *Gender Trouble: Feminism and the Subversion of Identity* (Bloomington: Indiana University Press, 1987). A compelling critique of queer theory is provided in *All the Rage: Reasserting Radical Lesbian Feminism,* ed. Lynne Harne and Elaine Miller (New York: Teachers College Press, 1996). See also the articles by Sheila Jeffreys, Sue Wilkinson, and Celia Kitzinger in *Radically Speaking,* ed. Bell and Klein.

73. Susan Bordo, "Feminism, Postmodernism, and Gender-Skepticism," in *Feminism/Postmodernism,* ed. Nicholson, p. 150. Further references follow in the text.

74. Barbara Christian, "The Race for Theory," *Cultural Critique* 6 (Spring 1987): 68, 71.

75. Marilyn Waring, Address to the 1999 Association for Women in Development Forum, Alexandria, Va., 11 Nov. 1999 (on C-SPAN). See also Waring's *If Women Counted* (New York: Harper, 1988); Maria Mies et al., *Women: The Last Colony* (London: Zed, 1988); Annette Fuentes and Barbara Ehrenreich, *Woman in the Global Factory* (New York: South End Press, 1983); and Maria Mies, *Patriarchy and Accumulation on a World Scale* (London: Zed, 1986).

76. See Cynthia Enloe, *Bananas, Beaches & Bases: Making Feminist Sense of International Politics* (Berkeley: University of California Press, 1990).

77. Uma Narayan, "Contesting Cultures: Westernization, Respect for Cultures, and Third-World Feminists," in *Second Wave,* ed. Nicholson, pp. 396–414. See also Evelyn Accad, "Truth versus Loyalty," in *Radically Speaking,* ed. Bell and Klein, pp. 465–69; Uma Narayan, *Dislocat-*

ing Cultures (New York: Routledge, 1997); and Susan Moller Okin et al., *Is Multiculturalism Bad for Women?* (Princeton, N.J.: Princeton University Press, 1999).

78. Charlotte Perkins Gilman, "A Study in Ethics," Typescript manuscript, Schlesinger Library, Radcliffe College, Cambridge, Mass.

79. See above, chap. 2, n. 7.

80. Coral Lansbury, *The Old Brown Dog: Women, Workers, and Vivisection in Edwardian England* (Madison: University of Wisconsin Press, 1985), pp. 82, 84. See also Donovan, "Animal Rights and Feminist Theory," in *Beyond Animal Rights,* ed. Donovan and Adams.

81. Marilyn French, *Beyond Power* (New York: Summit, 1985), p. 341. See also Carol J. Adams and Josephine Donovan, eds., *Animals and Women: Feminist Theoretical Explorations* (Durham, N.C.: Duke University Press, 1995).

82. Ynestra King, "Toward an Ecological Feminism," in *Machina ex Dea,* ed. Joan Rothchild (New York: Pergamon, 1983); rpt. in *Healing the Wounds,* ed. Plant.

83. Ynestra King, "Feminism and the Revolt of Nature," *Heresies* 4, no. 1 (1981): 14; an expanded version of this essay is in *Gender/Body/Knowledge,* ed. Jaggar and Bordo, and *Reweaving the World,* ed. Irene Diamond and Gloria Feman Orenstein (San Francisco: Sierra Club, 1990).

84. Vandama Shiva, *Staying Alive* (London: Zed, 1988), pp. xvi–xvii. See also Shiva, introduction to *Close to Home: Women Reconnect Ecology, Health and Development Worldwide* (Philadelphia: New Society, 1994), and Maria Mies and Vandama Shiva, eds., *Ecofeminism* (London: Zed, 1993).

85. Carol J. Adams' *The Sexual Politics of Meat* (1990) and Andrée Collard's *Rape of the Wild* (written with Joyce Contrucci). See also Carol J. Adams, "Ecofeminism and the Eating of Animals," *Hypatia* 6, no. 1 (Spring 1991): 127. Other important early works include Sheila D. Collins, *A Different Heaven and Earth* (Valley Forge, Pa.: Judson Press, 1974); Elizabeth Dodson Gray, *Green Paradise Lost* (Wellesley, Mass.: Roundtable Press, 1981), and *Reclaim the Earth,* ed. Leonie Caldecott and Stephanie Leland (London: Women's Press, 1983). For a useful summary of the historical development of ecofeminism, see Charlene Spretnak, "Ecofeminism: Our Roots and Flowering," in *Reweaving the World,* pp. 3–14.

86. Marti Kheel, "Ecofeminism and Deep Ecology: Reflections on Identity and Difference," in *Reweaving the World,* ed. Diamond and Orenstein, p. 129.

87. Karen J. Warren, "Feminism and Ecology: Making Connections," *Environmental Ethics* 9 (Spring 1987): 6.

88. Ruether, *Sexism and God-Talk,* p. 87.

89. Paula Gunn Allen, *The Sacred Hoop* (Boston: Beacon, 1986), pp. 1, 80, 100. See also p. 224. For a further discussion of such reconceptualization, see Donovan, "Animal Rights and Feminist Theory," pp. 369–74, and Marti Kheel, "The Liberation of Nature: A Circular Affair," *Environmental Ethics* 7 (Summer 1985): 142–49. Both the Donovan and Kheel articles are reprinted in *Beyond Animal Rights,* ed. Donovan and Adams.

90. Starhawk, "Feminist, Earth-based Spirituality and Ecofeminism," in *Healing the Wounds,* ed. Plant, p. 174. See also Charlene Spretnak, "Toward an Ecofeminist Spirituality," in *Healing the Wounds,* pp. 127–32. Other important recent ecofeminist works not mentioned elsewhere include: Greta Gaard, ed. *Ecofeminism: Women, Animals, Nature* (Philadelphia: Temple University Press, 1993); Val Plumwood, *Feminism and the Mastery of Nature* (New York: Routledge, 1993); Karen Warren, ed., *Ecological Feminism* (New York: Routledge, 1994); Carolyn Merchant, *Earthcare: Women and the Environment* (London: Routledge, 1996); and Joni Seager, *Earth Follies* (New York: Routledge, 1993).

91. Roderick Frazier Nash, *The Rights of Nature: A History of Environmental Ethics* (Madison: University of Wisconsin Press, 1989), pp. 70–71.

92. See Kheel, "Ecofeminism and Deep Ecology." Further references follow in the text. See also Ariel Kay Salleh, "Deeper Than Deep Ecology: The Eco-Feminist Connection," *Environmental Ethics* 6 (Winter 1984): 339–45.

93. Tom Regan, *The Case for Animal Rights* (Berkeley: University of California Press, 1983), p. 362.

94. Kheel, "Liberation of Nature," p. 137.

95. Regan's views are in *The Case for Animal Rights* (1983) and Singer's are in *Animal Liberation* (1975; rev. ed., 1989). See Donovan, "Animal Rights and Feminist Theory" for one feminist critique.

96. "A Declaration of Interdependence," *Ecofeminist Newsletter* 1, no. 1 (Spring 1990): p. 7. The declaration was originally issued by the organizers of the Women's Economic and Development Organization (WEDO) in 1989, according to Noël Sturgeon, *Ecofeminist Natures* (New York: Routledge, 1997), pp. 155–56.

Selected Bibliography

This bibliography includes only primary works of feminist theory and those secondary works that are immediately concerned with feminist theory. Intellectual antecedents such as works by Freud, Marx, Heidegger, Sartre, and others, although treated extensively in the text, are not included here. Books only are listed.

Abbott, Sidney, and Love, Barbara. *Sappho Was a Right-On Woman.* New York: Stein & Day, 1972.

Adams, Carol J. *The Sexual Politics of Meat: A Feminist-Vegetarian Critical Theory.* New York: Continuum, 1990.

Addams, Jane. *The Social Thought of Jane Addams,* ed. Christopher Lasch. Indianapolis: Bobbs-Merrill, 1965.

Addams, Jane; Balch, Emily Greene; and Hamilton, Alice. *Women at the Hague: the International Congress and its Results.* New York: Macmillan, 1915.

Allen, Jeffner, ed. *Lesbian Philosophies and Cultures.* Albany: State University of New York Press, 1990.

Allen, Pamela. *Free Space: A Perspective on the Small Group in Women's Liberation.* Washington, N.J.: Times Change, 1970.

Allen, Paula Gunn. *The Sacred Hoop: Recovering the Feminine in American Indian Traditions.* Boston: Beacon, 1986.

Altbach, Edith Hoshino, ed. *From Feminism to Liberation* (1971), 2d. rev. ed. Cambridge: Schenkman, 1980.

Amundsen, Kirsten. *The Silenced Majority.* Englewood Cliffs, N.J.: Prentice-Hall, 1971.

Anthony, Susan B., and Harper, Ida Husted, eds. *The History of Woman Suffrage.* Vol. 4. Indianapolis: Hollenbeck Press, 1902.

Atkinson, Ti-Grace. *Amazon Odyssey.* New York: Links, 1974.

Bardwick, Judith. *The Psychology of Women: A Study of Bio-Cultural Conflicts.* New York: Harper, 1971.

Barrett, Michèle. *Women's Oppression Today: Problems in Marxist Feminist Analysis.* London: Verso, 1980.

Bartky, Sandra Lee. *Femininity and Domination: Studies in the Phenomenology of Oppression.* New York: Routledge, 1990.

Beauvoir, Simone de. *The Second Sex* (1949). Translated by H. M. Parshley. New York: Bantam, 1961.

Bebel, August. *Women Under Socialism* (1883). New York: Schocken, 1971.

Beck, Evelyn Torton, ed. *Nice Jewish Girls: A Lesbian Anthology.* Watertown, Mass.: Persephone, 1982.

Belenky, Mary; Clichy, Blythe; Goldberger, Nancy; and Tarule, Jill. *Women's Ways of Knowing.* New York: Basic, 1987.

Bell, Diane, and Klein, Renate, eds. *Radically Speaking: Feminism Reclaimed.* North Melbourne, Australia: Spinfex, 1996.

Benhabib, Seyla, and Cornell, Drucilla, eds. *Feminism as Critique.* Minneapolis: University of Minnesota Press, 1987.

Benjamin, Jessica. *The Bonds of Love: Psychoanalysis, Feminism, and the Problem of Domination.* New York: Pantheon, 1988.

Bernard, Jessie. *The Female World.* New York: Free Press, 1981.

Birkby, Phyllis, ed. *Amazon Expedition: A Lesbian Feminist Anthology.* Washington, N.J.: Times Change, 1973.

Bird, Caroline. *Born Female: The High Cost of Keeping Women Down.* New York: McKay, 1968.

Bishop, Sharon, and Weinzweig, Marjorie, eds. *Philosophy and Women.* Belmont, Calif.: Wadsworth, 1979.

Bleier, Ruth, ed. *Feminist Approaches to Science.* New York: Pergamon, 1986.

Bordo, Susan. *The Flight to Objectivity: Essays on Cartesianism and Culture.* Albany: State University of New York, 1987.

Boxer, Marilyn, and Quataert, Jean. *Socialist Women: European Socialist Feminism in the Nineteenth and Early Twentieth Centuries.* New York: Elsevier, 1978.

Bridenthal, Renate, and Koontz, Claudia, eds. *Becoming Visible: Women in European History.* Boston: Houghton Mifflin, 1977.

Brownmiller, Susan. *Against Our Will: Men, Women and Rape.* New York: Simon and Schuster, 1975.

Buhle, Mari Jo. *Feminism and Its Discontents: A Century of Struggle with Psychoanalysis.* Cambridge: Harvard University Press, 1998.

———. *Women and American Socialism,* 1870–1920. Urbana: University of Illinois Press, 1981.

Bulkin, Elly; Pratt, Minnie Bruce; and Smith, Barbara. *Yours in Struggle: Three Feminist Perspectives on Anti-Semitism and Race.* Brooklyn: Long Haul Press, 1984.

Bunch, Charlotte, and Myron, Nancy. *Class and Feminism: A Collection of Essays from the Furies.* Baltimore: Diana Press, 1974.

Cade, Toni, ed. *The Black Woman: An Anthology.* New York: Signet, 1970.

Caldecott, Leonie, and Leland, Stephanie, eds. *Reclaim the Earth: Women Speak Out for Life on Earth.* London: Women's Press, 1983.

Carroll, Bernice A., ed. *Liberating Women's History.* Urbana: University of Illinois Press, 1976.

Chesler, Phyllis. *Women and Madness.* Garden City: Doubleday, 1972.

Chodorow, Nancy. *The Reproduction of Mothering: Psychoanalysis and the Sociology of Gender.* Berkeley: University of California Press, 1978.

Christ, Carol P., and Plaskow, Judith, eds. *Womanspirit Rising: A Feminist Reader in Religion.* San Francisco: Harper, 1979.

Clark, Lorenne M. G., and Lange, Lydia, eds. *The Sexism of Social and Political Theory: Women and Reproduction from Plato to Nietzsche.* Toronto: University of Toronto Press, 1979.

Code, Lorraine. *What Can She Know? Feminist Theory and Construction of Knowledge.* Ithaca: Cornell University Press, 1991.

Cole, Eve Browning, and Coultrap-McQuin, Susan, eds. *Explorations in Feminist Ethics: Theory and Practice.* Bloomington: Indiana University Press, 1992.

Collard, Andrée, with Contrucci, Joyce. *Rape of the Wild: Man's Violence against Animals and the Earth.* Bloomington: Indiana University Press, 1988.

Collins, Patricia Hill. *Black Feminist Thought: Knowledge, Consciousness and the Politics of Empowerment.* Boston: Unwin Hyman, 1990.

Cooper, James L., and McIsaac, Sheila, eds. *The Roots of American Feminist Thought.* Boston: Allyn and Bacon, 1973.

Cott, Nancy F. *The Grounding of Modern Feminism.* New Haven: Yale University Press, 1987.

Covina, Gina, and Galana, Laurel, eds. *The Lesbian Reader.* Oakland, Calif.: Amazon Press, 1975.

Daly, Mary. *Beyond God the Father: Toward a Philosophy of Women's Liberation.* Boston: Beacon, 1973.

———. *The Church and the Second Sex.* New York: Harper, 1968.

———. *Gyn/Ecology: The Metaethics of Radical Feminism.* Boston: Beacon, 1978.

———. *Pure Lust: Elemental Feminist Philosophy.* Boston: Beacon, 1984.

Davis, Angela Y. *Women, Race and Class.* New York: Random House, 1981.

Davis, Elizabeth Gould. *The First Sex* (1971). Baltimore: Penguin, 1972.

Diamond, Irene, and Orenstein, Gloria Feman, eds. *Reweaving the World: The Emergence of Ecofeminism.* San Francisco: Sierra Club, 1990.

Dinnerstein, Dorothy. *The Mermaid and the Minotaur: Sexual Arrangements and Human Malaise.* New York: Harper, 1977.

Douglass, Frederick. *Frederick Douglass on Women's Rights,* ed. Philip S. Foner. Westport, Conn.: Greenwood Press, 1976.

Dreifus, Claudia, ed. *Seizing Our Bodies: The Politics of Women's Health.* New York: Vintage, 1977.

DeBois, Ellen Carol. *Feminism and Suffrage: The Emergence of an Independent Women's Movement in America, 1848–1869.* Ithaca: Cornell University Press, 1978.

Dworkin, Andrea. *Our Blood: Prophesies and Discourses on Sexual Politics.* New York: Harper, 1976.

———. *Pornography: Men Possessing Women.* New York: Putnam, 1981.

———. *Woman Hating.* New York: Dutton, 1974.

Eastman, Crystal. *Crystal Eastman on Women and Revolution,* ed. Blanche Wiesen Cook. New York: Oxford, 1978.

Ebert, Teresa L. *Ludic Feminism and After: Postmodernism, Desire, and Labor in Late Capitalism.* Ann Arbor: University of Michigan Press, 1996.

Echols, Alice. *Daring to Be Bad: Radical Feminism in America 1967–1975.* Minneapolis: University of Minnesota Press, 1989.

Ehrenreich, Barbara, and English, Deidre. *For Her Own Good: 150 Years of the Experts' Advice to Women.* Garden City: Doubleday, 1978.

Eisenstein, Hester. *Contemporary Feminist Theory.* Boston: G. K. Hall, 1983.

——— **and Jardine, Alice, eds.** *The Future of Difference.* Boston: G. K. Hall, 1980.

Eisenstein, Zillah, ed. *Capitalist Patriarchy and the Case for Socialist Feminism.* New York: Monthly Review, 1979.

———. *The Radical Future of Liberal Feminism.* New York: Longman, 1981.

Elshtain, Jean Bethke. *Public Man, Private Woman: Women in Social and Political Thought.* Princeton: Princeton University Press, 1981.

Engels, Frederick. *The Origin of the Family, Private Property and the State* (1884). New York: International, 1942.

Enloe, Cynthia. *Does Khaki Become You? The Militarization of Women's Lives.* Boston: South End, 1983.

Estrich, Susan. *Real Rape.* Cambridge: Harvard University Press, 1987.

Evans, Sara. *Personal Politics: The Roots of Women's Liberation in the Civil Rights Movement and the New Left.* New York: Knopf, 1979.

Faderman, Lillian. *Surpassing the Love of Men: Romantic Friendship and Love between Women from the Renaissance to the Present.* New York: Morrow, 1981.

——— **and Eriksson, Brigitte.** *Lesbian-Feminism in Turn-of-the-Century-Germany.* Weatherby Lake, Mo.: Naiad Press, 1980.

Ferguson, Ann. *Blood at the Root: Motherhood, Sexuality and Male Dominance.* London: Pandora, 1989.

Ferguson, Kathy E., *The Feminist Case against Bureaucracy.* Philadelphia: Temple University Press, 1984.

Figes, Eva. *Patriarchal Attitudes.* New York: Fawcett, 1970.

Firestone, Shulamith. *The Dialectic of Sex: The Case for Feminist Revolution* (1970). New York: Bantam, 1971.

——— **and Koedt, Anne, eds.** *Notes from the Second Year: Radical Feminism.* New York: Bantam, 1970.

Flax, Jane. *Thinking Fragments: Psychoanalysis, Feminism, and Postmodernism in the Contemporary West.* Berkeley: University of California Press, 1990.

Flexner, Eleanor. *Century of Struggle: The Women's Rights Movement in the United States* (1959). New York: Athenaeum, 1972.

Foner, Philip S. *Women and the American Labor Movement: From Colonial Times to the Eve of World War I.* New York: Free Press, 1979.

Foreman, Ann. *Femininity as Alienation: Women and the Family in Marxism and Psychoanalysis.* London: Pluto, 1977.

Frankfort, Ellen. *Vaginal Politics.* New York: Bantam, 1973.

Freeman, Jo. *The Politics of Women's Liberation.* New York: McKay, 1975.

———, ed. *Women: A Feminist Perspective.* Palo Alto, Calif.: Mayfield, 1979.

French, Marilyn. *Beyond Power: On Women, Men and Morals.* New York: Summit, 1985.

———. *The War against Women.* New York: Ballantine, 1993.

Friedan, Betty. *The Feminine Mystique.* New York: Norton, 1963.

Frye, Marilyn. *The Politics of Reality: Essays in Feminist Theory.* Trumansburg, N.Y.: Crossing Press, 1983.

Fuentes, Annette, and Ehrenreich, Barbara. *Women in the Global Factory.* Boston: South End, 1983.

Fuller, Margaret. *Woman in the Nineteenth Century* (1845). New York: Norton, 1971.

Gaard, Greta, ed. *Ecofeminism: Women, Animals, Nature.* Philadelphia: Temple University Press, 1993.

Gage, Matilda Joslyn. *Woman, Church and State: A Historical Account of the Status of Women through the Christian Ages; With Reminiscences of the Matriarchate* (1893). Watertown, Mass.: Persephone Press, 1980.

Gallop, Jane. *The Daughter's Seduction: Feminism and Psychoanalysis.* Ithaca: Cornell University Press, 1982.

Gilligan, Carol. *In A Different Voice: Psychological Theory and Women's Development.* Cambridge: Harvard University Press, 1982.

Gilman, Charlotte Perkins. *The Home* (1903). Urbana: University of Illinois Press, 1972.

———. *His Religion and Hers: A Study of the Faith of Our Fathers and the Work of Our Mothers* (1923). Westport, Conn.: Hyperion, 1976.

———. *The Man-Made World; or, Our Androcentric Culture* (1911). New York: Johnson Reprint, 1971.

———. *Women and Economics: A Study in the Economic Relation between Men and Women as a Factor in Social Evolution* (1898). New York: Harper, 1966.

Goldenberg, Naomi R. *The Changing of the Gods: Feminism and the End of Traditional Religions.* Boston: Beacon, 1979.

Goldman, Emma. *Red Emma Speaks: Selected Writings and Speeches by Emma Goldman,* ed. Alix Kates Shulman. New York: Vintage, 1972.

———. *The Traffic in Women and Other Essays on Feminism.* New York: Times Change, 1970.

Gordon, Linda. *Woman's Body, Woman's Right: A Social History of Birth Control in America.* New York: Grossman, 1976.

Gornick, Vivian, and Moran, Barbara K., eds. *Woman in Sexist Society: Studies in Power and Powerlessness.* New York: Basic, 1971.

Gould, Carol, ed. *Beyond Domination: New Perspectives on Women and Philosophy.* Totowa, N.J.: Rowman & Allanheld, 1983.

Gould, Carol C., and Warshofsky, Marx W., eds. *Women and Philosophy: Toward a Theory of Liberation.* New York: Putnam's, 1976.

Greer, Germaine. *The Female Eunuch.* New York: McGraw-Hill, 1970.

Griffin, Susan. *Pornography and Silence: Culture's Revenge against Women.* New York: Harper, 1981.

———. *Rape and the Power of Consciousness.* New York: Harper, 1979.

———. *Woman and Nature: The Roaring Inside Her.* New York: Harper, 1978.

Grimes, Alan P. *The Puritan Ethic and Woman's Suffrage.* New York: Oxford, 1967.

Grimké, Sarah M. *Letters on the Equality of the Sexes and the Condition of Woman* (1838). New York: Burt Franklin, 1970.

Guettel, Charnie. *Marxism and Feminism.* Toronto: Women's Press, 1974.

Hanen, Marsha, and Nielsen, Kai, eds. *Science, Morality and Feminist Theory.* Calgary, Alberta, Canada: University of Calgary Press, 1987.

Harding, Sandra. *Is Science Multicultural? Postcolonialisms, Feminisms, and Epistemology.* Bloomington: Indiana University Press, 1998.

———. *The Science Question in Feminism.* Ithaca: Cornell University Press, 1986.

——— **and Hintikka, Merrill B., eds.** *Discovering Reality: Feminist Perspectives on Epistemology, Metaphysics, Methodology, and the Philosophy of Science.* Dordrecht: Reidel, 1983.

——— **and O'Barr, Jean F., eds.** *Sex and Scientific Inquiry.* Chicago: University of Chicago Press, 1987.

Harper, Ida Husted, ed. *The History of Woman Suffrage,* vols. 5 and 6. New York: J. J. Little and Ives, 1922.

Harris, Adrienne, and King, Ynestra, eds. *Rocking the Ship of State: Toward a Feminist Peace Politics.* Boulder, Colo.: Westview, 1989.

Hartman, Mary, and Banner, Lois W., eds. *Clio's Consciousness Raised: New Perspectives on the History of Women.* New York: Harper, 1974.

Hartsock, Nancy C. M. *The Feminist Standpoint Revisited and Other Essays.* Boulder, Colo.: Westview Press, 1998.

———. *Money, Sex, and Power: Toward a Feminist Historical Materialism.* New York: Longman, 1983.

Hawkesworth, M. E., *Beyond Oppression: Feminist Theory and Political Strategy.* New York: Continuum, 1990.

Hayden, Delores. *The Grand Domestic Revolution: A History of Feminist Designs for American Homes, Neighborhoods and Cities.* Cambridge: MIT Press, 1981.

Hekman, Susan J. *Gender and Knowledge.* Boston: Northeastern University Press, 1990.

Henschel, Susannah, ed. *On Being a Jewish Feminist: A Reader.* New York: Schocken, 1983.

Hershberger, Ruth. *Adam's Rib.* New York: Pellegrini & Cudahy, 1948.

Heywood, Leslie, and Drake, Jennifer, eds. *Third Wave Agenda: Being Feminist, Doing Feminism.* Minneapolis: Univeristy of Minnesota Press, 1997.

Hirsch, Marianne, and Keller, Evelyn Fox, eds. *Conflicts in Feminism.* New York: Routledge, 1990.

Hoagland, Sarah Lucia. *Lesbian Ethics: Toward New Value.* Palo Alto, Calif.: Institute of Lesbian Studies, 1988.

Hole, Judith, and Levine, Ellen. *Rebirth of Feminism.* New York: Quadrangle, 1971.

Holby, Winifred. *Women and a Changing Civilization* (1935). Chicago: Academy Press, 1978.

Hooks, Bell. *Ain't I A Woman: Black Women and Feminism.* Boston: South End Press, 1981.

———. *Feminist Theory: From Margin to Center.* Boston: South End, 1984.

Hubbard, Ruth; Henifin, Mary Sue; and Fried, Barbara, eds. *Biological Woman—The Convenient Myth: A Collection of Feminist Essays and a Comprehensive Bibliography.* Cambridge: Schenkman, 1983.

Hull, Gloria T.; Scott, Patricia Bell; and Smith, Barbara, eds. *But Some of Us Are Brave: Black Women's Studies.* Old Westbury, N.Y.: Feminist Press, 1982.

Jaggar, Alison M. *Feminist Politics and Human Nature.* Totowa, N.J.: Rowman & Allanheld, 1983.

——— and Bordo, Susan R., eds. *Gender/Body/Knowledge: Feminist Reconstruction of Being and Knowing.* New Brunswick, N.J.: Rutgers University Press, 1989.

——— and Struhl, Paula R., eds. *Feminist Frameworks: Alternative Accounts of the Relations between Men and Women.* New York: McGraw-Hill, 1978.

Janeway, Elizabeth. *Between Myth and Morning: Women Awakening.* New York: Morrow, 1974.

———. *Man's World, Woman's Place: A Study in Social Mythology.* New York: Morrow, 1971.

———. *Powers of the Weak.* New York: Knopf, 1980.

Johnston, Jill. *Lesbian Nation.* New York: Simon and Schuster, 1973.

Joseph, Gloria, and Lewis, Jill. *Common Differences: Conflicts in Black and White Feminist Perspectives.* Garden City: Anchor, 1981.

Kanowitz, Leo. *Women and the Law: The Unfinished Revolution.* Albuquerque: University of New Mexico Press, 1968.

Katz, Jonathan, ed. *Gay American History: Lesbians and Gay Men in the U.S.A.* (1976). New York: Avon, 1978.

Keohane, Nannerl O.; Rosaldo, Michelle Z.; and Gelpi, Barbara, eds. *Feminist Theory: A Critique of Ideology.* Chicago: University of Chicago Press, 1982.

Keller, Evelyn Fox. *Reflections on Gender and Science.* New Haven, Conn.: Yale University Press, 1985.

Kerber, Linda; Kessler-Harris, Alice; and Sklar, Kathryn Kish, eds. *U.S. History as Women's History.* Chapel Hill: University of North Carolina Press, 1995.

Key, Ellen. *The Morality of Women, and Other Essays.* New York: Ralph Fletcher Seymour, 1911.

———. *War, Peace and the Future, A Consideration of Nationalism and Internationalism, and the Relation of Women to War.* New York: Putnam's, 1914.

———. *The Woman Movement.* New York: Putnam's, 1912.

Kisner, Arlene, ed. *The Lives and Writings of Notorious Victoria Woodhull and Her Sister Tennessee Claflin.* Washington, N.J.: Times Change, 1972.

Kittay, Eva Feder, and Meyers, Diana T., eds. *Women and Moral Theory.* Totowa, N.J.: Rowman & Littlefield, 1987.

Klein, Viola. *The Feminine Character: The History of an Ideology* (1946). 2d. ed. London: Routledge & Kegan Paul, 1971.

Koedt, Anne, and Firestone, Shulamith, eds. *Notes from the Third Year: Women's Liberation.* New York: Notes from the Third Year, 1971.

Koedt, Anne; Levine, Ellen; and Rapone, Anita, eds. *Radical Feminism.* New York: Quadrangle, 1973.

Kraditor, Aileen S. *The Ideas of the Woman Suffrage Movement 1890–1920* (1968). Garden City, N.Y.: Anchor, 1971.

———, **ed.** *Up from the Pedestal: Selected Writings in the History of American Feminism.* Chicago: Quadrangle, 1968.

Kuhn, Annette, and Wolpe, Ann Marie, eds. *Feminism and Materialism.* London: Routledge & Kegan Paul, 1978.

LaFollette, Suzanne. *Concerning Women* (1926). New York: Arno, 1972.

Lederer, Laura, ed. *Take Back the Night: Women on Pornography.* New York: Morrow, 1980.

Lemons, J. Stanley. *The Woman Citizen: Social Feminism in the 1920s.* Urbana: University of Illinois Press, 1975.

Lenin, V. I. *The Emancipation of Women: From the Writings of V. I. Lenin.* New York: International, 1972.

Lerner, Gerda. *The Creation of Patriarchy.* New York: Oxford University Press, 1986.

———, **ed.** *Black Woman in White America: A Documentary History.* New York: Pantheon, 1972.

Lifton, Robert Jay, ed. *The Woman in America.* Boston: Beacon, 1967.

Linden, R. R.; Pagano, D. R.; Russell, D. E. H.; and Star, S. L., eds. *Against Sadomasochism: A Radical Feminist Analysis.* Palo Alto, Calif.: Frog in the Well Press, 1982.

Lloyd, Genevieve. *The Man of Reason: "Male" and "Female" in Western Philosophy.* Minneapolis: University of Minnesota Press, 1984.

Lorde, Audre. *Sister Outsider: Essays and Speeches.* Trumansburg, N.Y.: Crossing Press, 1984.

Maccoby, Eleanor E., and Jacklin, Carol N. *The Psychology of Sex Differences.* Stanford: Stanford University Press, 1974.

McAllister, Pam, ed. *Reweaving the Web of Life: Feminism and Nonviolence.* Philadelphia: New Society, 1982.

MacKinnon, Catharine A. *Feminism Unmodified.* Cambridge: Harvard University Press, 1987.

———. *Sexual Harassment of Working Women: A Case of Discrimination.* New Haven: Yale University Press, 1979.

———. *Toward a Feminist Theory of the State.* Cambridge: Harvard University Press, 1989.

Marks, Elaine, and de Courtivron, Isabelle, eds. *New French Feminisms: An Anthology* (1980). New York: Schocken, 1981.

Martin, Del, and Lyon, Phyllis. *Lesbian/Woman.* New York: Bantam, 1972.

Merchant, Carolyn. *The Death of Nature: Women, Ecology, and the Scientific Revolution.* New York: Harper, 1980.

Mies, Maria. *Patriarchy and Accumulation on a World Scale: Women in the International Division of Labour.* London: Zed, 1986.

——— **et al.** *Women: The Last Colony.* London: Zed, 1988.

——— **and Shiva, Vandama.** *Ecofeminism.* London: Zed, 1993.

Mill, John Stuart, and Mill, Harriet Taylor. *Essays on Sex Equality,* ed. Alice S. Rossi. Chicago: University of Chicago Press, 1970.

Miller, Jean Baker. *The New Psychology of Women.* Boston: Beacon, 1976.

———, **ed.** *Psychoanalysis and Women: Contributions to New Theory and Therapy.* New York: Brunner/Mazel, 1973.

Millett, Kate. *Sexual Politics* (1970). New York: Avon, 1971.

Mitchell, Juliet. *Psychoanalysis and Feminism: Freud, Reich, Lang and Women* (1974). New York: Vintage, 1975.

———. *Woman's Estate.* Baltimore: Penguin, 1974.

Moraga, Cherríe, and Anzaldúa, Gloria, eds. *This Bridge Called My Back: Writings by Radical Women of Color.* Watertown, Mass.: Persephone Press, 1981.

Morgan, Robin. *Anatomy of Freedom: Feminism, Physics and Global Politics.* Garden City, N.Y.: Doubleday, 1982.

———. *Going Too Far: The Personal Chronicle of a Feminist.* New York: Random, 1977.

———, **ed.** *Sisterhood Is Global: The International Women's Movement Anthology.* Garden City: Anchor, 1984.

———, **ed.** *Sisterhood Is Powerful: An Anthology of Writings from the Women's Liberation Movement.* New York: Vintage, 1970.

Myron, Nancy, and Bunch, Charlotte, eds. *Lesbianism and the Women's Movement.* Baltimore: Diana Press, 1975.

Narayan, Uma. *Dislocating Cultures: Identities, Traditions, and Third World Feminism.* New York: Routledge, 1997.

Nicholson, Linda J., ed. *Feminism/Postmodernism.* New York: Routledge, 1990.

———**, ed.** *The Second Wave: A Reader in Feminist Theory.* New York: Routledge, 1997.

Noddings, Nel. *Caring: A Feminine Approach to Ethics and Moral Education.* Berkeley: University of California Press, 1984.

Notes from the First Year. New York: New York Radical Women, 1968. Available online from *http://scriptorium.lib.duke.edu/wlm.*

O'Brien, Mary. *The Politics of Reproduction.* Boston: Routledge & Kegan Paul, 1981.

Ochs, Carol. *Behind the Sex of God: Toward a New Consciousness—Transcending Matriarchy and Patriarchy.* Boston: Beacon, 1977.

———. *Women and Spirituality.* Totowa, N.J.: Rowman & Allanheld, 1983.

Okin, Susan Moller. *Justice, Gender, and the Family.* New York: Basic, 1989.

———. *Women in Western Political Thought.* Princeton: Princeton University Press, 1979.

——— **et al.** *Is Multiculturalism Bad for Women?* Princeton, N.J.: Princeton University Press, 1999.

O'Neill, William. *Everyone Was Brave: The Rise and Fall of Feminism in America.* New York: Quadrangle, 1969.

Papachristou, Judith, ed. *Women Together: A History in Documents of the Women's Movement in the United States.* New York: Knopf, 1976.

Pateman, Carole. *The Sexual Contract.* Stanford: Stanford University Press, 1988.

——— **and Gross, Elizabeth, eds.** *Feminist Challenges: Social and Political Theory* (1986). Boston: Northeastern University Press, 1987.

Plant, Judith, ed. *Healing the Wounds: The Promise of Ecofeminism.* Philadelphia: New Society, 1989.

Plaskow, Judith, and Christ, Carol P., eds. *Weaving the Visions: New Patterns in Feminist Spirituality.* New York: Harper, 1989.

Plumwood, Val. *Feminism and the Mastery of Nature.* New York: Routledge, 1993.

The Quest Staff, ed. *Building Feminist Theory: Essays from Quest, a Feminist Quarterly.* New York: Longman, 1981.

Rabuzzi, Kathryn Allen. *The Sacred and the Feminine: Toward a Theology of Housework.* New York: Seabury, 1982.

Redstockings. *Feminist Revolution.* New Paltz, N.Y.: 1975.

Reiter, Rayna R., ed. *Towards an Anthropology of Women.* New York: Monthly Review, 1975.

Rich, Adrienne. *Of Woman Born: Motherhood as Experience and Institution.* New York: Norton, 1976.

———. *On Lies, Secrets and Silence: Selected Prose 1966–1978.* New York: Norton, 1979.

Rohrbach, Joanna Bunker. *Women: Psychology's Puzzle.* New York: Basic, 1979.

Rosaldo, Michelle Zimbalist, and Lamphere, Louise, eds. *Women, Culture, and Society.* Stanford: Stanford University Press, 1974.

Rosenberg, Rosalind. *Beyond Separate Spheres: Intellectual Roots of Modern Feminism.* New Haven: Yale University Press, 1983.

Rossi, Alice S., ed. *The Feminist Papers: From Adams to de Beauvoir* (1973). New York: Bantam, 1974.

Roszak, Betty, and Roszak, Theodore, eds. *Masculine/Feminine: Readings in Sexual Mythology and the Liberation of Women.* New York: Harper, 1969.

Rothchild, Joan, ed. *Machina Ex Dea: Feminist Perspectives on Technology.* New York: Pergamon, 1983.

Rowbotham, Sheila. *Women's Consciousness, Man's World.* Baltimore: Penquin, 1973.

Ruddick, Sara. *Maternal Thinking: Towards a Politics of Peace.* Boston: Beacon, 1989.

Ruiz, Vicki L., and DuBois, Ellen Carol, eds. *Unequal Sisters: A Multicultural Reader in U.S. Women's History,* 2d. ed. New York: Routledge, 1994.

Rupp, Leila, and Taylor, Verta. *Survival in the Doldrums: The American Women's Rights Movement 1945 to the 1960s.* New York: Oxford, 1987.

Russell, Dora. *Hypatia; or, Women and Knowledge.* New York: Dutton, 1925.

Russell, Letty M. *Human Liberation in a Feminist Perspective—A Theology.* Philadelphia: Westminster, 1974.

Ruether, Rosemary Radford. *New Woman/New Earth: Sexist Ideologies and Human Liberation.* New York: Seabury, 1975.

———. *Sexism and God-Talk: Toward a Feminist Theology.* Boston: Beacon, 1983.

———, ed. *Religion and Sexism: Images of Woman in the Jewish and Christian Traditions.* New York: Simon and Schuster, 1974.

Salper, Roberta, ed. *Female Liberation: History and Current Politics.* New York: Knopf, 1972.

Sanger, Margaret. *Woman and the New Race.* New York: Brentano, 1920.

Sargent, Lydia, ed. *Women and Revolution: A Discussion of the Unhappy Marriage of Marxism and Feminism.* Boston: South End, 1981.

Schaef, Anne Wilson. *Women's Reality: An Emerging Female System in the White Male Society.* Minneapolis: Winston, 1981.

Schneir, Miriam, ed. *Feminism: the Essential Historical Writings.* New York: Vintage, 1972.

Schramm, Sarah Slavin. *Plow Women Rather than Reapers: An Intellectual History of Feminism in the United States.* Metuchen, N.J.: Scarecrow, 1979.

Schreiner, Olive. *Women and Labor* (1911). New York: Johnson Reprint, 1972.

Seager, Joni. *Earth Follies: Coming to Feminist Terms with the Global Environmental Crisis.* New York: Routledge, 1993.

Shanley, Mary Lyndon, and Pateman, Carole, eds. *Feminist Interpretations and Political Theory.* University Park, Pa.: Pennsylvania State University Press, 1991.

Sherman, Julia A., and Beck, Evelyn Torton, eds. *The Prism of Sex: Essays in the Sociology of Knowledge.* Madison: University of Wisconsin Press, 1979.

Shiva, Vandama. *Staying Alive: Women, Ecology and Development.* London: Zed, 1988.

——— and Moser, Ingunn, eds. *Biopolitics: A Feminist and Ecological Reader on Biotechnology.* London: Zed, 1995.

Siegfried, Charlotte Haddock. *Pragmatism and Feminism: Reweaving the Social Fabric.* Chicago: University of Chicago Press, 1996.

Smith, Dorothy E. *Feminism and Marxism—A Place to Begin, a Way to Go.* Vancouver: New Star Books, 1977.

Smith, Hilda L. *Reason's Disciples: Seventeenth-Century English Feminists.* Urbana: University of Illinois Press, 1982.

Snitow, Ann; Stansell, Christine; and Thompson, Sharon, eds. *The Powers of Desire: The Politics of Sexuality.* New York: Monthly Review, 1983.

Sochen, June. *The New Woman: Feminism in Greenwich Village, 1910–20.* New York: Quadrangle, 1972.

Spelman, Elizabeth V. *Inessential Woman: Problems of Exclusion in Feminist Thought.* Boston: Beacon, 1988.

Spender, Dale, ed. *Feminist Theorists: Three Centuries of Key Women Thinkers.* New York: Pantheon, 1983.

Spretnak, Charlene, ed. *The Politics of Women's Spirituality: Essays on the Rise of Spiritual Power in the Movement.* Garden City, N.Y.: Doubleday, 1981.

Stambler, Sookie, ed. *Women's Liberation: Blueprint for the Future.* New York: Ace, 1970.

Stanton, Elizabeth Cady. *The Woman's Bible.* 2 vols. (1895 and 1899). New York: Arno, 1972.

Stanton, Elizabeth Cady; Anthony, Susan B.; and Gage, Matilda Joslyn, eds. *The History of Woman Suffrage,* vols. 1–3. Rochester: Charles Mann, 1881–86.

Starhawk. *The Spiral Dance: Rebirth of the Ancient Religion of the Goddess.* New York: Harper, 1979.

Steinem, Gloria. *Outrageous Acts and Everyday Rebellions.* New York: Holt, Rinehart & Winston, 1983.

Stites, Richard. *The Women's Liberation Movement in Russia: Feminism, Nihilism, and Bolshevism, 1860–1930.* Princeton: Princeton University Press, 1978.

Sturgeon, Noël. *Ecofeminist Natures: Race, Gender, Feminist Theory, and Political Action.* New York: Routledge, 1997.

Tanner, Leslie B., ed. *Voices from Women's Liberation.* New York: Signet, 1971.

Theobald, Robert, ed. *Dialogue on Women.* Indianapolis: Bobbs-Merrill, 1967.

Thompson, Mary Lou, ed. *Voices of the New Feminism.* Boston: Beacon, 1970.

Tong, Rosemarie. *Feminine and Feminist Ethics.* Belmont, Cal.: Wadsworth, 1993.

Tong, Rosemarie Putnam. *Feminist Thought: A More Comprehensive Introduction,* 2d. ed. Boulder, Colo.: Westview Press, 1998.

Trask, Haunani-Kay. *Eros and Power: The Promise of Feminist Theory.* Philadelphia: University of Pennsylvania Press, 1986.

Treblicot, Joyce, ed. *Mothering: Essays in Feminist Theory.* Totowa, N.J.: Rowman & Allanheld, 1983.

Vance, Carole S., ed. *Pleasure and Danger: Exploring Female Sexuality.* Boston: Routledge, 1984.

Vetterling-Braggin, Mary; Elliston, Frederick A.; and English, Jane, eds. *Feminism and Philosophy.* Totowa, N.J.: Littlefield, Adams, 1977.

Wagner, Sally Roesch. *The Untold Story of the Iroquois Influence on Early Feminists.* Aberdeen, S.D.: Sky Carrier Press, 1996.

Walker, Alice. *In Search of Our Mothers' Gardens: Womanist Prose.* New York: Harcourt, Brace, Jovanovich, 1983.

Wallace, Michele. *Black Macho and the Myth of the Super Woman.* New York: Dial, 1978.

Ware, Cellestine. *Woman Power: The Movement for Women's Liberation.* New York: Tower, 1970.

Waring, Marilyn. *If Women Counted: A New Feminist Economics.* New York: Harper, 1988.

Warren, Karen, ed. *Ecological Feminism.* New York: Routledge, 1994.

West, Robin. *Caring for Justice.* New York: New York University Press, 1997.

Wollstonecraft, Mary. *A Vindication of the Rights of Woman* (1792). Baltimore: Penguin, 1975.

The Woman Question: Selections from the Writings of Karl Marx, Frederick Engels, V. I. Lenin, Joseph Stalin. New York: International, 1951.

Woolf, Virginia. *A Room of One's Own* (1929). New York: Harcourt, Brace & World, 1957.

———. *Three Guineas* (1938). New York: Harcourt, Brace & World, 1957.

Wright, Frances. *Course of Popular Lectures* (1834). In Frances Wright D'Arusmont. *Life, Letters and Lectures, 1834–1844.* New York: Arno, 1972.

Yates, Gayle Graham. *What Women Want: The Ideas of the Movement.* Cambridge: Harvard University Press, 1975.

Young, Iris. *Justice and the Politics of Difference.* Princeton: Princeton University Press, 1990.

———. *Throwing Like a Girl and Other Essays in Feminist Philosophy.* Bloomington: Indiana University Press, 1990.

Zaretsky, Eli. *Capitalism, the Family and Personal Life.* New York: Harper, 1976.

INDEX